Chicano Culture, Ecology, Politics

Society, Environment, and Place

Series Editors: Andrew Kirby and Janice Monk

Chicano Culture, Ecology, Politics

Subversive Kin

Edited by Devon G. Peña

The University of Arizona Press   Tucson

For Corpus Aquino Gallegos and
to the future — Elaine, Elisa, Wayo, and Eliana

Chapter 4, by Laura Pulido, was originally published in *Capitalism, Nature, Socialism,* vol. 4, no. 7, pp. 27 — 58, and is reprinted in this volume by permission of The Guilford Press, New York.

The University of Arizona Press
© 1998 The Arizona Board of Regents
First Printing

⊛ This book is printed on acid-free, archival-quality paper.
Manufactured in the United States of America

03 02 01 00 99 98   6 5 4 3 2 1

Library of Congress Cataloging-in-Publication Data
Chicano culture, ecology, politics : subversive kin / edited by Devon G. Pena.
   p. cm. — (Society, environment, and place)
   Includes bibliographical references and index.
   ISBN 0-8165-1872-6 (acid-free paper)
   ISBN 0-8165-1873-4 (pbk. : acid-free paper)
   1. Mexican Americans — New Mexico — Rio Arriba County — Politics and government.   2. Mexican Americans — New Mexico — Rio Arriba County — Ethnic identity.   3. Ecology — New Mexico — Rio Arriba County.   4. Human ecology — New Mexico — Rio Arriba County.   5. Rio Arriba County (N.M.) — Environmental conditions.   I. Pena, Devon Gerardo.   II. Series.
F802.R4 C47 1999   98-25479
304.2'09789'52 — ddc21   CIP

British Library Cataloguing-in-Publication Data
A catalogue record for this book is available from the British Library.

Contents

Foreword   vii
VANDANA SHIVA

Acknowledgments   xi

Introduction   3
DEVON G. PEÑA

Part 1 — Indo-Hispano Land Ethics

1   Los Animalitos: Culture, Ecology, and the Politics of Place in the
Upper Rio Grande   25
DEVON G. PEÑA

2   Social Action Research, Bioregionalism, and the Upper Rio
Grande   58
RUBÉN O. MARTÍNEZ

3   Notes on (Home)Land Ethics: Ideas, Values, and the Land   79
REYES GARCÍA

Part 2 — Environmental History and Ecological Politics

4   Ecological Legitimacy and Cultural Essentialism: Hispano Grazing in
Northern New Mexico   121
LAURA PULIDO

5   The Capitalist Tool, the Lawless, and the Violent: A Critique of
Recent Southwestern Environmental History   141
DEVON G. PEÑA and RUBÉN O. MARTÍNEZ

6   Ecofeminism and Chicano Environmental Struggles: Bridges across
Gender and Race   177
GWYN KIRK

7   Philosophy Meets Practice: A Critique of Ecofeminism through the
Voices of Three Chicana Activists   201
MALIA DAVIS

Part 3 — Alternatives to Destruction
The Pasture Poacher (Poem)
JOSEPH C. GALLEGOS

8   Acequia Tales: Stories from a Chicano Centennial Farm   235
JOSEPH C. GALLEGOS

9   A Gold Mine, an Orchard, and an Eleventh Commandment   249
DEVON G. PEÑA

Bibliography   279

Index   305

Contributors   315

Foreword

Subversive Kin: A Politics of Diversity

Vandana Shiva

Whether it is ecological devastation or the destruction of diverse systems of knowledge, economic organization, and cultural patterns, the source is a common one; it lies in the dominant worldview that falsely universalizes the values, priorities, and truths of a small, privileged group based on class, gender, ethnicity, or religion. *Chicano Culture, Ecology, Politics: Subversive Kin* avoids the ineffective politics emerging from fragmented perspectives that focus exclusively on the politics of culture or the politics of ecology.

"Subversive kin" is an expression of an emergent politics of diversity that subverts the structures of dominant power and paradigms based on the idea of the dispensability of diverse peoples, diverse ecosystems, and diverse species. It puts in place a coherent philosophy of transformation that reverses the destruction of diverse cultures and diverse species which cohabit this beautiful earth.

The politics of diversity that combine the cultural and ecological aspects is the really subversive alternative of our times. This politics of diversity differs from the politics of difference in that the latter focuses only on race, class, and gender, ignoring the vital issues of survival linked to ecology and land-based and biodiversity-based livelihoods. The politics of difference in fact contributes to the annihilation of diversity because it empties the politics of identity of its material and ecological content and hence allows the consolidation and monopoly control over the earth's resources and the means of production by a handful of global corporations. Diverse cultures rooted in diverse ecosystems and supported through diverse livelihoods are thus eroded, even while the discourse on difference fills more books, journals, and conference and lecture halls.

The politics of diversity of subversive kin also differs from the narrow politics of species conservation, which privileges a few species over all others, including marginalized humans, and hence accepts their extinction as a rule, while defending preservation as an exception for a few places and a few species. By rooting identity in a "sense of place" as much as in gender, class, ethnicity, and other constructions of difference, identity politics, and the environmental movement are deepened and made more inclusive. They therefore become more subversive.

By establishing kinship with the earth and her other species, subversive kin can resist the culture of economic organization that destroys both cultural diversity and biodiversity by promoting and nurturing monocultures and monopolies. Diversity is the integrative force of the subjugated. It is the ground for rejuvenation of solidarity in a period when solidarity options are being closed from the top by the forces of globalization and from the bottom by the fragmentation of "post-modern deconstructions" — or what I have called "reductionist constructivism."

Karl Marx said that religion is the opiate of the people. One could stretch Marx to contemporary conditions and say that "post-modern deconstruction" carries the risk of being the opiate of the intellectuals, blinding and rendering them immune to the struggles people are engaged in in their everyday lives.

In an ironic and unpredictable twist, the globalizers, the difference theorists, and the narrow conservation movement activists converge in the shared assumption that the choice of how we live our everyday lives and the decision of who has a right to live and who will be a "threatened species" will be made by the not-so-invisible hand of the global corporations that control market forces. A politics of diversity that combines the ecological and the cultural does not leave the politics of everyday life to the market and to corporations. It also stakes a claim on the material and ecological basis of survival. It therefore provides a strong ground for resistance to globalization and the associated dispensability of diverse cultures, knowledge, economies, and species.

While the focus of this book is a particular community in a specific place — the Chicano rural land grant villages in the Río Arriba region of the southwestern United States — the patterns of solidarity and subversion are relevant to every community struggling to protect its cultural identity and survival base. An earth-centered movement for justice is not just a deep ecology movement; it is a *deep equity* movement. As Devon Peña states in his introduction, subversive kin are engaged in a search for equity and reciprocity among all species and communities.

Acknowledgments

Many people contributed to the development of this book. I would like to thank my dear friend and colleague Joe Gordon. As director of the Hulbert Center for Southwest Studies at Colorado College, Joe was the first person to encourage my research on the relationship between culture and nature in the Upper Rio Grande bioregion. I also gratefully acknowledge my colleagues with the Helen Hunt Jackson Faculty Fellows seminar at Colorado College for many stimulating discussions over the past seven years. I am especially indebted to Professor Mario Montaño, Professor Marianne Stoller, and Victor B. Nelson Cisneros.

Corpus A. Gallegos was a major inspiration for me in the preparation of this work. In fact, the idea for the "Upper Rio Grande Hispano Farms Study" was first hatched in 1989 in the kitchen of the Gallegos Ranch in San Luis, Colorado, during one of our many late-night visits over coffee.

Numerous other colleagues and friends assisted with this project by offering criticisms and insights. I acknowledge the generous contributions of Vandana Shiva, Shari Collins-Chobanian, George Sibley, Ed Quinn, Laura Pulido, Michael Soulé, Robert Curry, Christe Esquibel, Estevan Arellano, Luis and Bernice Torres, David and Trinidad Arguello, Arnold and Maria Valdéz, Adelmo Kaber, Cosme Gallegos, Praxedis Ortega, Jr., Sister Teresa Jaramillo, and Father Patrick Valdéz. Thanks are also due to the activists and organizers whose lives appear in these pages, including Lorraine Granado, Sonia Peña, and Rocky Rodriguez. I am grateful to the environmental activists with Ancient Forest Rescue, and I am especially thankful to Kirsten Atkins, Mike McGowan, and Heath Hansens.

The contributors to this volume have been patient over the many years of work that led to this publication. I am especially grateful to Ruben Martínez, Reyes García, Laura Pulido, Malia Davis, and Gwyn Kirk for their faithful dedication to critical and reflexive discourse on the politics of culture and ecology. And I am forever indebted to my dear friend,

Joseph C. Gallegos, who has given me more knowledge than I can ever repay. His is truly a love of the earth as provider of life.

The National Endowment for the Humanities (NEH) provided support for much of the research on which this book is based, through an interpretive and collaborative research grant (No. RO 22707–94). The NEH grant supports the work of the "Upper Rio Grande Hispano Farms: A Cultural and Natural History of Land Ethics in Transition, 1598–1998," a four-year study of Hispano family farms in northern New Mexico and southern Colorado. The views and opinions expressed by the authors are their own responsibility and should not be taken to reflect the official views or opinions of the NEH or the federal government.

The NEH grant enabled us to expand the research capabilities of the Rio Grande Bioregions Project, an independent research unit of the Colorado College. I would like to acknowledge the assistance of my staff at the Bioregions Project office, including Joanna Stewart, Ken Rubin, and Norma Flemming.

Finally, I would like to thank Christine Szuter, acquisitions editor at the University of Arizona Press. Christine believed in this work and faithfully supported its publication. Likewise, I would like to thank my manuscript editor, Patricia Shelton, for her untiring efforts in preparing the final manuscript for publication.

Chicano Culture, Ecology, Politics

Introduction

Devon G. Peña

The idea of a "subversive science" derives from the oppositional qualities of ecology.[1] As a scientific basis for social activism, ecology opposes the destruction by those with money of the conditions that support the diversity of life on Earth. As a philosophy of science, ecology respects the principle of "local knowledge" within the context of holism — the idea that the whole is greater than the sum of its parts. Thus, ecology opposes reductionist thinking, that is, the reduction of diversity to uniformity, of wholes to disconnected parts. The well-known adage, "Think globally, act locally," is a reflection of a place-centered, yet holistic worldview.

Ecology respects the situated nature of knowledge. The ecologist locates truth *in place,* within the contextual limits of both natural and cultural landscape mosaics that constitute a bioregion at a given point in time. Place-centered orientation conflicts with the dominant Western philosophy of science, a view in which the knowledge of experts is presumed to have absolute validity. The Western scientific worldview privileges expert universal knowledge against the traditional, place-bound, local knowledge of various unruly Others — women, workers, colonial subjects (Shiva 1988, Peña 1997a).

As an antidote to this sort of Western reductionism, ecology offers us another form of knowledge: The land speaks to the ecologist through the language of its place-specific biodiversity and thus sets the boundaries of knowledge; you can observe only what is already there. But ecologists also see nature through the lens of their time and place-bound location in human history and cultures. For example, classical ecology said that the boundaries of ecological knowledge were dictated by the natural tendency of the ecosystem to seek a state of equilibrium. This sort of ecological modeling may have reflected the postwar obsession with stability and security. The ideal ecosystem was viewed as one in which nature attained the characteristic features of a "climax successional" community in a state of dynamic equilibrium.[2]

More recently, with the emergence of a postmodern ecology of disturbance regimes, ecologists have gradually abandoned the search for a model of stable equilibria and are more likely to conceptualize the ecosystem as an unstable, ever-shifting mosaic of naturally *and* humanly disturbed landscapes. The diversity of life is seen to emerge from the edge of chaos instead of from a stable order. Disturbance rather than equilibrium is the dynamic basis of ecosystem evolution. In disturbance ecology, life is by nature chaotic and fragmentary rather than orderly and successional.[3] From the vantage point of this new ecology, there is no universal truth about the social construction of nature that we call "ecosystem," other than perhaps the unpredictability of human interference in the natural cycles of disturbance and regeneration. The diversity of landscape mosaics owes its existence to the unending cycles of destruction and rebirth of a place. Glaciers, earthquakes, tectonic shifts, wildfires, volcanoes, droughts, floods, and other natural disturbances constantly reshape the landscape. Watersheds were etched upon the changing face of Earth through this complex and epochal geomorphology.

The turn in ecology from a "stable climax community" toward an "unstable and shifting mosaic" probably reflected the social conditions during the mid- to late-twentieth century, conditions that provoked turbulent changes in civil society and social institutions. The sixties, after all, was a period of great social and cultural disturbance. The emergence of disturbance ecology coincided with the rise of identity politics in which the larger institutions of society experienced fragmentation from the pressures of organized social forces, such as the civil rights movement, which were led by racial and ethnic minorities and women. The collapse of the Eurocentric cultural order in the face of ethnic diversity coincided with the shift from stability to chaos in ecosystem theory. Was this a mere coincidence?

Ecology is not so much concerned with preventing disturbances in nature as with providing insight on human-induced environmental change (anthropogenesis) as an analog of natural chaos.[4] It is very difficult to mimic nature but easy to use anthropomorphic language to rationalize the destructiveness of the human species.[5] The subversive character of ecological knowledge is best understood, however, as an attempt to reintegrate humans into the natural world. Ecology, and especially conservation biology, envisions the possibility that human habitation within ecosystems can sustain and nurture wildness and biodiversity. As Arne Naess (1973) put it so long ago: We can relearn our citizenship in "mixed communities" of humans and nonhumans. Ecology merely reminds us how to live in our "niche," in our place.

What Vandana Shiva (1988) calls "reductionist science" involves a search for universal truths obtained through presumptively value-neutral and objective, experimental methods. Reductionist science, however, comes from a strait-jacketed separation of facts and values—a problem even the Manhattan Project scientific staff at Los Alamos ultimately recognized as calamitous.[6] The historical roots of this problem are deep. After the Baconian scientific revolution, the European (and neo-European) search was for a particular form of knowledge rising from the discovery of timeless and "placeless" truths. The discovery of this universal knowledge, however, implied the development of the technological means for global expansion. Reductionist science was thus radically cut off from ethics because it failed either to respect natural and cultural diversity or to recognize the situated nature of knowledge. The science of a globe-trotting culture is as destructive as are the imperialist desires it faithfully serves. Biological imperialism clearly has as its corollary the fitful child of cultural imperialism. The "law-making ability" of reductionist science is presumed superior because its codes and technological machinations *are* universally effective as tools of empire; apparently, they transcend the limits of local knowledge. In an often quoted passage from Plato's *Phaedrus*, Socrates said: "You must forgive me. . . . I am a lover of learning, and trees and open country won't teach me anything, whereas men in town do" (as quoted in Ariel and Kellen 1997, 13).

Reductionist knowledge brings the silence of the trees and the disappearance of rural people through loss of their means of livelihood. It openly devalues place-centered knowledge and rejects the right livelihoods that human communities have created on the basis of caring for their ecosystem rather than exploiting it. Local knowledge is displaced by the search for universal truths; this choice reinforces domination of the Other. The ultimate goal of reductionist thinking is the control and domination of nature through the mechanical arts of applied science and technology (Shiva 1988). The Baconian-Cartesian legacy of science says that

[k]nowledge is a power inimical to the Others, and its ultimate accomplishment is a world humankind creates through the science of the subordination of nature (Peña 1997a, 25–26).[7]

In the realm of politics—where "philosophy" presumably becomes "practice"—ecology challenges the growth-without-limits of capitalist exploitation of nature. Meanwhile, reductionist science continues to deliver the goods in the form of laser-guided weaponry, robotic factories, feller-forwarders, or genetically engineered crops sown from acts of biopiracy. Today, from the gene to the biosphere, capitalist interests patent life itself, while scientists continue their role as value-neutral servants of power.[8] Ecology poses the necessity of a transition to a *steady-state economy* that mimics the energy circuits of nature and so sustains ecosystemic integrity (i.e., an economy that preserves nature's ability to regenerate its life-sustaining diversity). In contrast, reductionism provides technological weaponry for use by those who seek to profit from global capitalism in a process that tears apart the planet's endangered ecosystems and local cultures. In this context, ecology can easily be read as an antireductionist and anticapitalist discourse. Its texts are grounded in the opposition of civil society to environmental destruction, and they provide a radical scientific basis from which to challenge the legitimacy of the fundamental economic laws of global capitalism. Ecology as a subversive science begets environmentalism as a new social movement.[9]

Putting Chicano Studies in Place

Within the intellectual history of Chicano Studies, ecological perspectives have seldom been expressed or debated.[10] In fact, until very recently, many Chicano scholars accepted the notion that ecology and environmentalism are primarily white, middle-class concerns. The emergence of the environmental justice movement changed that belief by challenging Chicano scholars to explore the issue of ecological degradation as a social problem. Despite the academic silence, our origin communities created ecologically sustainable livelihoods well before the term "conservation" entered the vernacular (see chapters 1, 3, 5, and 9). We have more recently recovered the idea that the land-based local cultures of the Río Arriba did not need Leopold, Muir, or Thoreau to develop environmental ethics. The essays in this anthology collectively chart the life stories of cultural, ecological, and political economic change within the land-based communities of the Río Arriba, or Upper Rio Grande, bioregion (see map). With this volume, we initiate a research program to restore well-deserved ecological legitimacy to our land-based communities.

Among students of Chicano Studies, theoretical discourse and political practice evidence confusion and fragmentation. Much of this confusion can be attributed to the currently fashionable flirtation by scholars with postmodern deconstruction, which asserts that all we can ever know about the world is a human construct. Thus, the prevailing truths of the time are merely the result of the assertion of power by specific human groups. Knowledge is power, and truth is thus situated; it is a by-product of whatever social group is positioned to impose its own version of the truth. This philosophical problem has haunted Chicano Studies since the questions of identity and subjectivity were cast out among the intersections of race, class, gender, and sexual difference. But much of this discourse seems cut off from collective expressions of struggle in our home communities.

This anthology directs the question of identity as much to our sense of place and our *biophysical* location as to gender, ethnicity, class, and other constructions of difference. We want to avoid the pitfalls of cultural essentialism. The problem of essentialism emerges whenever people (including scholars) construct categories of identity that are assumed to be representative of everyone in a socially defined group (see Fuss 1989). For example, to assume that all Chicanos have a strong sense of place simply because they identify themselves as Chicanos is to commit an essentialist error. There is nothing intrinsic to the varied forms of Chicano identity that would lead all people of Spanish or Mexican origin to connect with the protection of their land base as a principal source of collective ethnic identity. Nevertheless, students of Chicano Studies have largely overlooked the important socially constructed category of Other: nature. Thus, the intersections of place, identity, and politics remain largely unexamined.[11] A synthesis of ecology with cultural studies and political economy provides an alternative bioregional perspective from which to explore these connections and perhaps to make Chicano Studies more relevant to our communities while avoiding essentialist arguments about the uniqueness and profundity of land-based local cultures.

Our effort to reorient Chicano Studies through an epistemology of

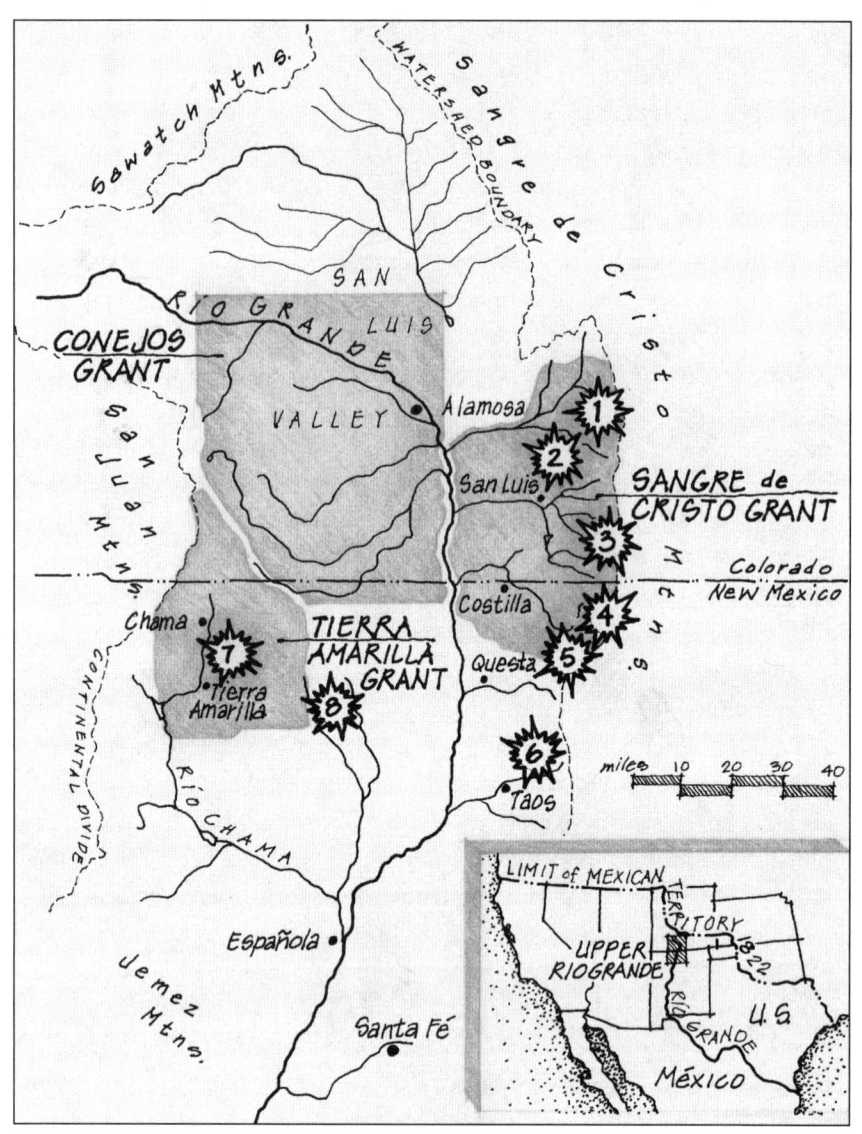

Map by Nina Veregge

Map of the Upper Rio Grande Bioregion

Principal Political-Ecological Disturbances

1 Malcolm Forbes Ranch properties of the Sangre de Cristo Land Grant. One in a series of large mountain estates owned by multimillionaires, this land has been extensively subdivided into second-home lots. The subdivisions in the montane zone include several hundred thousand acres of developed sites with more than four hundred miles of access roads. There is currently a conflict over the impact of this land-use development pattern on the watersheds of the Trinchera and Culebra Creeks. Logging in this area has also seriously damaged the watersheds.

2 Battle Mountain Gold (BMG) strip mine and cyanide-leach vat processing mill. Located in the Rito Seco watershed above the Chicano agricultural community of San Luis, Colorado, the BMG mine was the focus of a ten-year environmental-justice struggle, led by *acequia* farmers who see the mine and its tailing wastes as a long-term threat to the environment.

3 Massive logging operations on the 77,000-acre Taylor Ranch or "Mountain Tract" of the Sangre de Cristo Land Grant. A battle over logging on the common lands of the Sangre de Cristo Land Grant has been going on since June 1996.

4 "Ski Rio" ski area and resort in the southern portion of the Sangre de Cristo Land Grant (Costilla Creek watershed). This is the first in a series of ski areas and resorts that dot the Sangre de Cristo Mountain Range from the Colorado–New Mexico border to Santa Fe. The ski areas have produced a continuous battle over environmental impacts and economic dislocation waged by traditional Chicano farmers. Resort development is associated with a real-estate boom, which often results in the displacement of native families from ancestral lands due to skyrocketing property values and taxes. Some of the *acequias* in this area have lost their water rights to newly arrived agribusinesses.

5 Molycorp Molybdenum strip mine and tailings-waste facilities in the Red River watershed above Questa. Toxic wastes, including water tainted by heavy metals, has polluted portions of the Red River, rendering the water unsuitable for fishing, recreation, and irrigation. Local farmers and social activists have fought for pollution clean-up and reclamation over the past fifteen years.

6 Taos Ski Resort in the Sangre de Cristo Mountains above Taos. Continued development of this resort has led to battles over water quality, water rights, and land-use impacts since the mid-1970s. Sewage pollution of the watershed (Arroyo Hondo and Arroyo Seco) and condominium development in the foothills resulted in the organization of Chicano farmers, led by *acequia* associations.

7 Ganados del Valle wool producers' cooperative in the Tierra Amarilla Land Grant in the Upper Chama River watershed. Since the mid-1980s the Chicano wool growers' cooperative has waged a battle with the environmentalists over grazing rights on public lands that were once part of the commons of the Tierra Amarilla Land Grant. Ganados del Valle recently won a court decision against the Sierra Club Foundation for the return of more than $500,000, which the donor intended as assistance for wool producers in the Tierra Amarilla in finding grazing range for their herds.

8 La Manga Timber Sale in the Vallecitos Federal Sustained Yield Unit of the Kit Carson National Forest above the Chicano communities of La Madera, Vallecitos, and Ojo Caliente. This battle pits Chicano loggers against environmentalists in a conflict over management of public lands, traditional-use rights, and habitat protection for the endangered Mexican spotted owl. Most of the damage to this montane forest ecosystem, which was originally rich with old-growth Ponderosa, occurred during the industrialization of timber activity by the U.S. Forest Service after World War II. Throughout the 1970s and 1980s local Chicano loggers opposed the excessive volume of USFS harvest goals. The Chicano loggers sought a more sustainable and equitable timber-management policy that would favor small, locally owned timber, lumber, and wood-processing microenterprises over the large corporations that clear-cut their way through the area and then abandoned it.

place intends to open new avenues for the expression of the social and cultural practices of local, or situated, knowledge. By "situated knowledge" we understand a dialectical relationship of humans to the bio-geographical properties of place in which, over generations, the local culture accumulates a vast reservoir of knowledge dealing with the ecological limits of life in a specific locale. Norgaard (1994) describes this relationship as a "co-evolution" of culture and environment in which local communities become part of a "patchwork quilt" of diverse cultural and ecological landscapes.

The study of the relations of people, space, place, and physical objects reveals many hitherto unexamined dynamics of power. By studying the spatial dimensions of class, race, and gender boundaries, we can begin to map where and how people *place* themselves. As Harry Cleaver (1997, 2) recently noted: "Humans as corporeal beings always occupy space, and their personal and collective interactions structure and restructure that space." The social and political-economic organization of space has largely unexamined implications for the study of place as an aspect of identity.

Place — as articulated through peoples' contradictory spatial and social locations — is a primary repository for human constructions of meaning and identity. Humans create meaning in part by inscribing feelings and memories onto particular sites or shapes of their natural and cultural landscapes. This is the "interactivity" and "positionality" involved in the human experience of place and the crafting of self and identity.[12]

By recognizing the spatial dimensions of social, economic, political, and technological organization, we can better appreciate how a sense of place is itself contested terrain. This is evident in the conflicts over the *changing* physical shapes, feelings, meanings, and power of a place. The knowledge and experiences of people of color are particularly valuable to the study of the spatial dimensions of culture and lived experience. After all, people of color are accustomed to living in places constrained by clearly defined spatial boundaries born of racial, ethnic, and class segregation (e.g., living "across the tracks"). As one Hispano farmer said in reference to the enclosure of the Sangre de Cristo land-grant commons: *"Perdimos la libertad. Nos encercaron."* (We lost our liberty. They fenced us out.)

Lacking an epistemology of local knowledge, students of Chicano Studies will be left with few options for critically approaching and perhaps reversing the political-economic processes that destroy places. To explore the contested spatial dimensions of places, we must turn to eclectic mixtures of ecology, conservation biology, cultural ecology, cultural geography, environmental history, and political economy. The essays in this volume attempt an interdisciplinary synthesis of these disciplines. To grasp the contradictions of the social construction of place, we focus on how identities, struggles, and territorialities are built around the politics of cultural and economic subordination. Ecological and social domination will be shown to be interconnected, and the resistance such domination spawns reaches across differences of race, class, and gender. The first chapters in this volume focus on the role of the natural and built environments as experiential frameworks for the study of Chicano communities. The collective goal of the authors is to demonstrate how the ecological imagination provides an anchor from which to survey the vicissitudes of difference in their spatial and historical contexts. These essays will chart a course between ecology and Chicano Studies that is strengthening to both as subversive intellectual traditions.

Subversive Kin

Like ecology, Chicano Studies emerged to challenge the prevailing ways of thinking about things and doing them. It questioned the dictates of the "cult of objectivity"; confronted racist myths and stereotypical conventions about culture; and championed ideals of social action and change-oriented research.[13] As in the case of ecology, which rose to prominence with the modern environmental movement, the origins and evolution of Chicano Studies involved a search for critical knowledge that could be used in the service of community-based struggles. From the start, the Chicano critique of racial, class, gender, and sexual domination was an act by politically engaged intellectuals who were an integral part of a new social movement for social and economic justice.[14] Like ecology, Chicano Studies offered a critique of capitalist domination and provided an alternative vision of knowledge as a collaborative by-product of the work of hands-on intellectuals learning from and sharing with their communities. Chicano Studies sought local or situated knowledge, and its research program almost always addressed real social problems in specific communities. These epistemological and ethical similarities led us to a qualifying subtitle for this anthology that seems particularly appropriate: "Subversive Kin."

These essays articulate a dialogue between ecology and Chicano Studies. They are subversive in that the authors challenge the dominant ideologies and perspectives of conventional social science and humanities inquiry and that they were crafted by intellectuals who are committed environmental justice activists. All of us are grounded in the social- and environmental-justice struggles being waged by our communities — places wrestling with the harsh realities of environmental destruction, cultural extinction, and socioeconomic domination. But these essays also pose serious questions about the knowledge base of Chicano Studies. We explore new directions for framing critical, reflective inquiries by relating politics to culture, culture to economics, history to philosophy, and all these to ecological perspectives. These essays focus on the intersections of ecology with cultural and political-economic studies. But instead of inflating ethnicity and culture (a typically anthropocentric tendency within Chicano Studies), we argue that decolonizing ourselves (our communities and bodies) is inherently connected to the decolonization of nature.

Ecology and Chicano Studies share a vision of an emancipatory and transformative politics. Both seek alternatives to the dominant global capitalist system that is destroying biotic and cultural diversity. Both link the production of knowledge to lived experiences in real places. Both acknowledge the "edge of chaos" instead of becoming fixated on stability and order. In both cases, the transformative dynamics of disturbance (or domination) can be placed in spatial and historic context. As discursive practices, both derive from local knowledge and not from the construction of universal truths.

The concept of the ecosystem as a shifting and unstable landscape mosaic currently championed by conservation biologists is strikingly similar to the views that subordinated and colonized peoples long have had of the processes of social domination and conflict. Like the uncertainty facing wildlife in severely degraded ecosystems, local ethnic cultures experience fragmentation and displacement with each new wave of discriminatory legislation and each new intrusion by the forces of corporate economic subordination. Like the unstable, shifting mosaic of the disturbance regime, local cultures present a series of survival adaptations to capitalist domination. Thus, like the aspen groves that sprout in the aftermath of wildfires when disturbed land begins to heal, marginalized racial and ethnic communities continuously survive capital's "scorched earth" policies by reinventing themselves out of ecological, economic, and cultural devastation. The resulting unstable circumstances of local traditions and livelihoods are constantly threatened by an encroaching global market economy. We have often said within environmental justice circles: Ecocide and ethnocide go hand in hand, and people of color are also "endangered species."

Despite similarities to recent ecological thinking, Chicano Studies has been limited by a largely unquestioned and unchallenged anthropocentrism (human-centeredness).[15] Chicano Studies might have much to learn from the ecocentric (life-centered) perspectives of ecology. As we develop a more inclusive epistemology—one that is no longer human centered in outlook—we might discover and invent new tools for struggle. An earth-centered perspective should become intrinsic to our research activity. In this task we will surely have much to learn from our own local cultures.

The need for a change in perspective goes in the other direction as well. While ecology is a holistic and potentially subversive science,[16] its appropriation by the mainstream environmental movement has most often been narrow-minded, resulting in the politics of compromise and limited reform.[17] Mainstream American environmentalism has long ignored the class, race/ethnic, and gender dimensions of ecopolitics, and it remains a predominantly white, middle-class movement. Environmentalists have much to learn from Chicano land, labor, and civil rights struggles. For example, the environmental justice movement puts humans back in the picture by recognizing that the environment is the place where we live, work, and play. This simple expanded definition of the environment would help ecoactivists overcome the nature-culture dualism that limits their politics to "wilderness preservation" and wildlife protection. People are also poisoned by environmental degradation, and often the corporations that deforest the watersheds are the same ones that pollute the inner cities and rural areas with their toxic industrial wastes. Ecoactivists remain isolated from the broader social movements for ecological democracy and economic justice.

Ecology too has much to learn from the sustainable livelihoods of rural communities of color. Some conservation biologists are now willing to concede that native peoples often fulfill the critical ecological role of "keystone species." Through the disturbance ecology of their cultural landscapes, place-based communities create habitat niches and movement corridors that are vital to the survival of numerous native species of flora and fauna.[18] Environmentalists have been less adept at making this important concession to land-based communities. The result is a split between the social justice and environmental movements. In parallel fashion, ecology is too often split off from cultural studies and political-economy. As we will see, bioregionalism seeks to bridge this divide, but environmentalists (at least in the Upper Rio Grande watershed) have largely failed to bridge the gap that separates them from land-based communities that are dependent on the wilderness areas the ecoactivists seek to protect from corporate abuses.

Chicano environmentalism is not so much about the preservation of nature and wilderness as it is about struggles to confront daily hazards and threats to health and well-being in environments where we live and work. In rural areas these struggles focus on protecting the homeland environment from damage and expropriation. More importantly, Chicano environmentalism defines as part of its agenda the ideal of building sustainable alternatives to rampant capitalist maldevelopment. Laura Pulido (1996) calls this "the environmentalism of everyday life." With roots in inequities of class, race, and gender caused by the destruction and exploitation of nature under capitalism, these struggles link demands for social justice, sustainable development, workplace democracy, cultural endurance, and ecological soundness within a social movement that seeks a radical transformation of society. In this sense Chicano Studies and ecology are subversive kin in a search for equity and reciprocity among all species and communities.

The essays in this book are organized into three parts. In part 1, "Indo-Hispano Land Ethics," the authors outline the ethnophilosophical, ethnohistorical, and theoretical principles of a bioregional approach to Chicano Studies. Chapter 1 introduces a Chicano perspective on bioregionalism — the idea that the natural and cultural history of a place can be studied through a focus on the biogeographical and political-economic characteristics of watersheds. Using an interdisciplinary approach, I outline a model for collaborative social-action research: The insights of environmental history, cultural ecology, and land-grant studies are combined to achieve a more holistic view of regional processes of cultural and ecological change. The protection of Chicano land-grant communities, with their traditions of sustainable inhabitation of rural areas, requires restoration of the "homeland commons" in the Upper Rio Grande bioregion.

Chapter 2 refines the methods of bioregional inquiry through an exploration of discursive politics and the role of administrative regimes in local environmental conflicts. Rubén Martínez argues that bioregionalism can be strengthened through the incorporation of "textual analysis." Understanding the dialectics of text (discourse) is important to bioregional studies because it reveals the unfolding strategies and tactics of the dominant intrusive groups in expropriating and exploiting the homelands. The focus on discourse allows us to deconstruct the legal-political and administrative regimes that have usurped and mismanaged our homelands during the past 150 years of Euro-American domination in the Upper Rio Grande bioregion.

Chapter 3 contributes to the development of Indo-Hispano environmental ethics through an exploration of the concepts of "homeland" and "sense of place" as categories of ethnophilosophical reflection. Reyes García analyzes the ethnophilosophy of the homeland, noting that the concept itself has been appropriated by American tourists and environmentalists. Homeland is contested terrain. García writes that "where tourism, development, and environmentalism have severely undermined agropastoral traditions — in Taos, for example — homeland is conceived as theater much of the time. Homeland is not only a stage on which history is simultaneously imagined and acted out but [is] also a battlefield."

Part 2, "Environmental History and Ecological Politics," consists of four chapters dealing with various aspects of environmental history and contemporary ecological politics in the Upper Rio Grande watershed. Chapter 4 is a case study of the struggle by one rural, land-based New Mexican community to achieve ecological legitimacy under circumstances in which ecoactivists and environmental historians assume Chicanos are ignorant abusers of land and water resources. Laura Pulido poses important questions about culture and identity, sustainable development, indigenous land and water rights, and the future of the so-called public domain in the intermountain West.

Chapter 5 further examines the uses of environmental history in the context of ecological politics in northern New Mexico and southern Colorado, and it outlines an alternative approach for reconstructing the cultural and ecological history of the bioregion. Rubén Martínez and I critique the work of some leading environmental historians who have generally concluded that Hispanos in New Mexico and Colorado lack a conservation ethic. We conclude that ecological damage was primarily a result of the American railroad era of ranching, logging, and mining. We outline an alternative environmental history of the Río Arriba by reexamining evidence on the impact of logging and grazing and by taking a closer look at the relationship between natural and cultural landscapes in the Hispano villages. We argue for a synthesis of local ethnoscientific knowledge and conservation biology as a means to restore ecological legitimacy to the homeland commons.

Chapter 6 is a broad, critical examination of ecofeminism and Chicano environmentalism that assesses the prospects for building bridges across race, class, and gender. Gwyn Kirk explores common ground between ecofeminism and Chicano environmentalism, noting that both offer incisive critiques of mainstream environmentalism, capitalist domination, and institutionalized science. Both see people as "intimately connected to nature" and as "endangered species." But Kirk also poses a serious question for the politics of place-centered identities: "How can one guarantee that this lococenteredness does not become xenophobic, homophobic, racist, sexist: another version of redneck country?"

Chapter 7 presents oral histories of three Chicana activists from the Colorado Rocky Mountain region, women of color who are deeply connected to environmental justice struggles in various urban and rural communities. Malia Davis shows how these women activists recognize that "male dominance presumes a white agenda that is based on class-privileging." Poverty and economic discrimination, including the disparate impacts of environmental degradation in communities made up of people of color, provide a unified focus for both women and men. Yet, she writes, a conflict remains for gender issues within a culture where this is not the only locus of oppression, because there are also issues of racial and economic oppression.

Part 3, "Alternatives to Destruction," consists of a poem and two autobiographical essays reflecting on the prospects for sustainable human habitation of ecosystems in the Upper Rio Grande watershed. "The Pasture Poacher" by Joe Gallegos is a poem that defines cultural and ecological destruction as inextricably linked phenomena: The erosion of traditional land ethics is seen to accompany the erosion of the land through overgrazing.

In chapter 8 Joe Gallegos writes an autobiographical and semifictional essay that examines the daily life of an *acequia* (a gravity-driven irrigation ditch) in Colorado's San Luis Valley. He shows why the precious local knowledge of sustainable agroecological communities is endangered. Threats posed by water politics and practices of rural industrialization, like gold mining, are a constant force to be reckoned with by local water-rights users. The legal standing of water as a commodity is a fundamental source of conflict, and our legal system and laws distort the character of interpersonal relationships on traditional irrigation ditches.

Finally, chapter 9 is autobiographical, and I direct theoretical criticism at the commodification of land, water, and culture, while assessing the prospects for sustainable agriculture and the future well-being of Hispano communities in the Upper Rio Grande watershed. I revisit the infamous water trial involving the case of *San Luis Peoples Ditch et al. v. Battle Mountain Gold* to contrast the American legal system that treats water as a commodity and the Hispano view of water as a communal resource endowed with powerful cultural and ecological meaning. The acequia irrigation ditches are described as an "example of sustainable agriculture wedded to steady-state economics." The acequias increase biodiversity and provide a material basis for encouraging and instructing the local culture in the careful stewardship of the land, water, and wildlife. The historic acequia farming communities of the Culebra watershed are endangered by the destructive forces of mining and logging. The coming political struggles over land use and farmland preservation will determine the future of these historic communities.

Most of the essays in this collection focus on the Río Arriba bioregion, a place where Chicanos trace their ancestral roots deep into Native American, Spanish, and Mexican origins by five to thirty generations and more. While our focus is on a relatively small rural region of the Southwest, we expect that our readers will recognize the value of these historic acequia communities in the preservation of our nation's cultural heritage. As we explore the lessons to be learned from these rural pockets of *mestizo*, land-based cultures, we may better come to appreciate the broader environmental issues that face our communities in places as far-flung as Denver,

East Los Angeles, San Antonio, Laredo, Chicago, Detroit, and New York. As ecosystems vary, so too do the biogeographical cultures that develop in close relationship with nature's own designs. Such a relationship, as these essays will show, is possible for both rural *and* urban cultural landscapes. Cities and their neighborhood communities also exist in bioregional context, even if the built environments seemingly overpower the underlying ecosystemic basis of life.[19] Urban areas do not exist in an ecological vacuum. Rivers, land forms, plants, and animal life do not totally disappear simply because humans alter natural landscapes through the proliferation of built environments. If land-based cultures survive the current waves of ecocide and ethnocide, they might just provide the knowledge bases needed to reconstruct both rural and urban environments on the basis of more ecologically sustainable and socially just principles.

Notes

1. The title for this anthology is a "take" on Paul Shepard and David McKinley's *The Subversive Science: Essays toward an Ecology of Man.* See Shepard and McKinley 1969, who note that Sears (1964) first coined the phrase "subversive science."

2. In the 1950s and 1960s, Eugene Odum (1971) formulated the then most widely accepted interpretation of the principles of classical ecology in his book *Fundamentals of Ecology.* For an interesting discussion of the changing nature of ecology in historical and cultural context, see Worster 1995:65–86. On the ecology of "order" and "chaos," see Worster 1993:156–70. For more on the evolution of the ecosystem concept, see Golley 1993; also see Noss et al. 1994.

3. For more on the theory of the ecology of disturbance regimes, see Harris 1984, Grumbine 1992, and Noss et al. 1994.

4. Ecology underwent a significant paradigm shift in the 1960s and 1970s. Classical ecology (as formulated by Odum) sought to document the "equilibrium" and "stability" of ecosystems, which it fashioned in the form of the "climax community." With the advent of the "ecology of disturbance regimes," ecoscientists began to focus on the instability and uncertainty of the ecosystems that they fashioned in the form of the "shifting mosaic" of natural landscapes. Natural disturbances — fires, insect outbreaks, volcanic eruptions and landslides, floods, drought, and other catastrophic events — are said to continuously recreate the boundaries and edges of the various plant and animal communities that sustain the varied patterns of biodiversity. This shift to a focus on disturbance and instability

has led some to argue erroneously that human disturbances (e.g., mining, logging, grazing) are good for the ecosystem because they mimic natural disturbances. Human disturbance regimes, however, tend to reduce the diversity of the natural landscape mosaic. Anthropogenesis seldom maintains the regenerative qualities of ecosystems preserved by natural disturbances. For further discussion, see Noss 1993, Noss et al. 1994, Soulé and Lease 1995, and Peña (in press).

5. See the intriguing essays in Soulé and Lease 1995 for the proceedings of a conference on postmodern deconstruction and conservation biology.

6. For commentary from a scientist about the ethical dilemmas spawned by the Manhattan Project (and reductionist science in general), see Dyson 1979. Freeman Dyson, a mathematician and theoretical physicist who worked at Los Alamos with Oppenheimer, notes that the scientists involved in the Manhattan Project were enthralled with the logical and even aesthetic beauty of the mathematics underlying the invention of the A-bomb; they never paused to consider the ethical, cultural, and environmental implications of their research. According to Dyson, it was positivistic folly — the separation of facts from values — that blinded the scientists at Los Alamos.

7. See Oelschlaeger 1991 (80–82) for intriguing commentary on the implications of the Baconian model of science for environmental ethics.

8. On the "patenting of life," see Shiva 1997; see also Teitel and Shand 1997.

9. For recent commentaries along this line see Scheffer 1991, who sees the black civil rights, feminist, and antiwar movements as the "societal backdrop" for the emergence of environmentalism at a time when the science of ecology was attaining greater public visibility. Also see Paehlke 1989, Rifkin 1991, Pepper 1993, and Leff 1995.

10. Some recent works dealing with environmental issues and Chicanos include Peña 1989, 1992, 1997b, in press; Peña, Martínez, and McFarland 1993; Moses 1993; Peña and Gallegos 1993, 1997; Pulido 1993, 1996; Gutiérrez 1994; and Peña and Mondragon Valdéz 1998.

11. It is interesting that those Chicano authors who have most grappled with the dialectics of "place" and "identity" are novelists, poets, and other writers of fiction. One thinks of the work of authors as widely ranging as Tomás Rivera, Rudolfo Anaya, Jimmy Santiago Baca, Sandra Cisneros, and Gloria Anzaldúa as examples of authors whose writings embody a deep respect and concern for sense of place in Chicano identity politics. Of course, some of these authors (Anzaldúa especially) blur the boundaries between fiction, autobiography, and social theory — a particularly subversive quality of their contributions to Chicano discourse. Few nonfiction writers have expressed a similar awareness or concern for sense of place or, perhaps more precisely, topistics — the sociological study of placeways

(see Rosaldo 1989 and Saldívar 1990 for further discussion). But the spatial dimensions of social life, and thus sense of place, have remained largely outside the purview of social scientists in Chicano Studies; see Peña (in press) for further discussion of the spatiality of social life and the role of the biogeographical imagination in the construction of place-centered identities.

12. On "interactivity" and "positionality" as aspects of the human experience of place see Hayles 1995.

13. The earliest Chicano critic of the "myth of social science objectivity" is Romano (1970). Also see the recent commentary on Romano by García (1992). The ethics of social action research are outlined in the well-known preamble to the by-laws of the National Association for Chicano Studies (now National Association for Chicana and Chicano Studies).

14. For excellent critical historiographies of Chicano Studies, see Flores 1983 and 1986.

15. Examples of limitations due to anthropocentrism include essays in the recent anthologies edited by Anzaldúa (1990) and de la Torre and Pesquera (1993).

16. Actually, the development of ecology has followed a bifurcated direction in the past fifty years. A split has developed between a reductionist "microecology" that focuses on organisms from the perspective of "boundaries-inward," and a holistic "macroecology" that focuses on organisms from the perspective of "boundaries-outward." An example of this split is the opposition between a holistic agroecology and a reductionist molecular biology (qua: biotechnology). For further discussion, see Jackson 1987. On the history of the ecosystem concept in ecology see Golley 1993.

17. See Pulido 1990 and 1996; Peña 1992; and Peña, Martínez, and McFarland 1993.

18. On indigenous people as "keystone species," see Noss 1994 and Peña 1997b.

19. The recent rash of "natural disasters" (earthquakes, mudslides, brush fires, etc.) in the Los Angeles basin are remarkable evidence of the enduring ecosystemic basis of life. Nature does not disappear, no matter how grotesquely hyperurbanized and anthropogenic our built environment may appear.

Part 1

Indo-Hispano Land Ethics

1 Los Animalitos

Culture, Ecology, and the Politics of Place in the Upper Rio Grande

Devon G. Peña

> No *maten los animalitos, porque ellos también son muy inteligentes.*
> — Margarita Kuehner Peña

Storytelling is the source of much of my knowledge of the Greater Rio Grande bioregions, so I will begin with an anecdote. I was ten when my youngest uncle, José Eduardo, borrowed a Daisy BB gun from a neighbor. We set out into the brush mesquite and prickly pear *monte* that was our backyard in Three Points, a *barrio* in the South Texas border town of Laredo. We climbed down into the *arroyo* Chacón, a smelly, mucky, polluted tributary of the Rio Grande. Our quest was simple. Armed to the teeth, we hunted for birds. The slaughter was quick. The *pulguientos* were no match for the BB gun. My uncle was the marksman, and I acted as retriever. I fulfilled my role with pride and excitement. I'll never forget the quickening of my heartbeat after the kill or the smell of bird blood mixed with Rio Grande mud.

This was my only childhood hunting trip, and it was quite eventful as things turned out. On our return home, bloody prize trophies in hand, my grandmother Margarita strongly admonished us for this display of indecent behavior. I will never forget what she said to us: *"¡Sinvergüenzas! No deben de matar los pajaritos. No maten los animalitos, porque ellos también son muy inteligentes."* (No shame! You should not kill the little birds. Don't kill the little animals, because they too are very intelligent.) The wisdom guiding my grandmother's admonishment did not impress me at the time. I felt shame but did not fully understand why. I could see that my grandma thought it was wrong to kill another living being. But maybe a preadolescent boy, anxious to prove his worthiness as a companion to older male kin, is too perplexed with his place in the family to worry much about the ethical implications of such behavior. A ten-year-old might not fully comprehend why an elder treats animals with such a sense of respect and equality.

Many years later, long after her death, I am still conversing with my grandmother's ecological ghost. I am still trying to understand what lay beneath the egalitarian sensitivity she expressed in her beliefs about and relationships with animals and plants. Over the course of her sixty-three years, my grandmother raised ten of her own children and me; I was her first grandson. My childhood memories are rich with images of my grandmother on her hands and knees, working the soil of the bean, corn, pumpkin, and squash patch she kept in our backyard next to the *gallinero* (chicken coop) and horse corral. I also remember that my grandmother planted a cactus fence along the east side of the garden, a special edible cactus that lacked the hard spines of the prickly pear. It was soft, smooth, and cool to the touch. Margarita cooked the *nopalitos* for breakfast, diced and sauteed with onions, *serrano* peppers, tomatoes, garlic, and cilantro. If we were lucky, all the fixings came straight out of her garden. Lacking an item, she would often barter for a special ingredient with one of the neighbors. "Take these tortillas and go over to Elvira's," she would instruct me, "and bring me some of her delicious cilantro."

Over the years my grandmother assembled quite a menagerie of animals at home. She kept a *haula* (cage) full of pigeons underneath the old *huisache* tree that grew on the east side of our house. She trained the pigeons to fly away all day and to return home for their evening roosts. She raised chickens, turkeys, guinea fowl, and even rabbits. She never let us eat any of these animals and allowed us only to take eggs from the chickens. One time she even had a goat, but it kept getting into the garden and the cactus fence, so she gave it away to Don Amador, an old farmer who lived down the dirt road from her. With all the animals running around, she never let anyone keep caged birds. One time, my Tía Rosa brought her a pair of parakeets for her birthday. Margarita kindly refused the gift, saying: "It's wrong to keep them in cages. They belong in the trees. They should go home to the jungle." It just seems as if animals and plants occupied a central place in my grandmother's pleasures, and yet she refused to enslave the animals. She spared them the indignity that is too often carelessly heaped on pets. Even the pigeons spent most of their time away from the cage roost, and Grandma never locked the birds in as

prisoners; she closed the latch only at night to protect them from predatory visitors such as the neighbors' cats.

Once, two of my uncles shot the mother of some just-hatched barn
owls. They mercifully brought the two orphans home. My grandmother
cared for them for several months, keeping them in a makeshift cage,
feeding them small rodents, and giving them water. One morning she
released the toddler owls. She took them to a bluff overlooking the Chacón, opened the door to the cage, and released them. The owls flew into a
stand of Rio Grande salt cedar trees growing on the banks of the creek.
She called these *cubrevientos* (windbreak trees). She always had a name
for trees, shrubs, and plants, names that seemed fashioned out of some
ancient, secret language steeped in a deep memory of place. Another time,
she cared for a pair of young bobcats, again orphaned by my uncles.

Grandma was a seed saver. Every summer after harvest she left a few of
the cornstalks and bean bushes standing in the garden, gathering dust.
After the plants dried, she collected the crops and stripped the seeds from
them. She collected the seeds in mayonnaise jars, which she kept safe in a
kitchen cabinet next to the tin cans of marinated *chile chipotle* and *serrano*. I always wondered why she did this. Why not just buy the seeds at
the store? *"La semilla es la memoria de la planta,"* she said, *"y crece con lo
que vive en la tierra."* (The seed is the plant's memory and grows with
what lives in the soil.)

My grandmother introduced me to some of those creatures that "live
in the soil." *Los animalitos,* we call them. There were earthworms and
grubby things such as the little animals living in the dark, moist, and cool
soil under the shadow of her sour orange trees. As her stories, gardens,
and orchards are the persistent oases of my parched border homeland
memories, so too the seeds possessed spirit, a memory of earth places that
endured the passing of the seasons. I am left with memories of ghosts — the
owls and bobcats killed by kin. I also inherit Margarita's belief that the
spirit of the soil is in the seeds we save as precious heirlooms, and these are
the memories of place we find in our elders' wisdom of the land. As a child
I never appreciated my grandmother's ways. It was all too much a part of
my own daily routine to seem special.

Some thirty years and a dozen homes later, far removed from my place
of origin, I find myself wondering: What was it about my grandmother's
life experiences and knowledge that produced this love of nature and all

its life-forms? This question guides my current scholarly work, the study of *mexicano* culture from a bioregional perspective.

Bioregionalism

Studying the Interface of Culture with Nature

As scholars continue exploring the relationship between nature and culture, many are proposing the adoption of the bioregional paradigm as a singularly holistic perspective to guide inquiries about cultural and environmental change. Bioregionalists focus on the prospects for sustainable livelihoods and reinhabitation.[1] Sociologist Bill Devall offers one of the clearest statements regarding the bioregional perspective. The concept combines the terms *bio* (Greek for "life") and *regio* (Latin for "boundary"). The term "bioregionalism" refers to an intellectual perspective that links the study of cultural and natural areas. Devall emphasizes the interdisciplinary character of bioregionalism and points to its concern for the "restoration of the earth's natural plant and animal diversity within a 'regional framework' and of cultural adaptation to specific bioregions. . . . The central question for bioregional studies is what information do I need to know to live rightly and appropriately in this place?" (Devall 1988, 58).

Devall identifies four major criteria in the definition of a bioregion: biotic shift, watershed, sense of place, and cultural distinctiveness (Devall 1988, 61–64).[2] Biotic shift simply refers to the percentage change in plant and animal species from one region to another. (Usually a 15 to 25 percent change constitutes a biotic shift.) Watersheds are an important component of a bioregion because they define the basic hydrological units. The watershed contributes to biotic and cultural diversity. Water, in interaction with geography, creates the ecosystemic niches that give rise to specific biotic (and human) communities.[3]

The third criterion, sense of place (or spirit of place), is significant because it arises out of the local culture's understanding of ecosystemic conditions. Devall (1988, 62) quotes from bioregional poet Swan to elaborate this key point about sense of place: "Sacred places are the sites for ceremony and ritual healing, contemplation, and rites of passage. . . . In many cultures, such sacred places were seen and are seen today as the very cornerstone for cultural renewal." Devall's insistence on the centrality of sense of place in the study of bioregions reminds me of Ortega y Gasset's timeless adage, "Show me the landscape in which you live, and I will tell you who you are" (as quoted in Lane 1988, 64). Describing the qualities of cultural distinctiveness, Devall points to rituals, art forms, ways of living, and specialized terminology referring to land forms or weather or relationships with the landscape as indicative of a biogeographical culture (Devall 1988, 64).

Some bioregionalists emphasize the connections between ecological and cultural diversity to explain the emergence of a sense of place. The North American (now Turtle Island) Bioregional Congress defines bioregionalism as "a movement for strengthening and re-establishing the diversity of human cultures and their interconnections with their bioregion. . . . The boundaries of human cultures, before industrialization, were often the same as bioregional boundaries. The people who *lived* within each unique 'bioregion' evolved unique living patterns and cultures as a response to their bioregional resources and parameters" (as cited in Friends of the Trees 1988, 117). While this view recognizes that bioregional principles are rooted in the oldest, place-centered, human communities, it obscures the fact that many of these are still *living* cultures. This is why bioregionalists often speak of "people who lived" — in the past tense. Bioregionalists have tended to limit their thinking to the task of *reestablishing* cultural diversity instead of attending to the protection of existing, endangered local cultures. For a perspective that values cultural diversity, bioregionalism as currently constructed *in practice* is oddly silent on the infinite variations evident in existing human adaptations to and impacts on local ecosystems. Bioregionalists also are disconnected from the struggles of indigenous land-based communities.

Bioregionalism, Deep Ecology, and the Politics of Place

Most North American (primarily U.S.) bioregionalists derive their ethical values directly from "deep ecology," an environmental philosophy that embraces "biocentric" values. Deep ecologists ground their ontological and ethical program in a worldview that is centered on the concept of "interspecies equity," the belief that all life-forms are (or should be) equal partners, each deserving of safe and sacred habitat.[4] This idea of a "council of all beings" serves as a strong source of recent ethical thinking among bioregionalists. Thus, Jim Cheney outlines the concept of environmental ethics as deriving from place-centered, or bioregional, narratives. Places are constituted as the moral and physical spaces we share with other species, and bioregionalism is the narrative form humans use to create "storied residence" in a place (Cheney 1989). However, there is considerable ambiguity surrounding sense of place as a category of cultural-ecological value. This ambiguity stems from a tendency among bioregionalists to inflate symbolic (poetic) discourses and ritual as primary forces that shape the course of social, cultural, and environmental change. Bioregionalism inherits this tendency from deep ecology.

I see this tendency as a variant of "ecoidealism," in which ideas (ethics) are cast as determining the relationship of humans to the natural world. For a perspective that values the biophysical qualities of place (the material dimensions of human existence), deep ecology is silent on the role of modes of production and domination as social forces shaping the environment. In a feminist critique of deep ecology, Joni Seager (1993, 230) notes that "while there is an explicit criticism of destructive cultural attitudes toward nature, there is no apparent curiosity about the extent to which those 'cultural attitudes' may be gender, race, or class specific." While espousing nonhierarchical values of interspecies equity, deep ecologists remain silent on social inequities (on the basis of class, race, or gender differences) among human groups.

The reduction of agency to a mere discourse on ethical values is compounded by the misanthropic underpinnings of much of deep ecological thought. Oddly, radical environmentalists, many of whom profess deep ecological or bioregional values, have often presumed that humans can be destructive forces only in relation to nature.[5] Christopher Manes, Earth First! cofounder, once issued a call for "voluntary extinction" through mass suicide of humans as a final solution to the problem of the destruction of "wilderness" areas. I wondered then, Who would go first? — the overpopulating little brown people who were a political obsession for many "radical" environmentalists such as Edward Abbey in those heady Reagan days when it seemed to some that the border was overrun by Mexican wetbacks, or perhaps the transplanted deep ecologists sitting in their gentrified Taco Deco adobe mansions and "Earthships" on the outskirts of Taos, New Mexico, where the *acequias* once fed verdant fields? Manes was, presumably, the activist who used the pen name "Miss Ann

Thropy" to cast hilarious satirical diatribes against industrial civilization in the *Earth First!* journal.[6] But Mane's comedic and iconoclastic ramblings reflected a basic and widespread misunderstanding of the culture-nature interrelationship. The deep ecological standpoint, at that moment in its own contradictory discursive history, failed to acknowledge that some human cultures and social classes are *not* destructive in their relationship with nature.

This enduring philosophical position, uncritically embraced by some conservation biologists, denies the possibility for creative stewardship and inhabitation of ecosystems by humans. Against this misanthropic view, restoration and cultural ecologists propose that humans are as much a part of nature as other species. Humans can play a positive role by providing "ecological services" to the ecosystem:

> In the judgment of the [landscape] restorationists, the exclusion of humans from nature deforms both. Set off against nature, humans can only work harm in the world. Any possibility of constructive stewardship is denied them, and the best they can do for nature is depart it and leave it alone. But nature suffers as well in this separation from human beings, because it is deprived of the services that humans render as rightful citizens of the biotic community. Dramatic testimony to this is seen in . . . wilderness areas from which humans are systematically excluded [and which are] the most astonishingly unnatural places on earth. (Kane 1994, 70)

Another basic problem with the dominant North American varieties of bioregionalism is the exaggerated significance many activists attribute to "sacred place" in the struggle for cultural-ecological renewal. The intrinsic value of respect for sacred places as a basis from which to aim for cultural renewal must be understood in a broader historical and political-economic context than that posed by deep ecology in its chosen nemesis of "industrialism." It is simply not enough to reject industrialism (qua capitalism) as a lifestyle choice and then celebrate sense of place through earth-bonding rituals. It is especially problematic if the would-be natives (transplant ecoactivists) are accomplices in the conquest and extinction of the very communities they would emulate and protect. This is often the case wherever deep ecologists and ecoactivists have become part of the wave of post-1960s white immigrants who resettled in and gentrified many of the rural communities of the intermountain West. In Taos such environmentally correct members of the white middle class are now among the forces displacing natives.[7]

In addition, what of sacred places subject to the contradictory claims of "wise users" for recreational rights against deeply rooted Native American religious rights? The Rainbow Natural Bridge National Monument is a good example of how the politics of sacred places is ultimately limited by the ability of bureaucrats to mediate competing claims in a multiple-use-policy milieu that is decidedly stacked against the assertion of multicultural land-use ethics (see Smith and Manning 1997).

Be that as it may, surely the ethnic, class, and gender inequities reproduced across bioregions by colonizing settler states and the destructive boom-bust cycles of capitalist maldevelopment cannot be wished away simply by resorting to a philosophy whose politics ultimately reduce to reconstructed ritual; here I would include the spectacle of culturally decontextualized acts of civil disobedience as principled (but ultimately insufficient) tactics among those involved in the worthy search for a "wild" sense of place.[8] Most places are too chaotic as contested sites of political ecological struggle to serve as stable anchors for those who seek to retreat from the more misanthropic excesses of deep ecology by appealing to bioregional (and hence multicultural) ethics.

Devall's approach to the integration of cultural distinctiveness within bioregional theory is especially problematic because it overlooks two major conceptual problems in the study of multicultural relationships to nature:

1) Political economy, which refers, in bioregional framework, to the study of the territorial (spatial) inscription of relations of economic domination and the changing forms of human social organization; and

2) Ethnophilosophy, which refers, in bioregional framework, to indigenous, or better, autochthonous ontology, epistemology, metaphysics, aesthetics, ethics, and ethnoscience.[9]

By incorporating the study of the political economic and ethnophilosophical problems in a given biogeographical area, we can recognize how sacred places have been violated by locals and outsiders alike. Perhaps then we can approach the study of bioregions with a more critical and less romantic eye.

Deep ecologists, and by extension many bioregionalists, have long re-mained polarized around two constructions of culture *as relationship to nature:* One position scorns all human cultures and views them as equally destructive of nature (misanthropism). The other tendency laments native cultures as relics of a long-lost original unity with nature (exoticism).[10] Adherence to the desires of the exoticist carries the risk of reducing indige-nous traditions and practices to mere remnants in museum exhibits, archi-val collections, and decontextualized oratories in support of indigenous land rights. Worse yet is the reduction of endangered cultures to ab-stracted objects of amusement. In practice, "cultural" appreciation sucks the life out of "exotic" peoples. Local knowledge is appropriated and exploited by the insatiable market for traditional artifacts, rituals, and other expressive cultural practices.[11] The commercial venues present these as spectacles, stripped of their oppositional content, so that those who celebrate the presumed robustness of our nation's cultural and historic heritage can feel good about their contact with a "disappearing" Other.

There is clearly a need to move beyond deep ecological tendencies that too often misemphasize and exoticize sense of place as the conceptual basis of political action for cultural renewal, particularly when this con-cept is so easily misappropriated for commercial purposes. We are not only consuming the mountains as timber, ore, and pasture, but as scenery, spectacle, "wilderness," or even "power vortex."[12] The bioregionalist con-cept of "distinctive culture" must be clarified. If the ethical claims of local knowledge are to have effective standing within the politics of place, they must attain some semblance of "ecological legitimacy" on their own terms (see Pulido, chapter 4; Peña and Martínez, chapter 5).

From the vantage point of cultural ecology, the distinctiveness of local culture is by rule a function of the myriad expressive and material forms that specific land-based communities create to construct their own ethno-philosophical and ethnoscientific traditions. These place-centered knowl-edge systems have been widely documented and championed by natural and social scientists.[13] Bioregional study of cultural distinctiveness, how-ever, must recognize processes of change, which inevitably involves a more thorough analysis of the social conflicts that arise whenever colonizing forces seek to impose new social (and legal) relations of production and reproduction (see Martínez, chapter 2). Conflicted social forces (classes and other social groups) assert contested claims to places whenever they struggle to make their particular administrative regimes and land-use values dominant. These institutionalized and subaltern practices constitute the political economy of a bioregion, and they play a major role in the environmental history of places.

The approach proposed here for bioregional study emphasizes the need for a careful analysis of the local folk practices that constitute the ethnoscientific traditions. These autochthonous practices can be thought of as domains (discursive fields) of tacit, practical, and empirical knowledge developed by local communities over generations of interaction with their environments. Such place-centered knowledge systems (or *sapienza poetica,* to modify a term from Vico) may provide the semantic, normative, and ontological guideposts necessary for generating ecologically sustainable and culturally respectful forms of human social organization in given biogeographical contexts (see also García 1988). The bioregional approach to the study of cultural distinctiveness and renewal must include an accounting of these place-centered, and usually sustainable, folk practices and technologies (e.g., van Dresser 1964, 1972; Garcia 1988, 433–54; and Peña 1992).

The production and reproduction of material and symbolic culture in bioregional context is problematic in a more strictly political-economic sense. In areas such as the Río Arriba, battles between agropastoral and extractive industrial economies for control of the natural conditions of production are prime examples of the powerful and largely conflicted political-economic forces that shape places in ways that exceed the scope of more purely symbolic or ideological explanations. The large-scale destruction of watersheds and the resulting displacement of native communities; the chaotic transition from a sustainable agropastoral economy to an industrializing extractive resource colony; the enclosure of the commons and the disappearance and extinction of local knowledge — all these processes of change exceed the scope of the countless fanciful theoretical pirouettes concerned with the symbolic power, or spiritual ecology, of sacred places. By failing to incorporate the study of political-economic social forces and the oppositional practices generated by local cultures, bioregionalists will repeat idealized abstractions, or avoidance, of the Other; these tendencies have long characterized much of the historical discourse about the intermountain West. This ecophilosophical worldview neglects class, gender, and ethnic differences that unfold as politically located practices within the complex trajectories of social and environmental change.[14]

We must also guard against the romanticism identified by Ramón Gutiérrez (1989) in much of the work by "southwestern" cultural ecologists (see also Pulido, chapter 4). It is a romanticism not unlike that expressed in deep ecological fantasies about a return to an original unity with nature. We must remain critical and must not overlook the conflict generated by socially constructed differences, but we must also avoid romanticizing, or worse, "essentializing" local cultures. No one community is a home to natives in perfect harmony with nature. Instead, we must explore the contradictory ambiguities of local cultures' beliefs and practices. We must acknowledge and explore those uncomfortable locations of subjectivity that are filled with inconsistencies, instabilities, and ironies. For example, we may do well to examine the recurring disjunction between professed ethics and real actions (see Peña 1989 and in press). To remain critical in this fashion requires that we acknowledge power and inequity as factors that influence the evolution of the politics of place.

From this more critical political-economic perspective, we can consider the genesis of local cultures in the context of ecosystems (as per the typical bioregional tale), but we can go further and study the social forces and relations of production and reproduction, and we can also study how these are expressed in the politics of human spatial organization as economic forces alter the landscape. This approach ultimately leads us back to the study of the transformation of the natural conditions of production by capitalist development. Bioregionalism meets political economy on the conflicted terrain of environmental history, because capitalists are so good at transforming other peoples' natural and cultural landscapes. The political will that leads to power through economic domination is thus inscribed on bioregional homelands in the form of the highly disturbed landscape ecology of colonized areas.

To study the politics of locality without the fetters of romanticism and ritualizing spectacle, we must reexamine the problem of sense of place in the context of a discussion of how all "territorialities" are socially constructed (Grossberg 1993). In the context of the Upper Rio Grande there is an intensifying battle between three paradigms that pits resource extraction, wilderness preservation, and homeland commons as distinct and antagonistic locations in the unfolding politics for control of the natural conditions of existence. This clash of paradigms involves what I call the "politics of place." The resource extraction model is the dominant position and is clearly directed by the state and by capital to facilitate the exploitation of nature as a commodity. The wilderness preservation model had until recent times proved ascendant, and it privileges a policy agenda directed by environmentalists to manage or keep nature as separate from the detrimental effects of human culture as practicable (wilderness here, civilization there). The homeland-commons paradigm resonates with the claims of local cultures and favors a transition back to the stewardship traditions embodied in the principle of self-managed watershed commonwealths.[15]

My choice of a bioregional framework is tempered by a critical reading of research literature of two other comparative interdisciplinary fields that are usually overlooked in the bioregionalist discourse: cultural ecology and political economy. Cultural-ecological research shares many concerns and methods with bioregionalism, but at the heart of cultural-ecological inquiry is a commitment to the tenet that humans and nature are interrelated and that any separation of the two, whether conceptual or political, invites essentialist, exoticist, or misanthropic consequences. We must be clear that our own approach does not reproduce the ethnocentric ontological errors of American bioregionalism.

Political economy also shares some concerns with bioregionalism, especially those varieties of inquiry that focus on geographic, spatial, and regional dynamics (e.g., the study of uneven regional development). Guiding the practice of political-economic inquiry, however, is a commitment to (the undeniably anthropocentric) principle that human existence by definition requires production and reproduction of livelihoods, social organizations, ideologies, and so forth. Moreover, in radical political economics the transformation of material nature by humans acting in the world to produce and reproduce their species-life is a conflict-ridden process, largely shaped by the changing structures of power under conditions of social inequality and subaltern resistance. This, of course, is precisely what opens the possibility of sustainable human habitation of ecosystems, albeit within the limits of actual political power gained through the circulation of local struggle. Likewise, we must avoid the opposite tendency of political economists to underestimate the role of "ideology" as a force that constrains and redirects the processes of social, cultural, and environmental change. The struggle for ecological legitimacy among Chicano sheepherders is a good example of the important role of ideological dynamics in environmental conflicts (see Pulido, chapter 4).[16]

Bioregionalism's concern for a sense of place can provide a location from which to negotiate the legitimacy of the knowledge base of local cultures against the imperatives of intrusive political-economic forces. To do so effectively, however, bioregional study must provide ample room for practical critiques of the sociological and economic dimensions of inequality and injustice in specific places. Previous bioregional research identified sense of place as a key ecological value largely by appealing, somewhat naively, to the notion of cultural distinctiveness. Cultural ecology shows that many cultures are not destructive in relation to nature and that the path to sustainable livelihoods may be discovered by following the roads chosen by indigenous communities. Political economy initiates the effort to explain why indigenous communities might not have a workable approach as a consequence of the role that structured inequality plays in diminishing the intrinsic value of both natural areas and local human cultures.

The Cultural Ecology and Political Economy of the Río Arriba

Over the past thirty years, natural scientists, humanists, and social scientists have assembled an impressive body of original research on the cultural and ecological history of the Río Arriba bioregion.[17] Although this research has not been evaluated until now, a critical review and comparison reveals that it remains problematic in several fundamental ways. Of concern here are various problems that have been overlooked in the study of the forces described in this literature as underlying causes of environmental degradation, cultural extinction, injustice, and inequality:

1) cultural differences in the "demythologizing" of conservation ethics;
2) ethnoscience and the production and reproduction of place-centered knowledge;
3) political-economic conflict dynamics in the formation of bioregional distinctions;
4) exoticism in the (mis)construction of mexicano culture; and
5) exclusion of gender as a category of cultural ecological research.

Conservation Ethics and the Distinctiveness
of Spanish-Mexican Culture

The trend in the accumulated research of the past has been to stereotype mexicano (Spanish-Mexican or Hispano) culture. One recurrent construction involves the idea that mexicanos were historically insensitive toward ecological values and lacked a "conservation ethic." A proponent of this view is William deBuys, whose environmental history of the Sangre de Cristo Mountains remains an essential source among many contemporary students of this bioregion. We take up the critique of this environmental history in chapter 5. DeBuys's view is representative of the understanding of American scholars on the environmental history of the bioregion: The development of a conservation ethic had to wait for Aldo Leopold's arrival and genesis as the hallowed founder of "land ethics." Rural, land-based communities were, presumably, too primitive in their scientific understanding of nature to manage their resource domains in any thoughtful or sustainable manner (deBuys 1985). Native American, Hispano, and Anglo must all share blame for environmental degradation in the bioregion.

Everyone is equally to blame for the degradation of the mountain range over the past 150 years. This simplistic view obscures serious class, ethnic, and gender differences in land-use practices, the truth of which can be revealed through more careful study. It also overlooks the political-economic history of the bioregion and the tumultuous changes occasioned by the arrival of the railroad, loss of land grants, and the resulting contraction of grazing range, intensive commercialization of agriculture, and (urban) migration. These changes were key factors underlying the problems of mexicano (as well as Pueblo Indian) contributions to overgrazing and other types of land degradation. (See Peña and Martínez, chapter 5, for a more detailed critique of the controversies associated with the environmental history of the Río Arriba.)[18]

Labor historians of the bioregion are familiar with the fact that the period from the 1880s to the turn of the century corresponded with the widespread imposition of the *partido* form of ground-rent exchange relations in northern New Mexico. The *partido* (or rent-in-kind) system expanded largely as a consequence of the arrival of entrepreneurial land speculators such as Frank Bond in the Española area, Tom Burns in

Chama-Tierra Amarilla, and Alfred Manby in Taos. The *partido* system was important in incipient commercialization of local grazing economies. Commercialization implied increased "productivity," which obviously resulted in excessive demands being imposed on the natural carrying capacity of the land. Thus, at least in the case of Río Arriba, the destruction of ecological balance was more a consequence of capitalist intrusions than the direct result of traditional mexicano grazing practices.[19]

Many scholars — cultural ecologists and land-grant researchers among them — describe mexicano culture in terms of strong ties to the land, firm conservation ethics, and a history of sustainable land- and water-use practices.[20] Reyes García (1988, 298), reflecting on the philosophy of natural historian Barry Lopez, argues that land-based cultures derive their philosophical traditions from the local natural landscape. To repeat Lopez: "An indigenous philosophy — metaphysics, ethics, epistemology, aesthetics, and logic — may also derive from a people's continuous attentiveness to both the obvious (scientific) and ineffable (artistic) orders of the local landscape."

García's contribution to the ethnophilosophy of nature consists of recognizing (along with Gramsci) that all persons "are philosophers" and that agropastoralists in the Upper Rio Grande are no exception. Akin to the *emic* stance in contemporary social science discourse, this view affirms that truth claims are the province of a community of participants — in this case a local community defined by the dynamic, intense, and cyclical relations that join the human and the natural as partners in a mutual home space.[21]

García argues that in land-based cultures the ecology-human link is associated with the development of a "(home)land ethic," a relationship with nature that corresponds to the biogeographical regions that sustain local communities. Drawing on Aldo Leopold's founding contribution to land ethics, García pointedly argues that as biotic diversity is essential to the health of the land community, so too cultural diversity is essential to the health of both natural and human communities.[22] Thus, the drive toward conquest of nature (and exhaustion of wilderness as "self-willing land") is closely associated with the destruction of human cultural diversity (García 1988, 300; see also Peña 1992; and Peña and Mondragon Valdéz 1998).

In the homeland ethic the biogeographical marriage of cultural and ecological diversity becomes the essential source for autochthonous patterns of sustainable livelihood. The production of ethics is about social practices, about the rules governing interrelationships. These rules provide a code to differentiate between social and antisocial conduct (García 1988, 300). In the case of the discourse García identifies as the "Indo-Hispano" homeland ethic, the social practices guided by the code of *vergüenza* (shame) are critical in the crafting of the ecological sensibilities of land-based communities in the Río Arriba. One New Mexican *cuento* (folktale) tells the story of a man who is banished from the mountains by a Forest Spirit (Espíritu del Bosque) for being greedy and cutting too many trees (Peña 1992). Sanctions against the multiple forms of greed occupy a central position in the homeland ethic of these Hispano communities; yet the existence of such sanctions is not always motivated by affairs having to do with relations among humans. The motivation for such sanctions often derives from biocentric values that govern the affairs and relations *among equals within nature*. The Lacandón Maya say to the animals, plants, rivers, and mountains: *"In lak ech"* ("You are my other self").

In this version of *manito* bioregional narrative,[23] biocentric values are posed as an intrinsic property of land-based communities, because the health of land and water is a universal constant affecting the prospects for human survival. The evidence for this is embodied in traditional acequia (gravity-driven irrigation ditch) systems:

> Ditches themselves are innovations, though only elaborations on a natural process — the dynamics of the river. Dams installed by beavers or irrigators are transformative, however small [their impact]. Just as walking all day for weeks in the fields expands my blood and oxygen systems, so the irrigating itself expands the river's life systems. . . .
>
> Agropastoral enterprises have to be good for the land or they fail. The land must be kept happy for good to come from it. When I look . . . out at the fields through the window, I am faced by a denseness of life far exceeding the irrigator's intent to produce hay. Out there in the tall trees, grasses and flowers are an incredible number and variety of living beings. . . . By standards of pure economic profitability, that *bosque* might be considered almost superfluous, yet it is where there is most life. (García 1988, 371 and 373)

This ethical stance places biotic diversity above economic rationality, and it also recognizes the transformative qualities of human ecological adaptation. This resilience of local cultures is perhaps what most confounded the researchers associated with the 1935 Tewa Basin Study (reprinted in Weigle 1975; also cf. Forrest 1989). Today, as we look back on the social change of the past sixty years, we can more clearly see how such practices survive, because they are associated with the formation of conservation ethics as a deep and replicating narrative evoked by place-centered rural cultures (see García, chapter 3).

The endurance and "moral density" of homeland ethics are disturbed over time by the intrusion of capitalism and the geopolitical and bioregional changes this intrusion brings. The ecological attitudes of mexicanos are in a constant state of flux over time and in place. So too are their ethnoscientific knowledge bases. Thus, the "truth" is probably somewhere between an ultimately rushed indictment of a lack of conservation values and the agropastoral ideal described by various Chicano intellectuals. Some of the evidence does suggest that mexicanos have created sustainable patterns of bioregional habitation, but such cases have usually been treated by the literature in an uncritical manner that has lacked the substantive ethnographic detail needed to arrive at restorationist practice within the new social movements in the bioregion.[24]

The first point of contention between these two differing views is the extent to which rural Spanish-Mexican culture is capable of generating ecologically sustainable economic and social practices. Native ethnographers can provide a historical understanding of the oral traditions and site-specific contexts that inform Spanish-Mexican concepts of human nature, and especially of the relationship between humans and the natural world. The "cultural production of being" must be studied with an eye toward clarifying both concepts of self and of nature. What are the ecological consequences of Indo-Hispano (or Spanish Mexican) ontological predispositions in given bioregional settings? We want also to explore the contradictions of local cultures in our search for evidence of both anthropocentric (hierarchical) and biocentric (egalitarian) practices and worldviews.

Bioregionalism and Ethnoscience: The Search for Local Knowledge

In order to clarify and legitimize the regenerative capacities inherent in traditional ethnic folkways, an increasing number of scholars and activists are searching for alternatives to cultural destruction by promoting critical discourses within their origin communities.[25] The significance of this search for local knowledge is obvious when one considers that cultural diversity is the apparent source of creativity and right livelihood. The conservation of cultural diversity is emphasized by the American Folklife Center in the following urgent terms: "Productivity, freedom, and unity are . . . intimately connected with the nation's diverse cultural heritage" (Library of Congress 1983, 11).

In undertaking bioregional study of the Río Arriba, we need to develop comparative, site-specific studies that identify and document ethnoscientific knowledge bases and their associated placeways. I use the term "placeways" instead of the more conventional term "folkways" deliberately, because the spatial aspects of our cultural heritage are too often deemphasized. Historical and cultural preservationists tend to focus on folk arts and crafts, vernacular architecture, or archive-quality heirlooms. With few exceptions, this is detrimental to the ecological practices that evolve in tandem with both the natural landscapes of the watershed and the cultural landscapes constructed by distinctive ethnic communities.[26] Given the already well-known primacy of land-and-water resource management issues in the intermountain West, we can begin to outline an ethnoscientific inventory of placeways by modifying García's list (1988, 437) and emphasizing the following critical elements of local knowledge:

1) irrigation systems, practices, and rituals;
2) soil management techniques (both conservation and restoration practices);
3) crops, medicinals, and wild flora and fauna (agroecology and ethnobotany);
4) cultural landscapes, vernacular architecture, and topistics (i.e., placeways);
5) forestry and range-management practices;
6) labor processes (event-structures related to work cycles);
7) interpersonal relations (kin and friendship networks); and
8) foodways.

The search for local knowledge confronts a number of other methodological difficulties beyond those specifying the range of a knowledge-based inventory. There is the problem of the density of cultural traditions: How widespread must a given folk practice be to constitute itself as a cultural resource that can be protected? One indication comes from a commentary on the concept of *resolana,* which is instructive because it suggests that the density of cultural practices can be quite "thin" in the more or less insulated rural setting that characterizes the archetypical northern New Mexican agropastoral village (Atencio 1988).[27]

Other problems include moving from the identification to the documentation of collected knowledge and the related problem of moving from documentation to interpretation and finally to the reproduction of these knowledge traditions (i.e, to bioregional practice of cultural renewal for sustainable reinhabitation). Recall Sylvia Rodríguez's insightful advice about the crucial need for emic research methods (1987, 389). "With few exceptions, it seems to be the case that anthropologists have failed to capture an *emic* or native account of day-to-day Mexicano, Hispano, or Chicano social reality." (See also Paredes 1977.) Furthermore, there is incomplete documentation of the labor processes that intersect with event-structures organized on the basis of local knowledge. Here, we might explore the potential contradictions between homeland ethics and actual event-structures that unfold through unique patterns of social relations in given bioregional context. Such an exploration obviously requires a focus on political, economic, and sociological dynamics in the formation and transformation of bioregions.

Political Economy, Bioregionalism, and Sustainable Reinhabitation

Many students of Southwestern cultural ecology reject the possibility of economic development models to promote the preservation of village culture. Such strategies are seen as ill-advised and bound to fail because the objective of cultural preservation conflicts with the objective of economic modernization. American-derived norms and objectives are viewed as incompatible with the core values of *mestizo* (Spanish-Mexican) agropastoralism. The programmatic failures of the Tewa Basin Project can be read as definitive evidence of the inevitability of culture conflict.[28] This view persists in contemporary discussions of economic and natural resource policy. An example of such "uninformed analysis" is recent studies of economic efficiency which erroneously conclude that the land-use values of mexicanos, if not the internal qualities of the Spanish-Mexican culture as a whole, are ultimately incompatible with agricultural productivity.[29] Both of these views are reincarnations of cultural determinism in which

mexicano culture is seen as an impediment to development and modernization — a culture out of step with the rise of the "New West."[30]

The political-economic dimensions of human settlement patterns in the
Upper Rio Grande, as in other places, obviously revolve around the organization of life under rather extraordinary environmental conditions.[31]
Bioregional research must not limit itself to an evaluation of the presumed
"internal" attributes of a discrete mode of production (say, agropastoralism vis-à-vis industrial capitalism). Such a focus on "internal" (and eter-
nalized) qualities often results from analysis that has been based erroneously on stereotypes of a static, unchanging culture. The historical context
of Euro-American colonialism in the Río Arriba bioregion means that we
must examine the conflicted interaction of opposing modes of production.
After all, this bioregion is a *colonized* hinterland, an extractive resource
colony caught in the orbit of global capitalism.

The foremost political-economic problem in the bioregional study of
these processes of conflicted change is the legal and physical enclosure of
the commons of Spanish and Mexican land grants (*mercedes*). The enclosure of the commons should not be viewed as a *fait accompli,* for the
status of the land grants remains contested terrain. Mexicanos continue to
resist enclosure by asserting their historic rights of usufruct, even if they
must rely on the "subaltern crimes" of "trespass" into local landscapes
that have been legally (and spatially) restructured as part of the public and
private. The political-economic effects of enclosure are many, but the
fundamental process of change seems in part driven by the forcible transformation of independent traders, artisans, and farmers into members of a
highly segmented waged-labor force. The proletarianization of agropastoral communities is a major factor that has been almost universally overlooked by cultural ecologists and environmental historians.[32]

Another unresolved issue is the extent to which economic development
and wilderness conservation are compatible with the preservation of local
cultural integrity and autonomy. To address this issue, we must clarify
what we mean by mestizo agropastoralism. Then we must redirect the
study of material and symbolic practices toward an understanding of the
relationship between cultural landscapes and biodiversity, and of how
the relationship is disturbed by changing political-economic conditions
(e.g., real estate speculation, water transfers, rural gentrification, mining,
logging, etc.; Peña in press). Beyond careful study of land degradation by

capitalist interests, we must also examine how colonizing processes have historically limited local access to the natural conditions of production. This examination requires a study of the relationship between land degradation and poverty in the agropastoral communities. To reinhabit degraded homelands, we must embrace and ultimately resolve the struggle for local, democratic self-management of the watershed commonwealth. The restoration of natural areas must accompany the restoration of indigenous land and water rights in the commons.

Cultural Continuity and Change: Challenging Exoticism

One trailblazing historical study shows how Hispano villagers in northern New Mexico and southern Colorado created extensive kinship networks to bind rural- and urban-dwelling families during the emergence of a regional community between the 1880s and 1940s (Deutsch 1987); however, students of Río Arriba bioregional cultures have not explored the connections between urban and rural communities. Primary ethnographic and ethnohistorical research on rural-to-urban migration patterns remains to be done.

The mexicanos of the Río Arriba bioregion, taken as a whole, became predominantly urban dwellers during the years after the two world wars. Since the 1980s, however, the rural mexicano segment has been growing at a fairly rapid pace, presumably as a result of return migration and first births among baby-boomer parents. The recovery of the village-based Hispano population in the Río Arriba appears to be part of a more general process, described by agricultural economist Rochin (1993) as the "Latinoization" of rural America. Two complex issues have arisen as a result of these population shifts. On the one hand, changes related to the experience of migration to urban areas outside the homeland bioregion are evident in mexicano culture. On the other hand, the remaining rural pockets of the larger mexicano population are not static or exotic cultures and need not be romanticized for having the wisdom and good fortune to stay *in place* on ancestral lands, against the odds.[33]

Between 1960 and 1990, for example, close to two-thirds of the rural Hispano population of Costilla County, Colorado, migrated to cities such as Pueblo, Colorado; Colorado Springs; Denver; Greeley, Colorado; Laramie, Wyoming; Albuquerque; Phoenix; and even Los Angeles and Las

Vegas. This migration was largely precipitated by the collapse of the local independent sheep trade after the enclosure of the Culebra common lands on the Sangre de Cristo Land Grant (see chapter 9). Was the post-World War II migration out of the Culebra River agropastoral villages similar to earlier patterns that promoted the formation of a regional community? Little has been written about the experiences of Hispanos involved in this more recent (post-1950s) regional diaspora. Migration, urbanization, and the formation of a regional community are important forces to consider in accounting for the dynamic and changing character of Hispano culture in the bioregion.

The current popularity and marketing craze surrounding Hispano colonial arts and crafts (*santos, bultos, retablos*), "Sante Fe-style" architecture and furniture, coyote tales and accessories, and native recipes are indicative of exoticist placemaking, the reinvention of place and its material and symbolic trappings by the interloping and appreciative aficionados of the Other. Here we find a parallel intellectual legacy of both racism and exoticism: from Leonard Pitts's characterization of Chicanos as "swept into the dustbin of history" by the superior Anglo-Saxon civilization to the more recent constructions of environmental ethics and history by deBuys and Wolf, in which the Spanish-Mexican culture is safely reduced to quaint relics.[34]

Cultural ecologists and bioregionalists must also remain wary of these exoticist tendencies. In a commentary about the dangers of exoticism Darrell Posey states: "We have a legacy which is dangerous. One romantic Rousseauian view is that native peoples have lived in perfect harmony with nature and don't have any problems. The other one is that they are primitive. Somehow these fuse together to make an even larger myth, which is that primitive peoples are in harmony with nature and should stay there and never change" (as quoted in Hecht and Cockburn 1989, 218).

I believe the environmental history of the Río Arriba shows that Spanish-Mexican local cultures developed a more or less sustainable relationship with their watersheds but that the relationship of agropastoral communities to landscapes and watersheds was never static and unchanging. Euro-Americans were clearly not the only social group to provoke environmental change. The range of technologies used by humans in transforming the character of the Río Arriba bioregion was not limited to the machinery arriving with the Anglo railroads and sawmills. The acequias are also an example of a very ancient human technology that effected tremendous change in disturbed landscapes. Of course, the relative impact of acequias compared, say, to railroads is more than a matter of scale. The ramifications of environmental impact involve different cultural, political, and economic orientations to place (see Peña and Martínez, chapter 5).

At the same time, the existence of an enduring acequia tradition for watershed-based self-governance should not be construed to mean that mexicanos are forevermore natives in perfect harmony with nature. Overgrazing has occurred, for example, principally in the valleys surrounding larger towns such as Albuquerque and Santa Fe during the Spanish colonial and Mexican periods (see MacCameron 1994). Before 1848 the class structure of the Río Arriba included mercantile and large landowning strata (*ricos*) who made significant inroads toward large-scale commercialization of the livestock and carrying trades. Rich Hispanos contributed to land degradation as far back as the Spanish colonial era. After 1870 and the arrival of the railroad, when working-class mexicanos became waged workers in the timber, mining, and livestock industries, they also participated in numerous acts of environmental destruction. One of the great ironies of the environmental experience of Hispanos in the Río Arriba is that as rural proletarians and sharecroppers, the agropastoralists were recruited by mercantile, and later industrial, capital to partake of the laborious destruction of their own watersheds, the old land-grant commons (see Peña and Mondragon Valdéz 1998).

To avoid exoticism, we might examine the contradictory class location of mexicanos in light of the political-economic forces that transformed the natural conditions of existence in the bioregion. We might look for places and times when ruptures in cultural tradition and customary self-rule occurred. Deforestation induced by capitalist overexploitation of timber in the Río Arriba, for example, affected the ability of the agropastoralists to irrigate; in some cases acequias were abandoned. Sedimentation of ditches resulted from clear-cutting and overlogging, thereby disrupting the agricultural systems of Hispano villages by reducing in-stream flows available through the end of the irrigating season. (If the hydrology of a watershed is disturbed, the local acequia water users can no longer irrigate. The local culture begins to lose its ability to regenerate its land and hence its values. The land ethics and ethnoscientific traditions that bind a community to the land and water cannot be so easily replicated in a place where the material source of a right livelihood — the watershed — has been degraded and expropriated. Once the land is exhausted and its diversity of plants and animals reduced, it is more difficult for the local cultures to continue symbolic and material practices that are rooted in the existing biophysical qualities of a place.) Historically, deforestation and overgrazing changed more than the quality of grazing range or timber stands. They reduced the number of places available for people to harvest medicinal herbs, gather wild berries and edible plants, hunt for game, and collect firewood.

Beyond a reassessment of the changing relationship of mexicano agro-pastoralists to the environment, we must also address the experiences of city dwellers. Are city dwellers the "urban villagers" who maintain some cultural continuities? Do urban dwellers continue to maintain ties to family, land, and village economy? These are questions about change, for mexicanos are neither ecological thugs nor noble natives in perfect harmony with nature. We need to grasp the *changing* and contradictory character of Spanish-Mexican culture in both rural and urban milieus.

Finally, another type of exoticism occurs in the debate between wilderness preservationists and proponents of a Hispano homeland ethic. Deep ecologists fail to understand that what they call "wilderness" is the natives' homeland. They fail to recognize the socially constructed nature of nature.[35] Deep ecologists state that they want to preserve nature for its own intrinsic value, in a primordial or "wild" state, and free of the long-term presence or disturbances of human beings. But the entire planet, including the highest Himalayan peak and the remotest Arctic tundra, has long been touched by human habitation and use. Jeffrey A. McNeeley, the former chief conservation officer of the International Union for the Conservation of Nature (IUCN), clarifies this problem in no uncertain terms: "Conservation is linked in the public mind with wildlife. But humans have occupied this planet very thoroughly for thousands of years, and few real 'natural' habitats remain. Instead, the Planet Earth consists of a number of more or less anthropogenic habitats, originally occupied by people who developed cultural approaches to managing the resources of their local ecosystems in a reasonably sustainable fashion" (McNeely 1990, 1). As noted earlier, the tendency to insist on the separation of culture (civilization) and nature (wilderness) often carries misanthropic implications; but it can also be viewed as a type of exoticism in which nature is reconstructed as wild, untrammeled land. To the extent that deep ecology falsely dichotomizes the relationship of humans to ecology by declaring that humans are uniformly a plague on the land, it also exoticizes the environmental history of the planet by failing to recognize the cross-cultural variations of anthropogenesis.

In adapting to place some cultures are regenerative, while others are predatory. But the extinction of regenerative local cultures at the hands of more predatory modes of existence is a process that has been accelerating since the rise of global capitalism. The displacement of remaining land-based cultures by the forces of environmental degradation unleashed by the economic domination of capitalists has been widely documented. Unlike deep ecologists who emphasize nonhuman biodiversity, cultural ecologists recognize that regenerative local cultures are as endangered as spotted owls and marbled murrelets. In fact, the threats to species diversity are often the same as the threats to cultural diversity.

When is a local culture regenerative rather than predatory? Wherever anthropogenesis produces beneficial results for nonhuman life-forms and their habitats, a local culture can be seen as regenerative. For example, the acequias, like beaver dams and ponds, are clearly an ecological disturbance, but the earthen ditches, as Reyes García first noted, increase biodiversity and extend riparian wildlife habitat. Cultures should be judged by their contribution to nature's own biodiversity and not by the profits they make or the ethics they espouse on behalf of an inarticulate Other, that is, nature itself. In the practice of the wild, as Gary Snyder (1990) once phrased it, the bioregional community lives by an ethic of watershed reinhabitation and acts with a sense of awe and respect for all life-forms and their habitats, the homes of all beings. Arnie Naess (1973) calls this the "mixed community." The position of the human subject is decentered, and the ecosystemic webs of life — the watersheds themselves — become sites invested with the highest moral value. The decentered subject is thus repositioned within a complex mosaic of mutual relationships among all living beings inhabiting a shared place.

The local Indo-Hispano cultures of the Upper Rio Grande have a long-standing land ethic that has primarily been expressed through customary law and oral traditions. Songs, aphorisms, folktales, legends, and other types of lore have served as repositories of environmental ethics. So too have the customary laws governing the use and operation of acequias and common lands. The Spanish-Mexican people of the Río Arriba simply did not need Thoreau, Muir, Leopold, or Nash to develop environmental ethics.[36] This is a lesson all environmental researchers and activists would do well to learn if they want to move beyond exotic constructions of biological and cultural diversity.

Chicanas and Ecofeminism: Gender in Cultural Ecology

Throughout the Third World, women have played the leading role in environmental struggles (see Shiva 1988; Shiva 1993b). Women's leadership in the defense of the environment is attributable to their fundamental role as producers of the means of subsistence. "Since it is women's work that protects and conserves nature's life in forestry and in agriculture, and through such conservation work, sustains human life through ensuring the provision of food and water, the destruction of the integrity of forest ecosystems is most vividly and concretely experienced by peasant women" (Shiva 1988, 65). Thus, some argue that the destruction of natural resources most directly affects those who most often have a direct, intimate relationship with the land — women.

Have mexicanas played a similar role in the development of mestizo agropastoralism in the Río Arriba? Many studies have documented the role of women as migratory farmworkers, but fewer studies have broached the issue of mexicanas as farmers, ranchers, gardeners, or irrigators. One study indicates that Hispano women played a critical role in agricultural production in northern New Mexico's and southern Colorado's agropastoral villages. With the advent of the wage-labor migratory pattern, primarily involving male villagers, women's roles in agricultural production achieved greater importance. In the absence of men, women stepped into areas of production traditionally reserved for men under the agropastoralist division of labor (Deutsch 1987).

Historically, the gender division of labor in the villages has reserved much of agricultural activity, and specifically grazing and farming, for men. Nevertheless, mexicanas have long played a key role in agricultural production as caretakers of family subsistence garden plots, as processors and canners of farm produce, and as gatherers of healing herbs and makers of *remedios* (herbal remedies). The role of women as acequia ditchriders (*mayordomos*) is less well documented. One recent book identifies a woman in the role of ditchrider (Crawford 1988). Another study identifies a woman in the role of mayordomo for one of the acequias in the Costilla County Conservancy District in southern Colorado. The same source suggests that it is not uncommon to see women tending sheep and cattle or operating tractors with plows, mowers, or rakes (Peña 1990).

Recent research by the Upper Rio Grande Hispano Farms Study research group in the San Luis Valley indicates that women are still the principal labor for the planting, harvesting, and processing of produce from the family subsistence garden plots (Peña in press summarizes these findings). Even in those cases where men have taken over responsibility for gardening activities, the knowledge base for subsistence production has been acquired through female oral traditions. When asked to explain how he had learned to can fresh vegetables from the garden, Corpus A. Gallegos (the co-owner of the oldest family farm in Colorado) remarked that his wife had taught him and his two sons how to preserve and can the farm's produce. "You should talk to her," he remarked. "She is the one who really knows how to do this stuff!"

Mexicanas certainly continue to play key roles in agricultural production — as gardeners, food processors, herbalists, and even ranch hands. They also figure prominently as leaders and participants in environmental struggles.[37] Another study documents the leading role of women in the struggle against a strip mine and cyanide-leaching operation installed by Battle Mountain Gold in the foothills of the Sangre de Cristo Mountains above the town of San Luis in Costilla County.[38] Women of color, including mexicanas, are playing critical roles as leaders of new social-movement organizations such as the Southwest Network for Environmental and Economic Justice (SNEEJ), the Southwest Organizing Project (SWOP), the Land Rights Council, and Ganados del Valle.

There are many unanswered questions, however, about the dynamics in the construction of gender in the cultural ecology of the Río Arriba bioregion. Under what circumstances do Hispano women farm and ranch? How has the sexual division of labor changed over time, given the changes in local political economies and markets? Is the knowledge domain of women different from that of men, particularly in areas related to agricultural production, soil conservation, and natural resources management? When, and under what circumstances, do women assume what are traditionally defined as male spheres of labor activity? What are the intersections between domestic and farm production? What is the role of female oral traditions in the transmission of agropastoral knowledge bases? Is there a female emic perspective regarding concepts of nature and the place of humans in the natural world? Are there gender differences, within mexicano culture, in the pattern of attitudes and the values regarding ecological placeways? Ecofeminism posits that women and nature are organically connected, that women have a special, harmonious relationship with the natural world. To what extent do the experiences of Spanish-Mexican women affirm or reject this interpretation? What are the lessons that ecofeminists might learn from mexicanas?[39] Gender must figure prominently as a category of inquiry in future studies of the cultural ecology of the Río Arriba.

Reinventing Bioregionalism: Class, Culture, and Gender in the Politics of Place

Bioregionalism provides an interdisciplinary framework for critical study of the cultural and environmental history of the Río Arriba. It provides a holistic set of tools for the development of restorationist research that can play a positive role in the new social movements that seek to restore the health of the land and the traditions of local self-management of the homeland commons. The first steps in the development of the methodological and theoretical contours of such an approach are taken in this book. This introductory chapter has identified a series of issues, both methodological and theoretical, that point the way to a significant revision of bioregional inquiry in these multicultural and ecological contexts. The roles of political economy, material culture, and ethnoscientific discourses in the development of an Indo-Hispano cultural ecology and environmental history are the keys to this recasting of the bioregional paradigm.

Recognition of the issues outlined in this chapter encouraged a group of us—research scholars, farmers, and advocates of sustainable agriculture—to establish an interdisciplinary research team to address problems as disparate as soil conservation and range management, material culture and folklore, religious and spiritual beliefs, and ethnoscience. The Rio Grande Bioregions Project is a network of scholars, farmers, and land-use activists dedicated to the study and preservation of the historic acequia communities of the Río Arriba through the documentation and recovery of local ethnoscientific knowledge, including especially agroecological traditions.

Bioregionalism is a useful approach to the study of established and emerging links between cultural and ecological diversity. In terms of customary practices, it offers analytical strategies that unify the objectives of cultural and ecological preservation. More importantly, it relies on emic methodologies, such as native ethnography, which are essential to guard against exoticism and romanticism. Much of cultural ecological research in the Rio Grande bioregions is limited by a lack of comparative studies. Bioregionalism provides a framework to initiate comparative and site-specific (watershed-based) inquiries. To be effective in practice, however, bioregionalists must squarely confront the political-economic and socio-organizational challenges facing rural Hispano communities. Politics is intrinsically conflict-ridden, and people who are forced to engage in political struggles are always confronted by competing claims to Truth. Bioregionalists have a responsibility to link research with social action in a manner that gives voice to disempowered, endangered local cultures. Bioregional research can serve as an equalizer in arenas involving powerful political-economic forces that dominate the changing cultural and natural landscapes of the Rio Grande watershed.

The Rio Grande Bioregions Project is exploring new directions in social and ecological research, particularly by focusing on the recovery of ethnoscientific traditions and the protection of endangered watersheds associated with Hispano cultural landscapes and agroecosystems. The project is a first step toward comparative bioregional study of the Rio Grande watershed as a whole, and it consolidates existing research while generating new ethnographic sources. In the larger context of American ethnic folk-culture conservation, the project contributes the first comprehensive bioregional documentation of traditional mexicano environmental knowledge bases and folk practices at a time when the search for sustainable livelihoods may finally attain the prominence it has long deserved on the American social scientific and humanistic research agendas.

Notes

The generous support of the Hulbert Center for Southwestern Studies at Colorado College made this work possible. I am especially indebted to the former Hulbert Center director Joe Gordon. This work benefited from long discussions with several friends and colleagues, including Joe Gallegos, Rubén Martínez, Laura Pulido, Gwyn Kirk, and the participants in the Helen Hunt Jackson Faculty Fellows seminar program. The views expressed in this work remain my sole responsibility.

1. The bioregional concept of reinhabitation emphasizes the place of humans (as a species) within nature as residents of a mixed community of all life forms. Reinhabiting places means that humans practice not so much "sustainable development" as "regenerative residence."

2. Also see Sale (1985), who argues that watersheds produce distinctive human settlement and economic patterns.

3. Among the first social scientists to bring attention to the relationship between watersheds and the development of human cultures was Wittfogel (1968, 1972, 1981), who proposed a Marxist theory of hydraulic social formations (i.e., modes of production). See Worster (1985, 19–21), who declares: "The theory that underlies the specific problem of water and society in history comes out of the interdisciplinary study of culture and ecology." Brown and Ingram (1987) provide evidence of cultural differences in the valuing of water. The community value of water conflicts with the commodity value of water whenever differently positioned classes and cultures struggle over legal and economic definitions in the adjudication of water rights. The discipline of cultural ecology, like bioregionalism, unites the study of nature and culture through a focus on local cultures interacting with their watersheds. In the case of the Río Arriba, Artúro Campa (1963) was first in recognizing the significance of the Rio Grande watershed as a source of cultural innovation through human adaptation to environmental limits.

4. The principles of deep ecology were first outlined by Naess (1973); also see Devall and Sessions 1985; and Devall 1988. Cheney (1989) outlines the concept of postmodern environmental ethics as deriving from bioregional (or place-centered) narratives. On the ecofeminism-deep ecology debate, see Fox 1989.

5. For further discussion see, for example, Redclift 1987; Shiva 1988, 1993a, and 1993b; Norberg-Hodge 1991; Peña 1988a, 1992, and 1997a; and Peña and Mondragon Valdéz 1998.

6. Murray Bookchin and Dave Foreman discuss the misanthropic tendencies evident in the early years of Earth First! (i.e., early to mid-1980s); see Chase 1991. Also see Bradford 1989 and Seager 1993.

7. In a brilliant commentary on deep ecology and ecofeminism, political ethicist Joni Seager reveals the fundamental problem with the celebration of "native ways of being" (including white shamanist appropriations of Buddhism and Zen philosophies: "[T]he invocation of 'native ways of being' . . . is distressingly shallow, often coming down to little more . . . than a sentimentalized mythologizing of the 'noble savage' — a view that can, and does, easily slip into racist assumptions

and simplistic misrepresentations of a complex culture to which few white Americans can really claim access" (1993, 230).

8. As Edward Said (1993) has noted: "This cultural appropriation is a basic form of colonial domination. Is the 'Other' to be hated or loved into oblivion?"

9. Tomas Atencío (1964, 1988) was one of the earliest proponents of a Chicano social philosophy based on local knowledge of indigenous traditions. For a presentation of Chicano ethnophilosophy, see the important work of García (1988). Also cf. Olguín (1984 and 1989) and Martínez (1988a, 1988b).

10. For further discussion, cf. Olguín 1984, 1989; García 1988; and Martínez (1987, 1988b).

11. Sylvia Rodríguez (1987) provides a compelling view of this problem in her study of interethnic relations in the Taos Basin. McCannell (1984) points to the dangers inherent in "reconstructed ethnicity," which refers to "the kinds of ethnic identities which have emerged from the pressures of tourism" (as quoted in Rodríguez 1987, 324). This results in the *museumization* of living cultures such as those in the Indian Pueblos or surrounding Hispano villages.

12. See the significant collection of essays in Cronon 1996.

13. See, for example, Rappaport 1979; Goonatilake 1984; Caufield 1985; Shiva 1988; and Hecht and Cockburn 1989.

14. I am referring to the "triumphalist" perspective that taints much of the discourse on the history of the American (or intermountain) West. Triumphalist discourses equate Anglo-American culture with the ideals of progress, justice, and civilization.

15. See Quillen 1993 for more discussion; see also Peña (in press).

16. See Rosaldo 1989, Saldívar 1990, and Peña 1997a for discussion of the role of ideology as a force that constrains and redirects the processes of social change.

17. See, for example, the 1935 Tewa Basin Study (Weigle [1975] 1989); Van Dresser 1964, 1972; Bowden 1977; deBuys 1985; Worster 1985; Briggs and Van Ness 1987; Deutsch 1987; Upper Rio Grande Working Group 1987; García 1988; Rothman 1989; D. G. Peña 1992; Peña and Gallegos 1993; Pulido 1993, 1996; and Peña and Mondragon Valdéz 1998.

18. See, for example, Deutsch (1987); Upper Rio Grande Working Group (1987); Forrest (1989); D. G. Peña (1992); Peña and Gallegos (1993).

19. Oberg (1940), Leonard and Loomis (1941), Harper, Cordova and Oberg (1943), and Gelbach ([1981] 1993) are examples of researchers who have arrived at a similar conclusion.

20. See, for example, Van Dresser 1964 and 1972; Arellano 1972; Atencío and Pacheco 1980; Briggs and Van Ness 1987; Brown and Ingram 1987; Atencío 1988;

García 1988; D. G. Peña 1992; Peña and Gallegos 1993; Peña and Mondragon Valdéz 1998; and Upper Rio Grande Working Group 1987.

21. For a discussion of the *emic* and *etic* stance in social science see Harris 1976. The epistemological debate here centers around the nature of "truth claims." The *etic* stance envisions truth as a quality of the objective realities observed and documented by communities of "experts," while the *emic* stance envisions truth as a by-product of the intersubjective claims of communities of participants.

22. Cultural ecologists, botanists, and agroforestry scientists have uncovered substantial evidence to suggest that human-induced change in the environment often benefits wild plants and animals by creating and extending specific habitat niches and protecting movement corridors. This is particularly true in the case of polycultural agroecosystems. The research by Posey (1981) on the "forest islands" of the Kayapo indigenous communities of the Xingu watershed in Amazonas and by Caufield (1985) on the corn *milpas* of the Lacandón Maya in Mexico are exemplary samples of the available evidence. See also D. G. Peña 1992 and Hecht and Cockburn 1989 for further discussion, and Peña 1998 for similar evidence in a study of cultural landscapes and biodiversity in the Culebra watershed of southern Colorado.

23. *Manito* (literally, "little brother") is a term used in New Mexico to refer to native Spanish-Mexicans.

24. DeBuys 1985 and Carlson 1990 are examples of thin description. Some recent exceptions include Briggs and Van Ness (1987), Rodriguez (1987), and Brown and Ingram (1987).

25. For some examples of social action research in the Río Arriba, see Atencío 1988, García 1988, Peña 1992 and 1997b, Peña and Mondragon Valdéz 1998, Peña and Gallegos 1993 and 1997, Pulido 1993 and 1996, and Rodriguez 1987.

26. One important exception is Berger and Sinton (1985); see also Hufford (1994) on "folklife and land use" in the New Jersey Pine Barrens.

27. The concept of *resolana* refers to the grounding of local myth, legend, and cultural values in a particular space that is designated as the place for local story-telling, including the transmission of local lore across generations. In most Río Arriba agropastoral villages, this place is traditionally located on the sunny side of a building on the main plaza. Today, post offices often serve as sites for *resolana*, which is why many village communities have mobilized to prevent the U.S. Postal Service from closing smaller post offices in isolated rural areas. I believe the English language term that comes closest in meaning to *resolana* is conviviality, although this does not fully capture the specialized spatial dimension as clearly as *manito* vernacular.

28. For a critical analysis of the Tewa Basin Study, the Rio Grande Interdepart-

mental Board, and other federal programs in New Mexico during the New Deal, see Forrest 1989.

29. Libecap and Alter (1982) provide an example of what Van Ness (1987, 143–44) calls "uninformed analysis." See also Weber 1991 and Peña (in press) for more critical commentary.

30. For critiques, see Briggs and Van Ness 1987; and Forrest 1989.

31. See Peña 1997b for a discussion of the unique environmental qualities of the Río Arriba.

32. One important exception among students of the Río Arriba is Pulido (1996), who uses class and ethnic categories in her analysis of new social movements.

33. As Phillis Rose warns, "Compared with racism, exoticism is merely decorative and superficial. It doesn't exterminate. Exoticism cares mostly about its own amusement, and tends to find difference amusing where racism finds it threatening. . . . The racist is hedged by dangers, the exoticist by used-up toys (quoted in Hecht and Cockburn 1989, 209).

34. For a further critique see Peña and Mondragon Valdéz 1998.

35. On the social construction of nature see Dickens 1992, Evernden 1992, and Cronon 1996.

36. See García 1988 and D. G. Peña 1992 for further discussion of Chicano environmental ethics as an independent development; see also Peña and Martínez, chapter 5.

37. In chapter 7 Davis provides a set of in-depth life histories on four Chicana environmental activists from Colorado.

38. For example, Hispano women played a leading role in the Costilla County Committee for Environmental Soundness (CES) and the Land Rights Council (LRC); see Peña 1990; see also Pulido 1990, Gutiérrez 1994, and Krauss 1994 for more on Chicanas and other women of color in urban-based environmental struggles.

39. See Kirk, chapter 6, for a discussion of key issues in the emerging discourse between ecofeminists and environmental justice activists.

2 Social Action Research, Bioregionalism, and the Upper Rio Grande

Rubén O. Martínez

Much of Chicano/a research scholarship focuses on historical rather than contemporary features (see Camarillo 1979; Garcia 1981; and Romo 1983).[1] There also has been a tendency to focus on single communities rather than on regions (e.g., García 1991; Griswold del Castillo 1979; and Romo 1983). The suggestions by Galarza (1972) and Spicer (1972) that we examine Chicano/as in terms of regions and of landed and proletarian status have gone unnoticed by most Chicano/a researchers (except perhaps, Griswold del Castillo 1988–1990; Meinig 1971; and Montejano 1988). When several communities in a region have been studied, scholars often have covered too broad a social canvas and consequently glossed over many significant local processes (e.g., Barrera 1979; Mirandé 1985). Not only has Chicano/a research tended to focus on limited dimensions of the communities studied, it also has lacked any explicit emphasis on environmental history. This admission is significant because all communities exist in a spatial context that includes the natural conditions of production and reproduction. Historicism has obscured the spatial (regional) dimensions of our communities.

Chicano/a scholars are urged to identify general social and material relationships that exist across local communities in and among regions and to explain those relationships sufficiently well to be able to change or alter them in accordance with community needs. Otherwise, Chicano/a intellectuals and communities will continue to struggle separately, lacking a critical mass of resources and losing the struggle for authentic ethnic group survival. At a time when the United States negotiates with other countries to secure increased autonomy for ethnic minority groups (Palestinians, Kurds, etc.), Chicano/a nationalism, both as a cultural and separatist movement, is lost in a flood of apathy and disillusionment that seems headed toward capitalist totalitarianism. A bioregional framework that emphasizes the concrete problems of our communities may make it possible to bring the knowledge of the Ivory Tower of Chicano and Chicana Studies to our communities in the routine way that colleges and universities do for the dominant group.

The type of studies envisioned would attend to issues of knowledge production and stratification and would address practical questions about the problems that figure prominently in the lives of Chicano/as in specific localities — in our case, northern New Mexico and southern Colorado. Long ago termed "the Forgotten People" by George I. Sanchez ([1940] 1967), the indigenous Hispano/a peoples of this region have maintained salient aspects of their culture, although not without considerable adjustment to and acculturation with the ever-imposing American society (Mosk 1942; Mead 1953). They also have been able to retain ownership and control of some land, even though the land base that remained following the turn of the century is rapidly decreasing as more and more of it becomes the private property of dominant group members, especially in the present context of rural gentrification (Knowlton 1964a; Martínez 1987).

Much like George Sanchez's own work on Taoseños (1967), this project seeks to assess the life conditions of Chicano/as in the region.[2] It differs from previous work in that it employs a social action research model and attempts a pragmatic synthesis of aspects of political economy, cultural ecology, and environmental history with a bioregional approach that has practical utility for the local Chicano/a population. The practical questions to be addressed through systematic research should emerge from the needs, concerns, and objective interests of the local "communities" in the region. A bioregional approach asks important questions about possible locally driven economic and community development strategies that maintain both local culture and an acceptable and sustainable ecological balance in the region. Bioregionalism, from a Chicano/a perspective, proposes a full and complete research agenda that addresses ethnographic, social scientific, ethnoscientific, and philosophic issues and questions.

The bioregional perspective emphasizes political economy, cultural ecology, and environmental history. A bioregion, as defined by Sale, is "any part of the earth's surface whose rough boundaries are determined by natural characteristics rather than human dictates, distinguishable from other areas by particular attributes of flora, fauna, water, climate, soils, and landforms, and by the human settlements and cultures those attributes have given rise to." Sale argues that bioregions exist one within another, "forming a complex arrangement from the largest to the smallest, depending upon which natural characteristics are dominant." His definition, however, overlooks the anthropogenic character of existing bioregions and the influences of political economy, which greatly impact the cultural landscape and the natural dynamics of an area (Sale 1985, 55–56).

Political economy refers to the study of modes of production and their social relations. Bioregionalism emphasizes the study of the political economy of the bioregion as the primary mode of collective struggle against natural forces. It also examines the interaction among local, regional, and global modes of production (e.g., the influence of intensive capitalism on agropastoral autarchy). Cultural ecology refers to enduring cultural practices developed by human groups in their adaptation to the natural environment. By emphasizing the evolution of cultural practices and their consequences for both cultural and natural environments, bioregionalism explicitly includes reflexive human thought connected with the species' agency in the ecosystem (Netting 1977). In other words, the emphasis is on anthropogenesis, or the impact of humans on the natural landscape. Finally, environmental history is the study of the natural environment in human life, its variegated forms of fauna and flora, its geographical, geological, and hydrological features and processes, and the impact of these on human institutions (Worster 1988).

Concepts central to a bioregional perspective include ecology, ecosystems, biomes, human ecology, and local knowledge. Ecology, according to Amos Hawley, a pioneer in the field of human ecology (1944, 403), is a social science "concerned with the elemental problem of how growing, multiplying beings maintain themselves in a constantly changing but ever restricted environment." The basic unit of analysis in ecological studies is the community, with development studied relative to the limiting and supporting factors in the environment (cf. Hawley 1944, 1981). An ecosystem is "a community of interdependent organisms together with the environment they inhabit and with which they interact, and which is distinct from adjacent communities and environments." The emphasis is on the interconnectedness among organisms as well as between organisms and their environments. A biome is "a major ecological *community* of organisms, occupying a large area" (Allaby 1989, 136, 50). Finally, human ecology is "the study of the development and the form of communal structure as it occurs in varying environmental contexts" (Hawley 1944, 404). Sustenance relations are emphasized rather than the temporal distribution of persons and services.

The emphasis of bioregionalism is on the complex interdependency between human communities and their natural environments. These concepts point us to the basic relationships that local Chicano/a communities in the Upper Rio Grande bioregion have with the natural environment. Continuing invasion by the dominant group has altered those relationships, not only spatially, economically, and culturally, but also ecologically (see Peña and Martínez, chapter 5). Taken together, these overlapping areas of study provide the basis for an alternative approach to research and a new agenda for Chicano/a Studies that promise a more complete understanding of ourselves both as locals and as an ethnic group with distinct cultural orientations and behaviors toward nature and humankind. The term "bioregion" refers to a relatively large area that is naturally bounded in ways that make it distinct from other regions, a bioregion that encompasses human communities as well as other natural ecosystems. The study of bioregions emphasizes the maintenance of ecological balance and targets deviations from that balance.

Textual Analysis of Administrative Ideologies

The study of bioregions requires that we employ a variety of quantitative and qualitative methods. Etic and emic accounts of human ecology are necessary in bioregional research if we are to capture the utility of both scientific (expert) and ethnoscientific (native) perspectives. Also important is the study of state apparatuses that regulate the management and uses of national forests, public lands, waters, and other natural resources. The beliefs and practices of these agencies need to be studied in order to better understand how management and utilization practices have evolved over time and how they have impacted the natural and cultural ecology of specific bioregions. According to Dorothy Smith (1987, 1990) and George W. Smith (1990), textual analysis can provide a useful approach to the study of ideology and domination. Unlike the frameworks of deconstructionism and postmodernism, their approach avoids excesses in subjectivism and relativism. Dorothy Smith and George Smith encourage us to approach the body social as a material world that is constituted by the behaviors and practices of people as these activities are known and organized reflexively and recursively over time. From this approach, the social world must be known from the inside, from within the world of everyday life. As Dorothy Smith (1990, 22) states, "The only way of knowing a socially constructed world is knowing it from within. We can never stand outside of it."

Although this view needs to be tempered to allow for etic frameworks, I agree with Smith that the emic approach is crucial for understanding social reality. Like Dorothy Smith, George Smith believes that the everyday knowledge of members serves as the basis for understanding how a *regime* actually operates. He argues that "ideological practice operates as a set of procedures used to know theoretically, categorically, a social world with a view to administering it" (1990, 630). From this approach, extralocal ideological determinations of local events are organized through ruling practices that administer local activities on the basis of interpretations of texts. George Smith views the various institutional sites and practices of regulation and control as a more or less coherent politico-administrative regime. The notion serves as a heuristic device for studying how rulership actually works.

Dorothy Smith gives another useful insight when she uses "social relations" to refer to the actual practices of persons forming reflexive courses of action where "different moments are dependent upon one another and are articulated to one another functionally, but reflexively, as temporal sequences in which the foregoing intends the subsequent and in which the subsequent 'realizes' or accomplishes the social character of the preceding" (quoted in G. W. Smith 1990, 635). The concept of social relations is used by the researcher in the discovery of the recursive properties of spatial-temporal forms of social organizations, particularly those that are dependent on texts. Texts serve as active constituents of social relations by coordinating and temporally organizing a general form of social action (G. W. Smith 1990). Textually organized, local experiences of people have the same social configurations as the experiences of others; they are organized extra-locally through the same text.

There are bound to be variations in the local interpretations of text, however, so while the commonalities of social organizational forms lead to similar experiences among members, there also are local factors that mediate those experiences, giving them unique features. According to George Smith (1990), this recursive ontology makes it possible to go from particular events in local settings to a set of general, textually mediated social relations because they have the same social form.

In the conduct of study, the researcher brackets theory and other abstractions in order to study social phenomena that are concretely embedded in the social organization of everyday life. Members' knowledge as participants in a setting, their frustrations, and their perceptions of problems serve to orient researchers as they go about studying the social world. When studying the regime, researchers attempt to make sense of the setting on its own terms via the views of the representatives of the regime itself (politicians, bureaucrats, lawyers, etc.). Official interpretations of regime texts (laws, policies, etc.) provide important insight into the ways through which social reality is externally organized and imposed upon Chicana/o communities. The practices of such representatives are iterations of courses of action coordinated by the language of regime texts. The ontological property of social relations makes it possible to move from examinations of local levels to descriptions of general forms of organization, to social relations as a general course of action coordinated by official and unofficial texts and their interpretations (G. W. Smith 1990).

This approach is invaluable to understanding the dominant regime's apparatus of social control and its mode of operation in the Upper Rio Grande and other bioregions, particularly with regard to the evolving administration of land, water, and other natural resources. By examining the avowed purposes of governmental agencies along with the manner through which agency leaders have sought to realize them, we can gain a deeper understanding of the logic of the intrusive practices of the dominant group. For instance, the establishment and management of the national forests in northern New Mexico and southern Colorado reveal aspects of the dominant group's approach to controlling public *and* private uses of lands once under Chicano/a community control and management (Peña 1991). Moreover, it is through official reinterpretations of policies and laws that ownership and control of land and water are trans-

ferred from Chicano/as to the dominant group. Interpretations and reinterpretations become major mechanisms for displacing Chicano/as in the
Upper Rio Grande bioregion (Peña 1992).

Bioregionalism, Domination, and Resistance

As of the 1990s, competing interests over the control and uses of land,
water, and other natural resources are embedded in two contradictions:
(1) that between commodification and conservation and (2) that between
racial domination and ethnic group preservation (Pennick 1990). As the
hinterlands of this country's economy are brought more and more within
the hyperdynamics of contemporary capitalism, so the material and cultural influences on the Chicano/a communities of those hinterlands are
greater and more uniform. The transformation of indigenous life has occurred so extensively that some scholars are already lamenting the demise
of the oldest European cultural region (Carlson 1990; Martínez 1988b).
The complete proletarianization of Chicano/as of the Upper Rio Grande
bioregion threatens to have significant negative cultural consequences for
Chicano/as in general.

   The Western view that underpins the culture of the dominant group has
promoted the notions of industrialization, urbanization, and growth as
progress. The result has been alienated work, the atomization of family
and community life, and destruction of the environment on a massive scale
(Leiss 1974; Marglin 1990). "Free market economy" has come to mean the
pursuit of profits at the expense of human and natural resources, and material aggrandizement at the expense of human dignity, well-being, and
developmental growth among workers and the poor. The human side of
capitalism has shown only instrumental philanthropy (limited at that) and
deep human suffering. The Western Model of Development is contrary to
an emphasis on human development and ecological balance. It results in
the depletion of resources, the despoliation of the environment, and the
massification of society (i.e., atomized citizens maintained through mass
marketing, resulting in a loss of distinctiveness).

   At the same time, the intensification of capitalism in the hinterlands of
the United States has destroyed valuable stores of local Chicano/a knowledge—knowledge of farming, ranching, irrigation, mining, crafts, and

natural resource management. This type of knowledge is located at the realm of everyday experience among the members of the local Chicano/a populations. It emanates from a different logic than that of capitalism. This knowledge is embedded in a different understanding of human existence and in a different set of relations between communities and nature.

Among other things, local Chicano/a knowledge in northern New Mexico and southern Colorado stems from a traditional agropastoral culture that values human relationships more than profits, cooperation more than competition, and freedom more than control (Mead 1953). The local knowledge found in the Chicano/a communities of northern New Mexico and southern Colorado can make valuable contributions to a regional strategy for sustainable development. First, however, we need to clarify the differences between the modes of production (or vestiges of them) found in the Upper Rio Grande bioregion.

Modes of production can be compared on several levels. Peña and Martinez (1991) suggest that they be compared relative to objectives, macroeconomic orientations, definitions of productivity and efficiency, nature of technologies, systems of land tenure and water use, and the divisions of labor.[3] Use of these levels allows us to discern ideal types of a Traditional Sustainable Model (TSM) and a Capitalist Nonsustainable Model (CNM) of modes of production. In a TSM, production is for use rather than for exchange (CNM). Its economy is steady-state rather than growth-oriented. It emphasizes biological efficiency rather than mechanical efficiency. It is based on local cultural knowledge rather than expert scientific knowledge, and land and water are spiritual and familial patrimony rather than commodities. The TSM places emphasis on transgenerational capacity rather than on short-term profits (Altieri 1987; Shiva 1988).

The general approach outlined above can be used to provide locals with a greater understanding of their collective problems. Grounded in research that addresses local problems on a regional basis, a general strategy for Chicano/a community development could then be developed. The knowledge produced would encompass human ecological issues within the context of conflicts over land grants and land uses, water rights and water uses, economic development and sound ecological practices, natural resource management, and human resource development.

Each of these conflicts is greatly influenced by government involvement with agencies at the federal, state, county, and municipal levels having jurisdiction over the distribution and regulation of resources. At the federal level are a range of courts and legal decisions regarding land grants, water rights, and environmental conservation. The Department of Interior, the National Forest Service, the Soil Conservation Service, and several other agencies regulate and implement programs at the local level. At the state level there is a similar set of courts and natural resource management agencies, including environmental and wildlife management units. At the local level are county and municipal offices that carry out functions and administer programs in the broad areas of land and water use, conservation, and community development. At all levels there are programs for human resources and economic development.

Through a complex set of institutional arrangements and relationships, these agencies constitute a regime that attempts to administer the very nature of social life at the local level. Each of these agencies and their practices are structured by "texts," or rather by interpretations of those texts. These texts are comprised of the policies and procedures that prescribe the objectives, strategies, and dynamics of those agencies. The texts of the institutions of the dominant culture represent, to varying degrees, the Western view and its notions of profit, consumption, and conservation. All of these notions are based on assumptions about the separation of mind and body, instrumental reasoning, and universal knowledge (the understanding of persons and places out of the context of time), all of which assumptions are central to the modern Western view (Marglin 1990). It is through the codification of interests into laws that Americans have generally dominated ethnic minorities.

Fundamental shifts in the lives of Mexicans and other indigenous peoples of northern New Mexico and southern Colorado were formally set in motion when the United States and Mexico in 1846 went to war over territorial boundary disputes.[4] The social, economic, and political policies that were imposed on the first generation of Mexican Americans were of such a vastly different nature from their own that only recently have we become aware of ourselves as an ethnic group that has survived those changes. Our material conditions, culture, and sense of collective self have changed so much that many of us no longer feel the sense of community grounded in those values, beliefs, and practices that survived nearly three centuries in the Sangre de Cristo Mountains.

The "Epiphany of Landscape"

The Struggle for Water

Today, *la cuna de Aztlán,* the cradle of our ethnic group, *los Chicanos,* is under siege (Martínez 1988b). It submits to Western logic and the dynamics of advanced capitalism. Greed and domination supplant the "epiphany of landscape," and collectively we face complete and total cultural spoliation. Set in motion in the middle of the last century, these processes have been extant for 150 years. Increases in population size coupled with maladjusted methods of land and water uses have contributed to our problem: the impending total degradation of the lands, forests, wildlife, and ground and surface waters in the Upper Rio Grande region.

A century-and-a-quarter ago, many of our Chicano/a ancestors refused to participate in the American homesteading program because they did not perceive a need to do so; they had their plots of land, and from their point of view, there would always be land available for use. Their view was not grounded in a growth model; consequently, our great-grandparents could not have imagined the intensification of population density and land use that would follow them. After all, this was the "land of *poco tiempo.*" Social processes were slow as was any change. The tempo of life was in rhythm with a billowy white cloud slowly traversing a blue Southwestern sky on a long, hot, summer afternoon.

Our ancestors could not envision the scarcity of land and its degradation, and neither did Americans, who also were lulled into the view that there was an inexhaustible supply of land. Grounded in a philosophy that every man had the right to unrestricted ownership of a piece of land, U. S. land distribution policies near the turn of the twentieth century led to the "transplantation" of agricultural methods that were incompatible with efficient, long-range use of lands. According to Theodore Saloutos (1992, 446–47), a strongly individualistic way of life coupled with a seemingly inexhaustible supply of land led to degradation rather than conservation. He writes: "Hindsight and years of suffering have made obvious what foresight could not make obvious to policy makers at an earlier date. Authorities are generally agreed that the application of the homestead policy to the Great Plains was a serious mistake. The 160-acre units that were suited to farming conditions in the humid Mississippi valley proved highly unsuited to the arid conditions of the West." Today, major bio-regions such as the San Luis, Taos, Española, and Mora Valleys are under-going vast changes in population composition and landownership, and thus, in land and water uses (see Carlson 1990; Martinez 1988b; and Peña, Martinez, and McFarland 1993).

The study of land use includes the study of the hydrological cycle, and the cycle itself is tied to other natural resources and processes. Water use and management in the region have only recently begun to receive system-atic attention by social scientists. To date, only a few works have appeared that treat this topic in depth (see Clark 1987; Brown and Ingram 1987; and Ingram 1990). According to Clark, who studied water management and use in New Mexico, jurisdiction over water normally resides in the states, with the federal government asserting authority over some areas, such as federal public lands, Indian reservations, and so on (Clark 1987). Clark's work is significant in that it sketches water management in the area from the pre-Christian era to the present.

Explorations led by Coronado near the mid-sixteenth century noted the dependence of Pueblo Indians on agricultural products and reservoirs of water at Acoma. The Espejo expedition some forty years later noted in greater detail the agricultural methods at Acoma, indicating the use of canals to irrigate agricultural fields. Later explorers also noted the use of canals for irrigation. Community activities included maintenance of the *acequias* (ditches), water use, and harvest and storage of produce. Today's custom among "community users of irrigation water" to share in the repair and cleaning of ditches each spring is believed by many scholars to be of ancient indigenous origin (Clark 1987).

Despite 150 years of American domination, the amalgam of Indian and Spanish water practices continues to influence the use and management of water in the region today. Early legislatures incorporated the customs of the Spanish settlers and the Indians into territorial law, and "in 1891 the territorial supreme court reaffirmed an earlier decision which held prior appropriation to be the law of the territory" (Clark 1987, 671). Today, the "politics of water" in the arid Southwest is such that litigants are lined up to struggle in federal district courts over access to the groundwater. In-creased demands on water supplies (both ground and surface) continue to threaten the overall ecological stability of the region through the uncalcu-lated disruption of the hydrological cycle. In the northern part of the San

Luis Valley serious attempts by American Water Development, Inc. (AWDI) have been made to secure rights to mine the valley's confined aquifer, an attempt that raised many concerns on the part of locals (Peña and Martínez 1991). The few studies that have been conducted on the attitudes of northern New Mexico and southern Colorado Chicano/as toward water uses indicate that they are strongly opposed both to the sale of water and to its use for recreational purposes, preferring instead that it be used for agricultural and ranching activities (see Brown and Ingram 1987; Peña, Martinez, and McFarland 1993). At the same time that Chicano/a agricultural and ranching activities decline as a result of the negative impact of the larger social formation, the State of New Mexico takes away water rights on the basis of nonagricultural use, thereby ensuring that the agropastoral activities of Chicano/as are ultimately eradicated (Weber 1991). The situation calls for the serious consideration of alternative uses of land and water in a Chicano/a cultural bioregion that faces the local intensification of an environmentally destructive capitalist system (Atencio 1964).

In this context, self-determination, both at local and national levels, remains a variable inherent in and tied to the continued existence of Chicano/a communities over the next few decades. It is a contemporary ontological feature of our collective existence. To the extent that we struggle to address community issues in a concerted and systematic way, to that extent do we increase the level of self-determination which characterizes those communities. Rather than only theorize about self-determination, we must view it as a process to be sustained; it must be promoted and protected constantly. Like democracy, the price of self-determination is eternal vigilance.

Social Action Research in the Upper Rio Grande

Social action research seeks both to understand the phenomena under study and to change or transform them or the conditions from which they emanate. For Chicano/a scholars the primary problems that constrain community development are the structural features of the dominant society; these include specific forms of class, racial, and gender domination. The dynamics of domination work themselves out in concrete communities and have fairly clear ecological patterns and implications. It is at this level — the material existence of members of communities and their problems — that our cooperative research efforts should be grounded, irrespective of which regions scholarly teams decide to study.

The integration of scholarly research and Chicano/a community needs within contexts of competing "mainstream scholarship" demands by academic institutions requires that the research agenda be not only focused but fruitful. And it should be fruitful in ways that satisfy both academic and praxis demands. Chicano/a research must provide a basis for social action that secures for the community a vision of a better societal order. Collective action is grounded in a sense of purpose, a sense of improving debilitating human conditions, and in a vision of a better society. The "new society" must provide a sense of community for all those persons (dare we say, social identities) that comprise Chicano/as an ethnic minority group. Social theory should make comprehensible the new totalizations set in motion by capitalism in the realms of consumption, electronic media, and social control.

The Setting: Siete Condados del Norte. There are seven contiguous rural counties in northern New Mexico and southern Colorado that have Chicano/a demographic majorities. These counties are Costilla (75.9%) and Conejos (59.8%) in Colorado and Taos (64.9%), Río Arriba (72.7%), San Miguel (79.6%), Mora (85.0%), and Guadalupe (84.3%) in New Mexico.[5] These seven counties are characterized by severe economic problems and are similar to areas of the Appalachian region, which has some of the most economically depressed counties in the nation. The Chicano/a population is characterized by a local culture that has remained more or less intact over the past 150 years of American occupation. The indigenous Chicano/a culture is rooted in the Spanish/Pueblo Indian cultural amalgam that developed during the two hundred years preceding the American occupation. Manitos (and their South Texas counterparts) are perhaps the last Chicano/a indigenous rural cultures.

The seven counties offer exciting opportunities, not only to examine the intensified impact of the capitalist economy in the hinterlands, but to stem and alter that impact in ways compatible with local people's long-term objective interests. The bioregional approach can be applied in this region in ways that bring us, as intellectuals and scholars, back to the oldest indigenous culture of the Chicano/a, to decolonize and reorient our minds and to reexamine the possibilities for community and regional economic development. The aim of our research is to bring external political, economic. and cultural influences under the direction of the local Chicano/a culture so that it can maintain its sense of place, intergenerational vitality, and self-determination as it evolves into the future.

Regional development must be seen in the context of the many problems that attend the region. Gerrymandered councils of government and fragmented relations with a multiplicity of regulatory agencies attend many of the problems. The research must examine, among many other things, political network patterns both within and across Chicano/a communities in the region, and across them and the various institutional apparatuses of the dominant society. The purpose is to identify potential sources of political cooperation across Chicano/a communities that will set in motion a regional political consciousness that itself leads to development approaches on a regional level.

A bioregional approach to the study of Chicano/a communities in southern Colorado and northern New Mexico is similar to what in sociology has been called "grounded theory," that is, to build theory inductively by addressing issues and problems framed within the context of local communities. Initially, descriptive analyses are needed of the varied dimensions of group life. These include demographic factors, economics, kinship, community institutions, education, culture, ethnobotany, land grants, land and water policies, natural resource management, and ecological degradation.

Demographic Factors: "¿Es Raza?" Beyond providing mainstream descriptions of la Raza (the People or population) and the processes of fertility, mortality, and migration, we must address questions about the relationship between population dynamics and the environment. For instance, how are population changes leading to changes in land-use patterns? What impact are dominant-group settlement patterns having on the agropastoral activities of the local populations? What levels of population density are ecologically acceptable given specific sets of economic activities?

Economics: "Trabajando para sobrevivir." The social history of the region needs to be reconstructed using categories and emphases that reflect the objective interests of Chicano/a communities (Knowlton 1964b). An important part of this history is how people organize their work in order to survive. We should study the social relations of production and their transformation (e.g., patron/peon relations, the emergence and maintenance of the racial division of labor). Specific evolving forms of economic domination need to be identified and explained in order to gain a firm grasp of the present. The impact of capitalism on the local village economies also needs to be detailed and examined (see Cordoba 1976; Deutsch 1987; Forrest 1989; and Knowlton 1969). The partial autonomy that characterizes the region has to be understood in terms of its potential for local development. Patterns of market activity within indigenous production areas, such as crafts and farming, also demand attention, as do labor market characteristics and housing (Sargent, Lusk, Rívera, and Varela 1991; Peña 1992). Shifts in areas of economic expansion and their ecological consequences for Chicano/a communities deserve special attention in arriving at a strategy for the economic development of the region.

Finally, the cultural and spatial landscapes of Chicano/a ranches and farms need to be studied and preserved (see Sargent, Lusk, Rívera, and Varela 1991). The working knowledge of Chicano/a farmers and ranches deserves systematic ethnographic attention. The activities of ranching and farming — animal husbandry and agriculture — as well as the local knowledge systems that sustain them offer potential for local farmers and ranchers and for communities as a whole (Harper 1987).

Kinship: La Familia. La familia endures as the basic social unit in the lives of Chicana/os in the region. According to Florence Kluckhohn, "The central structuralizing principle is seen to be that of loyalty and responsibility for all members. And although the first loyalty and responsibility is for members of the immediate or extended family, the principle extends to all persons, related by blood or marriage" (quoted in Mead 1953, 170).

Changes in local kinship patterns should be identified and understood over time. These include relations with family members who moved to urban areas in search of economic survival and the interfamilial networks that developed between urban and rural areas. The indigenous communities of the region have served not only as sources of cheap labor, but also as "social sanctuaries" for the out-migrants, who return to the region repeatedly on vacations and family and business visits. Socialization practices, authority, extended kin, and other social patterns also should be recorded and examined, along with the impact of dominant group culture, where it can be isolated.

Community Institutions: Hermandades y Cofradías. Indigenous community organizations such as mutual aid societies and religious brotherhoods and sisterhoods should be examined and their positive roles in the larger community enhanced. Community organizations formed for the express purpose of resisting dominant group "encroachment and domination" should form a web of networks across the seven counties in order to enhance their power base and thus their effectiveness. Chicano/a participation patterns in policy and advisory committees of local governments (such as parks and recreation, local historical societies, etc.) also should be studied and their political implications made clear for the advancement of Chicana/o interests.

Education: "Iba uno nomás a comerse el lonchi." Problems of education from preschool to postsecondary levels cry out for attention and should be identified, their dynamics explained. For example, many Hispanos feel that the education system has not been sensitive to their needs — as reflected in the statement above, "One only went to eat lunch." Strategic plans with common educational objectives ought to be developed and implemented to address needs among the local populations, particularly as they relate to economic and community development. The chasm between schools and parents must be obliterated. Practical ways by which to implement relevant curricula and develop appropriate school climates and philosophies must be tested through praxis. At the postsecondary school level, two-year and four-year institutions need to strengthen cooperative relations in order to increase educational mobility among the local populations. The development of place-based curricula that value, preserve, and transmit local knowledge and ethnoscientific traditions is critical.

Culture: "Dando los años." Storytelling is a very important part of Hispano culture, as is reflected in the statement "Dando los años." The cosmological and philosophical aspects of the local culture provide the foundation upon which views of ourselves and our relationships to nature are founded. Local religions, customs, traditions, and folkways have ecological implications, and their meanings must be discerned. Another topic of study should be the social practices of congregating and having discussions *en la resolana* (sunny spaces around the *plazuelas,* where traditionally locals gathered to chat during cold weather). This and other indigenous social arenas of discourse are social spaces for the discussion and debate of matters of general community interest (e.g., Atencio 1988; Atencio and Pacheco 1980). Local forms of music, literature, and painting, as well as other local art forms also can be studied for their environmental meaning and implications.

Cuisine: "No tiene hambre y con el plato lleno." Knowledge of local cuisine can provide important leads in our coming to understand the ecological relations that characterize local communities (Darling 1951). For example, there are admonitions against waste as reflected in the statement in the title of this section, which translates "her eyes were bigger than her stomach." The centrality of gardens and orchards in the typical Chicano/a meal reveals not only the meaning of land and water in the lives of locals, but the extent of social change that has taken place in recent decades. Activities such as gardening and canning also can be further understood through this approach. Table etiquette can provide clues to patterns of authority and changes in it and other social relations. Further, both the study of gardening activities and table etiquette offer considerable potential for assessing the impact of the dominant culture on local, everyday patterns, particularly in terms of time orientations, relationships to nature, and technology.

Ethnobotany: "Andan cortando oshá." Local practices of folk healing and knowledge of medicinal herbs such as oshá (bear root) are vanishing quickly and demand immediate attention (Cordoba 1976). Left unattended, many practices will be lost forever in a society characterized by synthetic products and simulated realities. The categories of ethnobotanical knowledge must be reconstructed, and ways to integrate Chicano/a ethnobotany into local curricula, both within schools and in community education programs, need to be devised and implemented. Curricula guided by emic emphases can enhance the learning experiences of local youths.

Land Grants: "Sin tierra no hay ser." Land has been central to the lives of Chicano/as in the Sangre de Cristo Mountains, but the environmental history of Chicano land grants remains to be studied (see Brayer 1941; Gonzales 1969; Leonard 1970; Chavez 1984; and Briggs and Van Ness 1987). The current status of land grants should be identified and the *struggle* to reclaim them assessed in terms of effectiveness. Land grants need to be understood, not only in terms of legal and political struggles and the prospects of reclaiming them through these methods, but also in relation to broader social and economic processes that might provide new and more effective approaches to the restoration of lands. Clearly, restoration of communal lands remains a critical issue in the development of the region, and it demands the concerted attention of us all (Knowlton 1967, 1989). Finally, management and use of communal lands could be examined, particularly in relation to their ecological consequences and their future uses.

Land and Water Policies: "Entre verde y seco." Land and water policies in the region have put Hispanos "between a rock and a hard place"; disputes have intensified over the last two centuries (Lamar 1962; Knowlton 1964a, 1968, 1986; and Ortiz 1980). Current land and water policies need to be examined and a coherent analysis provided regarding their content, areas of dispute, and compatibility with sustainable development (Harper, Cordova, and Oberg 1943; Sargent, Lusk, Rívera, and Varela 1991). The impact of governmental management on indigenous uses of land and water, once understood, can help local ranchers and farmers develop an informed strategy in their struggle to survive. Indigenous practices of land and water distribution and their uses need to be reconstructed (Cabeza de Baca 1954; Carlson 1967). These include *el reparto de agua,* "agricultural methods," and grazing patterns (Gutiérrez and Eckert 1991). Land-grant issues continue to be central to the region, with hundreds of thousands of acres remaining in dispute (Knowlton 1976; Westphall 1983). El Instituto Tonantzín, a land institute, remains a vital organization in the land-grant struggle, and a bioregional approach would encompass its efforts and perhaps provide research support within the broader context of the region and its economic development. Other organizations addressing land problems include Ganados del Valle and the Rio Costilla Cooperative Livestock

Association. There is a tremendous gap in the cooperative extension service system with regard to *manito* agricultural communities. The establishment of permanent, on-site agricultural research institutes and centers in the bioregion is especially pressing.

Natural Resources Management: "La montaña será mantenida en su estado natural para todas las generaciones que vienen después de nosotros." As will be demonstrated in chapter 5, Hispanos have sought to maintain the environment in its pristine state for future generations to enjoy. But management of the Sangre de Cristo Mountains, their valleys, watersheds, and wildlife, for example, has been greatly impacted by the U.S. Forest Service (USFS) and by private landowners (Knowlton 1967). *La sierra* has provided not only an array of natural resources to the many communities nestled throughout the valleys and plains of the region, but also a sense of being, a sense of place. Indigenous use patterns and practices need to be counterposed to the policies imposed by the dominant group (Van Dresser 1972). Care should be taken to delineate the differences in conceptualizations of environmental and ecological concerns between Chicana/os and dominant-group environmental movements (Peña 1992). In addition, the history of USFS policies (e.g., Multiple Use Sustainable Yield Act, National Forest Management Act, and the General Mining Act of 1872) must be critically examined. Both qualitative and quantitative methods will be needed to make comparisons and to discern the meanings of indigenous practices and their objective consequences.

The Challenge to Be

Recuerden lo que se va acabando, gócen lo que hay, y luchen por lo que puede ser. (Remember what has happened, enjoy what you have, and fight for what can be.) As we stand on the eve of the twenty-first century, we are experiencing the totalizing processes of social domination and ecological degradation. Social domination maintains class, racial, and patriarchal structures that systematically deny Chicano/a communities access to scarce societal and environmental resources. The atomization of social life in a context of simulation and hyperreality is engendering an anomic period in society. Appearances of implosion are purely subjective, however, with objective processes of domination and control persisting over time.

Boundaries are reproduced and maintained through social practices in everyday life. Common experiences of simulated reality do not transform or eradicate institutionalized structures of domination. Chicano/a intellectuals can help forge a sense of our future as an ethnic group by addressing the objective needs of our communities through social action research. Such research would bring "community-oriented" Chicano/a scholars in direct cooperation with community leaders who articulate community problems and labor to address them. These scholars would be focused on recapturing and developing a collective sense of ethnic community rather than on describing the unique experiences of a myriad of marginalized groups. After all, we know that uniqueness is ever present in social reality and that its description, in and of itself, is not sufficient for the thorough understanding of our existence, particularly our collective existence. Without denying the unique in human experience, we can still maintain an emphasis on objective social-structural and social-ecological features and dynamics.

Proposed here are a general framework and a research agenda that promise to increase our knowledge about ourselves and our environments in order to regain community self-determination in a region where both demographic and cultural factors afford the greatest possibilities for self-determination to occur. Interdisciplinary teams of Chicano/a intellectuals in other regions could address questions of domination and self-determination through a bioregional perspective and thereby make significant contributions to our general understanding of our communities and of our collective ability to address community problems within regions with an eye toward long-term ecological and cultural viability.

Notes

Many of the ideas expressed here first appeared in a paper co-authored with Devon Peña and presented at the 33rd Annual Conference of the Western Social Science Association, Reno, Nevada, in April, 1991. I thank Devon Peña, Jeffrey Garcilazo, Jay Coakley, and Fred Bender for their critical comments and the Research Awards Committee at Pitzer College for its financial support.

   1. The difficulties that the terms Chicana and Chicano pose for discussing "community" are tremendous. Based on sex and gender distinctions, the terms

lend themselves too much to the fragmentation of community that unfortunately characterizes our lives. I considered using the term *la Chicanada* to refer broadly to the Chicano/a communities and peoples, including those who are more or less assimilating in and out of the diverse subcultures that traditionally have been referred to by scholars as "Mexican Americans." However, I concluded that some people might object to the written introduction of this term, which is used verbally in everyday life, and I therefore stayed with the more literary and avant-garde "Chicano/a."

2. Taoseños are a subset of Manitos, or Hispano New Mexicans, who are among the eldest settler groups of the Indo-Hispano communities of the Southwest and are known in relation to Californios and Tejanos. Chicano/as in this region, then, are known as Manitos. Historically, "Chicanos/as" evolved out of the regional subgroups.

3. See also Hawley 1984, Catton and Dunlap 1980, and Sale 1985.

4. Warring over territorial boundaries still occurs (e.g., the American-Iraq War; and the continuing conflicts between Israel and its neighboring countries).

5. These percentages were calculated by the author using 1990 census figures.

3 Notes on (Home)land Ethics

Ideas, Values, and the Land

Reyes García

June 18, Antonito, Colorado

At my ranch home, musing on the phenomenon of synchronicity after dreaming about a flicker fluttering at the bedroom window and then waking up to see one actually doing that, I wonder why being home feels so hollow today. Cradled in the amber morning light, I remember and look upon an entry from Leonardo da Vinci's *Notebooks* that had puzzled me:

> See: one's hopes and wishes to return to one's homeland and origin — they are just as moths trying to reach the light. And the man who is looking forward with joyful curiosity to the new years — and even if the time he is longing for ever comes, it will always seem to him too late — he does not notice that his longing carries within it the germ of his own death. But this longing is the quintessence, the spirit of the elements, which through the soul is enclosed in the human body. You must know that this very yearning is the quintessence of life, the handiwork of nature, and that man is the model of the world (MacCurdy 1938, 80–81).[1]

Although I am now, in fact, at home, sitting at my big wooden kitchen table, writing by candlelight in the house my great-great-grandfather built, nevertheless I experience this longing to be home. But I know this longing is insatiable, like the desire to bring justice to homelands.

Rudolfo Anaya touches on these themes when he declares that the revival of the idea of Aztlán by Indohispanos — Aztlán being the symbolic homeland of their indigenous ancestors, the Azteca/Mexica, in Nahuatl mythology — "attests to the role of myth in a culture where facts do not outweigh faith, beliefs, or the power of oral tradition. The legend of

Aztlán never died; it was only dormant in the collective unconscious. For people of Mexican descent, Aztlán exists at the level of symbol and archetype. It is a symbol which speaks of origins and ancestors, and it is a symbol of what we imagine ourselves to be" (Anaya 1989, iii).[2] Moral philosophies can be seated in the desire to be at home in the world. Indeed, the art of survival is a specialty of Mother Nature that binds each form of life to every other form, even as one devours the other: for all *must* find ourselves at home together *here*. Doesn't Nature stimulate cooperation through the homing archetype? Doesn't an ecosystem naturally take shape, and doesn't mythic imagination hold that story within it only when the world is a home?

Adding up the diverse and perhaps strange musings, this morning full of birdsong, I arrive at ideas about homeland and self that seem to converge onto a single archetype that I cannot yet name but which seems to me universal and absolute in its promise of part-becoming-whole and of finitude-touching-infinity, an expression of the fundamental ontological principle of belonging formulated in the Mayan saying, *"In Lak Ech,"* and in Spanish, *"Tu eres mi otro yo"* (You are my other self). Homeland can then be conceived of as a mesh of communities sustained by an ethics of reciprocity, whose motive power can be dream, symbol, myth, or only desire.

March 1, Antonito

On Head's Mill Road, a mile to the east and past the Rainbow Nite Club, my friend Cano Espinosa is running. Some days he runs fifteen or twenty miles to the San Luis Hills to the east and back. To my surprise, today he is leading on a rope a young horse who is trotting easily alongside him. Here in our hometown, Cano is a symbol simultaneously of terror and of blessing. He is to me a man both dangerous and holy because he is alive and alert at the margins of homeland. He is a model for me of purity and strength.

Yesterday was a leap-year day. I put four cattails on my mother's fresh grave to honor her eternal motherhood, and on the way back from the cemetery I saw flocks of great blue herons high overhead, and down in the meadow two bald eagles eating a calf.

Nine months after these first musings on homeland, and a week after my mother's death, I return to them. Here on the family ranch on the

Conejos River in the San Luis Valley of south-central Colorado, I feel close to the heart of Aztlán. Yet my mother is dead, and my heart is empty. Can there be a place called home for me without her?

March 8, Durango

Mass extinctions of species caused by massive human interference in the planetary ecosystem occur at the same sites in which indigenous peoples struggle to survive. The process by which natural as well as human histories are erased by the imperial/colonial ruling elites is beginning to be understood on all deep structural and cultural levels by Mexican American, Native American, African American, Asian American, and other ethnic and ecofeminist scholars whose work embodies the critical consciousness of the colonized peoples. These scholars have long served the liberation struggles of their peoples but must now move to disseminate place-based knowledge, not only in their own intellectual and community networks, but also in the natural ecosystems from which imbalances have ultimately arisen.

The water and soil systems of wetlands and rainforests are disappearing as the world's giant cities spread across the land like cancers; it will be only a short time before it is possible to imagine that the destruction of the wetlands above the Conejos River that flows through Antonito will be followed by the collapse of cities like Los Angeles. Consideration of human-origin disasters that could permanently damage Gaia's ecosystemic integrity frame any possible remarks on (home)land ethics much more urgently than a meditation, for example, on Greek moral philosophy.

March 10, Los Angeles

Driving to Twoheys Restaurant near Huntington Drive and Los Robles Avenue for fresh coffee at 6 A.M. before flying over the ocean to Kauai, Hawaii, I stop at a red light and watch a gray bird. It occurs to me that this bird is a city bird. She/he watches me as I swivel my neck to check the light, and she/he crosses quickly behind me as my car rolls on into the intersection. The bird stirs my compassion.

Sunday, as I placed four cattails on my mother's grave in Los Cerritos, a pair of bald eagles ate a calf below me on the valley floor. Several V's of

great blue herons flew overhead. There were young raccoons on García
Lane near my mother's ranch home when I arrived back from the cemetery.

Returning from Twoheys, I politely slow down to let a squirrel cross in
front of me to a tree on the other side of the street. I try to ask myself
questions about the meaning of Reality—about the True, the Good, and
the Beautiful!—mostly in terms of ecology and ecological *justice.*

When I get back to the house where I am staying, the elegant neighborhood is noisy from the high-pitched motors of grass and leaf blowers now
used by the gardeners instead of rakes and brooms. My recurrent an-
noyance at these blowers mirrors in reverse my yearning for the silences of
the meadows along the river back home, silences that are emblematic of a
profoundly stable moral order.

This feeling-memory of the river reorients me, but it is not a matter of
nostalgia. To be in a secure, *familiar* world is a basic need. Belonging—to
a family or even to a gang of "homeboys"—is a primordial mode of being
in-the-world, grounded in a sense of belonging *to a world.* To borrow a
phrase from Houston Baker, the "workings of the spirit" *of the land* shape
the methods and substance of eco/ethnophilosophical questions. And like
the planets, the orbits of familiar people, places, and events are elliptical:
they do not spin within perfectly concentric rings around Earth or around
man as Ptolemaic astronomers and Greek philosophers thought the heavens did. As I myself travel from el Río de los Conejos in south-central
Colorado to el Río de las Animas Perdidas, greening its way through
Durango or whirling on to the great city of Nuestra Señora de La Reina de
los Angeles, believe me I know: This world is not perfect in any Platonic
sense—this world we splice our way through, often laboriously conscious
of its thick paradoxes and ambiguities and brokenness.

Conejos County, where Antonito is located, is one of the economically
poorest counties in the United States, Los Angeles County one of the
richest. Conejos is one of the least populous areas of the United States; the
population of Los Angeles is now more than ten million. The contradictory realities of these places are linked today in such a manner that they
can be understood only dialectically, insofar as they are constituted by
actuality intersecting *ideality.*

After all, there is a way of conceiving mythic reality according to a type
of perfection that does not rely on Platonic abstractionism precisely be-

cause it is rooted in the ethnopoetic mythology intentionally rejected by Plato in the *Republic*. Among the Rio Grande Pueblos, for example, the mythic world of the kachinas is replicated in dance rituals wherein humans actually become kachinas while seeming only to imitate them. Mystical communal participation is achieved through music and dance and other sensuous components of ritual. Among the Pueblos the *koshare* (clowns) act as mediators between the human world and the divine world of the kachinas. (Socrates mediates between the human world of mere images and the divine world of ideas as an isolated thinker rather than as a member of a cohesive political-religious community.) As Jémez Pueblo elder José Rey Toledo notes: "Well, the clowns are symbolic of ignorant humans, you know. . . . It's so hilarious, that, and yet they don't know that they are trying to be converted to that perfect world [of kachinas] like everybody else. We all have a perfect world" (Toledo, in press). Again, reality can be understood to be constituted by social and historical *actuality* interacting with ethical or mythical *ideality* to create a human history that is both natural and spiritual, valued both in memory and imagination, both perfect and imperfect.

How do I judge the *value* of the *places* in which I dwell—the value of their relationships to one another, for example? Persuaded by a long search through the history of philosophy and religions and many other academic disciplines, and more recently by death itself, that there is no stepping back from this world in order to see it more clearly, that there is no other world from which to see this one and still be in it and of it, how can I begin to answer the most important questions in life?

I will have to relive journeys, think aloud, talk to you directly, tell you the stories in which this "I" disseminates itself into a multiplicity: for if the "I" of colonized, assimilated written discourse is to be replaced by the many voices of communal experience that bind knowledge to daily life, a new Self must be constructed from intimate encounters with Others, by an emergence from a more magical "We."

This last thought recalls the words spoken several years ago by my good friend Bill Lee, a Navajo artist and constant traveler, to his wife Carol on his way to give a guest lecture in my American Land Ethics class at the Baca campus of The Colorado College in Crestone, Colorado, which is on the lip of the Sangre de Cristo Mountains north of the Great Sand Dunes.

We passed a bald eagle perched high in a cottonwood who looked down at us with a sharp eye. After watching the eagle carefully for a while, Bill remarked, "It's enough just to know we are in *his* gaze, too."

March 11, The North Shore, Kauai

I finally understood what Bill had meant as I sat in Romero's Funeral Home in Antonito with my older brother and younger sister during the viewing of my mother's body. I felt she was looking down at me, like that eagle, a high-up representative of a very wide moral authority whose own matrix consisted of relatives, neighbors, and friends, both living and dead. As I stood up to greet the elders of the community who had come to pay their last respects to my mother, I realized that the oldest women seemed to understand my grief the best and that their words were the most comforting because they really *knew* my mother. "She was a good neighbor," la Señora Archuleta said to me very simply.

La Señora Cordova came with two of her children (both older than I), and like mine, her tears were an expression of both grief and hope, of relief but also of resignation to the great transformation her friend, my mother, had just experienced. I had never felt so much a part of my home community as on that afternoon and the next day at the funeral and cemetery, closing the long cycle bonding my old mother to her lifelong friends and wizened relatives.

In the oldest church in Colorado, Our Lady of Guadalupe Cathedral in Conejos, the funeral mass was conducted by our Theatine priest, Felix López, half in Spanish and half in English, as my mother herself usually talked at home. ("I'm a *coyota* from New Mexico," she would announce from time to time, "so my *palabra* is mixed *tambien*.") An altar boy and an altar girl assisted. He had light skin and black hair, while her skin was the color of dark honey, and she wore a coppery braid thicker than my wrist. Hermana Casimir read an epistle from St. Paul. My cousin Castelarito read from one of the Gospels. In both readings the agropastoral imagery was pronounced, and every detail was vivid and memorable. Padre Felix gave the sermon and then a eulogy. He had come to Antonito twenty years earlier from a tiny village in Andalusia. He was a priest much loved by the people, truly a servant of God. In his fifties, the priest was also an accomplished cyclist. I had encountered him at summer corn dances in the Pueblo villages of New Mexico, the last time at Jémez.

Padre Felix paused and faced the full church several minutes before speaking. He explained the Christian meaning of death and resurrection, of final forgiveness and ultimate hope. He reminisced about coming to my mother's house four miles outside Antonito to give her communion and finding her always waiting for him with coffee and orange juice. He described in general their conversations about her relatives mostly — the Gonzaleses and Sargents, the Gallegoses and Martinezes — and the dry humor with which she passed on to him stories passed down to her of great-great-aunts and uncles — Cleofas Jaramillo and Padre Antonio José Martínez of Taos. "The people she mentioned were makers of history," he said. "Doña Margarita," as he called her, "was my friend."

I told my children, Lana and Tania, what I had always told them: that when anything dies, even a mosquito, its spirit moves on, and that a spirit like their *nana*'s would be watching over us with the same steady love she had always given us in life, a love now rendered unconditional in death. They believed I was telling the truth, which I try always to do, and so they were calm and accepting of her passing even as they gazed shyly at the body she had left behind, awed by her mysteriously dignified and almost joyous repose. In such trust and continuance is perhaps the main moral lesson of these homeland musings.

We dwell in a natural matrix (from the Greek *mater*, "mother"), indeed. I hear and see its manifestation now as I recall a past very much alive in my own body-soul, listening to the pulse of innumerable waves, spellbound by the dark arch of a migrating whale off the north shore of this northernmost Hawaiian island and by its spume dispersing upward to merge with thick clouds nearly indistinguishable from the sea at twilight. *"La serena de la noche"* my mother used to call this time in the strange twilight between day and night, speaking softly in the fading light as she gazed out the big windows of her ranch home, past the big trees into the lilac-violet sunsets.

March 12, Kauai

After an introductory philosophy class one morning back in Durango, a Navajo student from Page, a town in the Lukachuchai Mountains south of the Four Corners, stopped by my office to discuss Plato. Michael wanted to know how the Theory of Forms underlay Socrates's moral defense of his occupation as a philosopher in the *Apology*. I told him we might cautiously try to make comparisons with Navajo thinking.

Socrates argues he cannot be guilty of "impiety" or "unholiness" as charged by the court of Athens. His philosophizing is a divine or holy activity, and his wisdom is produced by total "recollection" of and "participation" in the world of Ideas. Thinking this way myself for the first time, I asked Michael, my student, to imagine *hózhó* (Navajo for "harmony," "beauty," "balance," and "the good life") as the counterpart of the form of Good and the world of Navajo mythology as analogous to the world of Ideas. However, I postulated for him, Plato's perfect world is occupied by abstract concepts, while the Navajo world is inhabited by colorful persons such as the Hero Twins, Monster Slayer, and Born-for-Water, whose father is the Sun, or by White Shell Woman, who is the "inner life form" of Mount Blanca (just northeast of Antonito), as well as one of the multiple manifestations of Changing Woman, mother of the Hero Twins.

The comparison breaks down owing to the contradiction between Plato's abstractionism, on the one hand, and the personalism of the Navajo worldview on the other. I suggested to my student that the Theory of Forms is derivative, a result of Plato's general project: the decontextualization of Greek culture and the translation of the multiethnic religion and mythology epitomized in Homer's *Iliad* and *Odyssey* into a more uniform, and therefore more "universal," discourse—the discourse of a specialized conceptual, philosophical "culture." Of course, the Theory of Forms is most explicitly set forth by Socrates in *Book VI* of the *Republic,* immediately after he has banned the poets from his ideal *polis,* for their polyphonic songs are cacophony to Plato and his philosopher kings.

Earlier, in the *Euthyphro,* Socrates had railed against traditionalism and the authority of the sacred stories or myths of the poet-priests; group faith had to be superseded by the rationality of the individual emancipated from fetters of Greek religious culture. Plato's theory, as propagated through the mouth of Socrates in the text of the dialogues, represents a decisive step out of the oral tradition into the written.

Classical scholars such as R. G. Onians in *The Origins of European Thought* and Eric Havelock in *Preface to Plato* have both argued at great length that Plato's philosophy marks a radical discontinuity in the history of ideas (Onians [1951] 1989; also Havelock 1963). Yet, as I told the Navajo student, such scholars would probably view attempts to restore any type of personalized mythological specificity to Plato's theory as not only regressive, futile, and even ludicrous but also as impossible. There would be a variety of reasons for their probable denial of the possibility of such a project. Implicit within their positions, I could argue, is what contemporary anthropologist Johannes Fabian calls "denial of coevalness," which is in part a failure to acknowledge coevalness as "the *problematic* simultaneity of different, conflicting and contradictory forms of consciousness" (Fabian 1983, 146).

Onians and Havelock both treat Plato's attempted extirpation of the indigenous, oral, and religious Homeric culture he inherited as a fait accompli, as if for them the mythic imagination lay unavoidably buried in the childhood of humanity's evolutionary past. They assume final triumph by Plato on the field of ideas. Yet the finality of that conquest could never be justified adequately to Michael or me. We both know from experience that Plato failed to uproot tradition and that the West failed to replace myth with its empty, rectilinear, politicized cosmologies and its effete, racist, and sexist theories of progress. Onians and Havelock microscopically analyze the linkages between "traditional" and "modern" philosophical ideas, but they do not recognize the *living continuity* between them. Abstractionistic Platonic philosophies attempt to overcome the past by pointing toward a transcendent future outside time and beyond historical actuality. As Derrida has shown in *Of Spirit,* this abstractive tendency, already dominant in Plato, haunts Heidegger's influential philosophy, so that the dialectical tension between history and myth is denied by concealment of the *spiritual* paradox that makes the dialectic spin (Derrida [1987] 1991).

What we must keep in mind, I suggested to my Navajo student, is that the principle of transformation does not automatically translate into transcendence. The Navajo ideal of *hózhó* results from transformative dynamisms that incorporate natural history into the mythical and vice versa. Spirituality primarily involves reciprocal *transformation* rather than transcendence, and a dialectical hermeneutics of human existence retains its spontaneous dialogical, oral, open character only by emphasizing continuity through change.

Transcendental, idealist Western philosophies, therefore, tend to down-grade and underestimate nature, as in Plato and Hegel. Marx's counter-vailing efforts, however, also seem to be unbalanced — but in the direction of an exclusively *causal-material* explanation of history excessively focused on *human* forms of productivity. Further, this productivity is conceived in terms of *urban* scientific technology. Marx's moral analysis of the bad habits and bad character of capitalism — the word "ethics" derives from the Greek words for "habit" (*ethos*) and for "character" (*athos*) — falters when the analysis is applied to precapitalist "organic" societies.

Capitalism requires private property, which in turn requires the "dissolution of organic society." But strongly noncapitalist societies still exist within the world capitalist system. What is common and distinctive to them is that they are *ecological;* furthermore, organic societies are characterized by a relationship with nature so intimate as to be consistently or habitually mythological. It is this mythic element of their ecological character that has proven most resistant to domination throughout the history of capitalism and other hegemonic expropriative political economies.

Among Aboriginal Australians, for example, the "Dream Journey" (or "Walkabout") seasonally reincorporates human beings into an organic integral landscape whose dynamic patterns of meaning are established eternally by the events of the "Dreamtime." The ancestor beings or "Dreamings" are embodied in the Australian landscape, whose natural features are inhabited by and informed by the Dreamings.[3] Such a foundation of the truth of the world parallels the Navajo foundation of its truth by "inner life forms" such as White Shell Woman, who *is* Mount Blanca, and these *kinds* of "forms" are accessible to everyone — in archetypal dreams, for example. In these "pre-capitalist" societies, the forces of production themselves are not technological in a mechanical, scientific, and abstract sense: the forces of production and the mode of production literally embodied the labor-power generated by tribal wisdom. On these margins of capitalism, moreover, both work and ownership relations are not only communal, they are also mythical. The Dreamings are the physical/metaphysical core of a collective reality.

What I am suggesting is that conceptualization of ideals and values within the history of philosophy has been typically estranged from the collective experience of land-based peoples whose mythologized natural history is a primary source of their collective spiritual survival. Plato severed oral tradition from his written philosophy and made *ethics* a skeptical response to what he considered to be the *illusion* of democracy. Since then philosophy has tended to posit transcendental goals within reach of only an intellectualized elite who usually disdained manual labor (upon which their societies are always grounded) and condemned oral tradition to a dead, mythological past embodied in "lower" life-forms — to the illusory "mythic world" of Homer, in Plato's case. The universalization and eventual homogenization of ethical ideals and values wrought by the Platonic tradition perpetuated the very system of power — and slave labor — criticized by Socrates in the *Gorgias*.

A fascinating twist in the history of ideas led perhaps the most prolific and profound of ecophilosophers, Kentuckian Wendell Berry, to put into an essay his thoughts on slavery. In *The Hidden Wound,* Berry's central thesis (1970) reinforces one of my earlier points: that the dynamics of abstractionism display how philosophy and economics intersect to form a false morality — a morality that divides society into a plethora of *dualities:* male and female, master and slave, labor owner and laborer, intellectuals and manual laborers, primitive cultures and modern civilizations, and so forth.

For Berry, slavery not only reinforced the division of labor in American society in such a manner that civil war (which Greek philosophers thought to be the greatest of all evils) inevitably erupted, slavery also rendered the owner-elites ignorant of basic technologies/techniques of production. By so detaching themselves from the workers in order to exploit them as slaves, the plantation owners disconnected themselves from the very social class that knew most how to reproduce life out in the fields, since it was the slaves, of course, who did the real work on the southern plantations. Their *life on the land* and their *knowledge of the land* were devalued and relegated by the elite to the level of "folklore," far below the so-called productions of a "high culture," which becomes increasingly precious and abstracted from the natural origin and character of the agricultural forces of labor. The ideological superstructure was lifted off its economic base, and a "hyper-real" (illusory) *mass civilization* developed according to the accelerating dynamics of alienation, commodification, and fetishization fueled by advertising.

Mass civilization depends on the agricultural and cultural monocropping of the fields, and experience itself becomes an obviously reductive-abstractive practice; thus, there is an inevitable link in exploitative political economies between *abstraction* and *extraction*. Mining is definitely a bad habit of the mass civilizations that spread from Europe with Cristóbal Colón. The deforestation and the draining of wetlands that develop space for it are fundamental forms of *mining*. Characteristically, the means of production in societies of expropriation (as opposed to societies of appropriation) rarely embody basic natural principles of recycling or reciprocity. Raw materials are extracted and processed into obsolescent commodities. Returned to the system are waste products that become more and more toxic and nonrecyclable, while the means of production and labor-power become completely dominated by the capitalist mode of production that divides communities into owner and worker.

A hundred years after the *Communist Manifesto*, Aldo Leopold wrote in *The Sand County Almanac* that the two most significant developments of the modern age were the disappearance of wilderness and the hybridization of cultures. He noted the tight interdependence of these phenomena, recognizing that human cultures and civilizations emerge from nature, and that while the former beneficially extend, the latter detrimentally dominate nature. There are many different ways of conceiving nature and wilderness, one of the most philosophically fertile being that wilderness is a place (an ecosystem) where there is an unbroken continuity between the historical present and the very beginning of time. Conceived this way, wilderness stands as a bond between history and myth, since human comprehension of the origin of time is provided by myth. Both wilderness and myth are the ground of history (*historia* in Greek means "inquiry"), for they hold, carry, and preserve the sacred stories that tell people how to survive. Nature and myth are united by that common ideal of full knowledge of the continuance of life. The retelling of myths is thus important as a way of bringing nature and history together. When philosophers (or scientists) reject the sacred stories — the myths of the origins, emergence, and first adventures of a people searching for a homeland — as Socrates and Plato did, they cut themselves away from earth wisdom, severing their ties to their origins and from their primal languages of inquiry. For them, language itself goes on a holiday, as Wittgenstein would say, along with ethics as a vision of that total interconnectedness we call life.

Later that same day back in Durango, a different Navajo student, Ernest, from Rock Point, north of Chinle, Arizona, dropped by my office and asked me if I celebrated the New Year and other holidays like white people. I didn't know quite how to respond except to say to him that I was a *mestizo,* of mixed ancestry — Pueblo/Hispano from the Garcías who migrated north from San Juan Pueblo, mostly Mexicano/Chicano from my father's mother, Teodora Espinosa, and some English/Scotch/Irish from the Sargent/Burns ancestry of my mother's father, John Sargent; and also maybe Moorish and Sephardic through my mother's mother, Ludgarda Gonzales, whose exquisite watercolors of local flowers are hanging in my home on the Conejos River. I then recounted to him the conversation I had had with the other Navajo student, Michael, making the point that while my academic training and cultural background was substantially Euro-American, my area of specialization since late graduate school (after 1975) was ethnophilosophy. Thus I was aware of the background of indigenous Greek ideas behind Plato's Theory of Forms and also cognizant, for example, of the seasonal, nature-cycled ritual origins of both secular holidays and religious holy days in the Western traditions.

The previous conversation with Michael, which had been cut short by clock time earlier that day, seemed to fulfill itself in Ernest's differently measured account of how his people conceived and celebrated the major events of the year. He told me the New Year began in September, which the Navajos refer to by a word that means something akin to "when the mountains are half brown and half white," meaning "after the first snow has fallen." The other months have names similarly derived from significant local events. October is the time "when mountain sheep mate"; November, "when the wind is slender"; December, "when deer shed their antlers"; January, "when eagles are born"; February, "when baby eagles make their first sounds"; March, "when plants sprout stems"; April, "when plants sprout leaves" or "the month of delicate leaves"; May, "when antelope drop their fawns"; June, "when corn comes up"; July, "when fruits begin to ripen"; and August, "when the seeds are enlarging."

He told me the months and explained the seasons carefully, smiling. He said he could see that Plato's forms were quite removed from human experience in comparison to ideas in the calendar of a people for whom time could never be abstracted, detached from a local landscape and from the history and mythology of a particular people like his own *Dineh* — "the People."

March 26, Albuquerque

In the airport a well-dressed Chicano man speaks in Spanish in a telephone booth, wildly gesticulating with his free hand throughout his conversation of at least ten minutes.

Defining the cultural conditions of *liberation* in scholarly research, whereby traditional values and ideals are reconstructed on the basis of *personalized* inquiries into the moral past, is a moral/political task especially suited to ethnic writers and scholars. These scholars have a record of community cultural service, putting ethics into practice through family and regional histories as well as archival studies. There is an urgent need, I am convinced, to compare rural and urban life-styles so that resistance to and successful interventions against patterns of domination within each of them, and within rural/urban mixtures of life-styles, can be not only articulated but also rendered more effective. Such research would instigate new directions in social and cultural ecology, led by ethnic studies scholars and activists.

Certainly, social ecologist Devon Peña has listed in his writings important reasons why a *bioregional* model is most appropriate for such undertakings. Bioregional and eco/ethnophilosophical models would incorporate the four methodological vectors mentioned by Peña in a 1992 article, "The 'Brown' and 'Green':Chicanos and Environmental Politics in the Upper Rio Grande." The four vectors are (1) "biotic shift," a criterion for guiding studies of ecosystemic and cultural-ecological changes over time in a particular bioregion; (2) "watershed," considerations of which delimit or define a bioregion; (3) "sense of place" or *topophilia* ("love of place"), a cognitive/affective dimension of experience, leading to the strong emotional attachment required to care for widely diversified life-forms in a bioregion; and (4) "cultural distinctiveness," a criterion for studying the actual and imagined ways humans interact with their natural environment (all too often overlooked by so-called environmentalists). Attention to these factors would ensure an integrated ecological framework for academic research and political advocacy befitting the scholar/activist tradition in Chicano studies (Peña 1992, 84; see also Peña, chapter 1).[4]

Peña also calls for the inclusion of ethnoscience and ethnophilosophy in this scholarly framework. In his view ethnoscience encompasses ontology and epistemology, though these perhaps belong more properly to ethnophilosophy, which would include metaphysics, epistemology, logic, aesthetics, ethics, social and political theory, and so forth, but also philosophy of science, history, culture, and so on — insofar as these are self-consciously articulated from *culturally* distinctive perspectives. The social sciences and the natural sciences possess possible ethnophilosophical dimensions, of course, but "science" refers primarily to empirical observation rather than to conceptual reflexivity, insofar as the two can or should be distinguished. Perhaps Peña's use of the term "ethnoscience" is meant to dissolve this very division of the empirical from the introspective, since these are both phenomenological dimensions of existence that are not separable in either the study of nature or of humanity.

In any case, bioregional models overarch academic disciplines in the artificially separated human, social, and natural sciences insofar as they apply to all *renewable* forms of production/exchange/consumption grounded in ecosystemic cycles and in the life cycle as a whole. Homeland ethics would thus constitute fields of theory and action that are inherently bioregional. Many possible phenomenological fields or disciplines — biocultural, biomythological, alchemical, and so forth — might be included under some academic rubric of bioregionalism, since life and knowledge of life are reproduced in infinite ways. As the sociology of knowledge and the history of epistemology show, the wisdom associated with modern universities (which are tied to colonialism) has come to be legitimated by more and more specialized academic authorities. But exclusive modes of legitimation erode other sources of value within the academic channels of mass civilization. Ethnophilosophy and ethnoscience together — in a bioregional framework any homeland ethics must include both — move toward "reclamation" of those other sources of values and ideals delegitimated by the hegemonic colonialist ideologies that have developed by exclusion of indigenous knowledge and lifeways.

Values and ideals essential to any ethics must be seen to exist ultimately in relation to water and soil and light and air. From their immeasurable elemental interflux, distinctive life-forms and communities emerge. Furthermore, it is by participating in these material-spiritual archetypes that everything is finally united. The ultimate purpose or goal of the totality of systems may be ultimately unknowable or unimaginable; nevertheless, thinking bioregionally implies the "revaluation of all values" called for by

Nietzsche in his historical reflections on ethics. For him, not only was God dead, but so was Man. But that nihilistic turn need not be taken in philosophies of history and of culture reoriented by bioregionalism in the direction of remembering and reproducing life-styles and life stories that reincorporate nontranscendentalist and nonanthropocentric values and ideals and which thrive in personalized *collective* narratives about people recovering their lands. These forms of life augment rather than diminish the ancient myths—which remain cosmic, organic, systemic, and regional; which are able to incorporate all peoples from ant to star wherever they are; which are infinite in scope; and which at their margins merge with the Mystery.

The injustice, oppression, and brutality characteristic of urbanized industrial capitalism are the features of it most often documented and evaluated by ethnic and women's studies scholars. And there is an implicit ethics in this work precisely because it is motivated by and embodies values and ideals whose actualization is urgently needed by those dispossessed of their land and brutalized by city living, and also by the values and ideals that spring from life on the land. But such work will be devoured by the exploitative economism of modernity, which sucks all cultures into the soulless vortex of commodity worship, pollution, and waste. The sustaining natural resources and ecosystems will continue to be mined—unless intellectual and political work is undertaken within a matrix of bioregions in order to restore (ecosystemic) integrity to our actual living spaces.

If labor studies in the nineteenth century gave impetus to the study of cultures, it was the displacement of more or less indigenous rural peoples into cities as wage laborers for capital that made those labor studies necessary. Shifts from precapitalist to capitalist modes of production thus brought into being the contradictions between the indigenous lifeways and mass civilizations.

It is no accident of history, therefore, that some of the major concerns of both ecology and ethnic studies are noted by Peña in the important article cited earlier, which articulates, among a number of concerns, at least four general ones that would seem to be indispensable to bioregional methodologies: (1) cultural ecologists must first struggle to eliminate "environmental hazards people face daily in their living and work places" instead of wringing their hands over "the preservation of 'wilderness' for those privileged enough to engage in nature appreciation"; (2) ethnic scholars, especially, must focus their intellectual energies on the "critique of Western reductionist science," brilliantly initiated by Vandana Shiva, for example, in her analysis of "the dominant male-centered epistemology of international patriarchal capitalism"; (3) "the sustainable path recognizes nature as the embodiment of creativity, activity, and productivity"; and (4) theorists in all disciplines would do well to acknowledge the value of local, indigenous, or ethnoscientific knowledge (Peña 1992, 83).

The man on the telephone finishes and hangs up. He continues to gesticulate as he walks toward Gate 7. Modern technology has not been able to eradicate his cultural style: the oral tradition still within the gestures and face-to-face orientation of his Latino language habits, negating the depersonalization of telephonic communication.

March 27, San Antonio, Texas

José Barrera postulates, during the first panel I attend here at the National Association for Chicano Studies (NACS) conference, that the Spanish explorers were fueled by a medieval mythology that extended the patriarchal Hebrew conquest of the new land of Canaan to the New World, justified by an old-time *requerimiento* such as the one Moses and Aaron announced to the people of Jericho in the fourteenth century B.C.E..

Doug Monroy, another friend, recalled that when doing research on *Thrown Among Strangers,* he got chills, and his eyes teared up as he read in archival documents how Henry Dalton had paid the California Indians with alcohol. Doug said he felt as if he were "holding their deaths in his hands" (1990).

The coevalness or contemporaneity of history, it seems, makes a deeply emotional response to history inevitable at those times when we can "let the sources speak," as they did to José and Doug. Bioregional discourse works toward making whole the fragmented bodies of knowledge by referring to or reimagining the once-whole landscapes that have been damaged by human malpractices. Bioregional studies overlap with ethnic studies when scholars return to their communities with an eco/ethnic or culturally *situated* knowledge.

Such issues were brought home to me during the NACS plenary session orchestrated by Chicanas, one of the most inspirational sessions ever held at NACS. Another powerful NACS plenary session in Albuquerque two years earlier had featured Pedro Arechuleta from Tierra Amarilla, New Mexico, who spoke of the armed support of the ongoing struggle for land justice. "Don't forget why you're here," he warned. "Don't forget the people living back home on the land" (pers. comm. with the author).

Speaking from the heart intuitively and extemporaneously, Professor Inéz Talamantez set the tone of the session with her deeply female oratory and polyvalent *mestiza* presence, which to me seemed to threaten many of the Chicanos in the audience. She spoke the whole truth of her experience as a woman who was both a Chicana and a Mescalero Apache. Intellectually lucid, she stirred buried emotions in everyone listening. She analyzed the patriarchal atavisms recurrent at NACS and specified the crucial role of women in bringing a truly new, post-1992 world into being.

Professor Inéz Hernández, who is Chicana and Nimipu (called Nez Perce by the French colonizers), began with a poem about the mother that is "the most ancient mother of all—the original female energy, the female principle . . . who in her consolation validates me, as an *india* and as a woman, and teaches me how to have courage, to be brave" (Hernandez 1992, 154). She brought into sharp focus the ways in which the historic and mythic dimensions of women's experiences can coalesce to guide the revolutionary actions of all colonized peoples of color. Her poem is called "Mother's Song":

Don't cry my daughter
Don't cry
Don't allow those rages to
pass through you
so far into your soul
that you lose yourself
you lose yourself
and can't find yourself
Be calm, my little daughter
Everything passes
To be born
To be reborn. (Hernandez 1992, 154)

A flood of people, mostly women, surrounded the speakers after the session to express the vibrant sense of solidarity so eloquently evoked by those on the program. Although quite wide-eyed while offering my awe-struck words of thanks in turn, I too felt bonded to the two Inezes at an intimate level. For although I had spoken often to them at previous NACS meetings and at other conferences all over the country and though I knew them personally, I had not seen and heard them address a large group before. Witnessing these friends rising to an occasion like this as American Indian Chicana women responding to the quincentenary was empowering for me and for many others because the extraordinary strength of character and grace they embodied seemed to be generated by the experiences of a collective Self. The depth and force and richness of their presence emerged from the emotional details of a common life and from visions of a future rooted in communal history.

After the session, most of the thousand or more attendees exited the hotel and dispersed into this city with a river running through it. But in the quiet, elegant lobby of St. Anthony's Hotel, Professor Talamantez sat with two of her women graduate students. Drawn to them by their calmness and clarity, I sat with them and felt at home.

We talked for two hours. At one point I described my mother's death of the previous month and my recent trip to her grave, on which I had placed the four cattails. Her hands, lips, and eyes moving like small birds, Inéz carefully explained to me how to gather cattail pollen, with which her people prayed in ceremonies back home. Imagining the pollen in her cupped hand, I at once felt it radiate its healing, life-giving energy — even here in this natty bourgeois hotel. That imagined pollen in her hand will always stay with me.

April 10, Big Mountain, Navajo Nation

To find lasting value in life is what ethics is largely about. The mass civilizations of the last few hundred years, however, have tried to reduce everything to a monetary value, thereby obliterating heritages once passed down seven generations at a time. And it seems to me sometimes that no pure, good life is possible. Still there are *some* mixtures that are better than others. When I ride horseback among the very durable mixed-blood cattle my brother bought from "Dutch" Crowley of Chromo that have been engendered by many breeds of bulls and cows — Limousin, Shorthorn, and Hereford crosses — I am encouraged that my own children, who are *coyotas* like my mother, will be viable enough to carry on back home the agropastoral tradition flourishing here in Navajo country. Their blood ties to homeland incarnate the *mestizaje* (mixedness, hybridity) that is a crucial component of biodiversity, and through an ecologically conscious mixture of cultures it may be that the best of Western civilization will survive. When Aldo Leopold lamented the loss of distinct cultures along with wilderness, he did not yet have access to this new way of thinking about diversity, which has emerged from ethnic studies intersecting with ecological studies.

April 12, Big Mountain

Yesterday a Navajo man spoke aloud a prayer to the spirits of minerals. He asked those spirits not to allow the minerals mined by Peabody to be misused. "Everything here is controlled by a spirit. Unite all our hearts with mine," he asked us, "and send up a strong prayer to the spirit world in the smoke of the common fire."

There are various models and symbols of community. The circle arbor near the Teddy and Glenna Begay residence at Big Mountain serves as a *forum* or *resolana* for the people of this region to meet with one another but also to communicate with outside circles.[5] Today, just south of the Peabody mine on Black Mesa, whose mountains of coal are visible by day and whose lights twinkle by night behind the shimmering air, which are at the moment heated by the fires for the sweat lodges, there are many such overlapping and intersecting circles. From this unique center we touch them, intimately, by means of our good will.

As has always been true, I am aware of the spirit of my long-dead father in the afternoon sweat lodge ceremony, but this time my mother's spirit joins us. She is very much alive in my memory of holding her hand during her last moments before her transition to that other dimension beyond death. In her presence resides a moral energy that seems now to follow me everywhere and compel me toward goodness more forcefully than ever before. Her stories, her infinite kindness, and her stern love have formed my ideas of character and propriety, and now that she has passed on, memory alone connects me to the spiritual home to which she has returned. And in my mother's constant return, at the core of my homeland ethics, spins my own continual return home.

In my connection to her I am implicated in a web of synchronicities whose elemental forces are the spiritual causes of moral actions. Through her death, and eventually through my grieving for her, my petty pedantic ego has begun to dissolve within a more collective Self and to connect to a more ulterior source of continuance. Recovery of the sense of belonging to the world requires becoming connected to each other in new and mysterious ways, even as we are being rooted in the land, for as the Navajo man who prayed to the spirits of the minerals put it: "This earth is our home, the body of us all."

April 25, Los Angeles

Systematic philosophy from Plato through Hegel seems to have formed an important phase in the imposition of colonial structures of domination, characterized by cultural homogenization and conceptual abstractification, on traditional indigenous societies globally. By the Renaissance and its international rationalistic (Cartesian) phase, the mechanistic paradigm of the new science had seemed to usurp the organic paradigms of all the previous cultures. In Europe, and then increasingly worldwide, this mechanistic science, coupled with the expansion of Europe's empires, exerted an influence which drastically modified natural landscapes over nearly every region of the planet. Its paradigm of knowledge (where spirit and matter are mutually alienating) still *inhabits* the life patterns and daily practices of the mass of humanity today. Nevertheless, at a cultural level, modern, scientific, urban civilization superficially imitates ancient organic patterns of ritual in such a way that individuals are effectively depersonalized. One has only to think of the materialistic-consumptive insanity of the Christmas and New Year seasons to begin multiplying examples of the intended usurpation to which I refer.

On the other hand, there are lifeways and daily doings shaped by abiding ancient rituals, like the sweat lodge, that maintain themselves alongside premodern, preindustrial value systems, and they accomplish this precisely by integrating individuals into a web of natural cosmopolitical communities, revered as an all-encompassing matrix for their personal development, such that development means, essentially, "reciprocal spiritual metamorphosis." Because egalitarian communal rituals (as opposed to the manipulated-from-above homogeneities-in-action of colonizing empires) are heterarchical and heteroglossic, rather than hierarchical and monovocal, these rituals are powerfully transformative. When personal/ social identity is engendered within the diversified intimacies of an ecosystemically healthy community, historical meaning is constructed not only collectively but also synergistically: thus the world remains *organically potent* as well as coherent, and human life continues to be viable far into the future. It is the postmodern task of ethnophilosophy to reveal the *values* of ancient rituals as restorative sources of healing *power*.

April 26, Los Angeles to Albuquerque

Riding a bus to LAX airport through downtown Los Angeles, I notice a rock wall in a weedy field a hundred yards or so from a Holiday Inn. Glancing out the window of the speeding bus, I quickly examine a wickiup-like shelter, a hodgepodge of old chairs, a bookcase with odds and ends as neatly arranged in it as a museum storage shelf. The scene resembles those in other cities: Can Tho, South Vietnam, or la Ciudad Mexico — where I've marveled at the human ingenuity and persistence, which out of necessity makes nearly any space minimally livable.

Doris Lessing's novel *Memoirs of a Survivor* comes to mind amidst memories of my own experiences in the world's great cities. I wonder what future the rock wall shelter signifies? Does it mean the transformation of the United States into a Third World country? Am I witnessing the collapse of Western/Euro-American civilization in a time-warp breakthrough to a future that is a replay of the chaos of transitional upheavals of the past?

Steadily, and far down in my heart, burn images of homeland. I envision cranes or geese circling overhead; I hear coyotes howling their longings down by *El Río de los Conejos;* I smell the fresh-cut hay or the faintly familiar and, to me, beloved odor of the seemingly absentminded waddling skunks; I taste the cleanness of the sky and the purity of the ice-cold, deep-rock well water in my ranch house; I feel the silence of *las vegas y los alamos* in the thick fluids of my inner ears; I remember the story of my friend Robin, who put her hands in a river once and simultaneously felt the divine omnipresence of the water at the river's source, high in the mountains, and at the estuary where it emptied into the ocean.

Below us curves the shoreline of the City of Angels, the blue bowl of its harbor speckled with tiny white sails that seem like so many replicas of innocence itself, a scene that makes me think of times back home, lying on my back in the meadows, surrounded by lavender and pastel-yellow wild irises, looking up into clouds of tiny white butterflies. Closing my eyes, vaster visions surface in the dark circuits of memory: the night I lay on the edge of the Cumbres Lake between Antonito and Chama, staring up in awe at the starry night, then suddenly finding myself looking down in-stead of up—down, down, down into the unfathomable burning macro-cosmos. That is when I finally let go of fear.

Flying five miles high over the Nevada nuclear test site on the Shoshone Reservation (where students in my environmental ethics class had been arrested last week), my hope and inspiration returns. The words of Jimmy Santiago Baca, that great-hearted Chicano/Apache poet, wash into me like an ocean tide under the pull of a full moon in daylight:

> I was born a poet one noon, gazing at weeds and creosoted grass at the base of a telephone pole outside my grilled cell window. . . . The power to express myself was a welcome storm rasping at tendril roots, flood-ing my soul's cracked dirt. Writing was water that cleansed the wound and fed the parched root of my heart. . . . I wrote to sublimate my rage, from a place where all hope is gone, from a madness of having been damaged too much, from a silence of killing rage. I wrote to avenge the betrayals of a lifetime, to purge the bitterness of injustice.

These are the words that end "Coming into Language," the first essay in Jimmy Santiago Baca's book of essays, *Working in the Dark* (1992, 11). I treasure the time I took to savor the rest of it. Spiritual-visceral contact with such writing is a steady source of *value* and *power* to me and to many others whose "soul's cracked dirt" binds us all to one another. If I offer these musings and long quotes from friends new and old, it is because I cannot think or live without continual reference to those others whose ideas and values and very lives sing within my own. They are the radiant moral gossamers in which my life is suspended. Below, at this moment, El Río Grande roils brown between green banks, singing the goodness of life itself. This home landing is sweet, *dulce como miel.*

May 6, Antonito

Lying awake in my high-ceilinged bedroom, I am worrying about irrigat-ing these surrounding meadows, for there are those using water from the river system who consider only the economic dollar value of the land, who cut down trees, level their meadows, and plant monocrops. But to let the water run wild and the willows and cottonwoods spring up along the overflowing ditches is high on my agenda. If I let so much water flow that the old neighbors remind me that the Garcías seem to love water as much as the frogs do, it is because I want to increase the *total* value of the land in proportion to a standard of biodiversity, not to a monetary standard, according to some ultimate measure beyond my own or anyone's comprehension rather than according to some myopic short-term profit margin.

In early morning light, the still, small leaves trembling on the tall trees are uncommonly luminescent. The marshes will soon be thick with cattails, but now they are brittle, and the dried muck covers the sprouting, tiny, bright green grasses like a thick lace. Red-winged yellow-headed blackbirds flit off when they sense my crunchy footfalls.

Ten years ago my older brother, José Eduardo, laid upon me my irrigating responsibilities in a ritual event that changed my life forever. The marshes in these meadows were much smaller then. Only my vaguely calculating, intentional negligence allows the water in the myriad ditches to slow down, back up, spread out, and thus amplify these *vegas*. Of course there are those who misinterpret my intentions — usually *gringos* new to the area — and who treat me with stereotypical contempt, not because they are Euro-Americans, but more likely because they have little capacity for admiring nature. The swamps and big trees and wildlife are superfluous to them, I think, because their money-making cattle can't eat them. These kinds of men serve corporate interests. There are few of them here, fortunately. We stare at each other across ditches and fences and property boundaries like enemies, because we do not share the same values. The idea that I am an "environmentalist" sets their teeth on edge. The need to think and feel and act within ecosystems is, I believe, regulated by rhythms engendered by a universal Spirit or Mind. Only through such faith can those of us who live on the land sustain healing relationships with the nonhuman or more-than-human beings who surround and envelop us.

The birds on this ancestral ranch are especially delightful. Among the many animal peoples who live among these cottonwoods, the birds, whose polychrome plumage manifests the variegated beauty and wild radiance of the life-force, seem to me the most spiritual. They sit high in the trees, listening to the clouds thunder and watching the rain fall gently. They are singing softly, and the river is rising imperceptibly. Are you up there, Mother? Can you hear? Do you hear?

May 10, Boulder

Where are you, my dear Mother? Do you know of my great sadness today? I awoke with it and quickly put on my running clothes. Boulder Creek is itself running very full. The thick, fast-moving water absorbs my grief. I feel so very alone on this Mother's Day. It's my first without you and it's so very lonely.

May 11, Antonito

My friend Victor Nelson-Cisneros, the associate dean of The Colorado College, is from Brownsville, Texas. He is a big man who in a few moments of great tenderness told me that in order to grieve properly and go on with our lives we had to remember exactly how our mothers and grandmothers were and to cherish our memories of them. Five years ago he lost his mother, too. The moral and cultural ideals our mothers exemplified in their daily lives are still alive in us, he said, and they largely define who we are as Chicanos.

   What he says comforts me and makes me think of the Naskapi archetype of the Great Man, *Mista'peo,* a word which in their tongue means "soul-spirit."[6] The Naskapi of the Labrador Peninsula are caribou hunters who honor the caribou people in a ritual meal called "Mokoshan," which they eat before going hunting. Before, during, and after this meal, they make contact through the Great Man with the Caribou Master, who is the corresponding animal archetype within the caribou psyche. By means of these "inner life forms," the Naskapi learn how to hunt properly and, indeed, how to live properly. Contemplating my mother's death brings the meaning of her life closer to me, and I begin to see how the moral dynamism of archetypes illuminates the great patterns of spirit that are at work, not only in nature, but also in human relationships and in the profound feeling of kinship underlying them all. The good life is thus anchored in the Great Mother.

May 17, Hoh Rainforest

The spruce, hemlock, and cedar giants here are matrices for younger trees, but everywhere I also see trees of the same age fused together. It's when I see younger ones growing straight up through the older trees that I most understand what "heart" is and when I begin to understand that love is an outpouring of life and that the heart of life is love.

I see and even faintly smell very dark brown, very small Roosevelt elk munching ferns that sway up into their faces. They aren't afraid and don't move as I pass slowly by. The waters in El Río Hoh are pure, straight down from the center of the wilderness. I walk for miles just listening and look- ing and smelling and feeling and tasting the goodness of the world as it is.

May 23, Idylwild, California

One hundred miles east of Los Angeles at the Idylwild School of Music, there is a conference and festival celebrating the Native American music of California. They have named it "Ancient Songs in a Modern World," and I am attending the conference with Susan and our two girls, Lana and Tania. San Juan Pueblo ethnomusicologist Brenda Romero sings a song taught to the people by the dragonflies when they arrived at last where they were to remain. It is a very beautiful "circling-in-the-air-above-home- after-migrating" song. Local Cahuilla singer Brian Bubby says that among his people there are dances and songs performed on the shortest day of the year, when the first grasses start to come up. Human expressions of vitality — emotions and feelings and natural rhythms — reverberate in the heart of these songs and dances.

Bird Dancers come on stage with feathered skirts. They mimic bird actions with jerky neck and head movements. The Cahuilla people from around here compare their own migrations to those of the bird people, who are their neighbors here. Many of the male dancers display huge grins. Four women dance, swaying slowly, rocking their arms back and forth, holding bandanas folded in hanging-down triangles. The men at the end begin blowing short whistles in syncopation like many high-pitched trains tied to strings around their necks. Bare back-skin glistens with sweat.

The final dance is a blessing in the four directions. The Mojave people from around Needles, California, sing of "the beauty of the land." A singer comments, "A bird song brings water. It helps us get to our destinations." The singer speaks of mountains and rivers, always of land forms. Jimmy James, one of the most eminent of the elders here, tells us all to "love one another!" — my mother's last words, her final message in death.

As I listen to the Mojave singers, I am looking at a sepia-toned photo of Essie Parrish, Kashaga Pomo Spiritual Leader, who gave an oration here in front of the Center Pole in 1972, and I memorize her words: "They speak of who we are, and the families we're from, and about our relatives too. . . . People from different places will know about us and our ways by what we do, the things we say, how we act to each other, and how we act around those people when we are among them."

May 30, 6:56 P.M., Flagstaff, Arizona

Approaching Flagstaff, I am elated by the sight of the still snowcapped San Francisco Peaks. They are the borders of my vast Southwest homeland. Flapping up slowly to the side of the road is the ubiquitous Raven. Magpie I have seen only where there is water: they are for each other.

May 31, Acoma Pueblo, New Mexico

I find myself looking down on the flat valley from which old Acoma rises, where I was talking with Lilly Salvador two years ago. She has a workshop/store across from the Visitor's Center, and her son was a student at Fort Lewis College. Between the valley and where I stand, a stock pond nearly overflows after the last week of rain. Lilly told me that her pots call to her when she is away from working on them for more than a few days. She said she had gone to the Smithsonian in Washington, D.C., where she used a magnifying glass to study the Acoma pots. They seemed homesick there, all locked up, so she spoke to them. Although at first she thought maybe they should be brought home, they did seem to be well cared for. She showed us a pot with a parrot that looked like a swan that had a story to go with it about her son's taking his first deer after seeing a triple rainbow. The clay Lilly used for her pots came from stone, which she had ground up into a fine powder. I bought a cup and saucer her son had made. She said that the women make clouds on the pots to bring rain and that when they are up in the old village of Acoma, they throw them to the people. If the pots break, the rain will come. Her son understands animals, Lilly says. Even the cows keep calling him: "Come home. Come home. Come home. Come home."

May 31, Albuquerque

Truly, knowledge is power, but there are different kinds of knowledge and power. There is the cyclical knowledge generated and sustained within communities and ecosystems, but there is also the narcissistic knowledge generated by isolated individuals who use it to manipulate others instead of enhancing their mutual survival. Knowledge nourishes the good life when its complexity and richness are derived from its connections to networks of living communities. Ignorance makes the good life impossible for the few who pretend they know only in order to further their own interests rather than those of the common good.

June 1, Albuquerque

In an interview in *Crosswinds* (May 1992, 9), Stanley Crawford, author of the much-admired *Mayordomo* (Crawford 1988) says: "The development pressure is very high and getting higher every day, especially in Santa Fe and Taos. . . . [T]he only way to resist, or control, or direct what seems to be the inevitable development is to continue to encourage the traditional ways of life. . . . And that's why people are attracted to this place. The danger is that tourism will totally devour that which is feeding it."

Crawford's comments invoke, perhaps, a cultural manifestation of the Heisenberg uncertainty principle, applicable to cannibalistic tourists. They also bring to mind the paradoxical conflicts between modern and postmodern existence, conflicts wrought by failure to recognize the extent to which the actual, territorial Chicano homeland is given meaning by cultural symbolism. This knowledge is unknown to most outsiders, especially to tourists, but also to many so-called environmentalists who have been severely criticized recently by Estévan Arellano, Chicano editor and publisher of the northern New Mexico newspaper *Arellano*.

Recalling a few words from Hortense Spiller's *Mamma's Baby, Papa's Maybe: An American Grammar Book* helps me more fully comprehend

Crawford's comments.[7] Explicating the way Euro-Americans reified and commodified African Americans during the days of slavery by seeing them as material objects of possession, merely as bodies to be bought and sold to the highest bidder, Spiller writes: "I would make a distinction [in the case of the slave trade] between 'body' and 'flesh'" (Morrison 1987, 88–89). To have seen them as "flesh" and not as "body" would have required the masters to see their slaves as human beings whose real value was beyond price, as Kant would say. To see people as they really are is to see them in the context of their daily struggles, in the context of the great spiritual effort it takes to survive every day.

Value is derived from the spirit of that fleshly struggle. In a work of art such as *Beloved* by Toni Morrison, one of the world's greatest writers and an African American Princeton professor, the flesh of the African slave is given voice by the grandmother of Beloved, who is called "Baby Suggs, Holy" at special spots in the novel. For example, there is a scene in which the grandmother, out with her people in a forest clearing, delivers a sermon that is (to use a phrase from Spillers) one of her many *"figurations of the flesh"*: "Here," she said, "in this here place, we flesh; flesh that weeps, laughs, flesh that dances on bare feet in grass. Love it. Love it hard. Yonder they do not love your flesh. They despise it" (Morrison 1987, 88–89). Within this sublime moment in the novel, the grandmother is deeply embedded in the forest landscape on the edge of the city in the so-called free North to which she has migrated to escape slavery. In the forest they really are free, far from the reifying gazes of the white people but close to one another in this self-conscious collective experience of being the same flesh.

Land-based cultures and the traditional ways of life common to them are subtle and complex like the land from which they emerged and to which they are bonded mythically, even when cut off from the land. By outlasting and transforming systems that exist to dominate land and people, a land and a people sustain freedom enough to share a common flesh. Many of the most powerful and strangest scenes in *Beloved* come at the end of the novel, when the characters are closest to "rememory" of Africa in recalling images of passage and hearing stories in native dialects, and they affect me profoundly each time I reencounter them when I teach the novel in summer school. Asleep or awake, I often experience the presence of ancestors with the same dreamlike intensity. I dream in mythic imagery, and the words of my dreams are in archaic Spanish strongly associated with special places that are immediately and intuitively known to me even without having ever been there. The circuities uniting place and meaning are wired into my very flesh and bone and blood and nervous system.

Unintentionally, tourists and environmentalist newcomers often intrude upon people whose relationships with places may be invisible and inaudible to them at first, so delicately have they been inscribed — within the flesh and not merely upon the body. The deep-rooted relationships that have evolved between the land and the Chicano people (and men like Stanley Crawford who have become integrated into New Mexico ethnoecosystems through a long fragile process of adaptation) inevitably involve ecocultural practices only barely comprehensible to environmentalists who are unfamiliar with traditional fusions of the natural and the human. When people have learned how to belong to the land, their lifestyles become magnets to others not so fortunate but who can, with immense patience and steady tolerance, become her flesh too.

June 8, Durango, Colorado

My friend Jim Fitzgerald and I eat at Taco Delite, a family restaurant down the hill from the college. I first ate here while interviewing for the job I now have and meeting various faculty, including the man talking with me now.

The *comida* is wonderful, as usual. Fitz teaches sociology and Chicano Spanish and literature and lives on a ranch outside Bayfield. It is there that he and his wife, Teri, have raised two daughters as well as sheep and draft horses and countless other kinds of animals over the last twenty years. He's a sociologist/linguist who testified not long ago at the Tierra Amarilla trial of Amador Flores.

He is telling me about his "Mirror Project." I keep a copy of it in my office. In his research among Chicano/as in the region, he found three different but inseparable concepts of homeland. Where tourism, development, and environmentalism have severely undermined agropastoral traditions — in Taos, for example — homeland is conceived and acted out as theater much of the time. Homeland is not only a stage on which history is simultaneously imagined and acted out but also a battlefield. In a place like Tierra Amarilla, where the external forces of domination and expropriation have left many ecocultural practices intact, homeland signifies living on the land and remaining in place militantly, often successfully opposing incremental or accelerated development toward mass civilization.

To those born and raised in a city like Albuquerque, homeland may be a symbol such as Tierra Amarilla, a distant place to which urban Chicana/os are still connected by family visits, by property, by keeping a horse or cows there, and so forth. These different sample categories under which homeland stays alive in the minds and hearts of the people subtend a much larger experience. I am led to this belief by Jim's study, which incorporates these and other meanings of homeland: that the longing for homeland leads to greater depths of spirituality because it involves people in communal experiences larger than those of any individual.

July 8, Flying over Antonito

The spiritual principles of any ethics that yields survival and continuance, understood and lived out in accordance with natural laws and religious ideals, have consistently throughout history included: (1) the conviction that into a multiplicity of forms everything flows from a single source: the One, the Unborn, the Great Mystery or Great Spirit, Thought Woman, the Unconditioned, Chaos, Yahweh, God, Allah, The Creator, and so the list goes on; and (2) that everything is already and always connected to the Source and thus everything is interconnected and everywhere alive. Consciousness of these two basic truths renders reality sacred, so that the sacredness of the world and of existence itself is also a basic fact. Such realizations serve as the foundation for the possibility of Truth, Beauty, and Goodness — and of a real and lasting homeland ethics.

At this moment I see my ranch house, barn, corrals, and haystacks far below, straight down through the clouds, four miles northeast of Antonito. This vision is calming and centering, especially because the fluid, unbroken river-bottom ranchland possesses such a heightened natural look compared to the adjacent too-perfect circles of too-bright flat green fields irrigated twenty-four hours a day by automatic pivot sprinklers.

What I had suddenly realized earlier in the day, while listening to African music — "White Man Sleeps" in *Pieces of Africa* by the Kronos Quartet — was immediately confirmed by the land, it seemed to me. I couldn't help weeping. It was as if on the road to Albuquerque to get on this jet, my solitude and the sadness of being unable to share the beauty in which I felt submerged had disappeared, to be instantly replaced by an ineffable peace; I knew in my mind what my heart had always known—that the root of my being reached down into the Source itself. This intuitive indubitable conviction connected me to every other being in the universe, whose roots also touched the source of the web of life of which we were all strands. The Presence I experienced was the most intimate encounter I have had with the sacred, except during those very rare moments of lovemaking when I've felt myself falling ecstatically into starry heavens.

Surely, it is the oceanic feeling of oneness, unity, and totality that makes ethics possible by generating an equally all-encompassing compassion. Interacting with other beings as other selves—"Do unto others as you would have them do unto you" (Jesus); "Do not do to others what you would not want them to do to you" (Kung Fu-Tzu/Confucius); *"Tu eres mi otro yo"* (the Mayan *dicho*)—grounds every ethics of caring that aims to increase or intensify, through conscious action, the goodness of the world as intertwined systems of individuals—as a *whole.*

Like wilderness or paradise, such an ethics of connections and continuance can be described as an ultimately harmonious story of relationships established through an unbroken landscape of causes originating in the Creation. When Leslie Marmon Silko begins *Ceremony,* a novel I teach every summer, by rooting her own creative powers of storytelling in the creativeness of Grandmother Spider or Thought-Woman, the Keresan Creator Being, she situates her work within a spiritual reservoir that disseminates itself according to transtemporal energy patterns or psychic archetypes.

The ulterior dynamism of each life-form seems to involve archetypes such as the Great Man of the Naskapi or one of the Masters of Animals (the Caribou Master Beaver Chief, etc.) or of Plants (Mescalito). The ultra-archetype would then be The Great Mystery itself: the Nagual (Nahuatl-Mexican), Brahman (Sanskrit-Hindu), Yahweh (Hebrew), Wakan Tanka (Sioux), and so forth. Within indigenous human cultures, ideal natural beings of any species (Raven, Human, Frog, etc.) can energize individuals through dreams and visions (as happens frequently in James Welch's novel *Fool's Crow*). Humans can belong to the same spirit communities as nonhumans.

That great explorer of archetypal reality, C. G. Jung, writes in his memoirs of an experience that led to his discovery of "synchronicity" as a form of spiritual or psychic causality. He dreamed of "a winged being sailing across the sky. I saw it was an old man with the horns of a bull. . . . He had the wings of the kingfisher, with its characteristic colors. . . . During the days when I was occupied with the painting [which he had drawn of this being, whom he named Philemon], I found in my garden, by the lake shore, a dead kingfisher. I was thunderstruck, for kingfishers are quite rare in the vicinity of Zurich, and I have never since found a dead one" (Jung [1961] 1989, 183).

Kingfishers, which have appeared at critical times throughout my own spiritual life, symbolize the enduring goodness of nature. They have the power to calm waves on water (inner turbulence). They are solitary, ultimately, like each soul on its journey to the final homeland.

Many similar "organic symbols," as I call them, act as energy patterns to transform the meaning of geographical places into places in the heart, and I would claim that such transformations that enhance the "balance" of nature are inherently ecosystemic. Below me at this moment, the river systems of Oklahoma look like branches of an enormous tree of life. They spread across and down into the land while this jet races through aerial water systems swirled by winds high above the surface of the earth. These travel notes mirror a branching mind's ties to the world.

The homeland is a symbolic ideal within the inner geography of any genuine home. That ideal demands renewable innocence and purity of its indwellers, because it is the mythic place where the earth, the air, the water, and the fire are pure. Thus a sweat lodge is a primordial image of homeland. As Leonard Crow Dog says:

The *inipi* is probably our oldest ceremony because it is built around the simplest, basic, life-giving things: the fire that comes from the sun, warmth without which there can be no life; *inyan wakan* or *tunka*, the rock that was there when the earth began, that will still be there at the end of time; the earth, the mother womb; the water that all creatures need; our green brother, the sage; and encircled by all these, man, basic man, naked as he was born, feeling the weight, the spirit of endless generations before him, feeling himself part of the earth, nature's child, not her master. (Fisher and Luyster 1990, 20)

July 15, Albuquerque

Sitting outside by the ponds near the university library, I continue reading the journal entries of Jimmy Santiago Baca, the "Poet's Gleanings": "You must understand that there exist no pat formulas for mapping out one's journey. . . . It is a nameless lord that has come from the nameless land in which we search for our names, our faces: *we are the land becoming*. . . . Name ourselves tree, grass, sun. Start over again from that point" (Baca 1992). These memorable words form an important statement about organic symbols, images, and archetypes that can join inner and outer landscapes. Baca urges us into the cauldron of his life as it is lived in a context of Life as an infinitely jointed totality. Through Baca's writing I am led to renew all of my trust in the sources of life. In my heart I hold the image of the love in my mother's eyes for me, and through me, for a world broken and beautiful and mending . . . and still evolving. Baca teaches me to be at home with continuous metamorphosis, continuous rebirth.

July 17, Colorado Springs

Biotechnology moves humanity toward a *mechanical* rather than *cultural* transformation. Petroleum-based artificial fertilizers cannot be permanently integrated into the lifeways and soils of the bioregions in which they are used. Herbicides kill many more life-forms than they are intended to kill. Plants genetically engineered to be "pest"-resistant and/or self-fertilized are anthropocentric abstractions that betray a failure of imagination, whereby the Other is exterminated. Mechanical methods not only produce nonsustainable, opportunistic results, they also generate deadening systems of control that are out of control.

In cybernetic theory and in Gregory Bateson's extension of it to models of human ecology, any system is always considered as a whole, and it is in relation to this *wholeness* that Mind can be grasped as the most important intrinsic characteristic of systems; thus "mental characteristics are inherent in the ensemble as a whole." In a "schismogenic" system, however, where there is no "governor," "the system is constantly slipping into runaway" (Berman 1981, 243). The modernized, urbanized, industrialized dimensions of reality are centered on the Wall Streets and in the White Houses of the world, where the laws of nature and moral laws are totally subordinated to the pernicious principles of mining — expropriation and exploitation — that alienate the ruling class from the systems whose life-blood its economy of greed sucks out like a vampire. The Western addictive way of living stops evolution.

By various methods of artifice, addictions to the mining economy are institutionalized. Addiction is the perfect example of a runaway system. The heroin addict needs an increasingly larger fix; the sugar addict finds that the more pastry he eats, the more pastry he wants; the imperialist power starts out seeking particular foreign markets and eventually winds up trying to police the globe. . . . Addiction in one form or another characterizes every aspect of industrial society. It strangles life.

Morris Berman explains that one great danger in the runaway industrial civilization that mass produces is that it destroys its own "brain cells": "A mental system cannot remain in permanent runaway, cannot maximize variables and also retain characteristics of mind; it dies. On the individual level, we experience cirrhosis, heart attack, cancer, schizophrenia, and what has to be called living death. *The ethics of the system are implicit in its epistemology*" (Berman 1981, 244). In Berman's rendition (1981, 246) of Batesonian epistemology, "a social or political structure, a river, and a forest are all alive, and possess Mind." Mind is immanent in all *ecosystems* and by its very nature adapts to change in such a way that ecosystems *endure*.

Underlying these images of life and empowering them is the value of sovereignty, of a form of self-governance that does not detach its needs from the needs of communities that partake of wholeness. Sovereignty is a Native American value and a political issue par excellence today because Indian people — and we are all Indians if we could remember ourselves far enough back — need the freedom to live according to the natural/moral laws that have been passed down for tens of thousands of generations: freedom to live purely, cleanly, within the totality, according to the enduring ancient ways.

Coming down to Colorado Springs, I drove through San Luis, then over La Veta Pass into Walsenburg. The trip is beautiful because there's so much open, undamaged land. There are old dwellings on the prairie, foothills, and mountains that blend into the landscapes, and one gets a sense of the possibility of human beings belonging here, incorporated into the land, like Native Peoples traditionally have been. Who are the living persons and what are the ethical ideals that embody the results of purification? Where are there models of purity?

July 18, Antonito

My brother, José Eduardo, can you hear the frogs singing?

July 19, Antonito

Looking out at the gigantic *alamos*, at the tall yellow clover, purple alfalfa blossoms, at the birds and wind and clouds, in my heart I know why many of us travel too much, work too much, overcommit ourselves, and why we risk becoming addicted to trying to fix up everything. We do it for the future *wholeness* born into the world through our children and borne onward by them through the world into their own children's future, and so on and on.

The rain pours down out of the purple-gray sky. Is that you up there, Mother, showing me life flowing?

July 20, Antonito

Lying on my kitchen table with its richly colored cover of a painting of an African spirit-being, bell hooks's *Yearning* beckons me, so I pick it up and read the beginning of an essay called "Homeplace," where she recollects going to her grandmother's house: "Oh! That feeling of safety, of arrival, of homecoming when we finally reached the edges of her yard. . . . Such a contrast, that feeling of arrival, of homecoming, this sweetness and the bitterness of that journey, that constant reminder of white power and control. . . . There we learned dignity, integrity of being . . . faith" (hooks 1990, 49). For me, too, home is a place where women "nurture our spirits . . . that space where we return for renewal and self-recovery, where we can heal our wounds and become whole" (Jung 1960, 25). Yet I am puzzled by the emptiness caused by my mother's absence, as if her death were unfinished.

I walk from my house through the fields to hers. The grasses in the vegas are waist high and dark green. All the cottonwoods seem even bigger than usual. I pass a duck nest near a pond while the mother duck swims in little circles without taking her eyes off me. A skunk waddles near, snout scooting close to the ground, without seeming to notice me. A hawk circles the round meadow. There are billions of mosquitoes buzzing. Outside her bedroom window the hollyhocks she called *varas de San Jose (Bellis perennis)* stand seven feet high in full bloom.

Her house is still just the way she left it almost a year ago, she wearing her pajamas to the hospital, thinking she would return in a few days, but leaving her house forever. Her "old lady face powder," as she called it, rests in its usual place in the blue-tiled bathroom. On the mirrored mahogany dresser that was her mother's still stands the brass crucifix from her own mother's casket, and lined up in frames on either side of it, photographs of long-dead relatives from Abiquiu and El Rito, New Mexico, where she was born and raised *en español*. A trace of her, a characteristically discarded tissue, still lies on the floor near her bed. Everywhere throughout the house are pictures of her two grandchildren.

I sit in her favorite chair and watch the sunset through the big windows facing west, as she loved to do, and as we loved to do together. The tears come, for it is so very lonely without her. And I cry because I know she was lonely, living by herself way out here on this ranch for so many years, and because I waited too long to move back home.

Long after sundown I sit alone in her house. Then I hear the frogs singing. I rise and go outside into the night, glad the air has chilled and that there finally seem to be more stars than mosquitoes. It is a great comfort to know that soon the dragonflies arrive.

July 30, Cottonwood Lake Trail

Climbing the steep trail that will take me up tomorrow into the Sangre de Cristo Mountains to a lake just below Crestone Peak and the Needles, I once again ponder Jungian ideas, whose origins are ancient. In *Synchronicity* Jung defines this "acausal connecting principle" — an alternative to the principle of cause/effect — as "the simultaneous occurrence of a certain psychic state with one or more external events which appear as meaningful parallels to the momentary subjective state, and, in certain cases, vice versa." Synchronicity can thus be understood to consist of two factors: "a) An unconscious image comes into consciousness either directly (i.e., literally) or indirectly (symbolized or suggested) in the form of a dream, idea, or premonition. b) An objective situation coincides with this content" (Jung 1960, 31).

It is my birthday, and this misty forest trail vibrates with ulterior meanings. Rain pours down. Thunder and lightning rumble and flash. I am fortunate to be in a place of such power and purity, where the natural elements — water, earth, air, fire — evoke their primordial counterparts in the spirit. I have been thinking I must change my life and embark on a more genuinely spiritual journey that will bring me still closer to Aztlán, make me more useful to my people, and return me to the land more consistently. Perhaps after all these nights of sleeping out under the stars, a little of their steady light has sunk down into me.

On my birthday, therefore, I give thanks to my dead mother, listening perhaps from these mountains, and to all women for the gift of total birth — physical, emotional, intellectual, and spiritual. This rain and these feathers and these mountains make me aware of what is *given*. Life itself is the gift.

The feathers of a dead flicker lie in the rain in a perfect circle on the trail. I follow the trail down from the mountain between the stone cairns I restacked on the way up so that I could find my way back. Beyond all meaning is the great Mystery in which this small tragedy finds its proper place, marking in its turn a wider morality. This seemingly insignificant and puzzling array of feathers acquires immense and immanent meaning for me by virtue of its relation to death and eternity and to a matrix of meaning and being of which I avail myself only by an act of faith in Life, reflected back to me in every tranquil pool of water on the trail. *Gracias, mi mama.* You have taught me that we are all children, always within the great wholeness, and that we are cared for in varying degrees by the cosmos who is the mother of us all. You have taught me that during moments of synchronicity such as I experienced with these flicker feathers, we experience two or more different dimensions of reality, normally experienced separately or not at all in mass civilization. Synchronicity opens us toward the depth of the world, its unfathomable depth.

August 2, Jémez Pueblo

Today is *La Fiesta de Porcingula,* which comes to Jémez from the extinguished pueblo of Pecos, to the east of Santa Fe. Now merged into one, the people of Jémez are the only people in the world who speak Towa. The people here become plants and animals and dance for rain today. And it rained on them and on all of us at home here praying together.

Notes

I wish to thank the Chicano Studies Research Center at U.C.L.A for awarding me the Rockefeller Postdoctoral Fellowship that gave me the time and the place (and the computer) in 1992 to work on the manuscript of these selected journal entries for publication in *Subversive Kin*. In this regard I am particularly grateful to Assistant Director Antonio Serrata and Associate Vice Chancellor Raymund Paredes.

1. In an earlier entry in this first section of his notebooks entitled "Philosophy," Leonardo writes: "Every part is disposed to unite with the whole, that it may thereby escape from its own incompleteness" (MacCurdy 1938, 61).

The following autobiographical "Notes on (Home)land Ethics" were occasioned from March through August 1992 by personal experiences in different places that have stimulated my thinking on the borders of moral philosophy, Chicano studies, and ecology. For a more extensive, focused, and academic discussion of the themes explored in the present work, I refer readers to "Land and Story as Ethnophilosophical Archetypes" in my dissertation; see García 1988.

2. In an essay entitled "In Search of Aztlán" in Anaya and Lomellí (1989), Luis Leál states that even more important than being a "geographic" symbol during the early days of the Chicano Movement, "Aztlán symbolized the *spiritual union* of the Chicanos, something that is carried within the heart, *no matter where they may live or where they may find themselves*" (Leál 1989, 8, emphasis mine).

Nagy devotes three chapters to explicating Jung's theory of archetypes, which he himself understood to be thematic images of instincts. Commenting on "his reasons for positing archetypes" — reasons which were "thoroughly religious" — Nagy notes that "Jung wanted to save a place in the modern world for the human dream of *eternal life,* for the human sense of an ultimate meaningfulness in life, for human *moral ideals*" (1991, 161, emphasis mine).

3. See Cowan 1990 for a deeply empathetic and poetic account of the spiritual landscapes of the Aborigines. For more thoroughly academic and richly illustrated treatments see Sutton 1990 and Lawlor 1991.

4. In the present volume, Peña's "Los animalitos," originally presented as a lecture to the Jackson Faculty Research Fellows at Colorado College in February 1990, provides a well-considered overview of a culturally sensitive bioregionalism as well as a schema for immediate research.

5. Atencio writes: "The term Resolana derives from a real place — a space of smoothly trampled earth on the south side of a building or plaza. This place, protected on all sides from breezes, allows the south wall to receive the rays of the sun" (1988, 1).

6. See Speck [1935] 1977, 33–36 and Lopéz 1979, 90–93.

7. Spiller's article is quoted and discussed by Baker (1991, 37).

Part 2

Environmental History and Ecological Politics

4 Ecological Legitimacy and Cultural Essentialism

Hispano Grazing in Northern New Mexico

Laura Pulido

Governmental and other official and quasiofficial bodies commonly assume that the poor of the world are a major threat to the environment and that hence they lack what might be called "ecological legitimacy." Such legitimacy attaches to a group when it is seen as a valid environmental actor, when its commitment to preserving the environment is not regarded as suspect. Ecological legitimacy is associated with environmental stewardship, or the practice of caring for the land in a sustainable manner.

Ecological legitimacy often eludes poor rural populations because officialdom has long assumed that landless and land poor groups do not care about protecting their environments.[1] However, the rise of the environmental justice movement in the "First World" and the spread of peasant and indigenous struggles in the "Third World" have sharply challenged the ideology that the poor are incapable of caring for their own environmental conditions of life (Shiva 1988; Bullard 1990; Guha 1990; Bebbington et al. 1993; Friedmann and Rangan 1993; Gedicks 1993; Peet and Watts 1993; and Pulido 1996).

Ecological legitimacy may be drawn from different sources and crafted in various ways. One source that nonwhite and indigenous communities have used is what might be called (for lack of a better expression) romanticized cultural heritages (Bebbington 1993, 274–92). Such discourses are often predicated on cultural assumptions. This means, first, the practice of defining cultural differences as the principle determinant of intergroup conflict, and second, the assumption that some cultures are inherently more sensitive to nature than others, whether or not this is in fact true. Romanticized cultural heritages are a form of essentialism in that they regard the characteristics of a particular group as unitary and fixed or eternal. This kind of essentialism has been common with respect to gendered identity and is growing among indigenous environmental discourses.[2] Increasingly, the struggles of people of color in the United States and "Third World" peoples to assert their environmental legitimacy are cast within this kind of culturalist framework.

A number of writers — who insist that differences among various national and ethnic groups do in fact exist — have noted the dangers of cultural essentialism. One problem is that this type of cultural explanation is typically innocent of any analysis of socioeconomic (material and power) relationships and hence serves to essentialize ethnic differences. Cultural essentialism denies or obfuscates the whole problem of social or historical agency, obscuring dominant power dynamics such as the struggles between rich and poor, landowners and tenants, thus reifying cultural differences. Instead of examining how and why various constellations of wealth and power result in different environmental practices, cultural essentialism tends to view variations in environmental practices as originating in "natural" ethnic or cultural differences.[3]

Despite these and other problems associated with cultural essentialism, a seldom-noted fact is that the attainment of ecological legitimacy via one form or another of culturalism may serve at least three important purposes. First, the construction of an alternative narrative positing local peoples as capable ecological stewards is a form of resistance because it affirms a historically denigrated ethnic or national group. At the same time, it critically scrutinizes dominant modernist approaches to socioeconomic development and resource use (Shiva 1988). In this sense, culturalism offers a counterhegemonic discursive framework that is essential to the success of any oppositional struggle and alternative development path. Second, culturalism helps to consolidate the moral authority of the group in question. Moral authority, after all, is a form of power and legitimacy that arises from the belief that the relevant agents act in ethically sound ways and therefore are deserving of popular support. Examples of morally authoritative, ecologically legitimate struggles include the Chipko movement in India (Guha 1990; Rangan 1993) and the Brazilian rubbertappers (Hecht and Cockburn 1989). Third, resistance by definition develops within the context of socioeconomic or political oppression, and since culturalism is a readily available resource, it may be an effective, or even indispensable, strategy in the struggle for ecological legitimacy.

In this chapter, these general observations are applied to the process whereby a Hispano community development group in northern New Mexico, known as Ganados del Valle (Livestock of the Valley), sought to establish ecological legitimacy.[4] I examine the context in which romanticized, culturalist nature-society narratives emerged, and I explore some of the advantages and drawbacks of the use of these narratives. My thesis is that culturalism has served Ganados del Valle well, despite some serious theoretical and political problems. Ganados is a good example of the use of culturalism, because it has been struggling to gain access to grazing land by using various tactics, while at the same time being opposed by mainstream environmentalists and state resource managers who have denied Ganados ecological legitimacy by claiming that Hispanos are poor resource managers.[5] To counter this opposition and to challenge the historical vilification of Hispano resource practices, Ganados has often relied on culturalist arguments in its claim to ecological legitimacy. At the same time, supporters of Hispano grazing rights have employed both structural and culturalist arguments to account for the phenomena of overgrazing, emphasizing in particular the harmonious ecological relations of indigenous peoples in general.

First, I will situate this case study by presenting a brief overview of northern New Mexico; then I will explore the ways that scholars have characterized the links between Hispano resource use, poverty, and culture. In particular, I focus on those commentators who blame Hispanos for local poverty and environmental problems and on those who try to explain this poverty and soil erosion in structural terms. Both the "blame the victim" and "blame the structure" approaches suggest why Ganados has employed romanticized culturalist arguments in its efforts to establish ecological legitimacy. I then describe Ganados del Valle's struggles to win grazing rights. Finally, I explore the ways that culturalism has in fact been used by Ganados to assert its ecological legitimacy, and I also consider some of the larger political and theoretical issues associated with this strategy of "discourse of struggle."

Ecological Legitimacy: Hispano Resource Use, Poverty, and Culture

Northern New Mexico: For decades, scholars have been predicting the demise of Hispano village communities of the Upper Rio Grande. J. Russell Smith once noted that "the Rio Grande drainage area north of El Paso offers a more complete example of regional suicide than most people ever imagined" (Harper, Cordova, and Oberg 1943, 8). Yet there are many village communities that continue to struggle for survival. The Upper Chama Valley, the site of Ganados del Valle, is located in the northern Rio Grande watershed. It was inhabited by Apache and Navajo Indians until the late 1600s when Spanish explorers and *mestizo* settlers began permanent settlement of the region (Dunbar-Ortiz 1980). Hispanos initially settled the region through a system of land grants (*mercedes*) and developed an agropastoral system based on vertical transhumance grazing and subsistence agriculture.[6] Communities were organized to include private land for the home, garden, and feed production, and collective ownership of the highlands for grazing, timber, and other resources. Water was furnished by *acequias,* a gravity-based irrigation system well suited to arid environments.

Established as frontier outposts, Hispano villages were always oriented to subsistence, but their economic and social marginality escalated when the United States acquired New Mexico through the Treaty of Guadalupe Hidalgo in 1848 (Gonzalez 1969; Sanchez [1940] 1967). American control led to the loss of Hispano land and water rights through a variety of mechanisms, including the U.S. government's inability (or unwillingness) to recognize communal landownership, high legal fees, Hispanos swindling one another, and last but not least, outright fraud by land speculators and merchants. Regardless of the means, the end result was the commodification of land and American encroachment, which brought more intense patterns of grazing, hunting, logging, and other forms of resource extraction (Harper, Cordova, and Oberg 1943; Peña 1991).

As Hispanos' ability to make a living was eroded through the loss of grant lands, the villages slid into deep poverty. Faced with declining economic opportunities, Hispanos pursued seasonal work strategies, outmigrated, and occasionally rebelled (Gardner 1970; Blawis 1971; Rosenbaum 1980; Deutsch 1987; and Forrest 1989). Although the region has been the site of numerous studies and development projects, such efforts rarely addressed the fundamental problem of the loss of land. Instead, development agents sought to build a crafts economy, teach job skills, or promote the Americanization of villagers—all focused on changing the individual while ignoring the fact that a thriving rural economy is impossible without an adequate land base.

Poverty is highly racialized in the region. As retirees, telecommuters, and tourists (most of whom are white Americans) flock to "the land of enchantment," the resulting land speculation is undermining Hispanos' dreams of a viable rural economy. The newcomers drive up the cost of land, and as ex-urbanites they have values and goals different from those of low-income rural people, which further erodes Hispanos' efforts at community autonomy (see Peña, chapters 1 and 9; Peña and Martínez, chapter 5). In the face of seasonal unemployment of 18.9 percent in the Chama Valley (United States Census Bureau 1989),[7] the state has pushed tourism, based on wealthy outsiders' desire to consume the landscape, the cultural diversity, and the natural resources of the area.[8] The result has been the creation of tourist towns (Santa Fe and Taos), exclusive game ranches, luxury ski resorts, and a booming secondary home market. Such a strategy ensures the continued poverty of Hispanos because it is predicated on seasonal, low-wage tourist jobs.[9] The 1990 per capita income in Río Arriba county was $11,979 for whites as compared to $7,496 for Hispanics. The result is a highly polarized economy geared toward wildlife and wilderness production for the enjoyment of urban middle-class residents.

Economic polarization rests partly upon American romanticization of the nonwhite population. This continues a long tradition of white Americans desiring the landscape, artifacts, and sense of place associated with northern New Mexico Indians and Hispanos. Because white Americans have such contradictory ideological and material relationships with Hispanos, a rich and conflictual set of narratives has developed to explain persistent Hispano poverty and political resistance. Poor resource management—in particular, overgrazing—has been central to explanations of poverty. Not only do such narratives deny the ecological legitimacy of Hispanos, they exonerate white Americans and capitalism for the region's deep poverty and degraded land.

Culture, Resource Use, and Moral Authority

Although a large body of literature seeks to explain the "decline" of northern New Mexico, few scholars have critically examined the political subtext of the dominant arguments. Both past and contemporary studies of Hispano resource management have typically posited Hispanos as poor resource managers.[10] This literature has significantly shaped dominant perceptions of Hispano ecological practices. Certainly, whether Hispano resource management is considered environmentally sound or damaging has enormous implications for establishing the legitimacy of current Hispano grazing claims for and efforts toward local control (see Peña and Martínez, chapter 5). Two perspectives are presented here: the dominant one seeks to deny the ecological legitimacy of Hispanos, attributing persistent Hispano poverty to overgrazing; and an alternative view seeks to affirm the ecological legitimacy of Hispanos, and as a result, locates overgrazing and poverty within the context of American and capitalist domination.

The first perspective, which attributes Hispano "decline" to overpopulation and overgrazing (e.g., Weber 1991; Richardson 1990; Libecap and Alter 1982; and Scott 1967), is largely Malthusian in nature and clearly results in the denial of Hispanos' ecological legitimacy. In particular, this view identifies a number of specific causes of regional poverty, including general ignorance, partible inheritance (resulting in small farms), high birthrates, and a generally poor environmental ethic. It suggests that under Hispano practices agricultural productivity has declined by half. Soil erosion and loss of soil fertility result because Hispanos "tak[e] all from the land and return . . . nothing to it" (Redman 1947, 17–18). Moreover "the smallness of farms in northern New Mexico and the practice of subdividing land into strips perpendicular to rivers or irrigation ditches make conservation practices difficult to apply. . . . Continued overstocking and overgrazing have resulted in the deterioration of the land" (Redman 1947, 17–18).

The Hispano agropastoralists are portrayed as guilty of "poor farming practices" so that "the quality of product is frequently poor, resulting in low prices" (Cockerill 1947, 5–6). In this manner, poverty becomes a consequence of a cultural deficiency. Moreover, this perspective explicitly delegitimizes Hispano land and water rights claims: "For Spanish-Americans to blame their deficient economy upon the many rejected land-grant claims and loss of communal lands is an effort to divert attention from the many other problems that stem from the region's physical incompatibility with agriculture, as well as with its settlement and demographic patterns" (Carlson 1990, 110).

Because overgrazing leads to poverty, and because Hispanos are charged with overgrazing, they are viewed as responsible for their own poverty and also as bereft of ecological credibility. Such a perspective is held by a wide variety of New Mexicans and has serious consequences. For example, one member of the Audubon Society who resisted Ganados's grazing efforts explained that "[t]he population here [Hispanos] overdid it [overgrazed]. And to a large extent have been saved by outfits like Los Alamos who come in and hire 12,000 people" (T. Jervis, interview by Laura Pulido, July 1990, Audubon Society, Los Alamos, New Mexico). Clearly, for this "conservationist," Hispanos have no ecological legitimacy.

Other important elements in this argument pertain to history and culture. Emphasizing both the long duration of these problematic environmental practices, as well as associating these practices with an amorphous "Hispano culture," the perceived lack of Hispano stewardship is portrayed as natural and inevitable: "If there is a flaw in the relationship of the villagers to their environment, it is that they, like the people of pioneer and subsistence cultures everywhere, have consistently underestimated their capacity for injuring the land. The mesas and mountains may indeed be the alma, the soul of the village culture, but their elevated status has not protected them from abuse" (deBuys 1985, 297).

Considerable energy has been spent debating the grazing practices of Hispanos. Because this literature blames Hispanos for environmental degradation, they are delegitimized as successful resource managers. This delegitimization is based on specific grazing practices (e.g., overgrazing, grazing at the wrong time, too-small farm size for too large a livestock herd). But it also derives from the presumption of a general *moral* shortcoming as expressed in the *failure* to practice an appropriate environmental ethic. Delegitimization occurs because of the political need to clarify responsibility and to impose accountability on the agents of environmental degradation. Great weight is attached to environmental degradation/stewardship because it provides a necessary, but rarely articulated, moral subtext to environmental or developmental initiatives. Accordingly, those who are linked to ecological stewardship garner moral authority (whether they are the International Monetary Fund or the Moskito Indians). In the case of Hispanos, because they are not considered environmentally valid actors, their claims can be dismissed on the basis of their "proven track record" and their general moral shortcomings. Hispanos are denied "standing," as it were, in a discursive arena controlled by mainstream environmentalists, scientists, and resource professionals. I do not mean to imply that this is the *intention* of such actors, but I do argue that this is one *result*.

In response to such interpretations, others have developed critiques far more sympathetic to Hispanos, critiques rooted in structural analyses. Many of these arguments are drawn from political ecology, which suggests that colonialism, capitalism, and modernization outweigh individual agency, culture, or even sheer population numbers, in accounting for environmental change (Watts 1983; Wright 1992; and Thrupp 1993). Recognizing the consequences of conservative analyses, leftist scholars have depicted the economic problems of Hispanos as emanating from structural shifts, thereby leaving intact their ecological legitimacy, because "traditional" practices are associated with ecological stewardship (Harper, Cordova, and Oberg 1943; Eastman, Carruthers, and Leifer 1967; and Van Ness 1987).[11] Bobrow both characterizes and illustrates this practice: "Some academics and policy-makers . . . have criticized the practice of grazing on open [sic] common land. . . . These critics point to the scenario of land degradation laid out in biologist Garrett Hardin's 'tragedy of the commons'—open commons frequently become severely eroded, there is a decline in the quality and quantity of forage, and there is serious long-term ecological damage and accompanying economic decline" (Bobrow 1992; see also Eastman and Gray 1987). From this perspective the "tragedy of the commons" in New Mexico's Hispano land grants resulted not from subsistence grazing practices but from the imposition of a "foreign land tenure system which treats land as a commodity" (Bobrow 1992).

Devon Peña (1991, 3), in a critique of deBuys's cultural ecology analysis, also suggests that if Hispanos in fact contributed to environmental degradation, it was because of economic pressures: "[L]and degradation in Chicano community grants was the result of the partitioning and contraction of landholdings combined with the industrialization and commercialization of former common property resources. Evidence overwhelmingly demonstrates that environmental degradation in New Mexico was initiated in the 1870s after the arrival of the railroad, land speculators, and capitalist ranching, mining and lumber interests." This position clearly seeks to refute the "blame the victim" approach of previous analysts. In his detailed study of Hispano cultural ecology, Van Ness (1987, 194) argues that "from an ecological perspective the superiority of the Hispanic land tenure for a subsistence economy is clear." In a similar vein, Stoller (1985, 13) suggests: "This pattern of vertical transhumance for livestock raising is common among pastoral peoples in mountainous, high altitude areas around the world; it was well adapted to the topography of northern New Mexico and southern Colorado. . . . The Culebra river valley and its settlers are excellent examples of a group of people who developed a culture that was environmentally sound, sane and satisfying." Here, both authors seek not only to challenge dominant stereotypes, but to vindicate Hispano resource use patterns by emphasizing their sustainability.[12]

As in conservative analyses, political projects and moral positions underlie these arguments. But unlike the former arguments, these are used for oppositional purposes, with several consequences. First and foremost, these scholars seek to validate the ecological practices of a historically marginalized and dispossessed population by positing them as able and conscious ecological stewards. This position validates both their grazing practices as well as Hispano culture in general, because this culture is associated with good morals and ecological knowledge. A second consequence is that Hispano moral authority is enhanced by reintroducing the notion of victimization. Stressing Hispano dispossession (as opposed to blaming the victim) casts them in a light more conducive to public support. Victimization coupled with ecological legitimacy is a powerful combination for achieving moral authority. Finally, this scholarship sets the stage for activists to develop romanticized discourses and culturalist arguments. It provides the necessary intervention to create a new political space.

Thus, it should not surprise us when members of Ganados make conscious links between Hispano culture and sound resource management. As one local activist asserted, "We've been here for hundreds of years and the land is still here. We know how to take care of it; that's why they [environmentalists] want it so much" (S. Martínez, Ganados del Valle, interview by Laura Pulido, August 1991, Los Ojos). I will now turn to Ganados itself and its efforts to assert ecological legitimacy.

Ganados del Valle and Oppositional Environmental Discourses

Ganados del Valle was formed in the early 1980s when a few Hispanos decided to manage their flocks cooperatively.[13] Recognizing the need for meaningful economic development that was culturally and environmentally appropriate, activists created vertically integrated businesses based on grazing, lambs, and high-quality woven products. Although many Hispanos still owned a few head of sheep or cattle in the 1980s, their operations were not economically viable due to the small livestock numbers and limited range availability (P. Torres, Río Arriba County Extension, interview by Laura Pulido, August 1990, Española, New Mexico; see also Kutsche and Van Ness 1981, 45). Both land enclosure and land speculation have made the cost of land prohibitive for small farmers.[14] Accordingly, the hope was that what one could not do independently — run a viable operation — could be done collectively. By 1995 Ganados had five businesses, including weaving, sheep and grazing cooperatives, and several community projects, and was grossing more than three hundred thousand dollars annually.

Ganados is considered to be an economic success; it has increased the income of more than forty rural households. It is also considered to be environmentally responsible in that it promotes sustainable development. Despite severe regional poverty, for example, Ganados has consistently opposed manufacturing activities that pollute and environmentally damaging resource extraction, such as mining and luxury ski resorts. Moreover, Ganados has worked to develop land-use and zoning regulations to protect the county's environmental quality. This environmental consciousness is also apparent in Ganados's businesses. In addition to a recycling business, Ganados uses guard dogs instead of poison to protect its flocks against predators, produces organically grown lambs, and practices sustainable grazing.

In the late 1980s Ganados attempted to expand but was limited by a lack of grazing land. Given the shortage of grazing opportunities, Ganados asked the New Mexico Department of Game and Fish (NMDGF) to graze on Wildlife Management Areas (WMAS) in Río Arriba County. The WMAS were initially acquired by the NMDGF for the purpose of increasing elk habitat and hunting opportunities (New Mexico Department of Game and Fish 1980, 1984a, 1984b). Ganados proposed a project that would allow the cooperative to graze while conducting research in conjunction with New Mexico State University. Ganados argued that the WMAS had a dense matte covering that prevented plant growth and that use of a short-term grazing system could improve the grasses.[15]

The plan developed by Ganados, however, was opposed by both the NMDGF and local environmental groups.[16] Along with hunters, these groups constitute the agency's primary constituencies (W. Evans, New Mexico Department of Game and Fish, interview by Laura Pulido, July 1990, Santa Fe).[17] Throughout the struggle, Ganados's ecological legitimacy was questioned, both in terms of its ability to conduct sustainable grazing and in the sincerity of its environmental commitment. Ganados struggled for access to the land by participating in research projects, mediation, civil disobedience, and lobbying. At one point, in order to dramatize its plight, members of Ganados, along with two thousand sheep, trespassed on one of the WMAS. Although they attracted significant attention, the NMDGF eventually prohibited grazing on WMAS throughout the state.

The right to graze was fought over in other arenas as well, including a lawsuit against the Sierra Club Foundation filed decades after an aborted collaborative project. In the 1960s, prompted by renewed Hispano land-grant struggles, the Sierra Club Foundation embarked on a joint project to buy land with La Cooperativa Agrícola del Pueblo de Tierra Amarilla. "The preservation of land and the perpetuation of the economic and social values of an ethnic minority . . . [are] goals which are central to the philosophies of the Sierra Club Foundation and La Cooperativa" (Varela 1995, 1). The Foundation asked Albuquerque businessman Ray Graham to contribute one hundred thousand dollars toward the project, but despite these efforts, no land was ever purchased.

In 1989 Graham learned of Ganados's struggle with the NMDGF, and seeing the connection between his gift and Ganados's need for grazing land, he inquired how his donation had been spent. When the Foundation did not respond to Graham's inquiries, he sued. Meanwhile, Ganados persuaded the New Mexico attorney general to investigate the matter.

After several years of investigation, audits, and legal wrangling, a settlement was reached requiring the Foundation to make eight hundred thousand dollars available to Ganados. Ganados then set up a nonprofit land trust to purchase grazing land for its members' use.

The WMA struggle and, to a lesser extent, the lawsuit represent two discrete episodes in a much larger grazing conflict, one that goes back more than a century and demonstrates how ecological relations are the arena of both material and discursive power struggles. The land-grant struggles of the 1960s were crucial, not only because they inspired collaborative projects, but because they, along with leftist scholars, set the stage for contemporary oppositional discourses. Sylvia Rodríguez (1987) has shown, for example, how recent struggles in the Taos area have led to a rearticulation of land and Hispano identity. The oppositional discourse articulated by Ganados, and specifically its use of culturalism to promote ecological legitimacy, is but one example of many ongoing romanticized discourses of resistance.

Culturalism and Ecological Legitimacy

Ganados challenged the entrenched belief that Hispanos were responsible for regional soil erosion and poverty in many ways, and it used scientific, economic, legal, and, of course, culturalist arguments. The basis for establishing ecological legitimacy was the cooperative's self-definition as an ecological steward. Both "standing" as a valid environmental actor and authenticity in terms of its environmental commitment would flow from stewardship. Culturalism proved a useful way of establishing ecological stewardship because of the general exoticization of Hispanos by the dominant society, the regional reification of cultural differences, and the larger swirl of Hispano oppositional discourses.

Culturalist arguments served not only to validate Hispano resource practices but by extension Hispano culture as well. Specifically, the argument was that because Hispano culture was associated with ecological stewardship, any grazing program involving Hispanos would be a success. As a consequence, cultural preservation, in addition to grazing rights, emerged as a goal. In the narrative championed by Ganados, Hispano culture should be preserved because it is rich, associated with stewardship, and threatened. This last point was important, not only to Hispanos, but also potentially to other development interests since the region is increasingly relying on cultural tourism. Recognizing the extent to which the current fascination with Hispano culture is a function of tourism, one local research scholar explained, "You know, they are trying to make us into a colonial Williamsburg of the Southwest. . . . Tourism is so altered by . . . gas prices, tourist preferences, etc. It's cool to be Hispano now, but it may not be in ten years. Coyotes are in now, but where are they going to be in ten years, or furniture making?" (M. Valdéz, interview by D. Peña, September 1990, San Luis, Colorado.)

Aside from arguing that Hispano culture should be preserved because it is distinct, Ganados drew on other moral concerns, in particular the theme of dispossession/victimization first raised by oppositional scholars. The subtext to the argument was that Hispano culture had been victimized by the loss of grant lands, and this was all the more reason to support the project. Thus, access to grazing land would preserve an "endangered culture" and was morally desirable. "Elk and deer are not endangered in northern New Mexico. But the survival of New Mexico's Hispanic pastoral culture is endangered. Ganados del Valle's proposal to graze the wildlife refuges is an opportunity to strengthen one of the United States' richest cultures, improve the wildlife habitat and raise the standard of living in one of the nation's poorest rural counties" (Ganados del Valle, n.d.).

Having established a moral and economic basis to support its grazing claims, activists emphasized that Hispano culture is one of ecological stewardship. "Our fathers knew how to take care of the land. You get out of the land what you put into it" (M. Morales, interview by Laura Pulido, August 1990, Canjilon, New Mexico). This local resident, like many activists, firmly believed that Hispano culture was inherently more careful with natural resources than Euro-American culture. "Respect for water and land . . . is transmitted from generation to generation and has become a cultural characteristic of Indians and Indo-Hispanic people" (Atencio 1987, 11). Building on general romanticized images of Hispano history, landscape, folklore, and material culture suggests an environmental relationship that is "sound, sane and satisfying" (Stoller 1985). This relationship has enabled Ganados to argue that their proposed grazing effort would be a success precisely because it was rooted in Hispano history and culture: "We are a pastoral people. Our pastoral history goes back thousands of years spanning from the Iberian Peninsula to this continent. This pastoralism is reflected in the way the Spanish and then Mexican governments organized land use. . . . The common lands were used for moving large herds and flocks of livestock around the ecosystem which revitalized rangeland with each season. Under this system there was ample forage for domestic livestock and wildlife" (Varela 1995).

There is no doubt that culturalist arguments helped Ganados achieve ecological legitimacy. Moreover, ecological legitimacy, in addition to the moral authority cultivated on other fronts, contributed to very real gains. For one, culturalist arguments provided a means for Hispanos to challenge certain institutions and practices that were otherwise unassailable, such as private property. In effect, one subtext to Ganados's claims was an affirmation of communal landownership. Besides linking communal landownership to sound environmental management, Ganados offered an alternative to the dominant capitalist market ideology and private property relations that subsume our lives and which resonated with some Anglo supporters (K. Cassutt, Sierra Club member, interview by Laura Pulido, July 1990, Santa Fe).

Perhaps more importantly, the use of culturalist arguments has led to real changes in the social formation. The cultivation of ecological legitimacy, coupled with cultural distinctiveness, has been crucial in attracting public awareness and support. It was partly because of Ganados's compelling image that Graham and Ganados connected in the 1990s, eventually resulting in the beginnings of a community land trust. This is a clear example of how the engagement of social practices in a dialectic with structures of inequality is able to transform the prevailing material relations. Nevertheless, using culturalism to establish ecological legitimacy, as a general matter, is of great concern as the culture, morals, and everyday practices of poor and nonwhite people are under attack. This does not mean that such strategies should not be used, only that as academics and activists we should be conscious of their implications. One problem with romanticized ecological discourses is that they are often predicated on a unitary view of culture, one in which all Hispanos are thought to share the same culture, values, and practices. Though there is strong evidence that Hispanos did, in fact, produce far less environmental degradation than Anglos, emphasizing this position overlooks not only the considerable variation that exists within any social group but also the complexity of cultural evolution (Peña 1991, 1994b; see also MacCameron 1994).

Another consequence of culturalism is the reification of cultural differences between Anglos and Hispanos without paying sufficient attention to the social relations in which each group is embedded and the social practices that arise from those relations. Both Anglos and Hispanos suggested that cultural differences were an important source of the conflict, as different cultures (in this case, Euro-American and Hispano) approached land in entirely different ways. For instance, a common argument was that Hispano culture recognizes neither "nature" nor "wilderness" nor "wildness" (Peña 1991; Atencio 1987). In contrast, the Anglo land-use tradition embodies a dualism that sees humans as conceptually separate from nature. A New Mexican environmentalist has summarized well the distinctions: "In the eyes of land-based people, the environment is an ecosystem in which the people exist as one part of a harmonious whole, deriving food and materials, as needed, for their continued social, cultural, and economic existence. In the eyes of environmentalists, the same land may represent an area that should be protected for its own sake, for its beauty and pristine qualities, for wildlife habitat, or for recreation" (Taylor 1988, 90–100).

Cultural explanations such as Taylor's often account for a range of differences that arise from racism, imperialism, or class exploitation. Cultural essentialist arguments have important political consequences. For one, they compel us to forfeit the opportunity to make explicit the economic relationships among various groups. Overlooked is the fact that "culture" is partially constituted by a group's location within the historical trajectory of capitalism and its particular position within a geographically specific set of social relations. Even though Anglos and Hispanos may indeed conceptualize land differently, this practice is at least partially due to the fact that Hispanos were at one time part of a precapitalist empire (Spain), while contemporary Anglo land-use and environmental traditions were formed within the context of industrial capitalism.

The reification of cultural differences that seems to exist beyond, or independent of, economic structures also has the potential to reproduce the existing social formation. The extent to which mainstream environmental practices actively serve to reproduce inequalities of wealth and power is ignored by attributing conflicting land-use plans to vague cultural arguments. Consequently, mainstream environmentalists and professional resource managers are encouraged to continue their projects of land preservation and other environmental practices that lead to the further marginalization of oppressed groups. Arguments of cultural difference, which do not begin to address the structural and ideological relations that initially engendered such inequalities, may lead to a "multicultural" initiative of some type. An example of this lack of analysis of power relations comes from one Anglo writer's depiction of local ethnic relations: "As for Chama's personality, its special character springs from a blend of strong midwest Anglo [sic] and Southwest Spanish [sic] heritages blended so well within the last quarter century that neither culture dominates or struggles to dominate" (Daggett 1973, 42).

Another difficulty with culturalist arguments is that they are undergirded by a static conception of cultural change. The issue of "cultural preservation" is particularly important, in that it assumes that Hispano culture can or will die. Casting Hispanos as soon-to-be extinct people overlooks the fact that Hispano culture will continue to develop and evolve as long as there are people who identify themselves as Hispanos, regardless of where they live and work.

Anthony Bebbington has pointed out the complex ways in which "tradition" serves to inform the present, particularly in the quest for ecological legitimacy and cultural authenticity (Bebbington 1993). By pointing out how "tradition" can be used to overturn prevailing power relations, for example, we can avoid seeing minority cultures as either static and unitary (some activists' interpretation) or as embarked on unidirectional assimilation (modernist interpretation). Yet, by consistently stressing "traditional" culture, Ganados obscures both the phenomenal job it has done and also how the success of the project itself testifies to contemporary Hispano culture and its environmental ethic. Ganados is a remarkable example of cultural change within the context of inequality. It blends new and old by creating a viable alternative. It has successfully reclaimed a maligned cultural heritage and identity, but its operation draws upon the latest marketing innovations and technologies, scientific resource management, and academic arguments.

The fact that Ganados's dominant discourse is rooted in a series of problematic cultural formulations illustrates the extent to which structures of inequality set the terms of resistance. However, it is also worth noting that all the critiques of this strategy are largely theoretical, with *potentially* adverse consequences. In contrast, the use of culturalist arguments has resulted in real material gains. Finally, while I believe that all of the critiques are valid to varying degrees, inherent in them is the belief that the actors are not aware or conscious of the strategies they are using. Conventional critiques of strategic essentialism almost assume that marginalized groups are defined by romanticized discourses, regardless of other practices. Perhaps it is time to reconsider strategic essentialism in light of the goals and ambitions of marginalized communities. In some instances it is difficult to imagine a strategy of resistance that does *not* use the master's tools.

In this chapter I have tried to show not only the need for poor rural populations to establish ecological legitimacy but also the role of culturalism in developing this legitimacy. Ecological legitimacy is, I believe, a useful framework to understand romanticization, or other strategic tactics used by those fighting for environmental justice. I have pointed out that ecological legitimacy was useful in the public relations arena, but it was absolutely essential in order to challenge the dominant interpretation of Hispano grazing. Even though Ganados was not successful in changing the grazing policy of NMDGF, it waged an important battle and challenged conventional ideas about resource use, poverty, culture, and social justice — a battle that could not have occurred if Ganados had not established its ecological legitimacy.

The use of culturalism in the development of ecological legitimacy is situationally specific and reflects a particular form of oppression — exoticization. Culturalism is not a strategy available to those of despised and denigrated cultures, such as inner-city African Americans or recent Mexican immigrants. Other groups may develop moral authority based on other aspects of their experience. Given the material and ideological forces shaping the lives of Hispanos, including their insertion into a tourist economy, their relatively long history in the area, their attachment to a particular landscape, and the nature of Hispano poverty, it is hard to see how culturalism would not have emerged as an important element in the formation of an oppositional discourse. Nevertheless, it remains to develop a nonessentialist base for moral authority when there is an option to do so.

While some instances of romanticization and strategic essentialism result in serious problems, Ganados is not such a case;[18] overall, Ganados has been able to use strategic essentialism in a careful and responsible way. Moreover, it has not prevented the cooperative from working closely with other communities, such as with Navajos, in creating other rural cooperatives.

Perhaps of greatest concern is the shortchanging of contemporary Hispano culture. It is true that Ganados emerged from a long tradition of resistance and that its vision of development draws from the past; but neither of these facts should reduce Ganados to a project of historical preservation. The leadership required to undertake such an initiative, the level of commitment among cooperative members, their desire to protect a beloved landscape, and members' eagerness to build a viable economy for themselves and their children are all striking features of contemporary Hispano culture. Yet, many of these positive attributes get lost in culturalist arguments. Conversely, perhaps this is a relatively small price to pay when, by actively reshaping their material world and relations, Ganados is building a rare example of social and environmental justice, which in turn is creating a new Hispano culture.

Notes

This paper has benefited from conversations with Bill Lynn and the comments of Melissa Gilbert, Mike Murashige, Jim O'Connor, Devon Peña, Miguel de Oliver, Margaret Villanueva, and three anonymous reviewers. Partial research support for this chapter was provided by the Rio Grande Bioregions Project through a grant from the National Endowment for the Humanities (grant # RO-22707-94). I remain responsible for all interpretations contained herein.

1. For an excellent discussion see Zimmerer 1993.

2. For an overview of gender essentialism in nature-society relations, see Nesmith and Radcliffe 1993, 379–94. For specific critiques see Schroeder 1993, 349–65 and Seager 1993.

3. For general critiques and examples of strategic essentialism and cultural reification see Fuss 1989; Kobayashi and Peake 1994, 81–95; and Anderson 1994, 225–44.

4. The term *Hispano* refers to the Spanish-speaking population of northern New Mexico and southern Colorado. They are a subset of the larger Chicano population.

5. For two detailed analyses of this struggle, see D. G. Peña 1992 and Pulido 1993 and 1996.

6. Transhumance grazing is an extensive grazing system that takes advantage of changes in temperature and grasses by grazing through a range of environments over the seasons. See Gomez Ibañez (1977). For a complete discussion of Hispano cultural ecology in the region see Van Ness (1987).

7. Varela has calculated that 50 percent of the households in the Tierra Amarilla census district earned less than $10,000 in 1990; see Varela in U.S. Senate Committee on Energy and National Resources (1994).

8. A. Richardson, interview by Laura Pulido, July 1990, State of New Mexico Economic Development and Tourism Department, Santa Fe. For historical perspectives see Weigle 1975 and Works 1992.

9. For the early roots of this pattern see Bodine 1968; also see Rodríguez [1989] 1994.

10. See, for example, the reports of the Archdiocese of Santa Fe (1947); also Denevan (1967); deBuys (1985); Division of Research, Department of Government, University of New Mexico (1946); Harper, Cordova and Oberg (1943); Soil Conservation Service, Division of Regional Planning Southwest Region (1936); Weigle (1975).

11. This practice is common throughout the political ecology literature. As Ashish Kothari notes, "[P]overty or the lack of adequate economic opportunities often force people to degrade their own environment: for instance, firewood collection is a serious threat to forests in some places. What needs to be understood, however, is the genesis of this situation: more often than not, it lies in state policies which deprive the poor of their meager resources, and do not provide adequate alternative avenues for economic and social security" (quoted in Alier 1993, 113).

12. For a more nuanced discussion of the complexities and transgressions of Hispano resource management, see Peña 1994.

13. For the full history of Ganados and its connection to previous resistance struggles see D. G. Peña 1992 and Pulido 1996 (chapter 4).

14. Only 28 percent of the county is privately owned. More than 50 percent is held by the U.S. Forest Service in the Carson and Santa Fe National Forests, both of which have been reducing their stocking rates. It is important to realize that in order to qualify for a USFS permit, "base land" is required, which Ganados does not own. Another 17 percent of the county is owned by the Jicarilla Apache, who have in the past entered into leases with Ganados. Although the WMAS constitute only 2 percent of the county, this obscures the fact that they comprise 20 percent of the rangeland in the Chama area.

15. Ganados drew heavily on Savory's Holistic Resource Management No in formulating their proposal; see Savory 1989.

16. The Nature Conservancy, Audubon Society, National Wildlife Federation, and individual members of the Sierra Club.

17. This initiative was associated with Reies Lopez Tijerina and *la alianza;* see Bell Blawis 1971 and Gardner 1970.

18. For an interesting example of such problems, see Rangan 1993, 155–81.

5   The Capitalist Tool, the Lawless, and the Violent

A Critique of Recent Southwestern Environmental History

Devon G. Peña and Rubén O. Martínez

Many students of land-grant and Southwestern regional history have described the Chicano agropastoral village culture of the Upper Rio Grande
as uniquely well suited to maintain human settlements in arid and semiarid environments (e.g., see Oberg 1940; Harper, Cordova, and Oberg
1943; Van Dresser 1964; Knowlton 1964, 1967, and 1969; Leonard
1970; Rock 1976; Brown and Ingram 1987; Briggs and Van Ness 1987;
Martínez 1987; D. G. Peña 1992; and Ebright 1994). An important aspect
of the ecologically sound settlement pattern derives from local knowledge
of environmental conditions. Recent research by the Rio Grande Bioregions Project suggests that Hispano farmers are familiar with climate,
soil, water, and other environmental conditions affecting agricultural production and wildlife habitat (Peña 1998, in press). For example, in southern Colorado's Culebra watershed, Hispanos can predict whether irrigation runoff from the mountains will be "wet" or "dry" depending on the
timing for the appearance of a prominent snow-field shaped like a bird.
When the "bird" appears in June, the farmers surmise that it will be a good
"wet" year with plenty of irrigation water from the spring snowmelt. If the
"bird" appears earlier (in April or May), then farmers surmise that it will
be a poor or "dry" year with scarcity of irrigation water.

Hispanos use a variety of names for different soil types, which suggests
an awareness of ecological limits. For example, *tierra muerta* (dead soil) is
found in areas with dense, impermeable clay soil that inhibits drainage

from irrigation. Land with this underlying soil profile is generally left uncultivated. A frequent, and perhaps unintended, result is the preservation of native grass meadows (*vegas naturales*). Although tierra muerta is not good for farming, it is an essential ingredient for making strong and long-lasting adobe bricks in the construction of *hornos* (ovens) and farm buildings. Local Hispano farmers are also familiar with the location of natural plant communities that provide habitat for certain kinds of edible or medicinal wild plants (Salmon 1997) and can predict where piñon nut harvests will be concentrated in a particular year (Peña, in press).

For similar reasons related to an awareness of ecological limits, Chicano farmers are very strongly opposed to any destruction of their watersheds caused by industrial logging, mining, or subdividing practices. Farmers understand how the conditions that degrade wildlife habitat also undermine the integrity of the watershed and hence the ability of the irrigating community to manage its *acequia* system (see Peña 1998; Rívera, in press; and Rívera and Peña 1997).

This type of local knowledge extends to the specialized domains of crop genetic traits, livestock raising, and soil fertility. Elder Chicano farmers in the bioregion commonly describe *bolita* beans and alfalfa as crops that give *fuerza* (literally, life-force) to the soil, an emic reference to the nitrogen-fixing properties of those plants. One farmer describes intercropping as *el compadrazgo de las plantas* (plant godparentship), an emic reference to companion planting (Adelmo Kaber, conversation with Devon Peña, San Luis, Colorado, June 1997). Another farmer states that "he talks to the plants," listening for cues about what they need to grow (Joseph C. Gallegos, conversation with Erica Rubine, San Luis, Colorado, August 1996). Such observations, with their implied recognition of ecological limits, are an important and often overlooked aspect of local knowledge. We propose that this local knowledge plays a major and often overlooked role in the environmental history of the Río Arriba.[1]

The rediscovery and recovery of local knowledge may point us in new directions in the study of the environmental history of the Río Arriba, or Upper Rio Grande, bioregion. Local knowledge of ecological limits implies the existence of a "sense of place." Our reading of environmental history suggests that the multigenerational farming families of the Río Arriba have extensive knowledge of ecological limits precisely because they have lived "in place" for so long. Their knowledge is more directly place-bound than that of even the best scientific observers. Land-grant historians generally view Hispanos as ecologically well adapted to the limits of a high altitude semiarid environment. But land-grant historians have not systematically addressed the issue of land ethics or "ethics of place," in part because they have remained largely focused on legal, social, and economic history.[2]

One of the most remarkable features of the Chicano upland villages in the Río Arriba is the riparian long-lot and acequia cultural landscape (see Valdéz and Valdéz 1991 for an early and path-breaking study of Hispano vernacular architecture and cultural landscapes). The arid upland character of the Río Arriba bioregion presents a particularly challenging environment for sustainable human habitation. Chicanos adapted to these conditions by using irrigation technologies and customs brought by the Moors from North Africa to the Iberian Peninsula, and then to Mexico by the Spanish. The gravity-driven earthen ditch, or acequia, system allowed the Hispanos to settle and farm in small compact village clusters within the tributary valleys of the Upper Rio Grande watershed.

Over generations, these earthen ditches created vast riparian corridors — large plant communities of native cottonwood, alder, and willow that grow in profusion along the moist banks of the acequias. During the tenure of six generations, the arid upland valleys have been transformed into veritable puzzle parts of the natural landscape mosaic; the cottonwood bosques created by the acequias are now extensions of native wildlife habitat and movement corridors. In the acequias we have a clear case demonstrating how anthropogenesis can support and extend native biodiversity (Peña 1998; for a relevant discussion of cultural landscapes in formation of landscape linkages and biological corridors, see Hudson 1991).

Environmental History and Ecological Politics

Over the better part of four centuries, New Mexican Hispano people have effected significant and enduring changes in the natural and cultural landscapes that define the Río Arriba, or Upper Rio Grande, bioregion. Yet scholarly interest in this region among students of environmental history has emerged only over the past decade or so. The environmental history of the Upper Rio Grande is now part of a broader debate over the origins and nature of human disturbance and destruction of native ecosystems in

North America. This history also serves as a backdrop for an increasingly heated *political* debate over the future of land use in rural areas of the intermountain West. The central questions for the political debate are, What are the principal causes of ecological destruction, and how can we restore and protect the natural environment?

For some partisans in this debate, the question is perhaps best posed as, What are the prospects for sustainable stewardship of homeland areas by indigenous communities?[3] The insights of environmental history are of obvious import to the resolution of these issues. Much is at stake: Chicano land-grant and Pueblo Indian communities regard the upland forest eco-systems as watershed commons, the historic and cultural spaces of natural patrimony that once were governed on the basis of the customary laws of traditional clan, *ejido,* or acequia institutions. Some environmentalists envision a scenario in which a network of connected biodiversity reserves is placed in the hands of informed scientists who are presumably best equipped to understand and manage ecosystems.[4] Capital interests, on the other hand, seek to promote extractive uses of the "commons," while the so-called "wise users," "patriots," and "militias" clamor for less government, local autonomy, and the right of private property.[5]

Nowhere is the conflict over nature so intense as in the tri-ethnic bio-region of the Río Arriba where Pueblo Indians, Chicano land-grant heirs, American environmentalists, and logging, mining, and other development interests clash over land and water use policies (see map).[6] Some eco-activists argue that Hispano farming and ranching communities in the bioregion are archaic and largely insensitive to the environment. "Mis-recognizing" land-grant activists as mere "wise users," some American environmentalists in New Mexico have ridiculed Chicanos for presumably lacking awareness of ecological issues such as the importance of preserving habitat for biodiversity. These environmentalists, in turn, have been criticized for ignoring the land and water rights struggles of Chicanos and supporting the more narrow and misguided cause of "wilderness preservation."[7] There is no need to revisit this implied separation of nature and culture, wilderness and civilization, for it has already been soundly criticized in earlier chapters as an endemic and myopic feature of much radical environmental thought and action. The consequences of this conflict have been serious, for many American environmentalists in New Mexico are deeply divided from land-based communities. American ecoactivists have not been able to reconcile wilderness values with indigenous claims for autonomy in local land-use planning and watershed management. Rural Hispano communities in the region depend on the protection of the watershed for their survival, yet American environmentalists have not readily recognized the ecological values of indigenous communities or accommodated their demands for restoration of historic use rights.[8]

Some environmental historians have supported the political claims of the ecoactivists by invoking evidence of ecological damage during the "Spanish-Mexican era." These historians have sought to demonstrate that Chicanos did not have substantive knowledge of ecological systems or resource conservation (e.g., deBuys 1985 and Wolf 1995). Among American environmental historians, the Hispano is often viewed as an ignorant, if quaint, abuser of the natural environment. In this view, land and water conservation practices were presumably beyond the intellectual abilities or knowledge of the Spanish-Mexican settlers. Given the allegations of a culture deficient in land ethics, it seems the environmental history of Río Arriba is inextricably tied to the region's ecopolitics; it is also associated with conflicting concepts, not just of nature, but of class, race, culture, and cultural change.

This historiographic and interpretive essay offers a critique of recent research in the area of Southwestern environmental history. The focus is on a handful of prominent, often-cited studies on the environmental history of the Río Arriba bioregion — a seven county Hispano "homeland" core area in northern New Mexico and south-central Colorado, framed by the Sangre de Cristo and San Juan mountain ranges.[9] Several major arguments have been constructed by environmental historians in their treatment of northern New Mexico Chicanos. As we will see, these interpretive approaches obscure class, cultural, and geographic differences in land-use ethics and practices.

The cultural ambiguities and political-economic and social contradictions underlying processes of environmental change have been overlooked or mystified. Environmental historians and ecoactivists in this bioregion have tended to generalize the view that all cultures and social classes are destructive in their relationships to nature. As a consequence, they have also overlooked the fact that in certain discrete geographic settings rural communities have created cultural landscapes that protect native biodiversity and ecosystem integrity. In describing the beneficial landscape linkages created by Hispano irrigation systems, one astute observer has noted that "the meanderings of acequias . . . belie an obstinate rootedness, poke fun at rigid linearity, and symbolize an almost compulsive drive to link up and connect" (Nazarea, in press). The prolific connections between humans and their "lived" environment have been ignored by those who would breach the divide between nature and culture through the insights of environmental history. In this chapter we offer an alternative outline for a more balanced and nuanced approach to the study of cultural and environmental change in the Upper Rio Grande bioregion.

Recent American Environmental History of the Río Arriba

A stereotype recurs in the American environmental history of the Río Arriba. It is a ubiquitous figure: the picturesque but careless Hispano sheepherder who innocently overgrazes the land because of ignorance. Unaware of ecological damage caused by poor supervision of livestock, the Hispano sheepherder is cast as a primary culprit who stalks the land in the environmental history of this bioregion. For example, in a 1989 journal article published in the *New Mexico Historical Review,* Hal Rothman (1989) argues that "few people understood the concept of conservation" during the early part of the twentieth century. "American cattlemen and timber men and Hispano and Native American pastoralists alike in northern New Mexico were not among those who did." Rothman's case study centers on the Pajarito Plateau, an uplift west of the Española Valley that is roughly midway between Santa Fe and Taos. Inhabitants of this area witnessed the unfolding of the Manhattan Project and its aftermath at nearby Los Alamos.

In a more recent work, Rothman (1992) suggests that the rate of environmental change in northern New Mexico remained stable until 1880. The Hispano and Pueblo Indian sheepherders in the Pajarito Plateau overgrazed localized areas around water sources. But their practices of cyclic burning, rotational grazing, and preservation of old-growth forests contributed to a relatively stable ecosystem (the land could regenerate). As long as the local sheepherders were not trapped into the cash-based market economy, then an "open system" of free access to the commons prevailed and the use of the land remained within its carrying capacity. With the arrival of the railroad in 1880, the degradation of the area's rangelands accelerated. The excellent grazing conditions existing in 1880 allowed commercial sheep growers like Frank Bond to increase stocking rates by more than 100 to 120 percent. There was adequate grazing range left for the millions of sheep placed on northern New Mexican rangelands after 1880. By the early 1920s, as Rothman (1992) shows, the new American commercial operators had overstocked the short-grass prairie and montane meadows, a process that produced most of the severely degraded rangeland conditions seen in the Pajarito and other areas today. After 1880, the logging of old-growth forests became an additional new factor diminishing the ecological integrity of the Pajarito Plateau.

Rothman views the period before 1880 as involving a "pre-industrial pace" of life that was in the end a stabilizing force in the process of environmental change. But he also states that this slower pace did not mean that the Hispano and Pueblo peoples had an understanding of ecological principles or conservation ethics. Certainly, some of these changes would not have been easily discernable without the tools of ecological science. The introduction of exotic species that displaced native plants involved imperceptible changes that nonetheless had profound ecological consequences later.

Moreover, Rothman suggests that prior to the twentieth century and the advent of the American conservation movement, "[t]here was no cultural prohibition nor understanding of the land's fragile character to prevent herdsmen from overgrazing." While stocking levels were too low for mass destruction, "these patterns sowed the seeds of an ominous ecological future" by introducing livestock to a fragile upland environment (Rothman 1989, 197; also see Rothman 1992, 18–19). The economic demand for wool and mutton radically transformed livestock-grazing practices in the region. In most cases, subsistence stocking levels prior to the introduction of the railroad that served mass and military markets probably did not severely exceed the carrying capacity of the land as Rothman himself states. This was particularly the case wherever sheepherders practiced transhumance, that is, by rotating seasonal sheep camps to expand the range of forage and pasture areas within the intact common uplands and the private bottom lands.[10]

Plenty of evidence exists to suggest that rangelands in some microbasins within northern New Mexico and southern Colorado were largely intact as late as the turn of the century. There were high quality upland pastures resulting from the use of seasonal sheep camp rotations, low stocking levels, and cyclic fire regimes. However, as we suggest later, the relatively stable condition of Hispano rangelands, and by extension native wildlife habitat, was mostly a function of the lack of roads throughout the high country. Without roads there could be no industrial extraction of forest resources. The lack of roads also slowed the pace of the biological invasion of exotic flora that accompanied the Hispano sheep trade. For example, the introduction of exotic plant species by livestock did not affect interior forest species. Like overgrazing impacts before 1880, the displacement of native species was largely limited to localized areas around water sources and trails.

The absence of roads was an important factor in the pristine and wild condition of many of these upland commons areas. It is, however, currently difficult to gauge with any certainty what the condition of the range and forest lands in general was by 1880. We do know that by 1936, three-quarters of the watershed of the Rio Grande was suffering from serious degradation (deBuys 1985, 232). Perhaps the problem in many Hispano enclaves was not so much overgrazing but the introduction of exotic species that displaced the native varieties, as deBuys (1985, 215–220) suggests.

Rothman ultimately places blame for mass destruction on commercial American interests. Yet, he also concludes that "only the volume of use differentiated Americans from their [Hispano and Indian] predecessors" (1989, 210). Thus, all "frontier" cultures are guilty of ecological devastation. There were no significant class or cultural differences in the *ethics* governing the use of land, and everyone exploited nature to the maximum, albeit within the limits of their culturally determined technical abilities. Later, we want to demonstrate how Spanish and Mexican land and water use customs and regulations did in fact have an *ethical* basis and even a proven record of enforcement.

Rothman also seems to argue that culture makes a definitive difference although not in the universal lack of a land ethic. In his view, the principal factor that allowed Americans to have a greater impact was the more advanced technology introduced with the arrival of the railroad. It was "American culture" and its superior technology that were singularly adapted "to make a discernable and irrevocable difference" in augmenting the processes of land degradation (1989, 211). In this scenario, Hispanos were relegated to a position of dependency (which has some truth to it) in relation to the dominant and more dynamic and inventive American culture (which is largely untrue). The advent of the new industrial society (notice that Rothman does not say capitalist) meant that "Hispanos found themselves confronted with a set of forces that their culture had not taught them to address" (1989, 186).

Clearly, this approach presents a dichotomy between an active, inventive, and technologically advanced American culture as opposed to a passive, ignorant, and technically primitive Hispano culture. Actually, Hispanos actively responded to these new forces; the trajectory from the 1880s and the struggles of *las Gorras Blancas* to the 1990s and a revived Chicano land grant movement amply demonstrates this. That Hispanos did not always succeed in opposing these forces may be less a testament to the "backwardness" of their social movement than to the grotesque inequities imposed by the law under capitalism. It is this resistance to domination that Rothman overlooks in presenting an essentially false dichotomy of cultures in conflict.

William deBuys, a conservation activist in New Mexico, foreshadowed this view in his 1985 book, *Enchantment and Exploitation: The Life and Hard Times of a New Mexico Mountain Range*. DeBuys's historical study of the Sangre de Cristo Mountains sought to demonstrate how the collision of different cultures resulted in land degradation: Pueblo Indians viewed the land from the vantage point of "spiritual" values, Hispanos saw it as a "communal" resource, and Americans viewed it as a "commodity" (deBuys 1985, 9). It was the Hispanos' view of the land as a commons that presumably led them to damage the "Sangres" through overgrazing and excessive timbering. Later, as ecologists and land managers tried to restore the health of the watersheds, this legacy of common use would become an obstacle to sound scientific management of the forest and range lands. As deBuys notes: "The high country was conceived rather possessively as a large extended backyard — a commons — where people might make use of as many resources [as possible]" without the annoying limits and regulations imposed by "bully boys and bureaucrats" (deBuys 1985, 285). But this "free rider" interpretation overlooks the fact that the common lands were tightly regulated and protected by customary edict and practice (see, for example, Rock 1976 and Ebright 1994).

DeBuys (1985, 282ff) suggests that an environmental ethic as it developed in the Southwest was a distinct by-product of an early to mid-twentieth century American conservation movement inspired by Aldo Leopold. Leopold becomes the savior of an "American wilderness" in a (New) Mexican homeland that had been subjected to abuse by all cultures and classes. The Indian, Hispanic, and American people of the Río Arriba all abused the land, producing its "washed and worn" condition. DeBuys argues that Hispanos may have seen the land as their *alma* (soul), but this did not prevent them from abusing the land out of ecological ignorance.

This attitude brought the Hispanos into direct conflict with the U.S. Forest Service and other public land agencies that eventually came to manage most of the upland commons in the Upper Rio Grande. According to deBuys, the conflict between the "scientific" Forest Service and "traditional" Chicano villagers was unavoidable, because it grew out of "two radically different perceptions of the land. . . . Where the villagers saw a vast mountain range that had sustained their forefathers and would sustain them too, the Forest Rangers saw land in the dire final stages of a long-running ecological disaster" (deBuys 1985, 210).

The Chicano livestock permitees "resisted" more stringent scientific management of rangelands by the Forest Service. The rangers apparently had their hands full with the unruly villagers. And while American land speculators such as Frank Bond and Arthur Manby treated the land as a commodity, the bully boys and bureaucrats from the federal agencies tried their best to rescue the endangered forests by turning to the scientific management of wildlife and its habitat. This environmental history, then, perhaps inadvertently, privileges the ecological wisdom of a modernist conservation movement and diminishes the value of traditional place-based knowledge. It also overlooks differences in ecological impacts attributable to the length of tenure on the land and grazing practices under customary local self-regulation.

DeBuys minimizes the pattern of abusive land-use practices under the public domain regime. He downplays the Forest Service's role in bringing about ecological ruin precisely because its public land management mission catered to large-scale commercial logging and mining interests. There is an irony overlooked by deBuys. On the one hand, the Forest Service targeted Hispano sheepherders in its efforts to limit grazing to protect and restore the watersheds. On the other hand, the Forest Service promoted massive logging and mining operations which benefitted corporate interests to the detriment of the same objective of watershed protection. The Hispano livestock permitees, thus, rightly saw fundamental injustice in the apparently discriminatory enforcement of regulations in the quest by the agency to fulfill its worthy objective of watershed protection.

The irony is that the mandate of the Forest Service to manage for timber and mineral resources has been the principal cause of watershed degradation in the entire Southern Rockies ecosystem. The effects of clear-cutting, overstory removal, and skid trail and road construction are evident in the increasing sedimentation of watercourses and fragmentation of habitat.[11] Mining areas, for example at Questa on the Red River, have contaminated watercourses and acequias with acid mine drainage and increased sedimentation from soil erosion.[12]

By encouraging a shift to large-scale industrial logging and mining, the Forest Service inhibited Chicano smallholders from legally exercising self-managed control of use rights on ancestral common lands. This action had dire economic consequences as autonomous village-based pastoralists increasingly turned to seasonal migratory farm labor and other waged labor to survive. The timber and mining industries not only employed large numbers of Chicanos, they discouraged the acequia farmers from maintaining traditions that had earlier nurtured the economic stability and ecological integrity of the watershed communities.

We contend that "multiple-use" policies favored corporate economic interests to the detriment of ecological, cultural, and local community values.[13] In little more than a hundred years (i.e., since the creation of the USFS in 1891 and the first national forest reserve in New Mexico in 1892), logging and mining industries devastated large portions of the public domain on a scale that dwarfs the effects of four hundred years of traditional use rights by Pueblos and Chicanos.

"Nonextractive" industries have also played an often overlooked role in these processes of change. Skiing and related recreational industries and tourism have produced serious ecological damage. For example, ski industry facilities and their infrastructure — including slopes, lifts, auxiliary buildings, power stations, lodging, second homes, restaurants, roadways, parking lots, and sewage lagoons — have destroyed considerable wildlife habitat, reduced in-stream flows and water quality for fish habitat and downstream acequias, and undermined much of the rural character and ecological integrity of the existing, and more harmoniously integrated, cultural and natural landscape mosaic (see Rodriguez 1987, 1991, and [1989] 1994).[14]

In the post-hippie years of the seventies, continuous in-migration by Americans into northern New Mexico resulted in major development of leisure industries and tourism. An important economic side effect of in-migration and recreational industries was the escalation of property values by speculative real estate development. In Arroyo Seco, ten miles northeast of Taos, one rancher was reportedly offered a hundred thousand dollars per acre in 1996 for a piece of the family's historic *vara* strip, a part of the Lucero de Godoi or Antonio Martinez Land Grant. The highway to Taos Ski Valley cuts through the heart of the *plaza* of Arroyo Seco.[15] The family refused to sell, but the economic pressure produced by rural gentrification undermines the ability of many farm families to continue agricultural use of ancestral land. The result is a loss of open space as well. Often, displaced local residents cannot pay the inflated property tax rates; land in this manner is easily and cheaply acquired by developers through "tax sales." In the process, wildlife habitat and farmland are blacktopped to make room for more ski condos, second homes, or upscale boutiques and B&Bs throughout the Santa Fe-Taos-Red River-Angel Fire recreational hinterland.

DeBuys acknowledges the role of land grant speculation in the dismantling of the Hispano upland commons but does not provide a critical analysis of the dynamics described above. DeBuys states that the "Forest Service may not have been a perpetrator of land grant crime, but in many people's eyes it was an accessory after the fact" (1985, 257). But this view minimizes the fact that many of the upland commons of Spanish and Mexican land grants were forcibly converted to the public domain by federal decree and not just through purchase from speculators or timber companies. In the end, deBuys downplays wave after destructive wave of large-scale extractive industries throughout the railroad period of the late nineteenth and early twentieth centuries and chooses instead to emphasize the "real Third World problems" of poverty and overpopulation: "Those who argue that Hispanos of northern New Mexico . . . face the Third World problems of economic imperialism and cultural aggression should bear in mind that the most pressing and most serious problems of the Third World have little to do with imperialism or ideology. They are the demographic and environmental problems of desertification, deforestation, and erosion, all of which undermine the capacity of the land to meet the needs of growing populations" (deBuys 1985, 274-275). This is an ironic stance since deBuys outlines in great detail the destructive effects of industrial-scale logging by companies such as the Santa Barbara Tie and Pole Company which clearly acted in an imperialistic manner.

Since the 1970s, most students of environmental issues in a third world context have recognized that ecological damage results primarily from transnational capitalist exploitation of indigenous natural resources. Also recognized is the fact that native peoples in colonized areas offer important alternatives for sustainable self-management of the environment. Moreover, it is recognized that capitalist destruction of nature is everywhere accompanied by displacement and extinction of local cultures.[16] DeBuys ignores this contrary perspective.

By referring to specific "cultural traits," such as the attitude of "free and unrestricted use" of the commons, to explain overgrazing, deBuys argues that the Hispano culture could not comprehend ecological limits. The use of the commons in practice is neither "free" nor "unrestricted." The loss of use rights in the Hispano land grant common for violation of local norms and rules already is well documented (e.g., Rock 1976 and Tyler 1988). Therefore, the use of overpopulation in Chicano villages as an example of the demographic (and cultural) basis of ecological degradation in the bioregion seems rather disingenuous. Most of these villages have experienced dramatic out-migration since at least the 1930s and little internal growth from higher-than-average birth rates. Population growth in the "Hispanic" villages has been driven largely by a wave of post-1960s urban "white flight." In- and out-migration dynamics are best seen at Taos, New Mexico, where virtually 100 percent of the residents were Pueblo Indians and Chicanos in 1821. By 1970, these population groups together dropped to 60 percent and within another two decades hovered at 55 percent (Martinez 1988b). In this case, white-led gentrification accounted for population growth and many of the contemporary resource battles in that area (Martinez 1988b and Rodriguez 1987, 1991, and 1994). DeBuys's environmental history leaves no room for a critical appreciation of the deep ethnic and class divisions that underlie both historical and contemporary conflicts over the management and use of the land and water resources of the bioregion.[17]

The construction of Chicanos as violent and lawless land thugs is the interpretation of choice offered by Tom Wolf in *Colorado's Sangre de*

Cristo Mountains. Wolf's book (1995, 265) presents a more openly hostile view of Chicanos in Colorado's San Luis Valley: "After centuries on the nethermost fringes of many different empires, local Hispanics have evolved their own unique folkways. These include a long-memoried sense of justice and a porous wall between church and state. San Luis's *predominantly Roman Catholic culture harbors violence and lawlessness* as well as a profound love of land and community" (emphasis added). Wolf accuses Chicanos of destroying the land and then attacks them for "trespassing" on private property and trying to devalue the market price of land owned by the descendants of President Zachary Taylor: "With a knowing wink from Governor Roy Romer (Dem.), local lawlessness and state politics conspired to lower the ranch's market value" (Wolf 1995, 275).

Echoing Rothman and deBuys, Wolf argues that a "tragedy of the commons" damaged the environment well before the arrival of white settlers, and Chicanos must share blame for abusing the land. "[A]ll men rushed toward ruin, when everyone exploited, shot, gouged, and burned everything. . . . No one escapes whipping when it comes to land abuse in the Sangres" (Wolf 1995, xx, 265).

The idea that everyone shares blame for ecological degradation is a recurring construct in the environmental history of the Río Arriba. Wolf, however, takes this perspective a step further by arguing that the "capitalist tool[s]," namely Malcolm (now Steve and Kip) Forbes, and his neighbor, the southern plantation heir and descendant of President Zachary Taylor, Jack (now Zachary, Jr.) Taylor, are examples of wise and "sustainable" management of the Sangre de Cristo Mountains. Wolf portrays Forbes and Taylor as "unlikely environmental heroes" who saved the mountains from destruction by the ignorant Hispanos. He proposes that the coupling of a "new ecology" with the "market economy, individual liberty, and private property rights" is the best option for sustainable management of the "Sangres" (Wolf 1995, 264). Wolf never offers an in-depth examination of the concept of "sustainable management."

In part, these errors are a consequence of an inaccurate and distorted rendering of conservation biology and the theory of island biogeography. When Wolf calls Forbes and Taylor "unlikely environmental heroes," he overlooks the destructive impact of the four hundred miles of roads built for access to several thousand second-home lots in the Wagon Creek and Forbes Park subdivisions and the disastrous effects of severe logging on the Taylor Ranch. Conservation biologists have long recognized that roads and logging are the most destructive threats to wildlife, habitat, and watershed integrity. But Wolf misconstrues the excessive roads and timber cuts as examples of practices that create "edge" habitat for wildlife, and in particular elk (the most ruthlessly commodified species in the intermountain West). Using this muddled version of the theory of disturbance biogeography, Wolf argues that roads and timber cuts are good for the ecosystem because they sustain a diverse landscape mosaic that mimics the effects of natural disturbances such as fire and insect outbreaks.

By invoking this interpretation, Wolf seeks to justify the enclosure of Chicano common lands by capitalists who created the nation's largest privately owned mountain estates. He thereby justifies his argument that we should be cautious about current local efforts to restore control of these areas to land-grant heirs.[18] Where private stewardship is not possible, Wolf endorses the efforts of the federal government to apply principles of conservation biology in ecosystem management of the Sangre de Cristo Mountains. In this respect, Wolf notes that it was only during "the Progressive Era, [that] a truly *heroic* early Forest Service managed—emphatically managed—the forested watersheds of the Sangres back to their potential" (Wolf 1995, xx).

The carrying capacity of the upland commons in the Culebra Mountain Tract was not exceeded, however, until the early part of the twentieth century (1910) as a result of activities by mercantile capitalists and railroad links to distant markets. By blaming local *carneros* who owned handfuls of sheep for the tragedy of the commons, Wolf obscures the far more serious damage unleashed by the integration of this land-grant area, through enclosure, into an expanding regional capitalist market for wool and meat. The capital for the sheep industry clearly belonged to the mercantile and landed elite. It is this social class that must be seen as responsible for overgrazing the shortgrass prairies and montane meadows of the Culebra watershed. Contrary to Wolf's conclusion about a Hispanic tragedy of the commons, there were significant class differences in the stocking rates for the sheep industry, and small peasant farmers with a dozen sheep or fewer were not the cause of overgrazing in the mountains above San Luis. The privatization and enclosure of the commons led to overgrazing as mercantile interests dramatically increased the size of the flocks. We find this pattern repeated throughout much of the Upper Rio Grande.

Finally, Wolf argues that Chicanos in the San Luis Valley are veritable poachers of wildlife who have abused the private property rights of large landowners such as Malcolm Forbes and Jack Taylor by trespassing onto their lands to hunt for elk, deer, and other game. He notes that dozens of villagers from the San Luis area were arrested in a sting operation conducted in 1989 by the U.S. Fish and Wildlife Service (USFWS) and the Colorado Division of Wildlife (CDOW) to combat an out-of-control "poaching frenzy" by the villagers. Poaching shows an attitude of insensitivity toward wildlife, and so Wolf questions the ability of the Chicanos to manage the land themselves without causing more damage. Of the Culebra River basin ranchers Wolf says, "In effect, the stockmen [are] more interested in poaching than tending their stock" (Wolf 1995, 272).

The so-called poaching raid was based on the manipulation of people by a federal agent who encouraged locals to hunt for species not normally killed (black bear, cougar, golden eagle, etc.). With unemployment running at 20 to 25 percent and a below-poverty rate around 35 percent, it is easy to see why many local men responded to the agent's offers of from five hundred to a thousand dollars for certain carcasses. Wolf does not address the socioeconomic context of the raid and instead relies on stereotypical portrayals to argue that *all* Chicanos lack a conservation ethic. But there was also a political dimension to this raid, one which is evident today when many of the arrestees are now much more passive and quiescent, particularly with respect to the on-going land rights and antilogging struggles. Some opponents of Chicano land rights have drawn from Wolf's interpretation of the poaching raid, and overgrazing of La Vega, to argue against local participation in the management of the common lands.[19]

A more critical reading of the environmental history of the Culebra watershed reveals how complex class and race dynamics underlie the processes of cultural and ecological transformation. Wolf fails to appreciate the normative frameworks of the locals and how they make a serious distinction between subsistence hunters and unethical poachers.[20] The "ethical hunter" kills solely to supply meat for the family's table and does so on horseback along wildlife trails. The "unethical poacher," in contrast, is stigmatized and ridiculed for shooting bear, cougar, or eagle, taking money payments, and driving four-wheel drive vehicles on subdivision roads. The subsistence hunters see themselves as exercising a historic use right to the commons and engaging in a form of resistance to the enclosure of the land-grant commons. The poachers are abusing the wild-life while buying into the values of an acquisitive lifestyle (Peña 1994b and in press). Local people make these distinctions and play them out in their everyday lives. In this manner, every locality has internal contradictions as "stewards" clash with "poachers." Surely, do not the micropolitics of hunting (and grazing) play a significant role in the environmental history of a place? (see Peña 1994b).

Toward an Alternative Environmental History of the Río Arriba

Today a heated battle goes on for control of land-use planning and management throughout the intermountain West. The Río Arriba bioregion is very much at the center of this struggle. Those who actively oppose Chicano land and water claims have made use of the evidence proffered by environmental historians to argue against local self-management of watersheds or the restoration of common property resource rights. Tom Wolf's ill-informed assault on the farmers of the Culebra River watershed is the most obvious example of an unreflective academic exercise promoting racial domination. If we follow his logic, then surely a people who have damaged and abused the land in the past cannot be entrusted with the future of ecosystem protection.

We now want to offer the broad outlines of an alternative environmental history of the Río Arriba. We focus on direct evidence from four areas: (1) Spanish and Mexican era environmental regulations and Moorish-Iberian water allocation customs; (2) and (3) patterns of logging and grazing from Spanish-Mexican settlement to the present; and (4) the relationship of cultural landscapes to biodiversity as seen through an agroecological perspective. Our intent is to outline the general contours of an alternative environmental history to reveal the ambiguities and complexities of cultural and ecological change in the bioregion.

Conservation Ethics Reconsidered

Let us start with the notions of a conservation ethic and knowledge of ecological limits. Rothman, deBuys, and Wolf downplay the legacy of tragic mismanagement of the so-called public domain by the USFS and the Bureau of Land Management (BLM). They also trivialize the well-documented environmental regulations imposed by the Spanish laws of the Indies and Iberian-Moorish water allocation customs. Malcolm Ebright, a legal historian, has observed that conservation ethics and explicit environmental regulations were woven into Spanish-Mexican water and land laws. He quotes Gov. Cuervo y Valdéz of Spanish colonial New Mexico with respect to the management of Santa Fe's *la ciénaga* wetland commons in 1705: "[Livestock] shall not trample or eat the grass that grows there so that anyone who needs it [the grass] can mow it to feed their horses." In addition, Lt. Gov. Juan Paéz Hurtado is cited as saying in 1717 that "[at] this time every year [after peak spring snowmelt] a *bando* [ordinance] is promulgated ordering that all the pigs running loose in this Villa of Santa Fé be rounded up, so that no damage is done either to the planted fields, or to the Ciénaga of this said Villa, also that the same is done for the horses, cattle, sheep, and other animals, so that these [animals] will not trample or eat their [the Villa's common] grass" (Ebright 1994, 90).

Estevan Arellano's research (1996) demonstrates that the settlement of the Río Arriba acequia communities was regulated by longstanding legal custom and edict. The location of villages, plazas, acequias, field crops, row crops, common pasture, wood-gathering areas, and hunting zones were all clearly governed by rules derived from observation of local conditions of microclimate, topography, hydrology, soil, plant communities, and so forth. For example, swamp areas and wetlands were to be preserved; settlement or excessive use of such areas was discouraged for reasons of public health or safety. Arellano quotes from "Book Four, Title Seven" of the *Recopilación de leyes de los reynos de las indias* of 1681 to demonstrate the existence of colonial-era environmental regulations and knowledge of ecological limits: "It is ordered, that the land and surroundings, which are to be settled, be the most fertile, with abundant pasture, firewood, lumber, materials, sweet waters, natural people, transpiration, ingress and egress, and there be no lake close by, nor marsh lands where venomous animals live, nor there be any corruption of winds, or waters (Arellano 1996, 7).

Site-specific conditions for the establishment of land-grant settlements were one aspect of the environmental regulations imposed during the Spanish-Mexican period. The use and conservation of water also was a major consideration in defining the parameters for settlement. The management of water allocation under the acequia system was based on customary laws largely derived from the Islamic "Law of Thirst" (Clark 1987, 9, and Peña, in press). This law holds that all life-forms, all things with thirst, have a right to receive the life-giving liquid. The acequias are based on riparian principles, and these rules prohibit the severing of water from the land. Moreover, the water right is usufructuary, and the farmer has a right to use the water as long as it does not hurt other users on the ditch. The American system of water law, based on the doctrine of prior appropriation, allows water to be treated as a commodity that is for sale to the highest bidder. Clearly, the customary principles governing acequias are more environmentally sound (Peña 1998 and Rívera and Peña 1997). One of the conditions for the approval of land-grant settlements was that the water resources of the area had to be protected and preserved; watersheds were to remain in an undeveloped and wild state to protect the quality and quantity of the water flowing downstream into the dendritic network of irrigation ditches (Rock 1976, Tyler 1988, Baxter 1997, and Rívera and Peña 1997).

The legacy of Spanish colonial era and Mexican period environmental regulations is an interesting contrast to the numerous, poorly recast versions of Garrett Hardin's tragically inaccurate theory of the commons examined earlier.[21] Again we stress that such constructions of Hispano abuse of the land overlook the strong traditions of environmental self-management developed by the Spanish-Mexican people throughout the course of four hundred years in the Río Arriba.

History of Logging Impacts

The existence of environmental regulations from the earliest periods of Spanish and Mexican settlement is an important counterpoint to the idea that Hispanos "lacked cultural prohibitions" against ecological damage. But were these conservation ethics enforced in practice? Some historians (for example, MacCameron) have cited a case study by Marc Simmons (1988) for evidence of disregard for regulations in the colonial period. However, the case cited is likely exceptional, and the overall weight of the evidence on grazing and logging impacts suggests that the Río Arriba bioregion was not ecologically damaged in an extensive manner during this early period of settlement. Environmental regulations not only existed, but they were widely enforced.

The land-grant settlers made use of a wide variety of forest resources. Ponderosa pine was used for furniture; piñon was used to fashion saddles; cottonwood was used to make kitchen utensils; juniper was prominent in the construction of looms and beams. Hispano settlers also made use of Douglas fir for plows, corrals, and lumber as well as aspen for crafting musical instruments (guitars, violins, drums, and shakers). All these woods were used for firewood (U.S. Forest Service 1996, A–19). White fir, limber pine, blue spruce, and Engelmann spruce were little used because they grew at higher elevations and were not as suitable as the other woods. Fences were uncommon during this early period, so little wood was needed for this purpose. A 1996 Forest Service report notes that "[f]rom 1850 to 1875, a similar use of wood was made by the early Hispanic settlers of the SLV [San Luis Valley]. Their effect on forested communities was probably minimal due to their low population and correspondingly small use of resources. They mostly used resources found at lower elevations of [what is now] the RGNF [Rio Grande National Forest], located near settlements" (United States Forest Service 1996, A–19).

The evidence suggests that Hispanos did not have a major impact on the montane or subalpine forests throughout the period of land-grant settlement, but the more interesting point is that Hispanos developed a complex and rich material culture based on the careful use of wood products primarily harvested from lower elevation forests. From furniture to dwelling construction; from headgates to corrals; from carved saints to saddles—forest wood products permeated the material culture of the Hispanos, a remarkable characteristic completely overlooked by deBuys, Rothman, and Wolf.

An earlier study, published in 1956 for the Forest Service on the state of the Sangre de Cristo Mountains, shows that at least 80 percent of the forest stands in the Sangres were old-growth or late-successional communities. According to the author, E. J. Dortignac (1956), the impact of logging by Spanish-Mexican settlers in the Río Arriba was minimal because of a lack of industrial technology for large-scale cutting and little market demand for timber products beyond the traditional uses outlined above. Significantly, very few roads were built by Hispano land-grant settlers over the course of seven to thirteen generations of use, and most routes through the mountain areas followed Indian, sheep, and other livestock or wildlife trails. Road access was extremely limited and primitive, a condition that ultimately favored the integrity of wildlife habitat and movement corridors. For example, on the common lands of the Sangre de Cristo grant, as late as 1960 only two roads traversed above timberline on the 77,000-acre spread. (Neither road qualified as a mountain pass, although one did cross the range crest.) Finally, Hispano settlers did not disrupt the natural fire regime of the Sangres, a major factor that contributed (perhaps inadvertently) to the preservation of the bioregion's ecological integrity; for example, the lack of fire suppression encouraged the preservation of open park lands associated with old-growth Ponderosa plant communities.

There also is evidence of some deforestation, however, particularly in the areas of greatest population concentration (Albuquerque and Santa Fe). One historian makes note of these instances of deforestation but utilizes sources that may be culturally biased. MacCameron (1994, 25) cites W. W. H. Davis as observing the "exceedingly scarce" availability of wood in the entire region. Josiah Gregg also is cited as observing that "on the water-courses there is little timber . . . except cottonwoods, scantily scattered along their banks." But both of these researchers were "Easterners" who came from very humid areas; likely, their perceptions of native vegetation patterns in the semiarid conditions of New Mexico led them to conclude that these areas had been deforested when in fact the pattern of scarce vegetation was quite "natural" for the bioregion.[22] It also would take the acequia system several more generations to extend and protect the riparian life zones of the bioregion and thereby create more verdant cultural landscapes.

We can assess the state of these lands after they were converted to the public domain (i.e., the Kit Carson, Santa Fe, San Isabel, and Rio Grande National Forests) or enclosed by large private estates (e.g., Forbes and Taylor). It quickly becomes evident that the era of public (and private) land management, initiated since 1891–92, ushered boom-bust cycles of large-scale logging and road construction by corporate development interests. For example, more than half of the 240,000 acres owned by Forbes, Inc., was subdivided, and close to 480 miles of access roads were constructed after 1968–69 to serve second homeowners and logging operations. Today, conservation biologists decry this type of development as one of the most serious acts of habitat fragmentation and watershed degradation within the Southern Rocky Mountains biome (see, e.g., Curry, Soulé, Peña, and McGowan 1996; Noss et al. 1994; and Jones and Grant 1996). The exploitation of these large mountain estates can be attributed only to the desire for profit.

Logging volumes on public lands in the Río Arriba increased dramatically after 1892 and the establishment of the Kit Carson and Santa Fe National Forests. Over the ensuing decades, the industrialization of logging was encouraged by the USFS through the use of below-cost sales to the timber industry. Road building also was subsidized by the Forest Service to expand the total volume of board feet cut. Thus, within the Kit Carson, Santa Fe, and Rio Grande National Forests, logging levels grew by more than 3000 percent between 1892 and 1960, and most of this increase occurred after 1950, when a postwar logging boom fueled by home construction and the GI Bill occurred. Today, less than 10 percent of the forests in the Sangre de Cristo mountain range are old-growth or late-successional communities. More cutting took place in the fifty to seventy years of industrial logging than in four hundred years of Chicano settlement and use of common resources (Peña, in press). To compare the two uses is to discover not just a difference of magnitude but of vastly different modes of production. It is a matter of extremes: Under American control, the forests were managed for even-aged stands that were kept dense for logging purposes. Ironically, there are more trees today than there were a hundred years ago, just as the logging industry claims. While more trees are evident, however, the old-growth ecosystems have been thoroughly devastated.

Cultural prohibitions against greed (overgrazing and overcutting) in these Chicano communities have already been described elsewhere as enduring features of local customary control of land-use practices (e.g., see D. G. Peña 1992 on the "Forest Spirit" folktales of the Río Arriba). Hispanos cut less timber not just because of small, scattered populations, inadequate industrial technology, or limited market demand, but also because their land ethics discouraged the pursuit of such technology—the incentive of profit being largely absent. As we will see shortly, however, local knowledge was channeled in other scientific directions.

The Culebra mountain range provides a case of logging destruction by

Americans of the former land-grant commons. Like other mountainous areas of the Río Arriba, the Culebra common lands were largely uncut and roadless until 1960, when Jack Taylor first started building barricades to keep the locals out and access roads to bring the first wave of loggers into the area. Since 1995, Zachary Taylor has sold timber deeds for logging cuts of 80 to 100 million board feet in the Culebra mountain range over a period of five to ten years. The logging will eventually include all the merchantable timber on 34,000 out of 77,000 acres of enclosed common land and is the largest timber sale in Colorado history for a single contiguous area. The logging operations are principally contracted to out-of-state corporate logging interests, and they include some 20 million board feet to be extracted from the few remaining native old-growth and late-successional forests in ten thousand acres of previously roadless and unlogged areas. Could this sort of destruction of old-growth forests serve as a shining example of the "new ecology" wedded to the "free market?"

The suppression of fire on public lands also wreaked ecological havoc on the acequia communities. The USFS has suppressed natural fires for nearly a hundred years. The results are complex and disturbing. Fire suppression has eliminated natural processes of succession so that the conditions needed for old-growth Ponderosa have been impaired. Ponderosa pine communities require frequent, low-intensity fires to clear out understory and attain the structural characteristics of old growth. In addition, fire suppression has increased the available fuel for out-of-control, unnaturally hot, and devastating wildfires. The Yellowstone fire and the more recent but equally devastating Hondo-Questa fire in New Mexico are well-known examples of what can happen when wildfires develop under conditions of abnormal accumulation of biomass. Such massive fires further disrupt natural processes of ecological succession. Finally, fire suppression means that the forests are abnormally dense with young stands with little structural diversity (e.g., few dead snags) and thus less habitat. While there may be more trees today than a hundred years ago, the forests are more like overly managed monoculture tree plantations than natural forests. One negative consequence is that acequia irrigators receive less water downstream from abnormally thick forest stands. (For an example of this type of problem see Jones and Grant 1996).

On the other hand, timber practices tolerated by the USFS over the past hundred years, including clear-cuts, shelterwood cuts, and road-terrace patch cuts, have greatly damaged wildlife habitat and downstream water users. The acequias in several watersheds have been harmed by these practices as a consequence of increased coarse sediment loads in the watercourses, headgates, and ditches. Another effect of clear-cutting is a shortened irrigation season due to the fact that the snowpack melts at an accelerated rate in such openly logged areas.[23] The research of the past twenty years on the environmental effects of logging concludes, generally, that timber operations and road construction are the greatest threats to wildlife habitat, biodiversity, and watershed integrity (see Noss et al. 1994 for a good summary).

History of Grazing Impacts

As we have stressed repeatedly in this chapter, a wide variety of sources indicate that land degradation resulting from livestock overgrazing in the Río Arriba was principally associated with the arrival of the railroad after 1880. Commercialization of the livestock industry was accelerated by rail technology, and both the livestock industry and the railroad were promoted by regional and national capitalist interests.

   As early as 1936 the federal government reported that in the arid Southwest "abnormal erosion [had] caused some areas to resemble badlands" (Secretary of Agriculture 1936, 7). The most striking damage reported for the Rio Grande watershed was in the tributary Rio Puerco: "[W]here only small channels existed prior to 1885, destructive erosion [had] cut trenches 200 to 500 feet wide in the fertile soil of its floor" (Secretary of Agriculture 1936, 9; also see deBuys 1985). Similar processes of erosion occurred downstream of Embudo and in the vicinity of Elephant Butte reservoir.

   This federal study of the "Western range" notes that rangeland degradation in the public domain was mainly a result of "a no man's land without management prior to the creation of the grazing districts." It further concluded that the "traditional *American* (emphasis ours) attitude toward all natural resources" was "outstanding" among the causes of deterioration of the range. A "philosophy of inexhaustibility" furthered the "lavish" use of resources. This long and complex report suggests that an "unsound land policy" was the root of the problem of rangeland degradation. The policy had grown out of a "belief in private ownership of land" and an attempt to apply unmodified the practices of the humid East and Middle West to the semiarid West (Secretary of Agriculture 1936, 11).

The most striking evidence of this pattern is outlined in Victor Westphall's classic study (1965) of overgrazing in northern New Mexico's so-called public domain. Westphall demonstrates that the carrying capacity of New Mexico's fragile grasslands was exceeded only after the intrusion of American cattle and sheep-ranching interests.

Frederick Gelbach argues that the rangelands of the Upper and Middle Rio Grande watersheds were left largely intact during the Spanish and Mexican periods. Oñate's legacy, he states, was one of stewardship. Gelbach makes the strongest case against American capitalists by pointing to the arrival of the railroad and the commercialization of livestock as forces that opened the gates to land degradation in the region. Describing the observations of William Emory, who rode south from Santa Fe along the Rio Grande in 1846, Gelbach notes the existence of lush black grama grasslands. Emory and John Bartlett both noted that the uplands were "rich grazing country and the river valley was densely timbered with cottonwoods and mesquite." Gelbach (1993, 109) states that the military explorers "traveled along the Camino Real by following lines of mesquites planted by Spanish cattle two centuries earlier." According to Gelbach, "Rapid and extensive demise of grassland is the general outcome of American settlement. . . . Grass cover predominated in 1853 but began to disappear by the 1880's in concert with the postwar and railroad era of American ranching" (1993, 111). Gelbach, an unassuming island biogeographer, is very direct about assessing the American impact on the environment.

In another vein, Robert MacCameron suggests that overgrazing during the Spanish colonial period differed by geography, climate, topography, demography, and settlement patterns. Not all watersheds were subject to the same stresses. MacCameron strongly cautions against overgeneralization, noting that the Puerco basin, Albuquerque, and Santa Fe were perhaps exceptional in that stocking rates there quickly exceeded the carrying capacity of the range. But he also notes that an 1827 livestock enumeration reveals a total of 250,000 sheep and goats in New Mexico, with 217,000 of that number concentrated in Albuquerque and Santa Fe. It is easy to see why the rangelands in the northernmost regions of the Rio Grande watershed were largely intact until well past the turn of the twen-

tieth century; there simply were not enough sheep to damage the ecosystem seriously.[24]

Agroecology: Cultural Landscapes and Biodiversity

The environmental histories of deBuys, Rothman, and Wolf, as already
detailed in this and previous chapters, focus on changing ecological conditions in the mountain areas and forest ecosystems. We have sought in this
chapter to show how deBuys, Rothman, and Wolf have largely overlooked the landscape linkages between the Hispano villages and the watershed ecosystem. The relationship between the cultural landscapes of
agropastoral villages and biodiversity is a critical aspect of the bioregion's
environmental history and yet remains unexamined.[25]

In the context of the Southern Rockies ecosystem, the cottonwood,
willow, and alder riparian life zones are the principal "hotbeds" of biodiversity. These riparian zones play a critical role as wildlife habitat,
movement corridors, and migratory streams. And while the aforemen-
tioned environmental historians are quick to condemn Chicanos for introducing exotic flora and fauna — with sheep most often cast as the "hoofed
locusts" that invaded the montane grasslands — they completely overlook
the contribution of acequia irrigation systems to the preservation of native
biodiversity. In short, the acequia irrigation system provides critical ecological services for the broader regional economy on a scale that one study
(Peña 1997b) values at more than $260 million a year for the seven-
county bioregion (see also Peña 1997c; Rívera and Peña 1997).

We earlier noted that the riparian long-lot is another important feature
of cultural landscapes in the Río Arriba. The long-lot settlement pattern is
a rare and endangered farming landscape in which each family has a
ribbonlike strip of land whose dimensions are several hundred feet wide
and ten to twenty miles in length.[26] The length of the long-lot gives each
farming family access to different natural plant communities and topographical features (foothills, mesas, bottomlands, upland prairies, etc.).
The topographical diversity of the long-lot has been acknowledged as a
critical feature that protects wildlife habitat and movement corridors
(Peña 1998).

John B. Jackson's *A Sense of Place, A Sense of Time* is one of those rare
studies that goes to the heart of the matter without all the usual contor-

tion. Jackson's admiration for the acequias is apparent in his statement that the irrigation system is an "accomplishment deserving of more recognition than it has thus far received." The key to appreciating this system lies in the cultural landscape ecology of the farming communities: "[E]ach village created its own miniature landscape of gardens and orchards and fields and pastures, a landscape distinct from the surrounding wilderness. Farmers not only introduced new kinds of vegetation — crops and grasses and fruit trees — but also another climate, for their irrigation systems made them relatively independent of the unpredictable local rains" (Jackson 1994, 19). In fact, the acequia/long-lot cultural landscape creates its own microclimate, a point that was first made by Estevan Arellano, who describes it as "neo-Mediterranean." These microclimatic conditions are in part by-products of the expanded processes of evapotranspiration associated with the lush plant communities that grow along the banks of the irrigation ditches.

These "miniature landscapes" are perhaps best understood as puzzle parts of a complex "agroecosystem" in which livestock raising is combined with polycultures of row, field, and orchard crops. The place-based knowledge apparent in these arrangements is currently being documented through the use of "cognitive mapping" and "native cartography."[27] Farmers have specific place-names for different areas of the local cultural and natural landscapes. These place-names tend to be descriptive of some environmental quality inherent in the biophysical properties of the site. For example, local place names may refer to La Lumbriz (The Earthworm) as a place to gather bait for fishing. A spot with dense thickets of chokecherry is called Loma del Capulín (Chokecherry Hill). Such place-names are attached to areas within the long-lots or even refer to specific spots in an orchard or garden.[28]

Finally, recent agroecological research documents the role of Chicano farmers as conservers of horticultural varieties. As seed savers, Chicano farmers protect a wide variety of locally adapted landrace crops, which are species native to a region. Thus, their fields double as storehouses of genetically diverse native crops. These family heirlooms are examples of rare germ plasm of inestimable value to the future of agricultural security in a world dominated by monocultures and genetically engineered crops (Peña 1997a, 1997b, and 1997c).

These features of the Hispano village landscape ecology have been completely overlooked by environmental historians, and yet evidence suggests that Hispano settlement patterns and farming practices have long served to protect native domesticated and wild plant diversity. The riparian long-lot and acequia cultural landscapes are significant examples of human practices that extend native biodiversity. The ecological services rendered by these practices have not been acknowledged, in part because environmental historians have tended to focus more on natural landscapes than on cultural landscapes. And while Hispanos have introduced many exotic plants and animals to the bioregion, they have been equally adept at preserving many native species.

Beyond a Sense of Place

A few scholars have studied sense of place in the context of the Upper Rio Grande. For example, John B. Jackson and Charles H. Wilkinson have argued that Hispanos in the Río Arriba have a unique sense of place that has produced rich ethical traditions and sustainable land-use patterns. Describing the rural New Mexican Hispano sense of place, Jackson states, "There were still men and women who could identify the village a stranger came from by his or her accent, who knew the local name for every field, every hill, every wild plant. They knew their landscape by heart." This knowledge of place, Jackson suggests, is now threatened with extinction. Jackson sees the process of decay as resulting from modernization and "massification" of society, a process in which economic domination reduced the ability of the agropastoral villagers to remain independent and self-reliant. "Yet, some of the villages *have* survived. . . . Though the villages are probably just as poor, comparatively speaking, as they were in the past, some now have more movement and more vitality" (Jackson 1994, 20, 25, 58). For Jackson, the persistence of the Hispano villages is largely a consequence of the enduring sense of place that sustains the locals' deep attachment to ancestral lands.

Wilkinson echoes this view in his remarkable book *The Eagle Bird: Mapping a New West.* The existence of stable, tight-knit, and prosperous rural communities in the intermountain West is possible, Wilkinson argues, if we recognize that these "communities are bound together by the common love of this miraculous land." Wilkinson argues for "an ethic of place" that respects equally the people of a region and the land, animals, vegetation, water, and air. Such an ethic of place "ought to manifest itself in a dogged determination to treat the environment and its people as equals, to recognize both as sacred." The ethic of place, in practice, derives from basin and watershed demarcations and provides an alternative basis to concepts such as "multiple use" (Wilkinson 1992, 137–38.)

The struggle to protect the water rights of acequias in the Chama Valley in northern New Mexico is an example of the conflicts that arise between the homeland ethic of place and the unsound, and largely antidemocratic, policies governing resource use in the public and private domains. Citing a famous 1985 decision by District Judge Art Encinias, Wilkinson notes that "cultural considerations play a much greater role in law than we commonly realize" (1992, 159). The case involved an out-of-state developer's efforts to transfer water rights from agricultural uses by the acequias to a second-home subdivision in the foothills of the Chama watershed. Rejecting the transfer request, Judge Encinias noted that the region's "living culture" possessed significant values "not measurable in dollars and cents." Thus, "[t]he deep-felt and tradition-bound ties of northern New Mexico families to the land and water are central to the maintenance of that culture. . . . [T]o transfer water rights, devoted for more than a century to agricultural purposes, in order to construct a playground for those who can pay is a poor trade, indeed" (quoted in Wilkinson 1992, 158). A sense of place *can* find expression and legitimacy within the sphere of legal discourse and jurisprudence. But more often, the claims of local knowledge and local culture are devalued and excluded from the law and policy-making arenas (Peña and Gallegos 1997, 85–90).

While it is gratifying to see some scholars appreciate the value of a Chicano homeland ethic of place, there are also pragmatic limits to such an "idealistic" view of the conditions that would help resolve environmental conflicts in the Upper Rio Grande. The prospects for local self-management of the watershed commons, deriving from a respect for people and nature as equals, are severely limited by powerful political-economic interests. Again, the conclusion must be that any effort to reconcile the demands for "wilderness" protection with the demands for the restoration of Chicano and Pueblo Indian land rights must confront the inequities of power resulting from the dominant, multiple-use policies that are currently extant in the intermountain West.

A particularly troublesome feature of contemporary ecopolitics is that environmental impact assessment, ecosystem management, and wildlands preservation are all captive to the reifying primacy accorded the "sacred" law of private property rights. The language and values of the market system permeate the entire process of environmental protection and land-use management.[29] A "cult of expertise" that privileges the viewpoint of scientists who serve the interests of corporate power and the increasing bureaucratization and professionalization of ecosystem management tends to exclude local people from effective participation in land-use planning.[30] The crisis of a lack of "ecological democracy" is a more serious aspect of the problem facing the ethics of place than either Jackson or Wilkinson acknowledge.

Place-Centered Ethics, Local Knowledge, and Conservation Biology

The only way to empower an ethic of place against the discursive privilege accorded private property rights in legal and policy-making milieus is to integrate the claims of local ethnoscientific knowledge with the scientific methods of conservation biology. Only then, by scientifically verifying or rejecting the claims of local knowledge, will we democratize, and subvert, the entire institutional edifice that supports the current domination by capital of the land-use planning and ecosystem-management processes.

As the title of this anthology suggests, the local knowledge of rural land-based Chicano communities can be empowered through a more conscious association with the "subversive science" of ecology. Conservation biology, in particular, offers a potent ally for rural land-based communities interested in furthering the aims of ecological protection, cultural renewal, and local economic prosperity in a more holistic manner. Conservation biology holds the promise of reconciling humans in nature through its "core reserve–connecting corridor" model for ecologically sound inhabitation of watersheds.[31] The basic principles of the biological core reserve and connecting corridor design are really the best practice frontier for an ethic of place. They provide a framework to preserve biodiversity, protect watershed integrity, and promote local sustainable use of the environment. This zoning concept holds great promise for integrating conservation and human activities (Noss et al. 1994, 143).

The basic model of the biological core reserve and connecting corridor design integrates strictly protected core zones surrounded by one or more buffer and transitional zones. It also includes areas for research, restoration, monitoring, and compatible human settlements. This model does not prohibit human activity but manages it within the context of the overall objectives of biodiversity conservation and watershed protection. The simplest way to conceptualize this model is to envision a multiple-use module with an inviolate reserve at the core that is surrounded by a gradation of buffer zones, with intensity of human activity increasing outward and intensity of protection increasing inward (Curry, Soulé, Peña, and McGowan 1996, 15–17).

We believe that the environmental history of the Río Arriba suggests that traditional Chicano land-use practices anticipated many of the principles of conservation biology. The environmental rules and regulations governing the establishment of settlements and the use of water discussed earlier are indicative of a similar concern for ecosystem protection, especially the principle of interconnection between cultural and natural landscapes. Most of the montane watersheds in the land-grant region of northern New Mexico and south-central Colorado were left intact as wild lands, that is, roadless areas, until the arrival of the American-dominated railroad mass markets. Once again, we are stressing that this basic fact should inform the use of environmental history as a tool in the development of contemporary policies for the management and preservation of ecosystems. Such an approach may provide a framework to bridge the divide that currently separates environmentalists from Chicano land-grant activists in New Mexico.

An important exception to this pattern of divisiveness is found ironically in that "lawless and violent" cradle of rural Chicano Catholicism, San Luis and the surrounding Culebra River villages. In San Luis, environmentalists from Earth First!, Ancient Forest Rescue, Greenpeace, and other similar groups established a strong coalition with local farmers and land-grant activists to launch a year-long antilogging campaign that was recently characterized by *The New York Times* as "the hottest environmental dispute" in the Rocky Mountains (Brooke 1997). The reasons for the success of this Hispano-environmentalist coalition are complex, but an important aspect is that the ecoactivists recognize and respect the sustainable traditions of acequia communities while the farmers and land-grant activists recognize the need for continued ecological protection of the watershed. Conservation biology is expressed in the dialogue of the

coalition, which supports local self-management of the restored land-
grant commons on the basis of the principles of a democratized science. In
the Culebra watershed, the ethic of place and the subversive science of
ecology are coming together to strengthen the ecological legitimacy of
local knowledge. Environmental historians would do well to recognize
such creative permutations in the evolving contested terrain that pits the
capitalist tool against the lawless and the violent in the struggle for the
future of the commons in the Río Arriba.

Notes

Research support for this chapter was provided by the National Endowment for
the Humanities, Grant #RO-22707-94. The views expressed by the authors are
their sole responsibility and do not reflect the official views or policies of the NEH.

1. This research is being conducted under the auspices of the "Upper Rio
Grande Hispano Farms: A Cultural and Natural History of Land Ethics in Transition, 1598–1998," a four-year interpretive research project funded by the National Endowment for the Humanities and directed by the Rio Grande Bioregions
Project of the Colorado College.

2. One important exception here is Van Ness 1987. One of the first Chicano
scholars to address the issue of environmental ethics is Reyes García. See García
1988 and chapter 3 of this volume.

3. In most Native American and Chicano land rights struggles, a key issue is the
local self-management of ancestral areas. The case of the Blue Lake Wilderness
above Taos Pueblo is a significant example of a successful struggle for the restoration of local indigenous stewardship of homeland areas of cultural, historical, and
ecological significance to the aboriginal inhabitants. For further discussion of indigenous and Chicano land rights struggles see Briggs and Van Ness 1987, Churchill 1991, Jaimes 1992, and Ebright 1994.

4. The Wildlands Project is an example of an effort to use principles of conservation biology to establish a network of biodiversity "core reserves" connected by
biological corridors in a system of large roadless areas stretching from Canada to
Mexico. See the Winter 1995 issue of *WildEarth,* published by the Cenozoic Society, for a special thematic report on the first one thousand days of this conservation project.

5. On the militia presence in the southern Rocky Mountains, see Dawson 1995.
On the "sagebrush rebellion" and the "wise use" movement, see Woolf 1995 and
Christensen 1995a and 1995b.

6. For further discussion of these conflicts, see Peña and Mondragon Valdéz 1998.

7. Some critical studies of wilderness preservation in New Mexico include D. G. Peña 1992, Pulido 1993 and 1996, and Peña and Mondragon Valdéz 1998. For critiques of the "social construction" of wilderness see Cronon 1996. For a rejoinder, critical of the "postmodern deconstruction" of wilderness preservation, see Soulé and Lease 1995.

8. This has certainly been the case in New Mexico where environmentalists have long clashed with small-scale logging and woodworking cooperatives in the Chicano land-grant communities that use the Vallecitos Federal Sustained Yield Unit (VFSYU), a former land-grant commons now administered as part of the public domain by the Forest Service. The conflict between the Ganados del Valle sheep grazing co-op in the Tierra Amarilla Land Grant and environmentalists over grazing rights on public lands is another well-known example of such conflict. More recently (during 1996–97), an effort by some members of the New Mexico Wilderness Coalition to include Pueblo Indian (but ultimately not Hispano) communities in the management of proposed Bureau of Land Management (BLM) wilderness areas was defeated. The conflict within the environmental community over the historic rights of indigenous peoples led to a splintering of the coalition. (See D. G. Peña 1992; Pulido 1993, 1996, and chapter 4 in this volume; Wilmsen 1997; and Peña and Mondragon Valdéz 1998 for further discussion of these conflicts.)

9. The seven counties include Taos, Río Arriba, Mora, San Miguel, and Guadalupe in New Mexico and Conejos and Costilla in Colorado.

10. MacCameron 1994 provides evidence of localized overstocking by Hispano sheep growers during the colonial period. The foothill and montane meadows in areas adjacent to Santa Fe and Albuquerque were damaged by Hispano overstocking. MacCameron does not suggest that these conditions were replicated across the landscapes of the entire region. We are suggesting that economic, geographic, and cultural forces produced a wide variety of local patterns of ecological abuse and stewardship. On the practice of transhumance, see Pulido, chapter 4, this volume.

11. On the effects of logging destruction in the Southern Rockies ecosystem, see Herndon 1991 and Curry 1995. See also Jones and Grant 1996, Noss et al. 1994, Harris 1984, and Lansky 1992. Also consult the Web page maintained by the Culebra Coalition at http://bcn.boulder.co.us/environment/earthfirst/LaSierra/SanLuis.htm.

12. For example, Molycorp in Questa and Battle Mountain Gold in San Luis are both continuing sources of damage to water quality and habitat in the Red River and Culebra watersheds. See Peña and Gallegos 1993.

13. For a detailed critique of U. S. Forest Service policies in the Río Arriba, see Peña (in press).

14. Our own preliminary estimates on ski industry-related impacts follows (in acres of habitat and open-space land or farmland lost to infrastructure and real estate development): Santa Fe Ski Area (5,000 acres of habitat and 2,600 acres of farmland); Taos Ski Area (2,080 acres and 2,800 acres respectively); Red River Ski Area (860 acres and 1,300 acres); Angel Fire Ski Area (1240 acres and 640 acres); Ski Rio Ski Area (1800 acres but no lost farmland). These preliminary estimates are based on an admittedly conservative model that incorporates actual ski acreage with acres lost to auxiliary buildings and facilities such as sewage treatment, power generation and distribution, roads, highways, parking lots, and land with real estate developments (condos, lodges, second homes, restaurants, etc.) within ten miles of the core ski areas.

15. This pattern was repeated in most of northern New Mexico by the New Mexico State Highway Department through construction that eliminated all but a few traces of the original plaza structures that were the historic core of many Hispano communities. The roadway construction and modernization programs of the highway department led to the utter destruction of the architectural heart of most Hispano villages in northern New Mexico. This included the forcible relocation of many families from their multigenerational and ancestral homes, a process with its parallel in the "urban renewal" as "removal of the poor" strategies for "redevelopment" of the inner cities. Road and highway construction displaced the plaza as the social, economic, and cultural focal point of a community. For example, the sunny side of buildings in the plaza serves as the gathering place for *resolana,* a common space for the informal exchange of local news and knowledge (see Atencio 1987). Highway and road construction disrupt not just cultural landscapes, but natural ones as well, a point completely overlooked by most environmental historians of the bioregion.

16. The literature on the role of transnational capitalism in third-world environmental and cultural degradation is quite vast. DeBuys overlooks this body of research. See, for example, Blaikie and Brookfield 1987; Shiva 1988, 1990, 1992, and 1993a; Redclift 1987; Merchant 1992; Meyer and Moosang 1992; *The Ecologist* 1993; Pepper 1993; Nostrand 1992; Ghai and Vivian 1995. DeBuys might have consulted a body of distinguished research to acknowledge the role of capitalism in changing demographic, economic, and political dynamics associated with intensive industrial exploitation of natural resources; for examples see the pioneering research by Conklin 1954; Steward 1955; and Rappaport 1968 and 1979. He could also have consulted research on the ecological adaptations of Hispanos by scholars such as Oberg (1940), Harper, Cordova, and Oberg (1943),

Knowlton (1967 and 1969), Van Dresser (1964), and Rock (1976), all of whom contradict DeBuys's conclusions about Hispano environmental abuses.

17. For such analyses, see Martínez 1988b, Rodríguez 1987, 1990; D. G. Peña 1992; and Peña and Mondragon Valdéz 1998.

18. For more on the Sangre de Cristo land-grant struggle, see Peña and Mondragon Valdéz 1998.

19. The chair of Governor Romer's Sangre de Cristo Land Grant Commission invoked Wolf's arguments during the October 1995 meeting of the commission. A state wildlife commissioner later in the proceedings made similar arguments. Ironically, both are prominent Hispanic politicians.

20. Wolf's oversight is probably attributable to his not having interviewed any local persons about the "poaching raid." This seems to be a typical case of "remote" social commentary by someone completely unfamiliar with the locality that is the object of criticism.

21. For theoretical and historical critiques of the "tragedy of the commons," see Peña 1991 and Goldman 1993.

22. Jackson notes that nineteenth-century Euro-American explorers "believed the desert began somewhere in Kansas. To them, any region without trees and not adapted to traditional eastern methods of farming was desert" (1994, 23).

23. For comprehensive scientific discussions of the environmental effects of various logging practices, see Harris 1984; Grumbine 1992; Lansky 1992; Noss et al. 1994; Curry, Soulé, Peña, and McGowan 1996; and Jones and Grant 1996. See also Gardner (1951, 379–403).

24. For further varied discussion of the impact of Hispano agriculture on the environment in New Mexico, see Akins 1987; Baxter 1987, Baydo 1970, Carlson 1969, Deneven 1967, Eastman and Gray 1987, Humphrey 1953 and 1987, Jordan 1993, Nickerson 1945, Rowley 1985, Smith 1953, Widdison 1958, and Wooton 1908. An excellent review of this literature can be found in Wozniak 1995; see also Scurlock 1995.

25. In a more recent work, deBuys and Harris (1991) examine the cultural and natural landscapes of the Rio Trampas watershed in northern New Mexico. Even in this case, however, deBuys fails to acknowledge the relationship between *acequias* and biodiversity. For cultural ecological, ethnohistorical, and ethnoecological perspectives of this relationship, see respectively Van Ness 1987, Valdéz and Valdéz 1991, and Peña 1998.

26. The length and width of the *suertes* (riparian long-lots) varies considerably with influences from topography, social class background, land tenure practices (partible inheritance), and experiences with land loss and acquisition. In the case of the Culebra watershed, the original *suertes* granted to the Chicano settlers were

up to twenty or thirty miles long. See Carlson 1967, Stoller 1985, and Valdéz and Valdéz 1991. Over time, most of these long-lots have been severely fragmented through partible inheritance, title fraud, real estate development, encroachment, and other factors. Only a few examples remain of integrated long-lots that include all the varied topography of the original metes and bounds apportionments. For further discussion see Peña (in press).

27. The Rio Grande Bioregions Project is conducting this research. See Peña (in press).

28. Currently, we are studying the politics of place names and have found that there are significant differences between Hispanos' and Americans' means of arriving at place names. Generally, Hispanos tend to name places after characteristics or relationships embedded in the landscape features, while Americans tend to name places after important historical persons (military men, explorers, business leaders, etc.).

29. In another more recent book, *Crossing the Next Meridian,* Wilkinson (1993) examines the crucial role of political-economic power in his analysis of the four laws, or "Lords of the West," that shaped resource extraction policies in the intermountain West: the doctrine of prior appropriation, the Taylor Grazing Act, Forest Service timber-cut allocations, and the Mining Law of 1872. For commentary, see Quillen 1993.

30. See Levidow 1992; Peña 1992 and 1997a, 306–8; and Peña and Gallegos 1997, 85–91, for further discussion of the politics of environmental planning and regulation and the hegemony of market-oriented scientific discourse that excludes and denigrates local knowledge and citizen participation.

31. For more on the "biological core reserve–connecting corridor" or "biodiversity reserve" model, see Noss et al. 1994. For an example of this design applied to the Sangre de Cristo mountain range in southern Colorado, see Curry, Soulé, Peña, and McGowan 1996.

6 Ecofeminism and Chicano Environmental Struggles

Bridges across Gender and Race

Gwyn Kirk

The widespread and profoundly serious nature of environmental devastation means that ecological issues have great potential to bring people together across lines of race, class, and gender. My main focus in this chapter is on the interconnections, overlappings, disjunctions, and gaps between ecofeminist perspectives and Chicano environmental struggles. My interest in the Chicano environmental movement comes from networking with antimilitarist organizations in Texas and New Mexico and in living and teaching in Colorado and the San Francisco Bay area. I consider myself an insider with respect to ecofeminism; I want to be an ally to Chicano environmentalists. Here I explore common ground between ecofeminism and Chicano environmentalism to suggest what we can learn from each other. Neither ecofeminism nor Chicano environmentalism are unitary perspectives, of course, though I emphasize the points of comparison between them here, rather than their internal variations.

Ecofeminism: The Domination of Women and Nature

The term "ecofeminism" was first used by a group of feminists in France who established the Ecology-Feminism Center in 1974, based on their analysis of connections between male-dominated social institutions and the destruction of the physical environment (d'Eaubonne 1994, 174–97). A few years later in the United States, Susan Griffin and Carolyn Merchant each explored the connection between the domination of women and the domination of nature, where nature is often feminized and sexualized as in "virgin forest," "the rape of the earth," or "penetrating" the wilderness (see Griffin 1978; Merchant 1980). But the domination, I came to realize, applies more broadly than just to women and the nonhuman world. Patriarchal capitalist systems also involve exploitation based on race and class. The creation of inferiors and superiors is a core mechanism underlying systems of oppression including sexism, racism, militarism, colonialism, and the destruction of ecological systems. Val Plumwood argues that such hierarchies are mutually reinforcing and should be thought of as an interlocking set (Plumwood 1993, 41–68). Moreover, the capitalist economic system turns sources of life—whether forests, seeds, or women's bodies—into resources that are objectified, controlled, and used (Mies and Shiva 1993, 22–35; Shiva 1988, 1–37). Potentially, an ecofeminist perspective links the oppression of women, racism, economic exploitation, and the ecological crisis. It is concerned with personal and planetary survival and makes connections between the politics of food, health, population, land, development, and security. It is a politics of opposition and resistance as well as a politics of reconstruction and hope.[1]

In the United States, ecofeminism has activist antecedents in antinuclear and antimilitarist campaigns, workplace and community organizing, and the women's liberation movement of the 1970s. Various ecofeminist writers bring their own distinctive frameworks to the subject. Ynestra King emphasizes ecofeminism as political theory and practice. Starhawk and Charlene Spretnak give a central place to earth-centered spirituality and goddess reverence (King 1983c, 118–129; Spretnak 1990, 3–14; and Starhawk 1990, 73–86). Animal rights feminists emphasize the oppression of animals (Collard 1988; Adams 1990; Gaard 1993). Vandana Shiva critiques Western reductionist science and its counterpart—unsustainable development. She promotes traditional Indian concepts of sustainable agriculture and forestry (Shiva 1988, 55–217; Mies and Shiva 1993, 164–73).

This diversity of approaches raises the question of whether there is a sufficiently consistent, intellectually coherent, identifiable ecofeminist perspective, and many academics claim that there is not. Women of color critics argue that, as with much Western feminism, U.S. ecofeminism emphasizes gender over race and class (Smith 1983, 581–92; Amos and Parmer 1984, 3–19; Omolade 1989, 171–89). Some Third World feminists argue that ecofeminism has no material basis (Agarwal 1992, 119–

57). Some leftist radicals and socialist feminists reject ecofeminism as synonymous with goddess worship or on the grounds that it assumes women are essentially closer to nature than men (Biehl 1991). These criticisms are substantial, and some feminists who are concerned with environmental issues avoid the term ecofeminism because they consider it a liability (Seager 1993).

Worldwide, compared to men, women disproportionately are involved in campaigning around environmental issues at a grassroots level. I do not see women as somehow closer to nature than men, as is sometimes argued, or as having an essentially nurturing, caring nature. Rather, I see women's environmental activism as an extension of their roles as daughters, sisters, wives, and mothers, caring for families and communities. I agree that ecofeminists need to integrate issues of race and class with gender, and this chapter makes some suggestions for such integration. Monica Sjöö and Barbara Mor (1987) argue that all true spirituality is profoundly political and that all meaningful politics has a spiritual dimension. Many Native American, African American, and Chicano environmentalists do not seem to polarize spirituality and politics as some ecofeminists do (Sanchez 1993, 207–28). Even the most secular leftist theorists and activists derive their passion for social and economic justice from a fundamental *belief,* for example, in people's equality. As a way of resolving these theoretical problems, I argue for a *materialist ecological feminism* that focuses on the social and material reasons for women's environmental concerns and activism, that integrates gender, race, and class in its analysis, and that has an integrated view of spiritual politics (Kirk 1994, 69–89; 1997b, 345–63). This is what I mean when I use the term "ecofeminism."

Ecofeminist Practices

Such a broad, integrative body of ideas does not translate into one particular political practice, but antimilitarist protests such as the Women's Pentagon Action in the United States in the early 1980s and the peace camp at Greenham Common in England are good examples of ecofeminism in action (Cook and Kirk 1983; King 1983b, 40–46; Kirk 1989, 263–80). These protests focused on militarism as central to the oppression of women and the destruction of the nonhuman world. Military organizations cause more ecological destruction than any other social institutions.

They have massive budgets that might otherwise be used for socially useful programs, particularly those that support women and children who are the majority of the poor. The military generates a culture of violence that manifests itself in everything from war toys to video games and films. It involves the construction of a "militarized masculinity" (Enloe 1993, 52), especially during basic training, that connects violence and sexuality, that sees rape as a weapon of war, and pornography and sexual servicing as an integral part of military culture. At root, the military organizations are sexist and racist institutions (Reardon 1985; Omolade 1989, 171–89). The Women's Pentagon Action Unity Statement exemplifies the feminist critique of militarization. Although Grace Paley was a major influence on this piece, it was always understood that it was the outcome of a collective process and is never attributed to her.

During the 1980s, many thousands of women in North America, western Europe, Australia, and New Zealand participated in nonviolent antimilitarist protests. They maintained an oppositional presence outside military bases and weapons manufacturing plants, sometimes blockading the gates to close down these facilities. At the U.S. Air Force base at Greenham Common in England, for example, women climbed over and cut down the fence as a way of saying that we should not separate ourselves from military policy, that what goes on inside military bases should be open to public scrutiny. These actions manifest a deep concern for a life-sustaining future by using political confrontation and public education. This (largely white) women's peace movement led some commentators to suggest that a new global movement was taking root, but it did not sustain its early growth (Kamel 1985, 1). Ebbs and flows of activity are characteristic of informal organizing, where each person chooses what form her involvement will take and there are no paid staff. Such informal organization can suffer from strong personalities, from leadership that is not accountable and therefore hard to challenge, or from personality conflicts.

Differences of political opinion probably cannot and should not be "processed" away. Many who were previously involved in women's peace groups saw the myriad connections between militarism and many other issues. Some moved on to become involved in rape crisis centers, domestic violence work, campaigns for reproductive rights, Central America solidarity work, and environmental projects and protests. The movement was also limited by its theoretical perspectives. Fundamental connections between militarism and the oppression of women were emphasized, but the significance of racism and class oppression received little attention. Women of color critiqued these antimilitarist movements as racist, and this issue ultimately divided both the Women's Pentagon Action and Greenham networks.

Current ecofeminist practices in the United States include long-term women's land projects (Cheney 1985), ecofeminist newsletters and study groups, and animal rights organizing. Some ecofeminist writers and researchers work with local and regional activist groups and contribute to national and international debates. Examples include feminist work on industrial and environmental health; critiques of reproductive technology and genetic engineering; critiques of environmental approaches to population control; the development of a women's agenda for the U.N. Conference on Environment and Development in June 1992; and the promotion of economic development projects that serve women.[2] These projects draw on a variety of overlapping and somewhat disjointed frameworks and are not always explicitly defined as ecofeminist, especially in view of the problems associated with the term.

Those most affected by degraded physical environments in the United States are disproportionately women and children, particularly African Americans, Native Americans, and Latinas. Due to the gendered division of labor between home and work, women have a long-standing history of involvement in community organizing and urban politics — campaigning against bad housing conditions, high rents, unsafe streets, lead in gasoline, toxic dumps, and so on — and much urban environmental activism can be seen in this context (Cockburn 1977; McCourt 1977; Gilkes 1988; Krauss 1993). Sixty percent of the delegates to the First National People of Color Conference in October 1991 were women.

Many women first get involved in environmental activism because they become ill, or from the experience of caring for a sick relative, often a child. Women have persisted in raising questions and searching for plausible explanations for such illnesses. They have publicized their findings and taken on corporations and governmental agencies responsible for contamination (Zeff, Love, and Stults 1989; Pardo 1990; Krauss 1993; Gibbs

1995). In this process they are often ridiculed as "hysterical housewives" and their research trivialized as emotional and unscholarly. By contrast, Lin Nelson (1990, 172–87) honors this work as kitchen-table science.

The gap between much ecofeminist theorizing and women's grassroots activism has been significant, despite feminist aspirations to integrate theory and practice. Ecofeminists have often not taken into account the experiences and perspectives of many working-class women — Chicanas, Native Americans, and African Americans — working on ecological issues in the United States. Ecofeminism has been irrelevant for such activists. It is largely the preserve of writers and scholars, albeit often on the margins of the academy in precarious part-time or temporary positions. This leads to an "activism of scholarship" — by no means insignificant, as I suggested above — which does not often connect directly with the reality of life for many women organizing around environmental issues in their living and working spaces. Some ecofeminist writers and the editors of ecofeminist anthologies have attempted to bridge this gap by including a few articles by women of color, implying that these contributors subscribe to ecofeminist ideas. This appropriation may be inadvertent, but it is thoughtless and unscholarly. Those of us who write and teach about ecofeminism need to remedy the class, race, and ethnic limitations of our perspectives so as to build authentic alliances that can cross race and class lines.

Chicano Environmental Struggles

As evidenced by the work in this anthology, the Chicano environmental movement involves the struggle for economic and environmental justice, a demand for healthful living and working conditions, increased democracy in local communities and workplaces, and the maintenance of traditional agricultural practices that link ecological and cultural survival. This movement is based in the rural communities of southern Colorado, northern New Mexico, and Texas, in urban centers in the Southwest and California, and along the border between the United States and Mexico. Its roots are in civil rights organizing, labor unions, land-grant movements, *acequia* organizations that maintain collective irrigation systems, social-justice organizations, and liberation theology. Tactics include demonstrations and rallies, public education, research and monitoring of toxic sites, preparing and presenting expert testimony to government agencies such as water court or the Board of Mines, reclaiming land through direct action, and maintaining and teaching traditional agricultural practices. Particular organizations draw on these different strands in various ways, depending on their membership, geographical location, and key concerns.

The conviction that ecological, economic, and cultural survival are inextricably intertwined is an underlying theme within this movement. I briefly discuss a number of organizations below as examples of the scope and focus of Chicano ecoactivism. Some of these are multiracial and multicultural organizations, but Chicanos are very active in them.

Two multicultural coalitions comprised mainly of Chicanos, together with Native Americans and African Americans, are the Southwest Organizing Project (SWOP), based in Albuquerque, and the Southwest Network for Environmental and Economic Justice (SNEEJ), based in Albuquerque and Austin. Key issues for both organizations include toxins in communities of color, clean air and water, and labor struggles. A women's union, Fuerza Unida (United Force) is involved in struggles against plant closings and relocations by Levi Strauss in San Antonio. The Southwest Organizing Project is active at local, regional, and national levels and has taken a leading role in confronting the major established U.S. environmental organizations (e.g., the National Audubon Society, National Wildlife Federation, The Nature Conservancy, Sierra Club, Greenpeace, Wilderness Society, and the Environmental Defense Fund) with environmental racism.

Along with SWOP, SNEEJ was a founding organization in the First National People of Color Environmental Leadership Summit, held in Washington, D.C., in October 1991. This organization is also involved with environmental problems in the U.S.–Mexican border area as a result of *maquiladoras,* industrial production through subcontractors to U.S.-based corporations, and broader questions of economic democracy and social justice (Peña 1997a). For example, economic conversion from military production is an explicit goal. Through its connections with the Texas Farmworkers Union, SNEEJ is concerned with farmworkers' labor rights and campaigns against pesticides. Another important influence in SNEEJ comes from activists associated with Texas Center for Policy Studies, a left-liberal think tank that supports groups such as the Coalition for Justice in the Maquiladoras, an umbrella organization based in Austin and

Brownsville that works on environmental and labor issues in the maquila-doras. The coalition provides technical assistance to *maquila* workers wanting to organize against toxins and other hazards in the workplace. It actively monitors toxic waste discharges along the U.S.–Mexican border, and it pressures the Environmental Protection Agency and its Mexican counterpart, SEMARNAP (Secretary of Ecology, Oceans, and National Re-sources) for support.

Two local organizations in the Southwest concerned with the toxic waste impacts of industrial mining are Concerned Citizens of Questa (New Mexico), an all-male group comprised of local farmers, ranchers, educators, and residents opposed to the Molycorp mine; and the Costilla County Committee for Environmental Soundness (CES), based in San Luis, Colorado. The Committee for Environmental Soundness draws its mem-bership from similar groups, as well as land-grant activists, business peo-ple, and clergy; it also has key participation by women. It opposes the ex-pansion of the Battle Mountain Gold Mine and is active at state, regional, and national levels in leading opposition to the expansion of cyanide leach mining and milling in the Southwest (Peña and Gallegos 1993). Members of CES are involved in efforts to promote sustainable agriculture through producer cooperatives, to revive artisan crafts, and to advocate for ecolog-ically sound land-use planning. Some activists are involved in efforts to keep land in agricultural use and to protect natural areas, especially the sensitive headwaters of the acequia network. More recently, Chicano farmers, acequia groups, and land-grant activists have developed ties with radical environmentalists. As discussed in chapter 5, Chicano social justice activists in San Luis joined forces with Ancient Forest Rescue, Earth First!, and Greenpeace ecoactivists to form the Culebra Coalition, a multiracial grassroots group involved in an antilogging campaign to protect the wa-tersheds in the land-grant communities of southern Colorado.[3]

Given the crucial importance of water as a political issue in the South-west and in California, many Chicano environmentalists are involved in struggles to protect traditional water rights. Every watershed in northern New Mexico and southern Colorado has acequia associations that are directly involved in such struggles, but several regional organizations have emerged to focus on water rights. The Rio Grande Institute in Embudo, New Mexico, is a research organization made up of land-grant activists, researchers, and water lawyers, the majority of whom are Chicanos and Pueblo Indians. The institute advocates the protection of acequia water rights and clean water. The Water Information Network, a mainly Native American and Chicano umbrella organization in New Mexico and the Greater San Juan Basin area, provides technical assistance to grassroots organizations such as acequia associations and other water users. It concentrates on the protection of water rights and clean water and on the control of, and resistance to, strip mining.

The Taos Valley Acequia Association (TVAA), like many other acequia organizations, works to protect indigenous water rights in the Upper Rio Grande watershed. Key issues here range from protecting water quality and quantity from the effects of development — condos in the Taos Ski Basin, for example — to discussions about the designation of the Rio Grande from the Colorado border to Taos as a national natural resource conservation area, an issue that pits the white-water rafting industry and other recreational users against farmers and ranchers. In San Luis, the Costilla County Conservancy District (CCCD) and its Acequia Advisory Board have played a major role in Colorado water politics, working against the interbasin transfers or changes from agricultural to industrial and residential uses of water.

In California, Colorado, and Texas, many Chicanos are agricultural workers. A report of the University of California-Davis Pesticide Farm Safety Center advisory panel noted that chemically dependent, industrialized, corporate agricultural production is as dangerous to workers' health as mining.[4] The United Farmworkers of America, based in northern California and founded by the late Cesar Chavez and Dolores Huerta, veterans of the 1960s Chicano Movement, has negotiated collective bargaining agreements between farmworkers and growers and has also initiated some successful experiments in cooperative production. Currently, a key organizing issue is pesticides, and long-standing boycotts of table grapes have pushed growers to agree to contracts that safeguard workers' health.[5]

Chicanos are also involved in urban struggles around environmental racism, especially in Colorado, New Mexico, Texas, and California. The Center for Third World Organizing (CTWO), based in Oakland with a regional office in Denver, is a multicultural community organization with a strong presence of Latinos and African Americans. It focuses on toxic wastes and racial issues[6] and in Denver has been active against the ASARCO medical-waste incinerator through Neighbors for a Toxic-Free Community. In Oakland, CTWO is active against lead poisoning together with People United for a Better Oakland (PUEBLO). In Kettleman City, California, People for Clean Air and Water has opposed Waste Management, Inc., which planned to open a toxic waste processing and storage facility in the town. Local activists are predominantly Latino and African American residents — mainly women concerned with family health problems. Other members come from social justice organizations, especially CTWO in the nearby Bay Area. In Los Angeles, Chicanos have been active in numerous environmental justice campaigns through organizations such as the Labor/Community Strategy Center, Concerned Citizens of South Central Los Angeles, and the Mothers of East Los Angeles (Hamilton 1993, 67–75; Pardo 1990, 1–7).

Also in an urban context, SWOP and SNEEJ have more recently led a grassroots social and environmental justice campaign against the Intel Corporation, which recently built one of the world's largest semiconductor plants in what was once a rural farming area north of Albuquerque, New Mexico. Activists from SWOP and SNEEJ have remained opposed to Intel's plans to mine the groundwater aquifer for use in its industrial production processes.[7] They have also focused on problems related to environmental hazards as well as health and safety in the workplace and have worked with area native nations affected by the presence of the sprawling factory and subdivision developments.

Beyond antitoxin struggles in the cities and among farmworkers, Chicano activists are involved in initiating and supporting ecologically sound economic development projects such as Ganados del Valle/Tierra Wools in the Tierra Amarilla land-grant area of northern New Mexico (discussed by Pulido, chapter 4). This worker cooperative has raised large flocks of Churro sheep, well suited to local conditions. This hardy breed was nearly extinct as commercial ranchers favored other breeds. Ganados del Valle/ Tierra Wools produces high-quality, handwoven woolen rugs and clothing and organically produced lamb. The weavers design and undertake their own work, uniting mental and manual labor. This project seeks to integrate cultural revival and conservation, workplace democracy, and social justice. It also sponsors Pastores, a general store and meeting place that sells a wide variety of locally produced craftwork.[8] In Colorado's San Luis

Valley, the Culebra Cooperative Growers organization is involved in promoting organic farming among Chicanos and is working to increase the number of younger farmers and women farmers. Plans are afoot among co-op members to establish a Chicano farmer-to-farmer land-trust organization. This organization will acquire land for landless farmers and work to protect open space, farmland, and wildlife habitat from threats posed by extractive industries and subdivision developments.

Women play key roles in Chicano environmental organizing in urban and rural settings. Though many Chicano environmental and civil rights organizations have broad agendas, the women activists within these organizations are particularly involved in carrying forward feminist and environmental issues. Women hold influential positions on the coordinating committee of the Southwest Organizing Project, for example. They are predominant in People for Clean Air and Water (Kettleman City, California), Concerned Citizens of South Central Los Angeles, and the Mothers of East Los Angeles. Women had leadership roles in the Taos Valley "condo wars," and they continue to be active in organizations such as CES, LRC, and CTWO in Denver. The weavers of Tierra Wools are women, and María Varela has played a key role in initiating this project.

In rural areas, Chicanas work on family garden plots, planting, harvesting, and processing fruit and vegetables for home use. As ethnobotanists, some women know the backcountry in great detail because they go there at different seasons to gather herbs for medicinal purposes. *Curanderas*, traditional healers, continue to work with herbal remedies (Perrone, Stockel, and Kreuger 1989). They oppose the institutional framework of medicine and acquire their knowledge through female oral traditions. In Chicano bioregional narrative, women are the main storytellers.

Gender, then, is highly significant in Chicano environmentalism, but this is not a concept of gender separated from race and class perspectives. Chicana activists·see their identity as women integrated with their ethnic identity. Race as compared to gender is just as much, if not more, a place of empowerment for them. Malia Davis's respondents, for example, struggle with the difficulties of being strong women in a male-dominated culture and sometimes find themselves in conflict with their culture's traditional gender roles (see Davis, chapter 7). But such activists are not interested in separating themselves from the men of their community, and they frame their activism, as women, in class and race-conscious ways.

Ecofeminism and Chicano Environmental Struggles: Common Ground?

Despite the considerable differences in emphasis and approach suggested above, ecofeminists and Chicano environmental activists share crucial common ground. In this section, I will explore some of the commonalities in perspective and struggles before closing with some reflections on future prospects for cooperation across bridges of race, class, and gender.

Understanding the Economic Roots of Environmental Devastation

Many ecofeminists and Chicano environmental activists see environmental degradation as intrinsically related to the process of capital accumulation. The economic goal of profit entails great environmental damage with an all-too-familiar list of consequences, including, for example, air and water pollution, clear-cutting of timber, a loss of water in underground aquifers through the use of center-pivot irrigation systems, and the dereliction of inner-city areas. Environmental quality is often pitted against jobs by corporate employers, this on the argument that "cleaner" production processes are more costly. But toxic production methods are only part of the problem. An economy based on making a profit rather than meeting people's basic needs generates polluted environments, stress, and over-crowding as an integral part of its day-to-day operations. In rural areas traditional Chicano land-based culture is under pressure to assimilate into Anglo-American economic life and values, or become commodified through tourism, one of the few economic opportunities for Chicanos in the Southwest.[9]

Addressing Interlocking Structures of Domination

For ecofeminists, environmental degradation parallels the domination of "others" under patriarchal capitalism, particularly women and people of color, as mentioned above. Chicano environmentalists also see environmental issues in the wider context of race, class, and cultural oppression. Many ecofeminists and Chicano ecojustice activists offer incisive critiques of mainstream environmentalism as exemplified by the Big Ten environmental organizations as well as Earth First! and other "radical" environmental groups. Mainstream and radical approaches generally have remained blind to issues of gender, race, and class, and are often antiurban. They appear to have no analysis of structures of dominance among people in capitalist, patriarchal societies. As its name implies, Earth First! is more interested in "saving the earth" than in safeguarding the human population. This biocentric view, which emphasizes the intricate ecological connections of the entire biosphere, has led to outrageous claims — for example, that if AIDS didn't exist, it would have had to be invented, or that starving people in Africa should be left to die so that the human population can be brought back into balance with the carrying capacity of the land (Miss Ann Thropy 1991).

Currently, right-wing politicians are using radical environmentalist rhetoric to oppose immigration into the United States and Europe; they argue that immigration is a drain on natural resources and increases pollution (Schapiro 1992, 6–7; Political Ecology Group 1996, 37–38). This biocentric view also prevails within the largely white bioregional movement, which emphasizes decentralization, agricultural and economic self-sufficiency within bioregions, and a strongly developed attachment to place (Sale 1989). Many ecofeminists and Chicano environmentalists are critical of this strand of bioregionalism. Bioregionalism is not specifically committed to women's liberation or to opposing racism, and it has no principles for dealing with social and economic inequality within a bioregion. The assumption is that decentralized, small-scale regional structures and a shift from a human-centered to a biocentered perspective will solve all our environmental problems. Without an explicit social ethics this seems highly unlikely.

Reinforcing Connections between People and Nature

Nature is not just something out there to be experienced on occasional backpacking trips to remote locations. At its worst, this separation of people and nature produces a "nature good, people bad" view of the world, where nature is seen in terms of a pastoral fantasy, a romance with a virgin, feminized wilderness — vulnerable, innocent, and weak — and where protecting her draws on old militaristic iconography (King 1987).

Amongst many middle-class white environmentalists, wilderness is not thought of as the (home)land of indigenous peoples but as a place for city dwellers' leisuretime enjoyment.

Both ecofeminists and Chicano environmentalists see people as intimately connected to the nonhuman world in the most profound, yet mundane way: through the water we drink, the air we breathe, the food we eat, and our own bodily processes. As embodied human beings, we are part of the continuum of life. To imply a separation between people and nonhuman nature is to deny this very real day-to-day connection with nature through our sensuous, lived experience. This denial is also poor politics. Rainforests do not vote or engage in political activism, people do; and people should not be condemned as irredeemable if they are to change environmentally damaging habits and the economic structures that produce them. The connection between people and nonhuman nature cannot be overemphasized, and it needs to be remade for many in industrialized countries, perhaps especially those who live in urban areas.

Challenging Institutionalized Science

Starting with the ground-breaking work of Rachel Carson (1962) on the environmental dangers of chemical pesticides, there is a wealth of academic work by U.S. feminist scientists and philosophers of science that challenges the alleged objectivity and neutral values of institutionalized science and its masculine biases in methodology, content, and purposes (e.g., Fausto-Sterling 1985; Fox Keller 1985; Harding 1986; Haraway 1989; Tuana 1989). Many ecofeminists and Chicano environmental activists see institutionalized science as a major contributor to ecological destruction, indeed to the death of nature, as Carolyn Merchant (1980) put it; they offer trenchant critiques of models of development, science, and technology driven by an exploitative economy that puts profits before human needs.[10] Both perspectives are highly critical of the prevailing scientific approach which assumes that there will always be a "technical fix." In the context of Himalayan India, Vandana Shiva (1988 and 1993b) writes of ethnoscience, compared to the institutionalized science introduced by British imperial power, and about how sustainable agricultural practices are learned and passed on by indigenous farmers from generation to generation. Joni Seager (1993, 194–198) emphasizes the importance of "home-collected information" concerning toxins, information pieced together by U.S. women.

These critiques raise important questions about what constitutes valid knowledge and who can claim expertise and authoritativeness, key points also in Chicano critiques of science. Ecofeminists and Chicano environmentalists need to define research goals that will be of value to them and to policy makers rather than posit abstract notions of scholarship supposedly uncontaminated by political concerns (Peña and Gallegos 1997). Such a cooperative undertaking requires contexts where working relationships among activists, researchers, and policy makers can develop and where students can learn this approach by observing it in practice. In addition there need to be effective means for getting useful information out to ordinary people so that the knowledge is readily accessible.[11]

A Politics of Reconstruction

Ecofeminists and Chicano environmentalists share a concern for change. The goal of their struggles is not to pursue the liberal ideal of equal opportunity, an equal piece of a rotten carcinogenic pie (King 1987). Nor is it to buy "green" products, where the emphasis is still on consumption (Hynes 1991; Mies 1993). Instead, the goal is to transform relationships among people and between people and the nonhuman world, so that there is the possibility that our children's children will inherit a healthier planet. Ganados del Valle is just one exemplary Chicano project. In discussing women's peace activism above, I emphasized protest and resistance; but while saying NO to destruction and violence, women were also saying YES to life-affirming, sustainable ways of living. These visions are often fragmentary, and they are usually worked out in small-scale projects that are beset by the contradictions of trying to create genuinely alternative models in the dominant economic and cultural context. Examples include community gardens, farmers' markets, cooperative organic farming, seed banks that safeguard genetic diversity, ecohousing, recycling centers, and renovated land and buildings, especially in blighted post-industrial cities. Such a vision of transformation requires a much broader definition of wealth, a definition that goes beyond material amenities to place value on health, physical energy, security, time, skill, creativity, love, community support, a connection to one's history and cultural heritage, and a sense of belonging to a place and time.

Integrating Race, Class, and Gender

As I suggested above, U.S. ecofeminists need to place more emphasis on integrating race, ethnicity, and class with our analysis of gender and ecology; we have much to learn from Chicana environmental activists in this regard. This anthology is an important educational resource for ecofeminists. We need to know more about organizing for environmental justice, about Chicano land ethics, the connections between ecological and cultural survival, and about ecologically sound economic development projects currently being pursued in the United States.

A Sense of Place

A "sense of place" is also an important concept that few ecofeminists address, perhaps because many of us live in urban areas or are relatively mobile. Writing in the context of biocentered bioregionalism, Judith Plant (1990a, 1990b) is one of the few feminists who focuses on home, a place that has often been seen as limiting, oppressive, and unsafe for women. Elsewhere in this volume, Devon Peña argues that by emphasizing lococentrism — identity tied to locality — rather than biocentrism, activists can perhaps begin to avoid some of the problems associated with more conventional varieties of bioregionalism. He states that Chicano bioregional narratives locate us in a moral space that is also the physical space where we live. This assumes a profound shared connection to a particular place and to the people and other species who jointly inhabit it; within the experience of such sharing, people can be relied upon to act ethically toward one another as well as live in environmentally sound ways.

For people who have lived and farmed in one area for many generations, such as Chicano families in San Luis and Tierra Amarilla, or for extremely tight-knit urban neighborhoods, lococentrism may make sense. But this reformulation raises a number of questions. How do you learn this place-centered morality? Do you have to be born into it? City dwellers have little direct control over major environmental issues — where their water comes from, how it is used, whether it is polluted and by whom, where their food comes from, how it is produced, who their neighbors are, and so on. The exigencies of the job market mean that many people in the United States move several times in their adult lives. For many city dwellers there is little sense of connection to the land, which may be polluted by lead and other heavy metals or covered with asphalt. There is often little sense of the history of any given place. How does one develop this kind of lococentric consciousness as a city resident, as a newcomer to a particular area, as someone who either chooses or is forced to move regularly? How can one guarantee that this lococenteredness does not become xenophobic, homophobic, racist, or sexist? On the other hand, how do those who already have a "sense of place" learn to understand those who leave rural communities such as San Luis, especially young people, for what they perceive to be greater freedom and opportunities of urban life?

A sense of place needs to become a much wider concept that encompasses a sense of being connected to the whole planet so that I am not tempted to respect my place at the expense of yours, which gets back to the divisions of "not-in-my-backyard" thinking. I am not convinced that lococenteredness necessarily comes with a guarantee of social ethics any more than biocenteredness does.

Sexism as a Key Mechanism of Oppression

Ecofeminists can offer Chicano environmental activists an understanding of how the domination of nature is linked to the domination of women, and how sexism is a key mechanism of oppression with parallels to racial and class oppression. Understanding the parallels means seeing women's liberation as an integral part of creating a sustainable future, a point very often missing from Chicano environmental perspectives to date. Women of color often comment that white women conveniently ignore our privilege as white while emphasizing our oppression as women. To build bridges across gender and race for white feminists means understanding that we cannot separate race and ethnicity from gender. We have to make alliances with Chicanas and Chicanos, and in the process we may have to deal with what we consider to be sexist assumptions and behavior.

Ecofeminists and Chicano environmentalists can build on common ground in many practical ways. Ecofeminists need to consider how to support Chicano struggles against incinerators and toxic waste dumps, or against hazardous work conditions, whether in factories or on farms. They also need to support Chicano organic farming methods and ecologically sound development projects in inner cities and rural areas. It is important to make a distinction between a politics of solidarity, implying support for others in struggle, and a politics of engagement where we are struggling together — the "subversive kin" of this anthology — and hopefully becoming part of a wider, oppositional politics.

Subversive Kin: Toward a Wider Movement for Environmental Justice

I have argued elsewhere that a wider movement for environmental justice needs alliances between ecofeminists and environmental justice activists (Kirk 1997a). For such collaboration to take place, people need to have some basis for knowing one another, some shared stake in the community, and the prospect for developing trust despite differences in culture, ethnicity, and class. Such a coming together requires projects where people can work together as well as the development of a shared political culture and language, with a key role for individuals whose experience and connections enable them to cross lines of gender, race, ethnicity, and class.

One possible setting for such alliances may be through Women's Studies and Chicano Studies programs, with their origins in the women's liberation and Chicano movements of the 1960s and 1970s. These programs focus on the lived experiences of women and Chicanos respectively, through interdisciplinary studies that draw from literature, history, language, art, the natural and social sciences, religion, and law. They have generated a growing literature and are often on the cutting edge of academic disciplines, especially in the humanities and social sciences, though their significance is usually not accepted by established white male scholars. These programs offer critiques of current curriculum and pedagogy as well as evaluations of what constitutes valid scholarship and knowledge. Indeed, they repudiate the division between scholarship and activism that generally exists in academia. These programs, therefore, share a marginalized status and are most often poorly funded. They are under continual pressure to conform to traditional ways of teaching (even though the traditional ways are often the least effective for student learning) and to turn out scholarly work that is judged by very limited criteria.

I believe these pressures are designed to separate Women's Studies and Chicano Studies from their underlying social movements, that being the price of access to the academy (hooks 1992). I argue for a closer collaboration between these programs as a means of strengthening both and becoming an important alliance in an academic world that deals with multicultural education, for the most part, in highly token ways. By contrast, women of color have challenged Women's Studies programs to look at women's experiences from an integrated perspective that includes race, class, and gender, and to honor both the crucial differences among women and the things they hold in common. The work of Chicana scholars, writers, and activists provides an important bridge, as both Women's and Chicano Studies continue to redefine relevant notions of activist scholarship.

Issues such as environmental health, food production, and making cities livable are just three examples of environmental concerns that affect many people across lines of race, class, and gender. Pesticide poisoning of Chicano farmworkers, for example, should also be the concern of consumers who are buying contaminated produce. Middle-class mothers were responsible for getting the pesticide Alar banned in the United States in the late 1980s because it damages children's health, but they demonstrated no apparent awareness or concern for the health of farmworkers who had been exposed to it in their work (Mott and Snyder 1987; Garland 1989). Buying organically grown produce is an option for some people, though the produce is usually more expensive and not always widely available. But this sidesteps the issue of the farmworkers' health. Much more needs to be done to build alliances between farmworkers and consumer groups. An example might be campaigns to improve conditions for farmworkers, support for farmers' markets and producer/consumer cooperatives, and increase public education concerning the dangers of pesticides. Many ecofeminists are interested in holistic health based on a wholesome diet and the use of herbal remedies. Few of us were taught the medicinal properties of plants as we grew up, and we need to learn this lost information (Potts 1988).

Another environmental concern is the pollution of the Rio Grande by maquiladora factories along the U.S.–Mexican border. The global economy is structured so that transnational corporations exploit favorable production conditions in third-world countries with a fraction of the labor costs they would incur in the United States or western Europe, and without stringent environmental restrictions. Mexico is in a unique position in this regard, because it shares a border with the United States. Little explicit ecofeminist work has been done on this in the United States, but feminists in Mexico have been working through the Centro de Orientación de la Mujer Obrera (Center for the Orientation of Women Workers), the Coalition for Justice in the Maquiladoras, and the Centro del Obrero Fronterizo (Center for the Border Worker). There is great potential for collaboration among ecofeminists, maquila workers, labor activists, and Chicano environmentalists.[12]

Ecofeminists and Chicano environmental activists have crucial experiences and insights to bring to a broader movement for environmental justice. As subversive kin, we need to create an oppositional politics in the United States that radically challenges white-dominated, patriarchal, global capitalism and includes agendas and strategies for change to bring about sustainable living.

UNITY STATEMENT OF THE WOMEN'S PENTAGON ACTION (ABRIDGED)

We are gathering at the Pentagon on November 16 because we fear for our lives. We fear for the life of this planet, our Earth, and the life of the children who are our human future.

We are mostly women who come from the northeastern region of our United States. We are city women who know the wreckage and fear of city streets, we are country women who grieve the loss of the small farm and have lived on the poisoned earth. We are young and older, we are married, single, lesbian. We live in different kinds of households: in groups, families, alone; some are single parents.

We work at a variety of jobs. We are students, teachers, factory workers, office workers, lawyers, farmers, doctors, builders, waitresses, weavers, poets, engineers, homeworkers, electricians, artists, blacksmiths. We are all daughters and sisters.

We have come here to mourn and rage and defy the Pentagon because it is the workplace of the imperial power which threatens us all. . . .

The very same men, the same legislative committees that offer trillions of dollars to the Pentagon, have brutally cut day care, children's lunches, battered women's shelters. The same men have concocted the Family Protection Act which will mandate the strictly patriarchal family and thrust federal authority into our home life. They are preventing the passage of ERA's simple statement and supporting the Human Life Amendment which will deprive all women of choice and many women of life itself.

We are in the hands of men whose power and wealth have separated them from the reality of daily life and from the imagination. We are right to be afraid.

At the same time our cities are in ruins, bankrupt; they suffer the devastation of war. Hospitals are closed, our schools deprived of books and teachers. Our Black and Latino youth are without decent work. They will be forced, drafted to become the cannon fodder for the very power that oppresses them. Whatever help the poor receive is cut or withdrawn to feed the Pentagon which needs about $500,000,000 a day for its murderous health. It extracted $157 billion last year from our own tax money, $1,800 from a family of four.

With this wealth our scientists are corrupted; more than 40% work in government and corporate laboratories that refine the methods for destroying or deforming life. The lands of the Native American people have been turned into radioactive rubble in order to enlarge the nuclear warehouse. The uranium of South Africa, necessary to the nuclear enterprise, enriches the white minority and encourages the vicious system of racist oppression and war. . . .

We women are gathering because life on the precipice is intolerable. We want to know what anger in these men, what fear, which can only be satisfied by destruction, what coldness of heart and ambition drives their days.

What is it that we women need for our ordinary lives, that we want for ourselves and also for our sisters in new nations and old colonies who suffer the white man's exploitation and too often the oppression of their own countrymen?

We want enough good food, decent housing, communities with clean air and water, good care for our children while we work. We want work that is useful to a sensible society. . . .

We want health care which respects and understands our bodies. . . .

We want education for children which tells the true story of our women's lives, which describes the earth as our home to be cherished, to be fed as well as harvested.

We want to be free from violence in our streets and in our houses. One in every three of us will be raped in her lifetime. . . .

We want the right to have or not to have children — we do not want gangs of politicians and medical men to say we must be sterilized for the country's good. We know that this technique is the racists' method for controlling populations. . . .

We do not want to be drafted into the army. We do not want our young brothers drafted. We want them equal with us.

We want to see the pathology of racism ended in our time. It has been the imperial arrogance of white male power that has separated us from the suffering and wisdom of our sisters in Asia, Africa, South America and in our own country. Many North American women look down on the minority nearest them: the Black, the Hispanic, the Jew, the Native American, the Asian, the immigrant. Racism has offered them privilege and convenience; they often fail to see that they themselves have bent to the unnatural authority and violence of men in government, at work, at home. Privilege does not increase knowledge or spirit or understanding. There can be no peace while one race dominates another, one people, one nation, one sex despises another.

We must not forget the tens of thousands of American women who live much of their lives in cages, away from family, lovers, all the growing-up years of their children. Most of them were born at the intersection of oppressions: people of color, female, poor. Women on the outside have been taught to fear those sisters. We refuse that separation. We need each other's knowledge and anger in our common struggle against the builders of jails and bombs.

We want the uranium left in the earth and the earth given back to the people who tilled it. We want a system of energy which is renewable, which does not take resources out of the earth without returning them. We want those systems to belong to the people and their communities, not to the giant corporations which invariably turn knowledge into weaponry. . . .

We want an end to the arms race. No more bombs. No more amazing inventions for death.

We understand all is connectedness. We know the life and work of animals and plants in seeding, reseeding and in fact simply inhabiting this planet. Their exploitation and the organized destruction of never-to-be-seen-again species threatens and sorrows us. The earth nourishes us as we with our bodies will eventually feed it. Through us, our mothers connected the human past to the human future.

With that sense, that ecological right, we oppose the financial connections between the Pentagon and the multinational corporations and banks that the Pentagon serves. Those connections are made of gold and oil. We are made of blood and bone, we are made of the sweet and finite resource, water. We will not allow these violent games to continue. If we are here in our stubborn thousands today, we will certainly return in the hundreds of thousands in the months and years to come.

We know there is a healthy, sensible, loving way to live and we intend to live that way in our neighborhoods and our farms in these United States, and among our sisters and brothers in all the countries of the world.

Notes

This chapter comes out of many conversations, over a period of several years, with Devon Peña, a former colleague at Colorado College, who first started me thinking about Chicano environmental struggles.

    1. This paragraph is based on the introduction to *What Is Ecofeminism?*, a pamphlet consisting of Ynestra King's early essays, edited by Gwyn Kirk, and published privately in 1990.

    2. For information on these five groups, write to contacts listed below at addresses given or refer to books called out from the reference list as follows, respectively: The National Women's Health Network, 1325 G St. NW, Washington, D.C. 20005; Feminist Network of Resistance to Reproductive and Genetic Engineering (FINNRAGE), for which the U.S. contact is Janice Raymond, Women's Studies Department, University of Massachusetts, Amherst, MA 01003; Committee on Women, Population, and the Environment, Hampshire College, Amherst, MA 01002; Women's Action Agenda 21 (finalized at the World Women's Congress for a Healthy Planet, 8–12 November 1991, Miami), available from Women's Environment and Development Organization (WEDO), 845 Third Ave., 15th floor, New York, NY 10022; and finally, for the promotion of economic development projects that serve women, refer to Dankelman and Davidson 1988; Leonard 1989; and Rodda 1990.

    3. On the antilogging struggle in San Luis, see Brooke 1997 and Peña and Mondragon Valdéz 1998.

    4. The UC–Davis study of farmworkers is available from Migrant Legal Action Program, 2001 S St. NW, Washington D.C. 20009.

    5. See Pulido 1996 for a study of the early pesticides campaign among farmworkers in California.

    6. The address is The Center for Third World Organizing, 1218 East 21st Street, Oakland, CA 94606; it publishes a quarterly periodical, *Third Force*.

    7. SWOP and SNEEJ recently published a comprehensive study of the Intel struggle, *Intel inside New Mexico: A Case Study of Environmental and Economic Injustice*. See Southwest Organizing Project (1995).

    8. For more on Ganados del Valle and Tierra Wools (now Los Ojos Handweavers), see Jackson 1991; Sargent, Lusk, Rívera, and Varela 1991; S. Peña 1992; and Pulido 1993, 1996.

9. The distinction between urban and rural is not always meaningful. Both are the terrain of capitalist economics, and both are affected in various ways by industrialization.

10. Also see Peña 1997a (chapts. 6–7) for a more recent third-world, ecofeminist critique of science and technology.

11. Good examples are the Citizen's Clearinghouse for Hazardous Wastes newsletter, *Everyone's Backyard;* also *Science for the People.*

12. On *maquila* workers' struggles in the workplace and the community, see Peña 1997a.

7 Philosophy Meets Practice

A Critique of Ecofeminism through the Voices of Three
Chicana Activists

Malia Davis

Ynestra King (1983a) defines ecological feminism as a philosophy and a
political agenda about wholeness and connectedness. Ecofeminism respects the integrity of all living beings and opposes the devastation of the
earth by corporations, the government, and the military. Ecofeminists
argue that the domination of women, economic exploitation, racism
against indigenous peoples, and the domination of the earth are all rooted
in Western patriarchal ideology, theory, and practice (King 1983a, 13).
Ecofeminists oppose the violent military-industrial complex and focus on
promoting a way of living that honors and respects life instead of exploitation and death. As such, ecofeminists practice nonviolence.

Ynestra King emphasizes the importance of personal affinity among
women in their communities, as well as a sense of connection to the earth.
Ecofeminism politicizes the ecological concept of "unity in diversity"
(King 1983a, 15; 1990a). It opposes the definition of the environment as
an exploitable natural resource. It therefore opposes industrial technologies and market systems that transform nature into commodities. King
asserts that "politically, ecofeminism opposes the ways that differences
can separate women from each other through the oppressions of class
privilege, sexuality, and race." This perspective is associated with a political agenda that seeks to unite women by opposing Western patriarchal
beliefs and practices and focusing instead on values that respect the integrity of women and the earth (King 1983a, 15; 1990a, 32).

In shifting ethics to a life-affirming ideology, many ecofeminists discovered, and some rediscovered, past "goddess"-centered cultures that

honored the life-giving qualities of women, of natural cycles, and of future generations (Diamond and Orenstein 1990, xi). The study of ancient goddess-centered cultures serves as the philosophical foundation for much contemporary ecofeminist political practice in the form of woman-centered, Earth-bonding rituals (see Kirk, chapter 6).

Within the academic discourse of ecofeminism, much debate focuses on whether or not the female as subject is essentialized in the various reconstructions of religio-spiritual history. Critics argue that much of ecofeminist literature essentializes female characteristics as "life-giving" by emphasizing the "nurturing qualities of women" or women's "ability to heal" others. This controversy was sparked by criticism of the white-goddess spiritual tradition proposed as political practice by antinuclear activists Starhawk and Charlene Spretnak. White-goddess practice posits that a revival of women's Earth-centered spirituality is fundamental to effective ecofeminist political practice. Other ecofeminists see spirituality as optional, as a nonessential component for opposing the patriarchal domination of women and the earth.

The critique of the "essentialized female" divides the spiritual feminists from those who see patriarchy as oppressing nature and women but rejects the notion that women are "closer" to nature than men. Female essentialism becomes problematic by undermining the feminist opposition to a biologically determined view that women are indeed different from men because of their "natural" ability to mother, nurture, and heal. The spiritual ecofeminist perspective also overlooks the material, social, and economic conditions that frame the experiences of women and men in the natural world.

Beyond this mostly white, middle-class discourse are writings on ecofeminism and environmental justice by women of color, most notably Wilmette Brown (1983), Rachel Bagby (1990), Cynthia Hamilton (1990), Laura Pulido (1990, 1993, 1996), and Vandana Shiva (1988, 1990, 1993a, 1993b). Their writings share some common themes: issues of race and class, the misrepresentation of poor women of color, and the effects of a militarized, global capitalist system that institutionalizes racism, classism, and sexism. The spiritual perspective is evident in some of their writings, but it is not central; these women are fighting against patriarchy from a class- and race-conscious perspective.

Issues of racism and classism are central to these ecofeminists of color. Their identification is grounded in the problems of privilege. For example, each woman articulates aspects of the subjugation of women and nature within the context of a lack of health care and food, loss of common lands, or polluted water and air. These writers speak directly and personally to the disproportionate environmental degradation experienced by poor communities of color (Peña 1992 and Pulido 1993, 1996).

This chapter examines the viability of ecofeminism as a perspective that can inform people across race, gender, and class boundaries. The critical lenses for this appraisal are the perspectives of three women of color involved in social activism — in human rights, self-determination, and environmental justice struggles. Is there a gap between ecofeminist theory (the academic discourse) and community-based practice and activism? If so, how might this gap be bridged?

This chapter explores each woman's history as an activist, her educational and personal background, political and ethnic identity, as well as socioeconomic status and class experience. An understanding of each woman's material location in society is important in understanding her relationship to "activist" issues. The complex intersections of class, race, and gender identities are integral to the critique of a philosophy (movement) that claims to include women of all ethnicities and classes (King 1990a, 38).

Biographies of Struggle: On Becoming and Being Activists

The three women I interviewed currently live and work in Colorado. All three were born in Denver and now live and work there. The youngest woman was twenty-six at the time of the interviews, the oldest forty-three. The two older women are married and have children. All were raised in the Catholic faith, and all three now express discontent with the institutional church and its views on women and people of color. Two of the women identify themselves as Chicanas and one as a Mexican-American. All three women grew up in working-class conditions, and all of them have college or university degrees. Two of the women identify themselves as "radicals," and one defines herself as "progressive."

Roseanne "Rocky" Rodriguez:
"You are either a human being or a clone."

Rocky Rodriguez, thirty-seven, works for the National Chicano Human Rights Commission in Denver.[1] She also teaches English as a Second Language to workers. Much of her time in the months prior to 1992 was spent on organizing the Peace and Dignity Journey, which celebrated five hundred years of resistance by indigenous peoples in North and South America.

Rocky was born in Denver in November of 1954 and has lived there ever since. She is the middle child in her family that includes two biological siblings, twelve adopted brothers, and three adopted sisters. Rocky is a second-generation Denver resident: her grandparents came from Mexico to New Mexico, her parents' birthplace. Her parents moved to Denver to find jobs.

Rocky's grandmother played a very important role in her childhood. "She taught me a lot about *curanderismo* [folk medicine] because that's what she was, a *curandera* [folk healer]. She healed, she was a traditional doctor. . . . I guess her Indian ways rubbed off on me. That I always valued" (Rodriguez 1991, 1). Rocky was raised in the Catholic tradition but rejected Catholicism at age twelve because, she said, "it was too bull for me" (p. 21). Rocky refers to herself as the "black sheep" in the family because, she says, "I am also the one who has been real adamant about following our indigenous culture rather than the Hispanic culture" (p. 1). Rocky identifies herself as Chicana, a term she believes is used "to describe a brown population that . . . work[s] for self-determination and . . . social change" (p. 13).

Talking about the government, Rocky stated, "We have a government that says one thing and does another. People have to challenge that" (p. 29). Rocky advocates resistance to unrepresentative government when speaking about indigenous people: "[J]ust as we have always been ignored and not recognized, our laws, our government . . . our societies . . . now we have to say no, we're not going for this anymore . . . we're not going to obey your laws" (p. 29). Rocky's first "activist" experiences took place in the midst of national and international political turmoil in 1969 at North High School in Denver. She attended public school until 1969 when she was banned as a result of marching out of school with Chicanos and demanding to have their own history taught in schools, one part of the larger Chicano movement's goals. "We marched downtown, and it was a new experience for me because I had never had a sense of unity with my people. . . . We went to the state capitol and we said 'we want relevant education'" (p. 4).

This experience of unity and of developing identity led Rocky to become "turned off" by the class system (being classified as hippie-radical, jock, "rah-rah") and wanting to leave school, which she was not old enough to do. "I started being a radical," she says, "and arranged through a Vista worker (counselor) to get me out of school. I wanted to go to the school of life and have experience be my teacher. . . . [T]he Vista worker helped me get a document that said I was too 'emotionally disturbed' to be in school" (p. 5).

This proved effective enough to keep Rocky out of any public school. She eventually entered an alternative school, Escuela Tlatelolco, started by the Chicano organization called Crusade for Justice, and graduated as valedictorian.[2] She received her undergraduate degree in Chicano Studies at the same school (Colegio Tlatelolco) and did her student teaching there. Desiring to become a doctor in order to practice natural medicine, Rocky attended Metropolitan State College, Denver, then Auraria, also in Denver, where she also taught some concepts of curanderismo, focusing on the medicinal properties of Rocky Mountain herbs.

Rocky continued practicing her traditional beliefs, which became an issue while she was a student. "I went to one ceremony that said 'if you want to take the traditional road you can't even be in school because these concepts are 180 degrees apart. You cannot be in any institution that the white man has put out there.' I didn't finish my pre-med education. I dropped out of college and started focusing on traditional medicine. At the same time, I was still politically involved with the issues affecting my people" (p. 7).

Rocky identifies her greatest struggle as trying to unify and clarify the similarities of indigenous people and Chicanos. "I've been working all my life to unify brown and red people, because we are very similar. Our struggle is the same, our enemies are the same, and our goals are the same. . . . Once people understand . . . that every Mexican did not swim over the Atlantic Ocean to get here, they start to understand that we're not half-breeds. We're not Europeans" (p. 42).

Lorraine Granado:
"Responding to what people name as their own issues"

Lorraine Granado, age forty-three, works for the American Friends Service Committee in Denver.[3] She is the project director for Community Justice Organizing and is a main contributor to the Cross Community Coalition (C.C.C.) formed in May 1987 in response to issues of education, drug and alcohol abuse, better parent and child communication, and recreation opportunities. C.C.C.'s intention is to guide neighborhoods as they address, then solve, their self-identified problems. Lorraine is also one of the founders of Neighbors for a Toxic-Free Community, an organization that emerged from protests against the ASARCO Superfund site located in Globeville, Colorado, a low-income, working-class community in Denver with mostly black and Latino residents. The lack of city, county, or state regulations, coupled with a huge concern for the community's health, sparked the protests against the ASARCO Superfund site.

The oldest of eight children, Lorraine was born in Denver, Colorado, in April 1948. She still lives, works, and raises a family in Denver. Lorraine's father is originally from Mexico but came to the United States while a baby. His family was from a migrant farmworker background, and he grew up as a migrant farmworker after which he moved to Denver, where he worked at a packing house for twenty-seven years. Lorraine's mother is from northern New Mexico and grew up on a farm. She moved to Denver, met and married her husband, and raised eight children. Lorraine's seven siblings all live in Denver. She describes herself as coming from a large family and as being "definitely raised in my own culture. . . . [The] community we lived in was all Mexican Americans and Mexican Nationals. . . . I guess major influences were my own culture, my family, and church" (Granado 1992, 1). Now, however, Lorraine does not identify as much with the Catholic church. She says, "I think the Catholic church, at least, helped shape me in a very positive way . . . value systems, fundamental beliefs that we are all children of God, the beliefs of mercy, beliefs of patience, humility. Those values, I think, shaped who I am. But in terms of the doctrine and the policies of the Catholic church, I have great disagreements. . . . The Catholic church is not much different than most systems in the world. It's run by white males who have all the power, who have no room for women, who have no room for people of color" (p. 1).

Lorraine recognizes the good the Catholic church did for her in helping her shape her values, but she is acutely aware of the similarities in the doctrine and policies within institutions of power that exclude women and people of color from their structure.

Lorraine describes her ethnic identity as Mexican-American, and she defies being cast within rigid, conventional political labels or ideological persuasions. "I'm a progressive," she says. "I can't stand the term *left*. I can't stand the term *liberal*. . . . [W]e've been indoctrinated to believe there's a left and a right and you got to pick. I believe that's garbage. . . . I consider myself progressive—always looking for how do we learn, what do we know, how can we grow and not get locked into anybody's little box that says you have to belong to this ideology or the other" (p. 4).

When we talked about social class, Lorraine said, "It was the kind of thing where there was just enough money. Pay the bills and nothing extra. . . . [E]veryone was like us and we shared everything" (p .2). Throughout her childhood, though, Lorraine never felt like she was in an "upper-lower class" socioeconomic group, and she describes her childhood as extremely happy (p. 2). "It wasn't until I went . . . to a Catholic high school, which was not in my area. . . . In the whole school maybe four of us were Latino; no blacks, no Asians, no Indians. Everyone there was, I would say, middle- or upper-middle class. That's when I first learned that I was poor and that we were different. I'm glad it came so late. . . . I was who I was and proud of who I was . . . my people" (p. 2).

Lorraine emphasized her cultural identity and a positive upbringing. "[I] absolutely knew who I was and felt good about who I was and who I am. . . . I have no negative images. We were raised being told we were wonderful, we were beautiful, gosh we were smart. It came from everywhere: aunts, uncles, cousins, friends" (p. 2).

Lorraine did not go to college right after high school. Instead she got married and started a family. After her divorce she went back to school and obtained an associate's degree in recreational leadership, while raising two children. Lorraine then went to Denver's Metro State College and completed enough hours for a B.A. in Human Services and a second degree in administration for nonprofit organizations. I asked if being a single mother motivated her to go back to school, and Lorraine said, "No, I always wanted to go to school. I couldn't go to school because we just did not have the money" (p. 3). When I asked if financial aid was available,

Lorraine described her experience with the high school college counselor: "Actually it was a real racist thing. In our high school we had one person who met with the seniors. . . . I had met with him, just like all the kids did, and I told him I wanted to go to college. His response to me — I'll remember this until I die — was that my responsibility was to go to work and help my parents with the rest of the seven kids. I accepted that. He never mentioned that there was a thing called financial aid. . . . [H]e did not indicate to me that there were any avenues open to me to help finance that" (p. 3).

Lorraine's history as an activist began in high school, when she organized a group of students to spend time at an orphanage for disabled kids. She relates that her first real organizing began when she helped establish one of the first women's resource centers in Colorado at the community college. "[It was] because of the needs of women like me. I went back to school and had two kids. There were a lot of us, and there was no place for us to go to meet and talk" (p. 4).

Lorraine has now worked for American Friends Service Committee for ten years: "I love being here. . . . [W]e work truly as a community, we work cooperatively, [and] we do not have a hierarchy" (p. 5). Her work is joyful and the people she works with, she says, "are my friends and I truly love them" (p. 5).

The main reason Lorraine loves the work she does with AFSC is that the philosophies of the organization match her own personal beliefs. "I believe and practice nonviolence. I believe wholeheartedly that each of us is a child of God and that each of us has intrinsic value and worth, and that people deserve to be treated with respect. The AFSC believes that. . . . It spoke to who I am and what I believe. I came here to work because of that" (p. 5).

Lorraine is most concerned with issues of inequality, especially relating to women, children, and people of color. "Who suffers from inequality are people of color, women, children, the poor. . . . [W]hatever I do, it is based . . . [on] helping to change how this system relates to people of color, women, and so forth, in order to help bring a little more justice and help deal with the pain and hard lives those folks have. I think there's a price for the affluence in this country, and I think there's a segment of society that pays for that and that's the folks I want to work with" (p. 6).

Her professional work is in organizing, which she states takes some special skill. But "commitment comes straight from the people" (p. 6). Neighbors for a Toxic-Free Community is an example of the type of organizing done by the AFSC and is based in trust for the people who are affected directly. "There aren't organizations like the AFSC . . . that say 'go where the people are, work with them where they are, at what they perceive to be their problems' in a way that is respectful and trusting of them. It doesn't happen. Organizing so much in this country is around 'I have an issue and let me see who I can go out to get to work on my issue' " (p. 8).

Lorraine's position is one of organizing in response to what people "name as their own issues" (p. 8). The coalition of Neighbors for a Toxic-Free Community formed out of the need to address issues of environmental/health problems that a plant such as ASARCO would create. Says Lorraine:

> We were aware of the industry. We didn't like the smell. We didn't like the noise, all of that, but we even knew about the health stuff. We would wonder how come it seems like we have, every block, one, two, three people, with thyroid problems? How come so much asthma, God, so much asthma? . . . How come so many elders have emphysema? We had all those questions. This is not like in other neighborhoods, because these illnesses are too apparent. How come so many of our kids seem to have either learning disabilities or their parents are being told they are hyperactive? All of which we learned later on were symptoms of being exposed to lead. . . . [W]e knew all this stuff on a level, but we had no way to approach it, didn't know what to do with it. (p. 9)

"Neighbors for a Toxic-Free Community's goals were to educate themselves first, then to share that information with the community. After that, the question of what to do was discussed. Neighbors for a Toxic-Free Community is not based on distortion of facts, but on presenting the truth about hazardous industry, such as a Superfund site" (Granado 1992, 10).

Vast amounts of the organization's time are spent researching, investigating, and planning, then involving city and state health departments in situations and informing city councils about the effects that a site like ASARCO has on a community like Globeville.

Sonia Peña: "It's all disproportionately affecting communities of color."

Sonia Peña, age twenty-six, is the director for the Minority Activist Apprenticeship Program (MAAP) at the Center for Third World Organizing (CTWO) in Denver.[4] The program trains organizers from poor communities of color (the domestic Third World) and then places them within organizations that are working with communities of color. This includes working with direct-action organizations on issues that disproportionately affect communities of color. In the following statement, Sonia talks about people who participate in MAAP. "Somebody has to make a full-time commitment and be able to move around. . . . [T]he people that we have been able to get have been middle-class students of color who have been active on their campuses. . . . [T]he people we really want to train are low-income people of color who maybe have a shitty job, but who can't give it up because they have a family" (S. Peña 1992, 6).

The organization CTWO, therefore, has a mentorship program, which is a long-term placement program for people who cannot move. "It is a six-month placement one-on-one with somebody in an organization, that is a person of color, and that means they can be placed where they're from. . . . [W]e started last year. . . . [W]e did five placements" (p. 6). This is the alternative kind of leadership training that Sonia sees as essential to maintaining options within progressive organizing.

Sonia Peña was born in Eagle Pass, Texas, in 1965. Her mother left her father when Sonia was very young and supported the family by doing migrant farmwork in Arizona, New Mexico, and Colorado. Sonia spent some time in Oregon and northern California when her mother worked on farms there. She considers Colorado her home, however, where she and her family have lived for about sixteen years. One of the main reasons for staying in Colorado was that the state had good welfare and educational benefits at the time that Sonia's mother had become disabled from a work-related injury. Sonia's mother moved to Boulder after two of her children entered the University of Colorado-Boulder through the Migrant Action Program.

Sonia's two older sisters and older brother are attorneys. Sonia graduated from the University of Colorado with a degree in sociology. Sonia's mother still lives in Boulder in the housing projects where the family grew up. Sonia comes from a family of political organizers. Both her mother and sister were involved in United Farm Workers boycotts and organizing. They encouraged Sonia to attend college and then continue her education. Sonia saw her mother's and sister's political organizing as extra involvement, not as a career. She was exposed to "political action as organizing from a very young age" but never imagined it would be a career because "my mom and my sister had done a lot of this work but had never gotten paid for it. . . . [Y]ou went and became a UFW organizer . . . got paid five dollars a week and would have to figure out . . . housing. . . . [T]he connotation was that people that would do that were white people that could afford it. . . . [T]hat's mainly who I saw" (p. 2).

Sonia identifies herself as Chicana and middle class: "We definitely started low, working class." She explained that her mother was a single parent. "But right now," she says, "I think I'm middle class, just based on my education and experiences that I've had and the opportunities that I have. They are different than a lot of people with my same back ground" (p. 3).

Politically, Sonia identifies herself as progressive and says she doesn't get involved with electoral politics, nor does she identify with a particular political party. When explaining her religious or spiritual beliefs, Sonia states that religion does not play a big role in her life now. She was raised in the Catholic church but is no longer involved: "There are things I cannot agree with, especially the way that women are treated and the way women are expected to live, but I do believe there is a God. . . . I like the ceremonies, and I like the rituals, but I don't like what the meaning is behind them; like I don't like the fact that I never see a woman as the priest or never see a woman leading [the rituals]" (p. 4).

Sonia started organizing on campus at Colorado University and completed the Minority Activist Apprenticeship Program through CTWO in 1986. She was then asked to be director for MAAP in Oakland, California. Leaving Oakland after almost two years, she has now lived in Denver for almost a year. At present she is most concerned with training people to become community leaders. She makes a distinction between the types of leaders needed: [Some] "get by in the white male structure — that you can speak in public, that you can argue, that you can dress professionally, that you can get elected to office, which I don't think is the right way to go. I think we need to give people opportunities to explore other progressive careers and other types of leadership styles that I don't think are very much out there—especially to say to people, if you become an organizer you can make a living at it" (p. 4).

Activism and Chicana/o History

These profiles provide small glimpses of three women's personal histories and beliefs, ethnic and political identification, and activism. Each woman was influenced by her Chicana history and the role of family and community. Catholicism has also been a major influence in each of their lives, though each acknowledges that this Western patriarchal religion does not accommodate their needs as women of color.

Each woman's history of activism is grounded in the time in which she became active. Lorraine and Rocky were going to college at the time of the Chicano Movement, but a history of struggle and resistance by Chicanos goes back five hundred years. This adds a dimension in understanding their current personal connections to struggle, organizing, and activism in social and environmental justice issues with a strong antiracist bent.

Three Chicana Environmental Activists: An Oral History

The women in my study share common worldviews in which personal identification is rooted in social and political activism, feminism, and ethnicity. But these women redefine activism by building bridges across race, class, and gender and by defying conventional or feminist assumptions about political activism, ethnicity, and spirituality.

Redefining Activism

The three women discussed activism at length during each interview with me. Sonia referred to her work with CTWO as "organizing" and did not identify herself with the term "activist" (p. 8): "Activist . . . would apply to the different trainings that we do. . . . [W]e do some political education trainings; we do some organizer trainings. People who come to that are usually activists who don't do organizing or activist work for a living, but are very active" (p. 8).

Though CTWO uses strategies of direct-action work, Sonia does not connect her identity to these kinds of actions, even though she organizes and implements them. For example, CTWO protested the lack of free measles vaccinations in Oakland. This was a direct-action event, but for Sonia, "organizing" is the foundation for these kinds of events and therefore the basis on which she defines herself and her work.

Lorraine's explicit call to activism is based on a belief that she is part of a process for positive social change — the foundation for her involvement in issues such as the ASARCO Superfund site: "I know that to be a part of this system and the status quo and to reinforce that in any way is to choose . . . that which harms, which destroys. So I need to be a part of the other one, the part that is creative, the constructive, that heals, that brings peace. . . . I have to be a part of that change, again in a positive way. The answer is not to destroy back; the answer truly is change" (p. 12).

Processes of change derive from the AFSC philosophy of nonviolent, direct action by those affected by social injustice. Globeville is a good example of how a self-educated community can act out against powerful economic interests to prevent harmful developments.

Rocky's identity and beliefs are influenced by a very strong notion of decentralization. Her understanding of power structures and an unrepresentative government is closely tied to her history of direct political actions. Rocky is a student of curanderismo, and this is one source of her activism. She opposes the institutional framework of modern Western health care by helping people to become capable of healing themselves and preventing sickness. Brown (1983, 74–76) describes the "malignant kinship" of sex, race, and class in relation to disease and sickness and implies that the holistic health movement should describe getting well as "mobilizing body and soul to defeat more than illness or a disease; getting well means organizing to defeat the power relations of sex, race, and class that make cancer, illness and disease possible." Rocky's involvement in traditional medicine relates to Brown's views against the profit-oriented goals of Western medicine. Her beliefs are the antithesis of Western "fix-it" medicine. She says, "I thought people should have the means and knowledge to heal themselves. . . . [There] is basic stuff in their kitchen, in their medicine cabinet that they could use, especially, public health-care systems where the health-care delivery system doesn't really deliver unless you have the money" (p. 6). She explains why the American Medical Association does not want to implement more holistic and preventative medicine. "Because they (AMA) would like to present that alternative medicine is folklore, is superstition. Because what would happen if they really incorporated it into the system? More people would be getting well, fewer people would be getting sick, because of the preventative concept in there. . . . [B]eing sick is big business in this country. Alternative medicine could ultimately . . . kill capitalism within the AMA" (p. 7).

Rocky's activism manifests itself in education and, in particular, through her support of "deschooling": "[B]y deschooling society, the indigenous people . . . [through] 500 years of resistance . . . [are] rediscovering America. . . . [W]e have to rediscover this continent. . . . Teaching people about what really happened here, not just what the history books would like us to believe" (p. 15). Activism for social justice thus invokes a struggle for decolonizing (rediscovering) history through a proactive educational agenda.

Redefining/Challenging Feminism:
The Intersections of Class, Race, and Gender

Each of the Chicanas I interviewed associated feminism with white women's "liberation." Lorraine considers herself a feminist, but this stance is integrated with a strong ethnic identity. For all three women, ethnicity is just as important, if not more important, as a basis of identity (and place of empowerment) as gender is. Lorraine's comments on feminism echo this view: "My feminism . . . was not about the same thing as the feminist movement was about. . . . I'm a feminist, and in fact, when I went to work with the feminist movement, I could become very discouraged. . . . [I]t really seems to be about, and it's been said a million times, a lot of middle-class white women [who] are attempting to be upwardly mobile and open doors and stuff. For me, it's way back at ground zero, folks . . . you've got women here who don't even understand their own value. That's where it ought to be. Not taking care of a few who want to break the glass ceiling, but taking care of the many who need to understand that they are valuable and precious" (p. 13).

That Lorraine's first organizing work dealt with opening one of the first women's resource centers in Colorado indicates her recognition of and action around women's issues. Her framework for action extends beyond gender; it incorporates the intersection of gender, race, and class. For example, she frames health and child-care issues through two lenses, feminist and socioeconomic (access to resources): "[D]ealing with things like the mother who has a sick kid and doesn't have health care, and who has a right to that" (p. 13) followed her statement about "the many who need to understand they are valuable and precious." This consciousness started early for Lorraine. "[M]y feminism goes back to my mom and my dad, who I wouldn't say treated us equally. Clearly the girls had roles. The girls did the dishes, the boys did the yard work. But in terms of who we were, . . . they were proud of us, and one of us was not better than the other" (p. 13).

Drawing strength from her self-esteem, Lorraine went on to protest sexism. But her feminist identity is class, race, and gender-based: "[M]y feminism differs as a woman of color . . . who really sees [her]self as part of all those folks who are poor and struggling" (p. 13).

Rocky and Sonia do not identify themselves as feminists. Each of them feels that feminism as an identity is connected to white women, and therefore is exclusionist. Rocky says, "I always shied away from the word 'feminist' because I would equate it with the women's movement . . . because I used to feel like we were slighted by the women's movement. They didn't exactly reach out to women of color. Some of their issues we saw differently" (p. 36). After Rocky and I talked about some definitions of feminism, she said, "If a feminist means being a female who's actively resisting old standards created by men and is actively pursuing a progressive avenue towards . . . social change, then yes, in that respect I am a feminist. . . . [M]aybe it has progressed to those levels of including women of color and understanding some indigenous concepts. . . . For us it's not a man, a woman, or a child's struggle; it's a people's struggle. . . . [M]y brothers . . . are victims of racism, sexism, classism. . . . Granted there are men within our race that are chauvinist pigs (here I am using that word) . . . at the same time they are victims of oppression" (p. 36).

Later, Rocky says that it is the "separatism" she hates, the women versus men (p. 37), and that change can occur only by learning about and acting on the issues affecting us all. Rocky calls herself a feminist, according to the earlier quote, in a context of progressive social change, but she will not necessarily use the term in her cultural context, suggesting that her personal identification is associated primarily with ethnicity, secondarily with gender.

Sonia made some similar statements: "I have a cut around women's issues . . . [but] I have never called myself a feminist . . . like feminism to me was really equated to white women. . . . My issues around being a woman and my issues around being a Latina are really kind of at the same place. . . . I fight them at the same time" (p. 10).

All three women see feminism as related to the white women's movement. Lorraine's feminism "differs" because she does not readily self-identify as feminist and is working actively against the oppression of women, particularly women of color and "folks who are poor and struggling." This suggests a key difference in the way we "frame" the issues. For middle-class white feminists, issues of racism do not compound the issues of sexism. Sonia and Lorraine indicate that being women of color has framed issues of racism and sexism in a manner that gives them simultaneous importance. Their activist work is a direct result of their ethnicity, socioeconomic status, *and* gender. Gender is not seen as overly determining their concepts of self and activism.

Even more fundamental is their connection of racism and sexism to an inherently class-based, white-male privileging society. All three women, whether they identify as feminists or not, describe their conflicts with traditional family ideology's traditional gender roles, often explained as Chicana/o "culture." In fact, each of these women has a primary relationship with a man and chooses to negotiate within her culture's traditional roles for women and men. For these women, to see their struggle only as one of gender would mean excluding men from the culture. To see their struggle as singularly rooted in racism would deny the compounded reality of sexism. To see these two facets of oppression as integrally linked to classism explicates the fundamental differences between Anglo feminists and women-of-color feminists. Each of these women includes men in her struggles, which signifies the impact of racial and economic oppression linked to the compounded oppression of sexism. Their identity politics embodies not only gender oppression, but race and class as well.

Aida Hurtado (1989, 834) describes a linkage between the white man's oppression of both women and people of color. She brings the socioeconomic factors of oppression into what had traditionally been seen as a white-feminist versus feminist-of-color relationship. White women can access white men and their associated power and resources more easily than either women or men of color. Hurtado's theory is based on the process of distribution of wealth through class and race: white men need white women to produce offspring who will automatically inherit their power. (A black woman married to a white man will have offspring who do not inherit his power.) This creates a relational position of white women and black women to white men. Therefore, white women are subordinated through what Hurtado calls "seduction," and black women are subordinated through "rejection," where the probability of seduction or rejection is based on class position (1989, 847). White women, therefore, do not have a racial blockade to pass through in order to get access to resources. Hurtado gives the example of how a lower-class white woman could marry a middle-class white man and automatically benefit from those resources (as would their children). But a black woman would not. Hurtado demands that white feminists recognize their own subordination of women of color, based on class privileging, so as to recognize the differences in kinds of feminism.

That class so clearly differentiates women's experience illuminates what is often seen as simply ethnic differences. The women I interviewed are evidence of this. In critiquing Alison Jagger, Aida Hurtado (1989, 839) questions why Jagger does not see the reasons that black feminists might be reluctant to separate from black men while simultaneously recognizing their gender subordination. This is critical to the discussion of the views expressed by Rocky, Lorraine, and Sonia. All of them recognize that their men are subordinated by the system as well. These women are conscious of the complexity of their own oppression as women, but they choose to identify their oppression not by gender alone, but by class and race as well.

Ethnic Identity and Activism

A strong connection exists between ethnic identity and activism in the lives of these women. Ethnicity reinforces their activism and also involves a deep critique of capitalist and other interlocking systems of domination. Sonia said, "[N]ot just being a woman, but being a person of color really played a lot into what I am and the position that I'm in at CTWO. We're an organization that's probably like 98 percent people of color" (Peña 1992, 13). In Lorraine's words, "As a matter of fact, I wonder if I could be an activist if I wasn't [a woman of color]. . . . I think [if I was white] the system would have served me . . . and met my needs, and I still could have been a decent person and wanted to give something back and wanted to teach, and cared. But I would have missed what is the hidden story; deliberately the hidden story. So yeah, I mean it's the difference of being an activist or not being an activist; that's how fundamental it is" (Granado 1992, 15).

Rocky put it this way: "The enemy is imperialism, capitalism, racism, sexism. . . . There is a 'they', and they do exist, and they are the multinational corporate structure — to narrow it down, the United States government, in particular. I believe that they actually have programs that they have created to clone us all to act and live in a certain way to keep them in power and keep us all oppressed" (Rodriguez 1991, 44).

Implied in Lorraine's use of "hidden story" is the conscious effort to minimize the true history of people of color and white women in this country by the "enemy" that Rocky describes. The justification and rationalization of institutionalized "capitalist values" make up the illusory "American dream" of freedom and democracy.

Chicana Views of Ecofeminism and Mainstream Environmentalism

Much of the work that Rocky, Lorraine, and Sonia do, in conjunction with their personal philosophies, is based on exposing inequality and acting against oppressive organizations. From the ASARCO Superfund site to the lead abatement program of Oakland, California, the work of these women has social justice implications.[5] But these issues also connect directly to environmentalism. The shifting definition of environmentalism means recognizing that saving the environment is not exclusive to wilderness areas and specific endangered species. Environmentalism, as a movement, is being challenged to recognize and act on issues involving the people who pay for other people's environmental waste and contamination. All of these women are fighting against a corporate, capitalist-based structure that disproportionately affects both urban and rural, often poorer communities, as well as communities of color, women, and children.[6]

None of the three women interviewed identified with the term *ecofeminism*. None could define it. All had heard the term but had no connection to the philosophy. This may be due to the fact that most of these women completed their studies prior to the development of the ecofeminist philosophy/movement, but perhaps more salient is the framework in which ecofeminism developed. Rocky, Lorraine, and Sonia were provided a definition of ecofeminism (as described in the methodology section), and then asked whether or not they saw a special connection between women and nature. Many ecofeminists believe that because women have a special relationship to nature, a clear connection to the patriarchal abuse against the earth and women and people of color can be realized and simultaneously opposed. This is absolutely relevant to ecofeminism and the current academic debate around whether ecofeminism adequately addresses issues of race and class (if it does at all).

Critiques of Mainstream Environmentalism

Laura Pulido articulates the idea of mainstream environmentalism as a male agenda. She asserts that "few environmentalists have been able to forge a relationship between environmental quality, poverty, racism, and social justice." Since most groups work with reformist strategies, the questions about the roots of environmental problems and inequality are rarely questioned. The institutional framework within which these organizations work merely replicates the "domination by white males and their institutions" (Pulido 1990, 5; 1996).

The connection between women and nature exists with more complex health and environmental illness issues for poor communities, often communities of color, that bear a disproportionate share of the toxic contamination costs. "Three out of five black and Hispanic [sic] Americans live in communities with uncontrolled toxic waste sites" (Commission for Racial Justice 1987). Race and socioeconomic factors directly correlate to hazardous waste exposure. Resulting health issues are proof of this, as elucidated by Lorraine's definition of environmentalism. "[They (mainstream environmentalists) are not going to come down, and have not come down to Globeville to talk about ASARCO. They won't. . . . If you look at what we are really trying to do is to really preserve, enhance, heal life . . . you have to start looking first of all at the contamination, at the destruction, in terms of how it affects people and not just animals . . . because those people don't tend to be middle-class . . . or wealthy, they tend to be us" (Granado 1992, 14–15).

Rocky, Sonia, and Lorraine view the role of mainstream, male-dominated environmentalism in the same critical manner as they do exclusively feminist theory and practice. Lorraine's statement about the domination of women and nature follows the ecofeminism definition I provided to her. She said, "I believe that it's patriarchy, it's misogyny. However, I would say that probably, and my guess is, that ecofeminism is not coming out of women of color. . . ." Male-domination presumes a white agenda based on class privileging. And mainstream environmentalism has been (is) a predominantly white, middle-class movement. When Lorraine says, "God bless them for doing it; saving the whale, saving the owl," she is sincere. However, implied is the notion that the people who have time to spend in the wilderness are those people who can literally "afford" to be concerned with "environmental" issues as related to forests, wildlands, and non-urban environments. Lorraine's environmental issues exist in her own backyard at the ASARCO Superfund site (Granado 1992, 14).

These women of color do not identify with the mainstream environmental definition because it does not encompass the environment in which they live, the air they breathe, or the water they drink. Pulido correlates perception of environment to living and working conditions. For working-class people of color, the environment is not an "external" area or a "false" wilderness in need of preservation, but instead it is the immediate space where people live, work, and play (Peña 1992). For working-class or unemployed people (Pulido's example is south-central and east Los Angeles), the environment is just one of many problems facing Chicanas/os.

Sonia believes that the environmental movement is changing and talks about how her social justice issues are now being seen in an environmentalist context: "I still think it's a pretty white [movement], but I see that changing a lot, which I think is a really positive step forward. . . . When we were cutting this issue around lead in Oakland, we cut it as an environmental issue, which for us was the first time that the environmental movement or people in the environmental movement had looked at issues that really affect urban poor people, which primarily are people of color, and said, 'Yes, that's an environmental issue'" (S. Peña 1992, 12). Sonia touches on a fundamental problem with movements such as environmentalism and feminism: people's inability to confront their own classism, racism, or sexism. This confrontation would make possible a broader definition of environmentalism, hence the ability to link the domination of people of color, the earth, and women. Sonia explains: "I also see some resistance to that change and some resistance to cutting those issues of environment along justice lines, around race, and economic lines. . . . I think sometimes people say, 'Well, I want to deal with the environment because it is very clear-cut. It's not about racism, it's not about classism. It's about the environment and how we're going to save Mother Earth.' I think that for some people it can be hard to redefine that in their minds and say, 'Okay, it's not just about that. It's also about racism. So I'm going to have to deal with my own racism or I'm going to have to deal with the racism in my organization or the classism'" (S. Peña, 1992, 12).

Another problematic aspect of the mainstream environmental movement is the assumption that the Big Ten environmental groups are now more about the "protective" needs of the land than the people who live and subsist on the land. Rocky says, "[N]ow we have a lot of white people defending the earth, environmental groups. And it's good! Because there was a time when people didn't even look at that. . . . [O]n the other hand, we now have environmental racism . . . some groups, which we call the Big Ten, that raise thousands of dollars, even millions. They're the main spokespeople and recognized for environmental causes, but they never bother to ask the communities they claim to represent for their opinion, or direction" (S. Peña 1992, 25). This suggests the need to review traditional definitions of "environment" and "environmental issues" to include a deeper understanding and respect for self-determination and autonomy. Lorraine Granado asserts that we must go to and draw upon communities where the issues exist. Rocky Rodriguez calls for environmental organizations' increased sensitivity to self-determination. These comments highlight a gap between the traditional environmentalist focus and community-based, identified, and prioritized public health and environmental agendas. These women articulate the frustration of communities that have been traditionally overlooked or mistrusted to define their own issues, needs, and options for resolution.

Patriarchy and the Domination of Nature and Women

The key ecofeminist question posed to the women interviewed for this chapter was, "Do you see any connection between the domination of women and the domination of nature?" Lorraine responded in a manner reminiscent of Vandana Shiva's book (1988) *Staying Alive:*

I think it's about male systems and mostly Western European–thinking males, and the whole notion that things are to be conquered, subdued, used for the benefit of the folks doing the conquering and subduing. . . . Everything is objectified; things are objects. The earth is not living; it is an object to be used. The Indians were not people, blacks were not people; they were objects to be used. So it's a whole "conquer for my own benefit" because the notion was that people could accrue, should accrue, as much wealth as they could. In order to do that, all other things had to be devalued . . . and destroyed. That, I think, is the cause of it, and really is a way of looking at life. . . . [W]e call it progress, we call it development . . . but it's not about that, it's about exploitation (Granado 1992, 15).

Patriarchy is the basis of Western thought, as well as a rationalized approach to culture, politics, and economics. Shiva (1988) defines the root of domination over women, nature, and colonies as deriving from the legacy of androcentric Western science. The patriarchal paradigm infiltrates every aspect of modern culture. Lorraine describes objectification as the means to advocate for and rationalize exploitation of the earth's resources, with people being reduced to wealth accumulation mechanisms.

Rocky talks about the monopoly of wealth by a few, achieved by keeping the "other" (people of color, women) powerless (Rodriguez 1991, 44). Subverting this power cannot be accomplished by fighting back in a similar, oppressive way. Rather, other means must be employed. For example, Rocky's commitment to her indigenous beliefs and practices demonstrates how one can exist within a structure that places inherent value on people, other living things, and resources traditionally subjugated by patriarchy. "Our problem is the two-leggeds and the governments of the world that we are going to have to fight, because they are standing in the way of that. The governments are not stupid. Neither is the white man. He has a history. He knows what he is doing. . . . I don't even like to use the word white man, because there is an Indian word called *wasichu* that describes it better. . . . [I]t means fat-takers, take all the fat and leave people the bones" (Rodriguez 1991, 30).

To resist this domination, Rocky says, "people need courage." This courage is in living and acting in any way that dismantles the power of patriarchy. Becoming active in the Chicano human rights struggle is one aspect of a way to oppose patriarchy, as is following your "instinct" and defending yourself and the earth from that. "Every human being should defend the Earth. . . . The point is, without her, nobody could live. . . . [W]hen you defend Mother Earth you're defending your air; water; all the rock; the green; the vegetation; all the relatives; the swim, creep, crawl peoples; four-leggeds; two-leggeds; winged persons; star nations; cloud nations; thunder beings. You're defending the universe when you defend the earth" (Rodriguez 1991, 28, 42).

Rocky suggests that patriarchy's domination of women and nature stems from the same root. Sonia puts forth a similar viewpoint, although from a different angle: "I see similarities between the way women are oppressed and the way that people of color are oppressed. I see connections between how workers are oppressed and how poor people are oppressed in terms of health care. I see those connections. I think oppression takes very similar forms. . . . [C]ertainly that connection (women and nature) could be made. . . . I think it's all patriarchal" (Peña 1992, 11).

Each of these women has experienced racism directly, so she can make connections among the domination of women, nature, and people of color. Sonia also connects women and nature in a straightforward manner: "I think we do, because we have babies. We give birth, and I think that is something that gives us a special connection in terms of being able to regenerate and really have that connection with growth" (S. Peña 1992, 11).

Rocky feels a profound connection between women and nature; in fact, she believes that women must come together to heal the earth. She most closely echoes the approach heard in ecofeminist writings: "Women have to unite . . . spiritually to help heal the earth and themselves and save our species, because in the old way, society centered around the woman for that reason. . . . [S]he was the childbearer. Without the woman there is no nation, community, family; there ain't nothing. . . . Women are going to be at the center of society because we will have to defend the earth. All women, it doesn't matter what their color or culture, they all had a mother, and a grandmother, and a great-grandmother. . . . [I]t goes all the way back to the mother of the earth. . . . We have to look at where we are spiritually and how we are connected to the earth and the moon and the sun and those powers, those spirits . . . to heal the earth for now and future generations" (Rodriguez 1991, 17).

Rocky explains her deep spiritual connection to all living beings on

Earth. This is rooted in the indigenous concept she identifies as the "original instructions" of the Great Spirit. The original instructions are "like your instinct," the opposite of logic in which we are now schooled (p. 15). So for Rocky, a matrilineal connection exists for women, an instinct that exists in every woman, all the way back to Mother Earth.

Similarly, Lorraine makes a connection between women and nature based on childbearing and on health issues: "I think that as women we have a real direct connection to nature. I think that really comes around to the fact that we bear children. . . . So we have a connection to life that men cannot share. . . . Part of it is, of course, that they have been locked out because of their roles. . . . [I]f we're going to be environmentally conscious, we had better start talking about what is happening to our bodies, what is happening to our children; what is happening to the earth that then happens to our bodies and children." Though she agrees that women have a connection to nature through childbearing, Lorraine's comments centered on the health issues arising from environmental contamination and the environmental movement's failure to take a holistic enough approach. Therefore, health issues caused by environmental contamination are overlooked by mainstream organizations who are more focused on "saving the whale, saving the owl." Nonetheless, the mainstream also "buys into a male agenda, which does not get at the root of it" (Granado 1992, 14).

Origins of Environmental Degradation and a New Social Movement

Economic exploitation of the earth's natural resources, including human resources (labor), for personal gain, as expressed in the Western ideology of greed, domination, and short-run economic thinking, was a common theme in these women's responses. Sonia's view is pragmatic: "I would equate it [environmental degradation] to its resources. . . . [E]nvironmentally wise . . . struggles have really been around the resources . . . on the earth and how we're going to take advantage of them or exploit them without causing damage to ourselves" (S. Peña 1992, 12). Lorraine sees the origin of environmental degradation as rooted in the quest for personal gain. This is evident in her commentary about the "conquer for my own benefit" notion. The theme of exploitation as dictated (and justified) by capitalism is evident in her description of "greed" and "power" over resources. Exploiting the earth's resources is thus linked to the exploitation of people of color and workers in general (Granado 1992, 15).

The insights of Rocky, Sonia, and Lorraine on activism, feminism, environmentalism, and ecofeminism suggest a broader framework of social justice in relation to environmentalism and feminism. Defining the "environment" reflects the critical ethnic and socioeconomic standings of these women. Pulido describes this in the context of urban Chicano struggles. "[T]he objectives, dynamics, and concerns of Chicano environmentalists in Los Angeles differ . . . from the Anglo experience. . . . [T]his difference is a function of class position and socioeconomic status. . . . Because of their proximity to the means of production, and their economic vulnerability, [Chicanos] have a different perspective, . . . a unique vision of what environmental quality is and how it should be attained" (Pulido 1990, 4).

The origins of environmental degradation and the impact on us all are realized, confronted, and changed as we consider the differing perspectives of these women of color. Ecofeminism is trying to incorporate these differing perspectives by creating a political/spiritual agenda for all women, including women of color and indigenous people. Its feminist and mainstream environmentalist roots, however, are perceived as exclusive to the needs and perspectives of people of color and the poor, which inhibits its ability to broaden its appeal and application. The women interviewed in this chapter offered examples of the different perspectives Laura Pulido talks about. They framed their feminism and environmental activism in a class- and race-conscious way.

Ethnicity and Class in Ecofeminist Theory and Practice

While none of the informants identified with ecofeminism per se, each responded to the question about women and nature through a cultural, feminist framework. Each woman believes that women have a special connection to the earth and a greater understanding of life because of their capacity to bear children. These views echo an ecofeminist philosophical premise at the heart of the debate about the biological and social construction of women and their "qualities."

Even though these three women do not identify themselves as ecofeminists, their ideas about the connection of women and nature (through the ability to bear children) coincide with the associations made between women and nature in ecofeminist philosophy. Rocky talked about the "instinctive" role of women in redefining cultural values: "I think," she said, "that women, since we have had more of an opportunity to keep our instincts intact, we're obviously going to play a big role. . . . [T]he moon makes [us] bleed. . . . They play the role like the earth plays. Without the earth, there would be nothing. She feeds us, she nurtures us, she nourishes us. That's a woman's role. In some way, shape, or form you are going to be nurturing or nourishing, whether you are a mother or not. . . . [I]t is in your nature" (Rodriguez 1991, 16).

Essentializing the role of women is precisely what Janet Biehl and other socialist feminists dispute. Rocky's beliefs in the power of the universe and her view of the earth as the great mother are derived from her history as a (self-identified) indigenous person. She is not what she describes as a new-age "cosmic gypsy," out to make money by taking advantage of "spiritually deprived people." Her spirituality has its foundations in a deep, non-Western history. Ecofeminism's view of female essentialism is often closely linked with spirituality. But Rocky does not identify with ecofeminism, and she states that she keeps her personal spiritual beliefs separate from her politics. Her personal beliefs are, however, reflected in her activist work on behalf of self-determination and land rights for indigenous people.

Rocky's spiritual life has in no way depoliticized her. In fact, despite the issues around female essentialism, she has committed her life to resisting the institutions and ideologies that have historically oppressed her and her people. She refers more to her struggle as a people's struggle, not specifically a women's struggle. At the same time, she has stated that it is up to women "to unite . . . spiritually to help heal the earth and themselves and save our species" (Rodriguez 1991, 17). This is a significant task for women in a people's struggle. Women already bear the burdens of sexism, and for many, the additional burdens of racism and classism. A disproportionate number of women and children are unable to maintain a basic standard of living. Many women are the primary child rearers, while also working to pay for food, health care, housing, and other basic necessities. I would suggest that it is not a woman's *innate* responsibility to work for change. Women are often active on social justice issues, not because of their intrinsic nurturing qualities, but because they, and particularly women of color, are disproportionately affected by these issues. Women's material location is more precarious than men's. As such, they become likely leaders in these struggles.

Sonia's, Rocky's, and Lorraine's activism is connected to struggles against social and environmental injustice. Sonia Peña "organizes" so that communities have the leadership and skills to articulate and address their self-identified needs. The role women play in this crusade is crucial and was recognized by each woman interviewed. If Sonia focused solely on male community leaders, the unique perspectives, needs, and knowledge of women in the community would be overlooked. Social and environmental justice is based on opposing the systems that impose the burden of environmental degradation on poor communities of color.

These women are each an integral part of an environmental justice movement that simultaneously confronts racism and classism within the mainstream environmental movement. Their perspectives are critical, however, as they represent needs of women, cultures, and classes who historically have been marginalized by Western ideology.

Concluding Remarks

The intent of this chapter has been to assess the viability of ecofeminism as a holistic philosophy addressing environmental and women's issues across race and class. The research indicates that feminism and environmentalism are perceived mainly as white middle-class movements that are generally exclusive of the needs of people of color and the poor. The interviews excerpted in this chapter suggest that these women of color frame their activism differently from that of mainstream environmental movements.

The most germane finding is that these women connect environmental and social justice activism to class and race issues. Despite the overt sexism and racism encountered by the interviewees, they see their oppression as based fundamentally in an unequal distribution of wealth and therefore in inequitable access to resources and power.

Ecofeminist literature by women of color appears to include race and class in its agenda. Environmental justice and health issues are often at the forefront of the discourse. But women-of-color ecofeminists are in the minority. Most self-identified ecofeminists are white women who have focused on personal empowerment rather than confronting and resisting the racial and economic effects of Western patriarchal beliefs and practices. This reflects privileged access to resources. The type of oppression experienced and identified by most white ecofeminists (the majority of ecofeminists) is gender oppression, not classism or racism. Again this is seen in the "whiteness" of feminism and environmentalism, which, when explored, links to higher socioeconomic status.

Rocky, Lorraine, and Sonia reveal much about the lives of other women of color, who like themselves are active in issues that are closely connected to their own personal lives and beliefs, issues that are grounded in their ethnic, class, and gender identities. They are conscious and articulate about the effects that Western ideology has had on their history, their people, and themselves. They are deeply connected to the earth on a variety of levels; not only are they concerned about preservation of nonhuman living things, they are also deeply concerned about the health of their families and the land around them (urban and rural).

As we have shown, they view women and nature in ways similar to those found in the ecofeminist discourse. But to call them ecofeminists would be inappropriate. It would be an oversimplification to label their beliefs "ecofeminist," thereby implying that while some women are theorizing about the philosophy, others (like these women) are acting it out through the complex intersection of gender, race, and class in their communities.

The theme of self-determination resounds clearly and is a lesson to ecofeminists. These women work autonomously, which has implications for a philosophy such as ecofeminism that espouses a global movement. This research suggests that women of color or poor women might more rightly be concerned with local empowerment than with an agenda for global change such as that of ecofeminism. Identity politics (as it relates to self-determination and organizing styles that support autonomy) is a critical issue for ecofeminists. Is it possible to form coordinating and supportive networks of grassroots organizations without universalizing and homogenizing local differences and place-specific issues? Can ecofeminism truly attain "unity in diversity" as a mass movement?

The term "ecofeminism" itself may be detrimental. These interviews suggest that ecofeminism has, up to now, been unable to bridge the gaps of race, class, and gender, despite its well-meaning intentions to do so. That many women are drawn to ecofeminism, not so much for political reasons as for a place to find a spiritual connection and community, implies a need to address the issues of spiritual disconnection. The literature by women-of-color ecofeminists includes spirituality, yet locates it within a perspective that enables them to confront the effects of poverty and racism. That ecofeminist writings by women of color deal with issues of race and class suggests that there is much work to do if ecofeminism wants to cross race and class lines.

Rocky exemplifies what ecofeminism may need to do. She is a deeply spiritual person but is in no way depoliticized from the larger social issues of racism and classism. For a philosophy such as ecofeminism to claim itself to be political in nature connotes a determination to keep its political agendas political. This means that a thoughtful critique of racism, classism, and sexism must be the primary focus. If ecofeminism can reclaim this focus, it has the potential to evolve into more of a "social movement" and to organize around the issues of inequality that directly affect women, children, people of color, and the earth's natural resources. For ecofeminists to accomplish this in a framework of self-determination is the true challenge. Ecofeminists have much to learn from these women's self-determined, locally based and directed environmental and feminist activism.

Unresolved questions remain for ecofeminism. Where does the strategy against patriarchy locate itself if Chicanas refuse to disconnect from the men in their culture? Is it possible, in determining a course of action against Western (white) patriarchal beliefs and practices, for women of color and white women to include men of color who are oppressed through the same forms of racism and classism that poor women and women of color experience? A division exists here, in terms of identity politics, between ecofeminists who define their identities as woman-centered, and ecofeminists who remain inclusive of men. Women like Rocky, Sonia, and Lorraine are not likely to identify with a woman-centered agenda, because they refuse to categorize the issues of racism and classism as only women's issues. How does ecofeminism propose to be inclusive of women of color who are inclusive of men?

In the area of organizing, the difference between an academically and philosophically based activism such as ecofeminism and grassroots organizing (which is more appropriate and effective in communities where people are more directly in touch with the issues) must be explored. How do ecofeminists propose to include people who do not identify with the academic discourse and theory of the philosophy?

Ecofeminism must clarify its foundation and address these questions. Research such as this gives insight into deeper issues that delineate varying identities and forms of activism. Even within ethnicities, issues are perceived and confronted differently. The similarities and differences, as well as the in-depth examination of these three women's lives, reveals the complexity of critiquing a philosophy such as ecofeminism. At the same time, Rocky, Lorraine, and Sonia have helped clarify the issues that are in critical need of being addressed by ecofeminists. Perhaps in addressing classism and racism (and all of their effects and implications), a place may be found to unite so that women of color and white women can work for similar, even if differently articulated, goals in the process of overturning Western patriarchal ideology and practice.

Notes

I would like to thank Devon Peña for his assistance and guidance. An earlier version of this chapter was presented as my senior thesis in sociology at Colorado College, Colorado Springs.

1. The National Chicano Human Rights Commission was established in 1982 to promote indigenous status for Chicanos and to renegotiate the Treaty of Guadalupe Hidalgo. The NCHRC was accepted as an observer group by the International Indian Treaty Council in 1985.

2. The Crusade for Justice, founded in 1966 by Rodolfo "Corky" Gonzales, is based on community involvement and includes a school (two hundred preschool through college students) called Tlatelolco, a bookstore, a curio shop, and a social center. Crusade for Justice worked for community control of public schools and offered an alternative to public education during this protest movement.

3. The American Friends Service Committee is a Quaker organization working for social justice through humanitarian service. The focus of AFSC at local, national, and international levels is community justice, disarmament, and international affairs through organizing and educating.

4. The Center for Third World Organizing is a nonprofit organization working with activists and community organizers to promote the interests of Asian, African-American, Latin, and Native American peoples. CTWO is based in Oakland, California.

5. Sonia Peña worked with PUEBLO (People United for a Better Oakland) on a lead abatement plan in Oakland, California. PUEBLO, which developed out of CTWO in April 1990, is a multi-issue, multiracial community organization protesting the lack of education about and assistance in preventing lead poisoning in their communities.

6. See, for example, Brown 1983; Cone Newton and Ortega 1991; Kirk 1992; Pulido 1990; Mealy 1990; and D. G. Peña 1992.

Part 3

Alternatives to Destruction

The Pasture Poacher

by Joseph C. Gallegos

Well it happened again
Max's cows are out of their pen
Straight to my haystack a pair of ten
I'm pissed, I'm pissed, I'm burning inside
Them heifers are this time going to die.

For the rifle I make a dash
While loading it I get a flash
"The cows aren't at fault," let's not get rash
The saying is "shoot the owner not the cattle"
Or am I just a victim of a pasture poachers' battle?

I need a special psychology to combat this parasite
He watches my pastures till I'm out of eyesight
Then leads his herd in, Now is that right?
I've tried different methods to this day
Even the law in so many a way.

I'm tired, damned tired of this war
It seems endless and I want no more.
I have one idea ready to score
I'll corral his cows and load them all up
To the sale barn they'll go on the final roundup.

8   Acequia Tales

Stories from a Chicano Centennial Farm

Joseph C. Gallegos

It was a cool summer morning. The chirping of various birds mingled with the barnyard sounds—the morning concert. The sun was shining on the lifting dew, which made the fields glimmer in wet fox-fire green. The soothing sounds and majestic scenery are so common on the ranch that many times a person just gets used to it and forgets the surrounding beauty. This morning was different. Marlito was in a mood of heightened awareness. The sounds around him seemed louder than usual, the smells more pungent, and the colors brighter. "What a great morning," he sighed contentedly.

Marlito was soaking up the surroundings when he was suddenly interrupted by a loud noise. It was the loud but familiar bang of the ewes walking on the steel troughs. It was his signal that there were hungry sheep around.

The barnyard chores had to be done first, and like every other morning, the job seemed to involve little brains and a lot of sheep connivery. Marlito started by feeding the sheep a few bales of hay and a bucket of oats. The part he hated about feeding grain to the sheep was that it always seemed to become a race to the feeding trough.

Anytime sheep are fed in a trough, and the trough is in the middle of the corral, well . . . get your running shoes. When sheep see a person with a bucket, they become crazed, and they rush and crowd around the person. Many times they knock you down flat on your ass.

Last year, Marlito had to save his dad from becoming a victim of the daily feeding frenzy. Marlito's dad got caught with a bucket of oats in the middle of the sheep pen, and by the time Marlito got to him, he was at the bottom of the heap of an ovine free-for-all. Luckily, he survived the ordeal and the incident became a topic of conversation for a week or two. "Pobre hombre, ya mero lo mataban las borregas" (Poor man, the sheep almost killed him), you'd hear some old rancher saying at the cafe. "Si," another might pitch in, "las borregas te aplastan vivo, si te dejas" (Yes, the sheep will crush you to death, if you let them). And then someone else would start in with a story about way back when, in 1923, old man such-and-such had drowned in a sea of wool. "Mucha lana, te mueres sin lana" (Too much wool, you die without money).

When newcomers visit Marlito's ranch, they are usually sent to feed the sheep. What a comical display to see city folks fight off an onslaught of hungry ewes. Comic relief often quickly degenerates into a quick, on-the-spot rescue mission.

This morning, Marlito managed to sneak into the corral, so that by the time the sheep saw him, he had already emptied the bucket. Once the sheep were fed, he walked over to the barn where a few cows were waiting to be fed and watered. On the way there, Marlito crossed the *acequia* and saw something that almost took his breath away.

The ditch level had dropped during the night! Marlito left everything and went running to tell his father about the low water level. On the way to see his father, he recalled the last time the water level had been this low. He could not really understand why, but the low water level had caused his father to call the sheriff, and there was almost a fight with old man Evan Barato.

Stealing Water? Better to Shoot the Man!

Evan Barato was an old ex-mayordomo. He had been voted off the ditch association board because his drinking and cantankerous personality were affecting his ditch-riding duties. Evan had protested his political defeat by taking water from the ditch without getting permission from the newly elected mayordomo. It so happened that the new mayordomo was Marlito's Tio Cosme. When Cosme approached Barato about taking water, Evan flipped him the bird, and that's when all the trouble began. Cosme didn't take kindly to being flipped off, so he shoved Evan. At this moment, the story goes, Marlito's father, Cisco, the acequia's treasurer, entered the scene. Cisco tried to break up the fisticuffs, but the two stubborn goats kept shoving each other. That's when . . . well, no need to go into the gory details.

To make a long story short, Evan went to jail, and Cisco became an enemy of old man Barato. You see, Barato thought Cisco was siding with Cosme. The real reason Cisco called the sheriff was that he didn't want to have Cosme raising Evan's blood pressure. Evan had just received his pacemaker, and a slight rise in his blood pressure could have sent the old man to his grave. But the *parciantes* (irrigation-ditch members) always wondered: Wouldn't it be better to shoot the man instead of stealing his water?

Learning from Acequias

The preceding story is an example of what I call acequia tales. An acequia tale can deal with any aspect involving the irrigation ditch. There are stories about who gets the water and who doesn't. There are stories about goats, sheep, and cows drowning in the ditches. There are stories about that last miserable drought and even stories about *la llorona*.[1] I can recall many stories of battles over water. In my *paíz* (homeland), water is more valuable than gold.

The exciting part is that these stories are always being invented, even as I write this. There is always some kind of acequia problem, conflict, or strange situation. These irrigation associations are not some sort of perfect heaven on earth. It would take a lifetime to write all these stories down, but let me tell you, the acequias work only because the farmers depend on each other for the water. This is never an easy thing; fights and conflicts are an accepted part of the everyday life of acequias. Ditch stories are true-life tales and have lessons to teach us about mutual aid and cooperation among the parciantes. The stories show us how hard it is to keep the peace on the ditch.

I recall my first lesson on the importance of water. It happened not too long after I first heard the tale about Cosme, Evan, and Cisco. I was about eight years old when I opened my first *compuerta* (ditch gate).[2] I had watched my dad open the headgate several times, so I naively thought it was the thing to do. I opened la compuerta and proudly showed my Grandma the "great accomplishment." To my surprise, I was yelled at, spanked, and scorned for several hours. That night, *abuelita* Eliza told the famous story of how two of the ditch members had a conflict over water, and one of the parciantes was killed.

According to Eliza, who was the very best acequia storyteller, this murderous incident took place a few fields down the *acequia madre* from our home. As I recall the story, one member accused the other of taking his water. As the disagreement became heated, the accuser bent over to close the headgate and the accused hit him over the head with a shovel, killing him. Now, if this story didn't scare me, what would?

Frightful or not, these stories prepared me for the challenges that I had to face in learning to manage la acequia as an adult *mayordomo*.

I am presently the ditch rider of the San Luis Peoples Ditch Company.[3] I believe that many of the incidents that occur on the ditch are due to rivalries rooted in the past. Many of today's incidents follow the same patterns as the old stories. Just the other day, one of the newcomers on the ditch, a veteran marine by the name of Hank, was having trouble keeping the supply of water flowing into his reservoir. Hank is an odd type. He takes the water from the ditch, stores it in the reservoir, and then pumps it into a seventy-thousand-dollar center-pivot irrigation sprinkler. He's the only one on the ditch who does this. He has never liked the ditch method and thinks it's too primitive a way to irrigate. "It's too inefficient," he says with a sneer. Hank is a retired colonel who loves his daily spirits. Sometimes the spirits seem to overtake him, but if you can talk to him before 10 A.M., he is a very normal cattleman.

On this day, Hank was his usual self, drunk. I had been at the sale barn and was in no mood to deal with Hank's obnoxious ways. When he approached me, it was obvious that he was really plastered. His first words from slurred out, "Ware's myah waaahtah?" My first reaction to that statement was to think calmly, "Who could possibly have the old man's water?" Before I could come up with a response, Hank went into some type of conniption fit. He started in with wild language and then in a burst of anger blurted out, "I bet you stole my water, you shithead."

With that comment, my "be calm" attitude went to the dogs. I didn't mind the fact that he called me a shithead, but a water thief? That is a horse of a different color. I instantly went into a rage and was cursing him worse than he could ever imagine possible. The situation had deteriorated to the point of near violence when my brother intervened.

As Hank and I argued, my brother came rumbling into the yard in his truck. He instantly realized what was going on and called the cops. The cops hauled Hank to jail to sober up and warned me about controlling my temper. The next day, Hank drove up and apologized for his behavior. Now that I recall the incident, I could have been a little more controlled. I remember many times that my dad was accused of stealing water and all hell would break out. I guess that's where the saying "You can steal a man's wife, but never his water" came from.

This statement may seem insensitive to the female gender, but it is part of our local lore, and so it is foolish to pretend such a saying does not exist. This statement is never made in the presence of a man's wife. It shows the importance of water to agriculture in this alpine desert region. The ranch revolves around water. If there is drought, your land use will change to a completely different mode. Plowing and soil tilling happen earlier in the year, and the cattle grazing takes different rotations. Lack of water causes the plant life to grow at a slower rate, and the recovery of grazed grass takes longer. The slower recovery makes the operation depend on the areas that are impacted less by the drought. For example, during a wet year, the uplands of the San Francisco Creek can be grazed until September, but during a dry year they can be grazed only until late July.[4] I'm sure most farmers here agree: The availability of water determines the way you run the business.

There are many different types of farm/ranch operations throughout the world. My ranch is a hybrid, because it is also a farm. I grow grass for the cattle, but I also grow other crops. The farms in this region are unique. They have a long and rich history. Our crops, animals, and production techniques are from both the old and new worlds. We have borrowed a lot from the Pueblos, Hopis, and the Navajos. And we have also shared wisdom, seeds, and animals with our Indian brothers and sisters.

The one thing that makes us unique is our irrigation tradition. I am told by the academics that the acequia comes from the Moors of North Africa. That is something, how we are irrigating in the middle of North America with techniques that came from Africa.

The acequias are good for the land. They have to be. The ditches make a lot of plant life possible in what is really a cold, barren desert. More plants means that the wildlife — birds and mammals — have a home. The ecologists call this "biodiversity." I call it life, *tierra y vida*.

That is the other thing that makes these farms special. We manage our lands to produce not just alfalfa, hay, corn, and beans. These lands are sanctuaries for wildlife. What is good for the farmer, the rancher, and livestock can also be good for the mountain lion, the owls and hawks, and the coyotes. When I see all this wildlife around me, it tells me that the land is healthy enough to sustain many different forms of life. A good farmer will not destroy the land or poison the water. A good farmer will not kill the wildlife or destroy its home.

Water Hogs, Thieves, and the Devil

The Corpus Aquino Gallegos Ranch is situated in a high-altitude desert, the San Luis Valley. The annual precipitation is about the same as that of Death Valley in California. The major difference between our desert and Death Valley is that we have snowpack in the mountains. Slow spring melt from the fourteen- and thirteen-thousand-foot peaks allows us to utilize the moisture during the summer growing months and deliver water at constant rates. The consistent water supply during the dry summer months is the major reason the farmers can irrigate, and that means good production. Without the snowpack there would be no farms in this area. In the mid-summer days there is very little rainfall, and this is the time when most crops require irrigation in order to flourish.

The technicalities of the water situation are very complex; to explain these technicalities requires much time and space, for the way irrigation water is allocated and delivered is very intricate. The interesting aspect of water politics is how it determines much of the human behavior patterns in the agricultural community. When the snowpack is plentiful and the spring has plenty of rainfall, members of the ditch company are much more cooperative and friendly. There is usually a good harvest, and that means more economic prosperity with many smiling faces. It's a great time to be a ditch rider. Most of what a mayordomo does in a wet year is to drink coffee with the members of the ditch. On the other hand, a dry year will bring out the worst in people. Members seem to complain more, and tempers often flare. The idle chats and hot coffee take a back seat to verbal jousts and cold stares.

The problem with dry years is that every ditch member will accuse the other members of being water hogs. "Water hog" is a local term that is used to describe a person who takes too long to irrigate and wastes water. As far as local insults, it ranks way up there with "water thief." The only thing *worse* than a water hog is a water thief.

To be a good ditch rider means you also have to be a good psychologist — you have to be in a position to understand human behavior and to resolve conflicts that could spiral out of control. In farming the arid lands of the San Luis Valley, a good psychologist abides by the cycles of the water. You have to watch the seasonal cycles and plan ahead. If the snowfall is light during the winter, you'd better start planning for a rough irrigation season.

The problem with the water hog is that the behavior affects everyone. So you have to make sure no one gets too greedy or too desperate with the scarce water. In dry years the mayordomo works a lot harder, because he has to help everyone irrigate to get the job done more efficiently. That way, you control the water hogging, and everyone gets enough water to irrigate.

The personal relationships on the ditch are changing. Managing the ditch is less personal and more formal each passing year. I was hoping that many of these ideas wouldn't have to be heavily analyzed, or certain words given definitions. For example, the term "water availability" can be defined, and I will not leave all the analyzing and defining to the lawyers of the world. I would prefer to let the free-minded men and women who use the water rights express themselves. Water law, and the Denver elite lawyers who design and defend the law, are causing these changes. It used to be that the ditch was managed on a person-to-person level. The members' word was the law. The human aspect was foremost, and the law was distant and removed from the everyday work of the ditch. Today, it is getting more formal, and this can create problems, because the law does not abide by the land.

Also, with more newcomers on the ditch, well, they want to follow everything by the book. They already think the old way is a wasteful manner to manage water, and with changing laws, new technologies, and more complexity, the potential for conflict is increased. The law is not designed to serve the needs of the land or the farmer. The critics will tell you that farmers have too much water and that they waste it. They attack the acequias as wasteful and inefficient. The urban developers and politicians want the water so they can support economic growth in the sprawling cities. So they change the laws and make it difficult for us to manage the water resources. The lawyers and engineers create more situations that become ripe for conflict.

Whose point of view is this? The cottonwood trees that line the acequia banks don't think the leaking water is wasted. Nor do the birds and other animals that live in the trees. The ditches create habitat niches for wildlife, and that is a good thing for the animals and the farmers. It is not wasteful, unless of course you are an urban developer greedily looking for more water for the cities' maniacal growth needs. The gringo treats water like a commodity.[5] You know the saying, "In Colorado water flows uphill, towards money."

Whatever changes have occurred in water law, the threats to our irrigation traditions do not stop with the law books. There is now tremendous pressure to transfer agricultural water rights to urban and industrial uses, which are economically more profitable than farming. This is what happened with the Battle Mountain Gold Mine in the Rito Seco watershed.[6] The water court in Alamosa let the mining company transfer water from agricultural to industrial uses. The transfer of water is bad enough, but the mine waste pollution is an even more serious, long-term threat to the quantity and quality of water in the ditches.

Water rights are being threatened. Like I said earlier, without water there can be no farming. Without farming there can be no community here; it's just a desert. And you can't live in a desert for too long. I always say that farming is not an occupation; it is a way of life. And that is what is at stake here, a way of life.

My family has farmed this land for five generations, since my great-great-grandfather, Dario Gallegos, settled here in 1851. I do not want to see this way of life destroyed. If I wanted to leave farming, I would have stayed in the oil business ten years ago and made a lot more money doing something that is a lot easier than working the land. This is not about making money; it is about protecting a way of life that is in balance with the land.

To live on this land, you have to feel her emotions; you have to nurture her. Mining is not nurturing. It is the rape of the earth. Mining is abusive—like punching your spouse in the stomach and tearing her apart from limb to limb. People sometimes use the term "husbandry" to describe farming. I like the term because it shows that men can establish nurturing relations with nature. You cannot be abusive to the land and survive as a farmer. This is why the farmers in this area are opposed to mining in principle. Now we will have to live with an abusive, violent neighbor. There is a new saying in San Luis: "The devil has arrived, and he drives an eighty-ton earth mover."

Return to *la Sierra*

As there are acequia tales, there are also *la Sierra,* or "mountain," tales. La Sierra tales are also exciting and like the acequia tales, they involve many personalities and conflicts. La Sierra is our name for the Sangre de Cristo mountain range that rises east of our rancho. La Sierra is our watershed. That means that all the snowpack from the mountain peaks will melt and run off into the creeks and rivers. This is where our acequia water supply comes from. Because la Sierra has been the source of our lifeblood and the basis of our agricultural existence for nearly two centuries, the protection of the watershed is an extremely important task.

Before experiencing la Sierra for myself, I was told many stories about the great mountains. Most of these tales were shared by the *viejitos* (elders) of our family. But after years of working on la Sierra, I now have a few tales of my own. The tale that comes to mind is about how a practical joke to get revenge can turn into a nearly tragic childhood episode.

It was a mean, hot summer when I was the age of twelve. It was the summer when I finally got to work herding sheep in la Sierra. Being old enough to herd sheep was a turning point in a young boy's life. It was the time to celebrate the transition from childhood to manhood. Herding sheep in la Sierra meant that I would be leaving home for the first time in my life. It was the first time I would join and work in the company of the *borregeros* (sheepherders) and learn about the mountains. Sheepherding and hard work were not new to me. It was la Sierra that made the difference. I would no longer have to stay in the lowlands doing the monotonous, backbreaking jobs of hoeing and irrigating the crops. I had the prestigious job of summer borregero apprentice.

La familia didn't have many sheep to run on la Sierra that year, but it was enough to justify hiring a summer borregero. Most of the local borregeros went to Wyoming where the big herds were. So that year, la familia hired a borregero from New Mexico. Felipe was an older man. In his younger days he had been a superb *tresquilador* (sheepshearer) and he followed the big herds. As Felipe got to be elderly, he declined the long migration to the north and took up herding closer to home.

When I first met old man Felipe, I really liked him. His low monotone voice made him seem extremely timid. As I later found out, this was not the case! Felipe was a real storyteller, who loved a good laugh. Away from his *patrones* (bosses), the timid, obedient sheepherder became a loud, talkative jokester.

As a first-timer in la Sierra, my gullibility was exposed by this old borrego. I put great faith in what Felipe told me, hanging on his every word. He had so much to teach me about sheepherding and about la Sierra. But I eventually found out that his stories or words of advice often left me as the butt end of a joke. As the summer wore on and I became more learned about mountain herding, my confidence in handling the sheep increased. The price I had to pay for this mountain training was to put up with Felipe's constant joking.

The joking was tolerable until Felipe instructed me to do the mid-summer task of *soltando cola* (tail loosening). According to Felipe's instructions, soltando cola was done only to the bucks of the herd in order to increase their fertility. "To do this job," he explained, "you first have to gather all the bucks in a corral. Then you capture each buck, throw it down on the ground, and get it facing belly up. Then you quickly grab the tail and point it at a full moon. . . . Yes," Felipe continued, "this means the job has to be done at night."

So one night in late July, Felipe had me go into the aspen log corral where he had gathered the bucks. I tried to capture the bucks. This whole job proved to be a real fiasco. The bucks had never been held down in their lives. The meanest buck saw me, charged, and knocked me out! The next thing I knew, I was looking up at Felipe's face, which at that moment was about to burst into laughter. Rather jovially, Felipe asked me if I was all right, and when I said, "I think so," he broke out in an uncontrollable guffaw.

Well, at that moment, a bit too late, I realized that the whole soltando cola job was a hoax. Felipe had made a big fool out of me. I knew that revenge was the only sure way to restore my honor and dignity. The retaliation had to be timely and good enough to fool Felipe. I especially wanted to time it for that moment when Felipe was ready to pull another joke on me. This way he would never, ever pull a dirty joke on me again, or at least he'd think twice about it.

It was difficult to come up with an idea. Then one day I was herding the sheep near an aspen grove. The sheep were grazing steadily that day, so I walked off to explore an opening in the aspens. The aspen grove was thick with white-barked and quakey trees and knee-high mountain grasses. In the midst of the grove, I discovered the key to my revenge: an old, abandoned aspen log corral. When I first saw the corral, I didn't immediately think of the possibilities for revenge. It was later that day, as Felipe and I were doing the evening corralling at the main camp, that the idea came to mind.

Knowing that Felipe would use my gullibility as a tool for his practical jokes, I constantly searched for his weakness. When he told me to let a ewe out of the corral and pointed at our white sheepdog, I finally realized his weakness. Felipe was nearsighted when he didn't have his spectacles on.

Every day, Felipe and I would take the herd to some grassy mountain parks near the aspen grove. On the way to the parks, the herd had to pass through a narrow trail above a rocky cliff. The sheep passed along this part of the trail for several hundred feet, and I started to wonder what would happen if a sheep fell off the two-hundred-foot cliff. With this thought in mind, I went about planning my own practical joke.

The borregeros usually take Sundays off to go to the nearest village for supplies or to take care of whatever errand needs to get done. As usual, Felipe prepared his horse and the burro for the weekly trip. He had no idea what would be in store for him when he returned. With the good-byes said, I set out on my quest.

Like every morning, I grazed the sheep in the meadows near the aspen grove. This morning was a little different. Once in the meadows, I herded the sheep up against the aspens. The herd got into morning grazing, and then I raced into the aspens and started fixing the abandoned log corral. It was a small corral, so fixing the structure was easy and took little time. Once the corral was repaired, I went back to the herd and split it into two groups. I took one of the groups into the corral, where there was some grass. I then took the other group back down the trail toward the main camp. Stopping at the cliff, I broke out the remnants of an old sheep tent and some white rags. Climbing down a rocky ledge, I took the tent and all the rags to the bottom of the cliff. At the bottom, I ripped the white rags into pieces and draped them over the shrubs, logs, trees, and so on. I climbed back up and took the half-herd back to the main camp.

Felipe arrived at camp later that evening, and I started acting out my role. With a sobbing voice, I told Felipe: *"Se hicieron locos casi todos los borregos y brincaron al cañon y todos se murieron"* (Almost all of the sheep went crazy and jumped into the canyon and all of them died). At first, Felipe did not believe me. He then looked at the herd and noticed that a good number were indeed missing! He instantly became concerned and started asking questions. That night, I hid Felipe's glasses.

Felipe couldn't wait to see the remains of the "crazed ewes." Early in the morning, I led him down the sheep trail to the site of my dirty joke. He looked over the cliff. His squinting eyes told me that he could barely make out the patchy pieces of white rag, especially without his spectacles. I could tell immediately that my contrivance probably looked like real dead sheep to him. He was seeing all the evidence necessary to believe my story. And boy, let me tell you he was sorry, panicky, and very disturbed!

After Felipe saw the make-believe carcasses, he took off grumbling toward the main camp. I followed him into the sheep tent and noticed that he was shaking. This borregero was extremely nervous, and for a moment I saw tears welling up in his eyes. He muttered something about, *"Se va enojar el patrón"* (The boss will be angry). I have to admit that I started to feel pretty bad about my stunt. I was about to tell him about the whole charade. Then I thought about the madness he had put me through all summer long, and for the moment I decided not to confess. Felipe must not have slept that night, because I heard him moaning and cursing about his poor luck.

I woke up early and immediately knew something was wrong. Felipe had not awakened me, and it was late for our morning chores. I yelled for Felipe a couple of times, but he didn't respond. I got up and dressed, only to find that the sheep were still in the corral and none of the morning chores were done. I yelled out a few more times, but still no response. After a couple of hours searching for the borregero, a scary thought came to me that made me very nervous. Could it be that Felipe had run away? I went back to the tent and looked for Felipe's personal items. All his things were gone! *He* was gone! Felipe had left me! My predicament was terrible. What was I to do? Thinking about my situation for a long time, I decided to get help. I now had to face up to my family about the problem caused by a vengeful practical joke gone awry.

The next morning I left the sheep in the corral and went for help. It was really hard to face my father *y los hermanos* with this joke turned into a big problem. I told the whole truth and got my butt kicked. I shall never forget *la patada* (the butt kicking), nor will I ever forget Felipe, the borregero, whom I never saw again in this part of the country.

My tale is typical of the stories about la Sierra. And hundreds more remain to be told. My story has been changed over the years. In one version, the storyteller meets the devil by the cliffs and barely escapes with his tanned hide. Stories like this give life and meaning to la Sierra. Through such tales we learn to make our home in the mountain. I have many memories of sheepherding, cattle driving, horseback riding, hunting, fishing, and hiking. These memories are what made me who I am. La Sierra is the place where I grew up. She gives me a place of belonging. Something bigger than one person or family.

Every day I awaken, the first thing I see is la Sierra. This has been our home for almost two centuries. The common land has been taken from us for some thirty-seven years. We have been here a long time. But it will never really feel like we are home, not as long as the mountain is kept under lock and key. Many in my generation were the first to grow up without a chance to really know the mountain as a home. My hope is that our children grow up in a world my grandparents knew and come back home to be with the mountain. In the end, no one owns la Sierra. The mountain owns us: She cares for us and makes our livelihoods possible. As long as the snowpack is up there in the mountains — sheltered by the shadows of the forests — we will be here, irrigating with the clear spring water that makes its way from the peaks to the lowlands.

Notes

I want to thank Devon Peña for his knowledge shared and Rose Mendoza-Green for her help in the preparation of this chapter.

1. The legend of *la llorona* [the weeper] runs the course of the Rio Grande from the river's headwaters in Colorado to its mouth in South Texas. The local version tells of *la llorona* as the ghost of a woman who long ago drowned her children. She

is now condemned to roam at night along rivers, creeks, ditches, and other water-courses, wailing as she searches for her children.

2. The *compuerta* is a gate used to divert water from the *acequia madre* (mother ditch) to the *sangrias* (lateral ditches used to irrigate the farmers' fields). The largest *compuerta* is the headgate. It is used to control the flow of water from the source stream into the *acequia madre*.

3. The San Luis Peoples Ditch holds the oldest surface water rights in the State of Colorado, with a decree dating back in 1852 and adjudicated in 1889. There are some twenty-three ditches in the area of San Luis with mid-nineteenth century water rights, the oldest in Colorado.

4. The description by Gallegos of the effects of drought on grass recovery and different grazing rotations is a good example of the practice of "transhumance" described by Laura Pulido, chapter 4.

5. In this context the use of the term "gringo" is meant to convey a critique of a particular ideology. The ideology is associated with the commodification of land; it refers not to the "white race" but to a way of looking at issues. An example is the gringo attitude toward water, an attitude which fails to respect ecological limits (particularly evident among those who came out West from more temperate and rainy regions).

6. See Peña, chapter 9. See also Peña and Gallegos 1993, 1997.

9   A Gold Mine, an Orchard,
and an Eleventh Commandment

Devon G. Peña

Over the past century and a half, Western water law largely has been shaped by a struggle amongst private, public, and common property values. Nowhere is this more apparent than in the rural intermountain regions of northern New Mexico and southern Colorado, where Hispano communal land and water rights have been subordinated to private capitalist and state bureaucratic control after enclosure. As Stanley Crawford (1988, 267) states: "Water should go . . . to those who tend it, who use it, who love it, who dance for it. . . . Yet we have licensed our society to scheme for [water] to flow toward those with money and power. . . . [W]e have, in effect, given them the keys to the treasury so that no expense will be spared in drawing lines, making maps, conducting research, making surveys, and filling vaults and basements with mountains of legal testimony."

The legal reduction of land and water to mere commodities is much more than just a key to the treasury. It is the linchpin of a legal system designed by a colonizing settler state to expropriate the land and water of indigenous homelands. The ancestral Hispano watershed commonwealths of the Río Arriba were forcibly converted into exploitable natural resource colonies. They are now scientifically managed by the state and capital for the sake of economic development. The rule of water law in these intermountain bioregions is grotesquely inequitable. It privileges the sacred right of private property against presumably more vulgar, primitive, and inefficient rights vested in ancient customary practices that hold land and water in usufruct (see Rock 1976, D. G. Peña 1992, Wilkinson 1992, and Goldman 1993).

The American legal tradition poses serious long-term threats to the legal standing of Hispano and Pueblo Indian water rights and land-use practices. The fundamental problem is that the law artificially and unwisely separates water and land from their cultural-ecological contexts. By defining water and land as commodities, the Euro-American legal system allows capital to cannibalize cultural and natural landscapes, to transform the diversity of life itself into exploitable commercial objects that exist in a state without rights before the law. On private property, trees have no standing.

The enclosure of ancestral Spanish and Mexican common lands eliminated local management of the watersheds. This expropriation of the land base eventually provoked an increasingly fierce battle over senior surface water rights, the existence of which depends on the protection of the watersheds. Water law, that is, the doctrine of prior appropriation (first in use, first in right), has been used by the state to further limit the ability of local cultures to protect the customary rights of senior agricultural water users by promoting the industrial and commercial exploitation of mineral deposits, timber, wildlife, and even scenery. This attack by the legal system has unleashed deathly economic forces. These forces are undermining the integrity of a fragile and limited resource base through processes of social displacement and ecological destruction that are endangering the survival of sustainable rural human communities in the arid intermountain environment.

The legal system privileges an ownership regime that treats water as a commodity to be bought and sold. So, of course, those with the most money play the game. Making it legal to buy and sell water physically severs the water from the land. This legal code differs dramatically when compared to the treatment of water in the Upper Rio Grande bioregion; there water is under a system of customary rules that emerged from a confluence of Moorish, Spanish, Mexican, and Puebloan practices. These traditions treat water as a common good with use values inhering in and inseparable from the land.[1] This basic contradiction between private and common property regimes is the most serious threat to the protection and survival of the water rights of *acequias,* the irrigation systems that are the material basis for the Hispano agropastoral communities in this bioregion.

The attack on common property rights involves the legal codification of production that produces violent but legally sanctioned invasions, enclosures, and expropriations of *space.* The law itself violates the integrity of places as habitat for mixed communities of humans and nonhumans. Yet, in many parts of the world, marginal hill populations have resisted this misuse of the laws of the land and water.

The drawing of lines, like the production of surveys, maps, and legal testimony, culturally disrupts customary patterns of sustainable water and land use (Ebright 1994). Developers are supported by a legal system that endorses the right to industrialize and commercialize water rights, even at the expense of environmental and cultural integrity.[2] In his book *Crossing the Next Meridian* Charles Wilkinson (1993) attacks the "lords of yesterday" — mining, cattle, timber, and water barons — and the laws perpetuated to facilitate the extraction of natural resources during the American conquest of the intermountain West.[3] While the "lords of yesterday" are presumably on the decline, in San Luis, Colorado, a struggle is unfolding between the acequia-based farmers and "the lords of things with a price," the water and timber barons, land developers, and government bureaucrats who promote the marketing of nature.

The Semiotics of Water Court, or Long Live the Vadose Zone!

Joe Gallegos and I walked into Colorado water court in Alamosa. It was an unusually warm morning for late fall in the San Luis Valley. The trial of the San Luis Peoples Ditch and Others vs. Battle Mountain Gold was about to begin. In retrospect I can see the irony of the legal language used to describe those who filed as joint opponents to the proposed water right transfer and augmentation plan of BMG — The San Luis Peoples Ditch and "Others." The history of capitalism charts this process of the exploitation of Others. Joe and I, along with the rest of the joint opponents, were really Others, not just in the sense of the lingo of legal proceedings but more disturbingly in the minds of the corporate lawyers from BMG. They were already comfortably situated in Judge Robert Ogburn's courtroom when we arrived.

We were more than opponents. We were from a different culture, a different world than the lawyers from Denver and Houston. We were bronze-skinned, rag-tag types. We were the unruly Others who refused to wear their Sunday best to court: We, the Others, who allegedly speak a funny type of English, "Ees lek dis"; we, who are presumably prone to irrationality and emotionalism; we, Others who actually care more about the health of the land, for it is part of the family, than we do for the bottom line. How irrational can you get in a competitive, individualistic society that rewards acquisition above all else? Joe and I shared the feeling that something really bad was about to happen to us.

The judge spoke first, and what he said confirmed our worst fears, for he said something about not wanting this "to get emotional." This was a purely legal and scientific matter. Water court, he explained, was a very serious legal process, and the opponents would not be allowed to parade a bunch of emotional people in front of the bench. I nudged Joe and asked, "Do you think he feels that way about all environmentalists, or just Mexicans?" The judge went on about the necessity to stick to facts and procedures; none of this fuzzy environmental stuff. This was good legal positivism, a calculated separation of "facts" from "values." Talk about anticipating the fall. The reductionist logic of water law combined with the rigid formality of its overseers is a very effective strategy for keeping monied power in control of the rules and the outcome of public discourses. Here was a perfect example of how the values of environmental protection and cultural conservation are not given equal weight when forced to confront the apparently sacred claims of private property.

Throughout the trial, BMG did most, nay all, of the parading. The trial was an obscene, one-sided, five-day exhibition by expert hydrologists, geologists, engineers, and lawyers who stalked well-worn legal and scientific terrain. It was a virtual, nonstop scientific battering ram. All of the experts were snappy looking in their three-piece, shark-skin suits and alligator boots — all sharper than a nail on the stand.

The experts' testimony seemed rational enough. It was coherent . . . rigorous. They cited all the correct sources and outlined all the appropriate water law case histories. The piles of charts, maps, surveys, and expert depositions were all neatly in place (and so terribly inaccessible). The absurdity of the arguments made by the opposing legal and scientific team members was obvious to us, but they really seemed to believe that cyanide leaching and strip-mining are environmentally sound. Scientists can be perpetrators and victims of their own scientific delusions. They worship at the altar of technological fixes. As a student of mine, Michelle Kaye, says, "They are up to their modern scientific elbows in the myth of objectivity." And money easily buys their expertise, which is to say, their loyalty to blind faith in science and technology as obfuscating servants of power.

It seemed to me that the acequia representatives were the ones with the ethnoscientific argument. After all, they view water as part of a complex ecological system. Interacting with geography, water creates the conditions that encourage the emergence of diverse life-forms. These life-forms — plant, animal, human — interact to create life regions that are based on close relationships between the various members of the mixed community. Some people call this a bioregional way of life. It means living in harmony with the local environment. It means having the sense of place and local knowledge necessary to develop human cultures that are in harmony with the ecological limits of the bioregion. It means being able to live with a "steady-state economy" and recognizing that water, land, and air are not "things with a price." They are the essential natural conditions that make life on the planet possible. A bioregional way of life means understanding that water has a health of its own and sustains a dynamic equilibrium in terms of mass, flow rate, and water quality. Those who understand this way of life guard against abuses of water that undermine the resilience, carrying capacity, and regenerative properties of a sensitive ecosystem.

Water is often described around San Luis through the metaphor of the cardiovascular system. People around San Luis can often be heard saying, "Water is our lifeblood." As in the cardiovascular system, when the human heart is affected because the arteries are clogged, people get sick and die. Pollution (cholesterol) damages the circulatory system and endangers the health of the overall organism. Creeks, rivers, aquifers, clouds, rain cycles, and the microclimatic dynamics of evaporation, evapotranspiration, and convection *are* the circulatory system of a watershed, providing for an "elegant balance."[4] Pollute, destroy, or disrupt the hydrological cycles of the watershed, and you endanger the balance and health of the entire ecosystem.[5]

Obfuscating rhetoric was the order of five long days in a courtroom crowded with hostile experts. The contempt they held for us was thick enough to smell, like polyurethane mixed with sulfur. Despite this parade, the acequias of the Culebra River basin forced a few major, somewhat costly, concessions from the corporation (see Peña and Gallegos 1993). By the time the opponents were called to the stand, everyone, including the judge and lawyers, was weary. The experts of BMG had put us all through the grinding mill. Joe and I felt violated, wounded, and exhausted. I imagined that this is how the earth must feel under the incessant grinding and pounding of the gargantuan ore crushers and earth movers at the Rito Seco mine.

Maclovio Martínez, president of the Costilla County Conservancy District, another of the joint objectors, and Joe Gallegos, *mayordomo* of the San Luis Peoples Ditch, were the only local people who testified. Josephine Lucero, whose deposition had been taken earlier, was already on her deathbed and could not make it to Alamosa. The opponents' testimonies were over in a matter of minutes! No one, it seemed, had time to listen to the people who had the most direct knowledge of the situation—the local farmers who understood what it takes to work sustainedly with the land. But the legal system does not recognize the legitimacy of the place-centered land ethics and ecological wisdom held by the acequia farmers and ranchers. With the silencing of local knowledge, ecological concerns could be more easily dismissed as irrelevant to the case. Through a perniciously disrespectful derogation of local knowledge, the case was reconstructed as being primarily concerned with a much more narrow task—determining the quantitative criteria to be used in adjudicating the right of BMG to transfer a given quantity of water from one site to another so as to effect a change from agricultural to industrial uses of the water. At a critical point in the deliberations, when the issue of water quality versus water quantity occupied center stage, the judge stated: "I don't think there are any endangered species in there. There are no snail-darters in those creeks." The trial was a mean spectacle featuring the indisputably objective knowledge of experts against the quaint, unscientific voices of the noble but ignorant natives. As Paul Feyerabend (1988, 25) states: "The theoretical approach is conceited, ignorant, superficial, incomplete, and dishonest. . . . It is conceited because it takes for granted that only intellectuals have worthwhile ideas."[6] Through hyperbole, the judge obscured the presence in the Culebra watershed of endangered native Rio Grande cutthroat trout by referring to a species from another part of the United States, where the Tennessee Valley Authority's dam-building projects were delayed by a famous little fish.

Of course, the legal system would not entertain the possibility that the agropastoralists of the Culebra microbasin also are endangered species. In the end, the judge decided that the Colorado Mined Land Reclamation Board (MLRB) had already resolved the environmental concerns by issuing a mining permit to BMG. Water court is not the place to rehash ecological arguments. Issues of historic and cultural conservation were reduced to a one-page memo issued by the Colorado State Historical Society in which the "aesthetic" (i.e., visual) impact of the mine on the San Luis National Historic District was deemed to be minimal. Indeed, living culture was once again reduced by the law to an empty tourist spectacle.

The experts were peddling ideological thinking as objective scientific fact. Battle Mountain Gold and the court ultimately defined water as a commodity. It is up for sale to the highest bidder. You can move it around from here to there. You can sell it across mountains toward money. You can suck the farms dry and pipe the water to Denver, Phoenix, Las Vegas, or Los Angeles. Water is movable property. Water is money. Money gets and makes water, and water gets you more money. Quickly, like sparse raindrops on a parched and thirsty *playa,* the abstractions fizzle out. The commodification of water ultimately gives us dry lake beds blowing away in the wind, abandoned farms and shattered local economies, and dead lawns covered over with green paint in drought-stricken Los Angeles. What type of worldview does it take to come up with a concept like the commodity? To do this you have to be willing to treat water and people as objects, objects with a price. As the Zapatistas in Chiapas say, "Here you can buy and sell anything except indigenous dignity. Here everything is expensive except death."

Capitalists are quite emotional about the bottom line, so they have learned to exploit a legal system that serves the profit motive well because it too measures productivity, efficiency, and equity in terms of what best promotes economic growth for private gain. Ecological and bioregional scientific facts notwithstanding, capitalists are not going to let the health of land, water, and people stand in the way of their zealously protected legal right to make profits. The emotions tied up with the commodification of water and land are slippery and evasive. This emotion of greed is hidden beneath a veneer of rational choice, a choice legitimized by the power of expert knowledge and subservient to the predatory logic of market economics.

This emotion evokes the politicized desire of capital to possess and dominate objects. But this is cleverly and conveniently disguised as an immutable right deriving from natural law. The law reifies culture-bound ideological values: The beliefs and legal principles specific to one social class and culture are proclaimed universal truths, applicable to all classes, cultures, and places. Western water law, as embodied in the doctrine of prior appropriation, is a derivative of the primacy accorded private property rights. The claims of capital are given a privileged position in legal discourse. The law devalues the claims deriving from the place-centered land ethics of Hispano agropastoralists. Water law privileges an economic rationality that is in opposition to nature and defined by fraudulent science, based on dubious technology, and mired in questionable ethics (Rodgers 1982, 248–50).

In opening arguments, BMG attorney Bob Krassa described the cyanide vat leach technology at BMG as a "system of multiple redundancies," implying that it is completely accident proof. Krassa used the terminology of cybernetics to lend an air of technical mystique and infallibility to the BMG project. I often think of laws as dead letters. But this was more a case of the law using language, stripped of its ethical core, to legitimize the destruction of life and make death acceptable.

Anyone familiar with the history of cybernetic technology is aware of some humbling facts. Cybernetic systems, as first outlined by Norbert Weiner (1948, 1950) in the late 1940s and early 1950s, are self-enclosed technologies with multiple redundancies and human "feedback loops." Some familiar examples of cybernetic systems are the continuous-cycle petrochemical plant and the desktop computer. The feedback loops provide instant information on system conditions to the operator (the automobile speedometer is an example of a primitive feedback loop). The multiple redundancies are supposed to prevent catastrophic failures. That is how the experts described the allegedly "self-enclosed, zero-discharge" system built outside San Luis to process the gold and contain mine wastes.

Two of the most technologically advanced cybernetic systems in the world today are nuclear power plants and the space shuttle. People familiar with these highly automated technologies know they are based on a "system logic of multiple redundancies." In other words, you have a back-up computer to the back-up computer for the main computer. The breakdown of this system was the subject of the 1950s cold war film *Fail Safe*. These systems are obviously not fail safe as demonstrated by the accidents involving the nuclear power plants at Three Mile Island and Chernobyl, the chemical refineries at Bhopal in India and San Juan de Ixhuatepec in

Mexico, and the Space Shuttle Challenger. In all five cases, the back-up systems failed. In all five cases, lives were lost.

Multiple redundancies do not make for an infallible technology. In fact, cybernetic systems can be even more dangerous than mechanical systems because of the increased magnitude of the consequences of human error and technological failure. These failures tend to unfold at catastrophic scales (Peña 1997a). For example, feedback-loop errors such as misreading pressure gages in the control room of a nuclear power plant can lead to events that affect entire ecosystems, if not the biosphere as a whole. The safety and reliability of cybernetic systems are notoriously limited due to the uncertainties induced by human error. Somehow, the experts encourage the rest of us to blindly trust in these sophisticated technological systems; then they expect us to do nothing in the face of catastrophic system changes. Cybernetic systems are supposedly flexible and responsive, but the interface of humans and technology is really not predictable or controllable enough to avoid catastrophes (Hirschhorn 1984).

Walter Wise, BMG general counsel, was proud of the performance by the Halepaska engineering crew. The mining corporation's legal and scientific staffs were quite impressive, especially to anyone unfamiliar with the history of cybernetic catastrophes. Despite the experts' cleverness with abstractions, it was not something I recommend as entertainment, even for those who can patiently sit through the Santa Fe Opera or a golf tournament in a sunny poolside Taco Deco Arizona suburb like Scottsdale.

I was hoping to see the acequia farmers make a bit of history by persuading the judge that Colorado water law was ripe for a revolution. It was time to bring our water laws back into harmony with the environment, as they once were under Pueblo Indian and Mexican traditions, before the lords of yesterday turned water and land into commodities. I really thought that we might have a chance at getting the judge to consider seriously testimony on environmental and cultural protection in a water rights trial. After all, how could anyone really separate water quantity from water quality? How could anyone ignore the fact that watershed protection is essential to the viability of local cultures and ecosystems alike? I was to be disappointed with the court's myopic decision, a choice based in pure market logic and a corresponding inability to view the world more holistically: BMG owns the water. It can use it as it pleases. And if any other water rights are damaged, BMG can do the damage and then compensate the parties. The law calls this "augmentation," but the only things enhanced are corporate profit margins.

December 4, 1990, was the last day of the trial. As we drove back to San Luis, I asked Joe about the clear-cuts on the alluvial slopes of the Mount Blanca massif, just south of the Sand Dunes National Monument. "BLM (Bureau of Land Management) came and chained it," was Joe's brief reply.[7] It was one of those misbegotten experiments to expand grazing range for cattle ranchers on public lands. We drove a bit farther. I thought about parallels to the sadistic sexual metaphors Francis Bacon used to describe the "nature of nature" in reductionist science: To boldly go and forcibly penetrate "Her." Science, according to Bacon, involves forcing nature to give up "Her" secrets through the use of the so-called mechanical arts. Whips, chains, and machines are to be used to extract "goods" from nature, for "She" is barren and unproductive and must be made fertile and productive by the seed of man's knowledge (Merchant 1980; Shiva 1988).

Driving into Ft. Garland, we passed the highway sign that announces Kit Carson's reign as commandant at the old military fort. Joe breathed deeply and added, "Fifty years have passed since the BLM chained the piñon-juniper on Blanca. In that time, it hasn't grown back. All you have up there is eroding land, arroyo cuts, and wasteland scrub. What do you think BMG is gonna leave us after they're gone? Nice green pastures for elk and cattle? A healthier watershed?" I did not have to answer that question. Three miles northeast of San Luis the landscape provides an all-too-stark response: growing scars in the foothills of the Shining Mountains. Here, "development" is revealed in all its destructive grandeur — a predatory machine capable of devouring entire mountains and watersheds. Gleaming in the sun, the cyanide leach mill is a precise, efficient, and stainless-steel automaton, managed with computers and capable of destroying the life that sustains the acequia communities.

The Black Hole of Industrial Mining

The Rito Seco originates in snowmelts that spring from a series of wondrous water meadows lying from ten to twelve thousand feet in high subalpine forest terrain. Cascading down toward the wide valley bottomlands of the Rio Culebra, the headwaters of the Rito Seco cut through pre-Cambrian rock until they reach the montane Douglas fir, ponderosa, and aspen stands that rim Rito Seco Park just upstream of El Plomo, an old Mexican mining prospect that is but a remnant cave in a cliff wall.

The creek has been intensely modified by the work of beavers, creating a series of ponds and wetlands that are home and a stopover for a variety of birds, mammals, and other wildlife. The terrain gradually yields to a widening alluvial floodplain carved by the creek in budding canyonlands surrounded by piñon-juniper foothills and sagebrush prairies. At depths ranging in thickness from one hundred to five hundred feet under the Rito Seco creek bed is the Santa Fe conglomerate. Below this "overburden" is the pre-Cambrian basement rock that contains microscopic specks of gold. This is the "molecular" gold hunted by mining predators from San Luis to Santa Fe.

Crossing the boundary into the mine property, just downstream from the Rito Seco Park beaver ponds, I feel as if I am entering a war zone—a war that is between Man and Nature. The Rito Seco foothills have been transformed into a ghostly, barren landscape—a black hole in the Culebra basin. Vegetation all around is dead or dying, choked and crushed by dust, noise, dynamite, and chains. The beaver ponds in the Rito Seco downstream from the strip mine are choked with sediment.

Commenting on the degraded condition of the Rito Seco beaver ponds, Praxedis Ortega, Jr., once told me, "The water in there looks like cyanide chocolate syrup"; he was amazed at how quickly the watershed had become damaged. During class trips to the ravaged site, the mine-safety engineer never passed up the opportunity to tell my students that the half-mile-long strip mine was the very latest in "habitat friendly" earth-moving technology. During one field trip with a class, we stood perched on the precipice of a two-hundred-foot deep hole where a piñon-juniper woodland once grew on a south-facing slope. "It's great for elk, deer, and even the bighorn sheep love to be around the [mine] pit!" he exclaimed. I guess he did not realize that the closest bighorn herds are across La Veta Pass, some twenty miles to the north in the Mt. Blanca massif. I'm sure they will stay there, away from the mine. The operations manager chimed in, "Why not think of it as a huge sculpture? It'll be a great tourist attraction," he said, greedily eying the black hole.

Water Webs

Leaving this tortured piece of earth, the Rito Seco gradually winds back to more familiar and friendly terrain, the headgates and acequias of San Luis. The ditches are a network of water webs. They respectfully invite the snowmelt waters of the Rito Seco for a detour to the fertile bottomlands of the Culebra. The Rito Seco commingles with the Rio Culebra to feed the oldest surface water rights in Colorado, the San Luis Peoples Ditch.[8]

West of San Luis, the bottomlands of the Culebra lie between two volcanic mesas. This fertile site offers protection from the elements — strong wind and dust storms that frequent other parts of the valley. San Pedro Mesa rises south of the bottomlands. To the north, La Mesa de Misericordia y Piedad offers shelter from winds that sweep in from the wide spaces that lie below Sìs Naajinìì. The craggy rocklands on top of La Piedad are a refuge for a Stations of the Cross shrine, a religious site with fourteen bronze statues sculpted by a local artisan, Huberto Maestas. It is also home to La Capilla de Todos los Santos, a three-dome adobe mission, handcrafted and designed by local artisans, carpenters, and architects.[9]

The road from San Luis to Antonito takes you west on a drive between La Piedad and the Culebra bottomlands. The Corpus A. Gallegos Ranch is a historic *extensión* that is centered in a core of four hundred acres in the Culebra bottomlands due west of San Luis.[10] This land has been in the family for five generations, since the time Dario Gallegos settled it in 1851. The waters of the Rito Seco course through the San Luis Peoples Ditch, which cuts across the northern end of the Gallegos extensión between the ranch and the Antonito highway. From the highway looking south, you can see the twin volcanic domes of San Antonio Peak and Cerro de los Utos (Ute Mountain), which frame a gateway for the Rio Grande as it leaves the San Luis Valley and enters the Taos Plateau to carve a series of deep and wild *cañadas*.

I learned to appreciate the acequia system by working at the Gallegos Ranch. Acequias respect the contours of the land. These irrigation systems rely on the natural force of gravity, and like rivers, they tend to follow the path of least resistance. Acequias are a good example of a system based on principles of biological efficiency and natural traction. Mechanical center-pivot sprinklers, popular in other parts of the San Luis Valley, are not evident in this archaic cultural landscape. Center-pivots are based on a technology that mimics mining; they have a ravenous appetite for fossil fuels, pesticides, and fertilizers. The industrial mining of water, whether by corporate agribusiness people such as the potato farmers in the northern end of the valley or by companies such as American Water Development, Inc. (AWDI), now defunct, is not exactly a sustainable practice. It is part of an agricultural system that homogenizes the land. Only one type of one species of crop is grown, and the land grows dusty and tired under the onslaught of chemical residues and erosion. These industrial systems are enslaved to heavy debt, addicted to toxic agrochemicals, hopelessly dependent on mechanical efficiency, and guilty of farmworker exploitation.[11]

The acequia farmers, in contrast, are practitioners of sustainable agriculture and steady-state economics. The acequia network remains free of pesticides, fertilizers, and fossil fuels. It is also very labor-intensive and requires great skill to control field flooding with minimal soil erosion or water waste. The acequia irrigation system is a cultural institution sustained by intense social relations. For the mayordomo there is always the prospect of a struggle about the ditch. To maintain the cohesion of the group of irrigators, the ditch rider must encourage reciprocity and mutual aid. This is not easy, because the membership of ditches is changing and the law provides little refuge for the maintenance of customary practices. Nature can also take its toll. As a bad drought demonstrates, good-natured neighbors quickly get vile when water is scarce (see Gallegos, chapter 8).

Acequias increase biological diversity. Wetlands and farmlands are cloistered together in neighborly balance (see Peña 1997b; Rívera and Peña 1997; Rívera [in press]). This agropastoral system encourages diversity by integrating wildlife habitats and farming landscapes (Peña 1998). The farmlands of the Culebra microbasin actually look more wild than the orderly circles and linear crop fields of the center-pivot irrigation systems that sprawl across the desert prairies on township quarter sections in the communities of Center, Ft. Garland, and Monte Vista. In the short term, center-pivots are likely more profitable and efficient, but they eventually work against the limits imposed by biogeographical conditions. Center-pivot irrigation systems bankrupt the soil and water. They starve the land of natural nutrients and soil microflora, producing in nature a sort of artificial sterility. The fertilizers used in these operations can gradually turn the aquifers into depleted underground salt marshes.

The agropastoral tradition of Hispano agroecosystems is ecologically well adapted to arid land. There is an extraordinary diversity of native crops and wild flora on the Gallegos Ranch. The landrace pastures include fields of native blue fescue, blue grama, red top, brome, orchard, and timothy grasses. Joe Gallegos has restored a dry-land prairie on a five hundred acre extensión located west-northwest of La Piedad. This land was long ago lost to the family patrimony and was severely overgrazed by commercial sheep operators pushing eastward from Conejos County across the Rio Grande. Joe recently bought this land and decided to restore the old prairie grasses that were succeeded by big blue sagebrush. This dry-land restoration involved reseeding the prairie with blue grama, a native, drought-resistant bunchgrass, as well as two crested wheat varieties imported from arid Asian steppes and one crested wheat variety from the Great Basin Desert.

Like his progenitors, Joe Gallegos avoids the temptations of an alfalfa monoculture. The ranch is really a complex agroecological community because it mimics nature's own diversity. The extensión includes at least four life zones: (1) a piñon-juniper woodland on top of San Pedro mesa; (2) a sagebrush ecotone (transition zone) between the mesa top and the creek; (3) the Culebra creek riparian zone (with its dense corridor of cottonwood, alder, and willow stands); and (4) the bottom wetlands and various *vegas* (subirrigated meadows) with profuse communities of native grasses. In addition to wildlife habitat and pasture lands, the rancho includes several rotating alfalfa- and row-crop plots, which are traversed by willow communities growing along the earthen *espinazo* ditch banks.

An old heirloom stock orchard is one of the most enduring features of this cultural landscape. In another area of the ranch, new orchard trees have been planted within the irrigated family garden plots. These plots are thoroughly intercropped with numerous horticultural varieties, centered on the corn-bean-squash polycultures. Locally adapted *habas* (horsebeans) are one of several "naturalized" exotic varieties found in the family garden plots. These heirloom crops are sown from seed stocks handed down across the generations.

The crops grown by the Gallegos family are genetic storehouses of native agrobiodiversity. Planting involves the more traditional patterns of intercropping, minimal tillage, the use of organic pest controls, and rotations with oats, alfalfa, and winter wheat. The white maize *milpas* (corn gardens) are perhaps the most amazing cradles of biodiversity on the Gallegos Ranch. The maize grown by the family is a multigenerational heirloom landrace variety used for *chicos* and *posole*.[12] Chicos are made from rare, white, milky corn during the early harvest when the kernels are still tender. The corn is roasted in adobe *hornos,* woven into *ristras,* and hung to dry on wooden racks. Once dried, the kernels are stripped from the *mazorca* (cob) and stored for use in pork, beef, venison, or elk stews prepared with *chile colorado,* onions, and garlic. For making posole, some of the white maize is left standing until it matures on the stalk. The maize kernels are stripped from the cob and soaked in lime for use in the manner of hominy for *menudo.*

The milpas are intercropped with legumes such as the equally rare *bolita* beans (another landrace crop). In one field, I identified and collected six different varieties of white corn and two of bolita. Another field yielded another eight varieties of white corn. This means that in Joe's two fields, totaling no more than ten or twelve acres, crop biodiversity is eight times greater than in a monoculture field covering four sections (640 acres) planted in one or two genetically altered hybrids.[13]

The maize, bolita, habas, and other crops are planted from seed stocks that have been in the Gallegos family for at least three or four generations. Joe's brother, Jerry, is especially proud of a Mexican squash variety, *calabasita.* Jerry calls it the "Eliza Special," in honor of his grandmother who first cultivated it. The germ plasm of these landraces contains several hundred, if not a thousand, years of genetic code, recording the evolution and adaptation of heirloom crop varieties to the high altitude and arid land conditions. These heirloom seeds have been selected for specific qualities over generations of observation. The ancestral seeds are an alternative to a steady diet of genetically engineered, sterile hybrids controlled by biotechnology companies. Joe believes these native seeds are important, if only because farmers can remain independent of the corporate merchants who peddle hybrids with agrochemicals needed to produce high yields from the monocultures.[14]

Thinking about the complexity of this agroecosystem, I am struck by how these irrigation and farming traditions often have been described derisively as "primitive" and "inefficient." Gilbert C. Fite (1966, 185), expressing a widespread opinion, states that "the Spanish-Americans [sic] continued a primitive, self-sufficient type of agriculture." A renowned chronicler of Colorado agricultural history, Alvin J. Steinel (1926, 174), was more crudely ethnocentric in his description of Chicano agricultural traditions: "Farming did not advance under Spanish-American rule in the Southwest." The "crude implements" and "primitive methods" made Hispanos unproductive and inefficient as farmers. "It was only through the cultural influences of the minority of the better class of Spanish-Americans that complete stagnation was prevented. . . . [A] half century of contact with American educational influences has revived the spark and given the Mexican people a place of economic importance in our agricultural system." In other words, we mexicanos needed gringo schools to teach us how to accept the theft of land grants, destruction of the commons, and a position at the bottom of the occupational hierarchy as underpaid, overworked, and pesticide-contaminated seasonal migratory farmworkers or displaced independent farmers. The *gachupines* (i.e., Spanish Americans) would provide a more solid foundation for our advancement through their European cultural influences. In this version of a degenerate Mexican culture, being "primitive" is equated with the sin of "self-reliance," a quality despised and "misrecognized" by the would-be apologists of modern capitalist monocultures.

The acequias are criticized as wasteful and inefficient because the earthen ditch banks are moist, and flood-irrigating creates wetlands. This is why the State Engineers Office and the Army Corp of Engineers have tried for so long to modernize the ditches by insisting that the *parciantes* pave the dirt-lined channels. For example, the San Luis Peoples Ditch was lined with concrete in the mid-1960s to reduce the amount of "wasted" water. Hydrologists and capitalists alike tend to view this "leakage" as wasteful, since it represents water that is not used directly to serve human needs. They never seem to consider that water shortage crises are byproducts of a continuing failure to recognize environmental limits. They do not appreciate the finer points of steady-state economics. Capitalist development, or maldevelopment, is antinature in its celebration of the cult of mechanical efficiency. Yet this obscures the basic ways in which the emphasis placed on economic objectives undermines nature's own standard of productivity — the biodiversity of the land organism (Leopold 1968).

The Chicano agropastoralists disagree; they believe that the water from acequias supports wildlife and its habitat. How can that be nonbeneficial? Obviously, we are dealing with a conflict between human-centered and earth-centered value systems. This is not just a simple matter of water conservation and greater efficiency in the delivery of water rights. The acequias may appear inefficient from the vantage point of individual economic rationality or water conservation, but when viewed in the holistic context of mixed plant, animal, and human communities, acequias are equal opportunity providers. They do not discriminate against wild animals and plants because these life-forms yield no obvious economic gain for human beings. Water shortages are not caused by leaking acequias but by the increasing overappropriation and misdirection of water to industrial and urban uses — including industrialized agriculture.

The water webs criss-cross the bottomlands of the Culebra and Rito Seco. Except for the concrete channel of the mother ditch, the *sangria, lateral,* and espinazo ditches are still earthen works.[15] The terminology of acequias derives from a language constructed by an earth-centered culture. Give heed: the mother ditch (*acequia madre*), bleeding ditch (sangria), and spinal ditch (espinazo) — this is the language of bodies, mothers, blood, and of life. Wherever the flow of water goes, life also flourishes. Through acequias, humans extend the domains of riparian habitat. Wetlands are abundant. The farmers protect them because they attract wildlife and also serve as windbreaks to help control soil erosion. It has never occurred to local farmers that such a use of water might be considered "nonbeneficial evapotranspiration."[16] The acequia is a cultural institution that firmly rejects the unholy alliance between the scientific jargon of hydrology and the commodifying value system of capitalism.[17]

An Heirloom Orchard

In the northeastern corner of the Gallegos extensión is one of Colorado's oldest orchards. The waters of the Rito Seco and Rio Culebra, fed from the acequia madre, allow the orchard to thrive in the somewhat dry and rocky soil alongside the road to Antonito. The orchard is the by-product of the sustainable interaction between water and culture, of a balance between natural and cultural landscapes. The oldest trees in the orchard were planted by the Gallegos family more than 105 years ago. The San Luis Peoples Ditch borders the orchard on the north side. During the fall harvest, some of the fruit drops into the acequia madre and floats downstream toward the Gallegos homestead and barnyard. The decaying fruit from the ditch is a favorite of the horses, goats, sheep, pigs, and geese. Everything is consumed; there is no waste here. Cattle occasionally stray into the orchard to munch on the thick carpet of gooey, bittersweet fruit that lies decaying on the ground. The smell of natural pectin is pervasive.

The Gallegos orchard has red and yellow transparent apple trees. It also has trees bearing red and yellow plums. The unique *cirhuelita del indio* (wild miniature black plum) is also plentiful. Pears, apricots, and choke-cherries complete the tree stocks in the orchard. Although it is located on private land, the orchard serves as a communal resource. The neighboring honey bees are the first beneficiaries of the spring blossoms. Myriad birds enjoy the harvest, and a horned owl has made one old apple tree her spring hatchling roost. Residents from the neighboring area visit the orchard in late September and early October. The blazing aspen in the mountains east of San Luis are a sure sign that harvesttime has arrived. People don't need calendars or digital clocks to figure out when it is time for fruit picking. All they need to see is the turning of the aspen groves on the flanks of Culebra Peak. And so they come to harvest. Climbing trees, singing low guttural tones, the harvesters arrive over the course of two months. Many soon return, bearing gifts of jams, jellies, preserves, and pastries. The Gallegos orchard keeps several age-old traditions alive: fruit canning and preserving, gift-giving, and barter. Apples into jam, chokecherries into wine, and fruit pastries and other delights find their way into the Gal-legos's kitchen and a dozen others. The fruit of the orchard travels far from San Luis to Colorado Springs, Denver, and Pueblo.

In February 1991 I brought a class of students from Colorado College to live and work in San Luis for ten days. Our third day in San Luis was a gloriously warm and windless Sunday. We worked at pruning the trees in the orchard. Corpus Gallegos came out to greet us, and we talked about the work for a while. He said the orchard had not been pruned since the 1950s. Forty years of neglect had left the orchard struggling to survive, and the harvests seemed less bountiful each passing year. We wondered why and asked for an explanation.

Corpus lamented the decline of communal values. The local youth, it seems, traditionally pruned the orchard right after the fall harvest, but the passage of time had brought changes and neglected traditions. "Just like the other things that have died," he said. "You know, like the festival of San Ysidro Labrador during the spring ditch cleaning. That is also gone."[18]

My reply was an overgeneralization: "These are the cultural casualties of changing times." One student suggested, "Youth are more interested in MTV, VCRs, and fast cars." Corpus defended the local youth. "You can't really blame them. There is not much left here for the young people. Not enough jobs, no land. There are few opportunities to stay at home and make a living." The CC students didn't seem to understand. One asked, somewhat sheepishly, "Well, if they studied harder, you know went to college and such, they could get better jobs in the city, right?"

The Gallegos orchard is a symbol of the struggle in San Luis for cultural survival. It is painful to me that a group of mainly white, middle-class students from an exclusive liberal arts college would take responsibility for the health and renewal of an orchard planted with carefully nurtured heirloom trees. And they did so, often without recognizing their tendency to romanticize the farmers. That outsiders were here to do the work traditionally done by the locals did not seem to bother Corpus. His eyes lit up and a glowing smile marked his face when we drove up and asked to borrow some saws and a few axes to do the job. We were about to give the orchard a new lease on life, and for now all that mattered to him was our commitment to the chore.

An Eleventh Commandment

I was in the San Luis church again today, my first time back there since the day before the start of the Battle Mountain water trial. I am feeling despondent, tired of how the struggle against BMG has come to dominate the life of the community in such a pervasive way. For almost two years now, there has been nothing but talk of the mine tinged with a fear for what the future will bring. The mined waste ponds are already leaking. Since the arrival of BMG in 1987, the community has been forced to direct its creativity and resources into a struggle to prevent the destruction of the ecological basis of an endangered local culture.[19] The community could be using these same resources to sustain its momentum toward an environmentally sustainable economic revival.

San Luis has been pursuing a plan for sustainable development based on a long-term revival of artisan crafts such as weaving and furniture making, organic farming and ranching, and the conservation of historic and natural areas. The legal struggle against BMG is an enormous drain on the already limited resources available for sustainable and culturally respect-ful development projects in the Culebra microbasin. In the absence of BMG, this community could be channeling its energies and creativity to protecting and reviving the vitality of the local culture and economy. It could turn to the task of restoring its historic-use rights to the land-grant commons, now "owned" by the descendants of President Zachary Taylor.

Battle Mountain Gold could suffocate the bioregional impulse of the community. This is the source of my despair. The acequias, and the agro-pastoral traditions they support, are endangered. Their protection and conservation are critical to the survival of mestizo, land-based local cul-tures in the Upper Rio Grande bioregion. The survival of these local cul-tures is the key to the environmental health and economic future of the bioregion. In 1991, BMG received the largest fine in Colorado history for violating its operating permit by exceeding the parts per million of cyanide allowed in its toxic tailings pond (Peña and Gallegos 1993). Any future mining disaster will likely damage the already frail local agropastoral economy.[20] The contamination of water, soil erosion, and destruction of wildlife habitat and wetlands disrupt other types of economic activities. Water pollution and soil erosion caused by mining endanger farming and ranching activities. We need to recognize that these local communities offer sustainable alternatives to extractive development. Industrialization of land and water more than anything else actually limits the options for other types of economic activities such as farming, ranching, artisan crafts, and recreation.

That Sunday two years ago, I made one of my infrequent visits to the Sangre de Cristo church to hear Father Pat deliver a sermon. I remember that he spoke about the delusion of powerlessness. "The delusion of powerlessness," he said, "leads us to accept pain, suffering, and tragedy without any hope of change." This is nothing like "the meek shall inherit the earth." Father Pat said that we must conquer our fears and especially our fear of powerlessness. We all have inner power. Some see this inner power as God. Others might see it as the strength that comes from realiz-ing that everything and everyone is interconnected. We must conquer the delusion of powerlessness or else suffer oppression without hope of relief. This was an appropriate message for those of us who were fearful of the events that would unfold in water court, an alien realm in which we truly felt powerless.

After mass, I shared some coffee and conversation with Joe and Corpus, then went for a walk into town. I had not seen the mural on the north wall of the rectory in some time, and so I walked over behind the San Luis Visitors Center toward the church buildings. The mural depicts people from the Rio Culebra villages gathered together in family groups around an image of Father Pat. There is hope and determination in the faces of the people in the mural. A green frog sits at Father Pat's feet, indomitable in its dignity. I have always been so enthralled by the faces of the people in this mural and by the many smiles of the people I actually know that I never before noticed the commandments painted on a utility pole in front of the mural. Reading the commandments, I found that there were eleven instead of ten. The eleventh was "Take care of God's world." This seems an appropriate expression that captures the sentiments of the local people who are struggling to conserve their love of the land through this sense of place.

Every Creature Will Tell You

Sister Teresa Jaramillo is a fifth-generation San Luiseña and has dedicated much of her life's work to medical missions in Latin America, especially Nicaragua. Sister Teresa is the spiritual adviser of the Committee for Environmental Soundness, a grassroots organization fighting BMG and other ecological threats based in San Luis. She believes in sisterhood with the earth. I remember a poem she wrote in honor of the resistance against BMG:

There's such freedom here
In this high retreat
Every creature will tell you.

Sister Teresa sees this self-confirming life present in all of nature's ways: "Every creature will tell you." Lessons from the mountains she calls them: *"Todos somos niños de la sierra y ella nos enseña como vivir y convivir"* (All of us are children of the mountain and she teaches us how to live and live together). For Sister Teresa, the mountains are not a wilderness but a homeland, neighbor, friend, and teacher. It is her space for conviviality.

Why does the wind
Motion like some thing
Of a thousand wings?

It's as though I, too,
Have some place to go.
Some place no one else can lead me.

Sister Teresa's wisdom is founded on an appreciation for the spirit of locality, for having a place to call home. She is not lost in the frosty meadows of the Rito Seco headwaters or the dry, windswept prairies of the Ventero. This is her home, and with the knowledge of the local landscape she weaves the wondrous tapestry of her identity as woman, Chicana, Catholic medical missionary, teacher, and environmentalist. Teresa has lots of places to go: Nicaragua, The Vatican, Guatemala. But she always returns to the place of her birth, San Luis de la Culebra. The sister's work for global peace and social justice is matched only by her deep commitment to and involvement with the local community on issues ranging from recycling to clean water and air. During our struggle against Battle Mountain, Sister Teresa provided the community with tremendous spiritual energy and guidance to carry forth the resistance. She generated a sense of place and power-within equal to the task of confronting those who would exercise power over others.

Changing without Dying

I prepare to leave San Luis after more than eighteen months of struggle against the mine. Months of hard work with irrigation, planting, cultivation, harvest, cattle drives, and auction sales have challenged my physical limits, the product of a too fat, middle-class life-style wrought by the advantages of being a member of a campus-bound, petit bourgeois intelligentsia. Life in the real world has humbled me. It has been almost precisely two years since the fateful BMG water trial. Joe Gallegos hugs me. Holding me at the shoulders, he says: "A lot of things have happened since you came. Lots of changes. You ask questions all the time about what is important here and what are we really fighting for. I've told you before, my philosophy is simple, you have to change but you don't have to die."

Joe was simply repeating a lesson we have all learned the hard way: The modern world exerts incredible pressures on people to abandon their archaic placeways. We try to adapt and in the process often lose more than we have gained. Joe's view is that we have to adapt but in the process should keep our culture, language, and customs intact. Like me, Joe is not outwardly religious, but he has a strong sense of the sacredness of his locality, an identity centered on the land and water that comes from the knowledge that these natural elements keep his family farm thriving. Joe's connection to the local landscape is something I really appreciate. As a result of my growing friendship with Joe, I too have developed a strong attachment to the Rio Culebra bottomlands.

As I leave the Gallegos Ranch to go back to teaching at Colorado College, Joe gives me a copy of a poem, his response to my grandmother's advice that "the animals are also intelligent." He calls the poem "Salva Tu Sierra":

Rezan todos a San Ysidro	Everyone pray to Saint Ysidro
el Rito Seco nunca será lo mismo	the Rito Seco will never be the same
también los animalitos son inteligentes	the animals are also intelligent
lloran porque su bosque a caido	they cry because their forest has fallen
en manos de malas gentes.	into evil peoples' hands.
Destruyen la sierra sin pensar	They destroy the mountain without thinking
dejan las ruinas para cobrar	leave ruins behind as our charge
químicos tóxicos donde habia vida	toxic chemicals where once was life
truchas muertas, nomás mira!	dead trout, just look!
Ayúdale a tu sierra	Help your mountain
para que no muera. . . . .Amen.	So she will not die. . . . Amen.

Postscript: 24 de julio 1997—En la Cuenca del Pico de las Animas Perdidas en Purgatorio

Yesterday morning at 4 A.M. "Local Woman" locked herself down at a gate to block logging crews trying to enter the Taylor Ranch. She calls herself Local Woman to answer those who allege that the antilogging protesters are all outside agitators. She kept the loggers out. Describing herself as a concerned mother of three, she said her children have a right to inherit a happy earth. She has arrived at the gate to prevent further logging destruction. She is not an environmental activist and has never engaged in civil disobedience. During Local Woman's lock-down, grandmothers, relatives, and friends from nearby villages come by with food, water, and words of encouragement. Overnight, Local Woman metamorphoses into Dreadlock Boulder Earth First!er, when lock-down duty passes to her out-of-town supporter. Local Woman and Dreadlock EarthFirst!er are acting together to stop the cruelest bit of ecological and cultural destruction in the intermountain West—the 210-million-board-foot liquidation of the Culebra watershed forests in south-central Colorado's San Luis Valley. The logging threatens the livelihood of Colorado's oldest farming families who irrigate twenty-two thousand acres of cropland with the water that courses down from the mountain forests.

This part of the Sangre de Cristo Mountain Range is punctuated by a 14,000-foot-high peak known as La Culebra, "Water Snake." There are eight other nearby peaks towering above 13,000 feet elevation. These alpine peaks are "owned" by Zachary Taylor, a direct descendent of the presidential namesake. Taylor apparently does not know that the Mexican-American War is over. Only now, instead of Winchesters and cannonballs, the weapons of choice are feller-forwarders, skidders, and chain saws.

Well into the evening, Joe Gallegos comes by my ranchito for a visit; he's accompanied by some colleagues from the Ancient Forest Rescue contingent. We drink plenty of coffee and smoke tons of cigars and cigarettes to make sure our discussion is adequately subversive. Chain-smoking Ed Quillen says, "Revolutions are hatched in smoke-filled rooms." I am playing guitar, practicing a song for Saturday's patron-saint feast-day celebration. The song is called "Sierra Vida" (Life Mountain). Joe reads it and starts scribbling on the sheet, rewriting the song. It goes like this, following Joe's strike-outs:

Sierra ~~Vida~~ Muerta   ~~Life~~ Death Mountain
por la sierra   through the mountain
mueren ~~viven~~ todos   everyone ~~lives~~ dies
estas ~~vidas~~ muertes   these ~~lives~~ deaths
tan ~~sagradas~~ cortadas   ~~sacred~~ cut so short
sierra ~~vida~~ muerta   ~~living~~ dead mountain
mir'a hijita   look my daughter

voces ~~aves~~ serpientes	~~bird~~ serpent voices
canto en ~~flores~~ mierda	songs in ~~flowers~~ excrement
sierra ~~verde~~ gris	~~green~~ gray mountain
bosque ~~libre~~ encarcelado	~~free~~ caged forest
por la gente	for the people
y ~~Dios vigente~~ Diablo	and ~~God in force~~ Demon
Serpiente	Serpent
sierra en ~~nieve~~ hielo	mountain in ~~snow~~ ice
sol ~~caliente~~ frio	~~hot~~ cold sun
y en ~~agua~~ fuego	and in ~~water~~ fire
se ~~convierte~~ quema.	it ~~becomes~~ burns.

He hands it back to me, and I read the changes. Joe has spontaneously converted "Life Mountain" song into "Death Mountain" song. Bird voices become serpent voices; flowers become excrement; the green mountain becomes a gray mountain; the free (wild) forest becomes a caged forest.

My feebly romantic effort to impart some good cheer and hope for the future at Saturday's festivities is reduced in a matter of minutes to the dust that is left when trees die in the Culebra, in the turbulent wake of the relentless slashing and cutting that is occurring above us in the mountain forest. The weight of a year-long antilogging campaign implodes the song, returning its animating pursuit of resistance back to its source in the heartless vortex of destruction.[21] I fear these words. They seem to extinguish hope for the future.

Surely there is a lesson to be drawn here. Joe and I have been fighting mining and logging destruction of the Culebra watershed since 1989. We are tired. Despite my effort to put our best heart forward in this song, Joe's revisions remind me that our watershed is threatened by industrial logging. I realize now how differently positioned Joe and I are with respect to our local sense of place. There is little room for celebration, however innocently contrived to relieve us of sadness, if the place we grew up in and loved as children is being mutilated every day by feller-forwarders, "cherry-pickers," and skidders. From emerald sanctuary and sacred homeland to clear-cut, strip-mined wasteland in a matter of one too-fast-moving decade. Over that time, the source that grounds our sense of place—the wild mountain—is rapidly disappearing under the mechanical onslaught of the logging crews. Instead of snow turning to life-giving water, we have ice, cold sun, and fire burning on the mountain. The acequias are choked with the death of the mountain. The trees are silenced.

This waste and destruction need not be. William H. Rodgers, Jr., a renowned legal theorist, provides a compelling case for a "natural use rights theory" that privileges the protection of common over private property rights. Of particular relevance to the survival of the acequias is the "law of waste," which states that "assaults against the long run productivity of [land], by loss of topsoil, destruction of watercourses, and elimination of vegetation, have been forbidden in waste litigation. A standard of 'good husbandry' is often invoked, sometimes even to forbid changes in land use. . . . The waste cases support recognition of a universal 'good husbandry' use restriction on all natural resources" (Rodgers 1982, 249).

It may seem appropriate to conclude this essay with some reflections on contemporary legal theory. The experiences of the past nine years — from the campaign against the BMG mine through the current struggle against logging destruction of the Culebra watershed — have taught us that the law is contested terrain. If acequia farming communities are to survive the current wave of destructive exploitation, the lords of things with a price must be challenged in the courts as well as in the streets. The only inner strength the people of the Culebra River villages need against BMG or the logging crews from Southwest Forest Industries can emanate from their traditions of "good husbandry." The acequia farmers have been here, *in place,* for six generations. They have successfully lived and prospered in a harsh, punishing, and unforgiving environment for as long as they have only because they have protected and nurtured the land and water and respected the limits imposed by the place.

As this book goes to press, the historic acequia communities of the Upper Rio Grande from San Luis to Santa Fe increasingly are threatened by a continuous assault on the land. Extractive industries, resort developers, second-home buyers, and real estate speculators are undermining both ecological and cultural integrity. The response of these communities — either through the establishment of new agricultural cooperatives and land trusts, the development of land-use regulations, litigation, or direct action against ecological damage — is a new social movement for social, economic, and environmental justice. This is a battle of paradigms: a bureaucratic model of state and capitalist control of nature as a commodity and the indigenous model of sustainable local stewardship of the homeland. At stake is the future of the commons, not just in San Luis, but throughout the intermountain West. Justice, common sense, and scientific prudence dictate that we protect these communities, for they are cradles of ecological democracy and sustainable livelihood. We must not allow our society to eliminate the ancient common property tradition and its sole remaining legacy — the watershed democracy of the acequias.

Notes

Thanks to Corpus Aquino Gallegos, Joe Gallegos, Adrienne Seward, and Victor Nelson Cisneros for their assistance. Minor portions of this essay first were published in an editorial series in *The Valley Courier* (November 28–29, and December 1, 1990). The author wishes to acknowledge the support of the National Endowment for the Humanities, Grant #RO-22707-94. The views expressed by the author do not reflect the policies or views of the NEH or the federal government.

1. For example, the Ladahk of the high alpine steppes of northern India share much in common with Mexicans in the Upper Rio Grande: Both are land-based cultures which have adapted successfully to arid intermountain environments and both share a long history of resistance to political economic subordination by intrusive colonizing forces. See Norberg-Hodge (1991); also see D. G. Peña (1992).

2. Rívera (in press) and Rívera and Peña (1997) provide examples and case histories of this problem.

3. The "lords of yesterday" include the doctrine of prior appropriation, "organic" timber acts (creating the national forests), general mining law of 1872, and various grazing district laws for publicly owned range lands.

4. Curry (1976–77) outlines the concept of the watershed as a combination of elements that includes the water, soil, the underlying geologic formations (bedrock, faults, etc.), the vegetative cover, and the climatic regime.

5. Water exists within a complex hydrological and geochemical system, which can be described as a closed system in which mass, flow rate, and quality of water are all interconnected. The function of a vadose zone (which includes soil and flora) is to regulate the filtering and releasing of water into the local aquifer system.

6. See also Peña and Gallegos 1997.

7. Environmentalists call the BLM the "Bureau of Livestock and Mining" because the agency is seen as responsible for causing major environmental degradation through policies which have historically favored extractive uses of the public domain.

8. The Peoples Ditch was hand dug in 1852, decreed in 1862, and adjudicated in 1889.

9. The architect of the adobe *Capilla* is Arnold Valdéz, a fifth-generation native of San Luis. See Peña and Mondragon Valdéz 1998.

10. The *extensión* is the riparian long-lot parcel that is typical of the cultural landscape in compact agropastoral communities such as San Luis. The riparian long-lot is traditionally one to two hundred yards wide and three to five miles long. It includes nearly every ecotone in the bioregion from the piñon-juniper woodlands on the mesa tops to the native grasslands and wetlands close to the river bottoms. For further discussion and sources see Peña, chapter 1, this volume.

11. For a comparison of acequias and mechanical center-pivot sprinklers see Peña 1997b.

12. A land race is a horticultural variety derived from crops that are native to the biome and cultivated by seed-saving farmers who hand the seeds down from one generation to the next.

13. For a study of the genetics of maize grown on the Gallegos land, see Bertrand 1996.

14. On biotechnology threats to Hispano agroecosystems, see Peña 1997b.

15. The *lateral* ditches deliver water from the mother ditch to individual riparian long-lots. The *sangria* (bleeding) ditches are used to distribute water evenly within the farming and gardening plots, and the *espinazo* (spinal) ditches are used to deliver water to the middle of the fields.

16. "Nonbeneficial evapotranspiration" is the term used by hydrologists to describe the "loss" of water through the evaporative processes of riparian plant life. The "culprits" responsible for nonbeneficial evapotranspiration are the *phreatophytes* (i.e., in the San Luis Valley, cottonwood and birch trees, riparian willow, saltbrush and rabbitbrush and exotic [imported] species such as Russian olive). Of course, the water is not "lost," but appropriated by nonhuman life forms in a beneficial way. This perception of beneficial versus nonbeneficial depends on one's philosophy. If you are anthropocentric and care only about human needs and priorities, then cottonwoods are the enemies of efficiency, unfairly taking a share of water away from human agricultural, industrial, and domestic uses. If you are biocentric, or lococentric (place-centered), then the use of water by nonhuman life is beneficial in its own right. Perhaps this place-centered ethic of water use derives more from the classic Islamic "law of thirst" than from Judeo-Christian principles. See Clark 1987; Peña 1997b and in press.

17. For further discussion, see Peña 1991, 1992, and 1997b.

18. Recently, Father Pat Valdéz reinstituted the spring ditch blessing ceremony on May 15 of each year, the feast day of the patron saint of the farmer, San Ysidro Labrador.

19. For more on the history of the struggle against BMG, see Peña and Gallegos 1993 and 1997.

20. The damage has already been done at the Summitville mine west of San Luis across the valley in the Alamosa River watershed. The Summitville mine is an EPA-designated Superfund site. Contamination from leaking mine wastes, which have leached cyanide and heavy metals, has killed all aquatic life in an 18-mile stretch of the river. This contamination has affected more than 30,000 acres of irrigated farmland.

21. For a detailed history of the antilogging struggle, see Peña and Mondragon Valdéz 1998.

Bibliography

Acuña, R. 1988. *Occupied America: A history of Chicanos*. New York: Harper and Row.

Adair, M., and S. Howell. 1990. *Breaking old patterns, weaving new ties*. San Francisco: Tools for Change.

Adams, C. J. 1990. *The sexual politics of meat: A feminist perspective*. New York: Continuum Books.

Agarwal, B. 1992. The gender and environment debate: Lessons from India. *Feminist review* 18 (1): 157–91.

Akins, N. 1987. Animal utilization in the Middle Rio Grande Valley area. In *Secrets of the city: Papers on Albuquerque area archaeology in honor of Richard A. Bice*. Papers of the Archaeological Society of New Mexico, no. 13. Santa Fe: Ancient City Press.

Albrecht, L., and R. M. Brewer, eds. 1990. *Bridges of power: Women's multicultural alliances*. Philadelphia: New Society Publishers.

Alier, J. M. 1993. Ecological struggles in India: Interview with Ashish Kothari. *Capitalism, Nature, Socialism* 4:113.

Allaby, M. 1989. *Dictionary of the environment*. 3d ed. New York: New York University Press.

Altieri, M. 1987. *Agroecology: The scientific basis of alternative agriculture*. Boulder, CO: Westview Press, Inc.

Amos, V., and P. Parmer. 1984. Challenging imperial feminism. *Feminist review* 17:3–19.

Anaya, R. A. 1989. Introduction to *Aztlán: Essays on the Chicano homeland*, ed. R. A. Anaya and F. Lomellí, pp. 1–11. Albuquerque: University of New Mexico Press.

Anaya, R. A., and F. Lomellí, eds. 1989. *Aztlán: Essays on the Chicano homeland*. Albuquerque: University of New Mexico Press.

Anderson, K. 1994. Constructing geographies: "Race," place and the making of Sydney's aboriginal Redfern. In *Constructions of "race," place and nation*, ed. J. Penrose and P. Jackson, pp. 81–99. Minneapolis: University of Minnesota Press.

Anzaldúa, G. 1987. *Borderlands, La Frontera: The new mestiza*. San Francisco: Aunt Lute Books.

Anzaldúa, G., ed. 1990. *Making face, making soul, Haciendo Caras: Creative and critical perspectives by feminists of color*. San Francisco: Aunt Lute Books.

Archdiocese of Santa Fe. 1947. Archdiocesan Rural Life Conference on Rural Problems of New Mexico. Rio Grande Bioregions Project Archive, Hulbert Center for Southwestern Studies, Colorado College, Colorado Springs, "Agricultural Studies and Agroecology" vertical file collection.

Arellano, E. 1972. *Entre verde y seco.* Dixon, NM: La Academia de la Nueva Raza.

——. 1996. *Querencia:* La Raza bioregionalism. Unpublished research report, Upper Rio Grande Hispano Farms Study. Rio Grande Bioregions Project, Hulbert Center for Southwestern Studies, Colorado College, Colorado Springs.

Ariel, B., and L. Kellen. 1997. Cutting words against the trees. *Earth First! Journal* 17 (6): 12–13.

Atencio, T. 1964. The human dimensions in land use and displacement in northern New Mexico, 44–52. In *Indian and Spanish American adjustments to arid and semiarid environments,* ed. C. Knowlton, 44–52. Lubbock, TX: Texas Technological College.

——. 1987. Cultural philosophy: A common sense perspective. In *Upper Rio Grande waters: Strategies: A conference on traditional water use,* ed. The Upper Rio Grande Working Group (Santa Fe, October). Albuquerque: Southwest Hispanic Research Institute and Native American Studies Center.

——. 1988. Resolana: A Chicano pathway to knowledge. Ernesto Galarza Commemorative Lecture, 3d Annual Lecture. Stanford: Stanford Center for Chicano Research.

Atencio, T., and C. Pacheco. 1980. The concept of *la resolana. Agenda* 10 (1): 14, 34.

Baca, J. S. 1992. *Working in the dark: Reflections of a poet of the barrio.* Santa Fe, NM: Red Crane Books.

Bagby, R. 1990. Daughters of growing things. In *Reweaving the world: The emergence of ecofeminism,* ed. I. Diamond and G. Orenstein, 231–48. San Francisco: Sierra Club Books.

Baker, H. A., Jr. 1991. *Workings of the spirit: The poetics of Afro-American women's writing.* Chicago: University of Chicago Press.

Baker, R. D., R. S. Maxwell, V. H. Treat, and H. D. Dethloff. 1988. *Timeless heritage: A history of the Forest Service in the Southwest.* U.S. Forest Service, U.S. Department of Agriculture, Washington, D.C.

Barrera, M. 1979. *Race and class in the Southwest.* Notre Dame, IN: University of Notre Dame Press.

Baxter, John O. 1987. *Las carneradas: Sheep trade in New Mexico.* Albuquerque: University of New Mexico Press.

——. 1997. *Dividing New Mexico's water: 1700–1912.* Albuquerque: University of New Mexico Press.

Baydo, G. R. 1970. *Cattle ranching in territorial New Mexico.* Ph.D. diss. Department of History, University of New Mexico, Albuquerque.

Bebbington, Anthony. 1993. Modernization from below: An alternative indigenous development? *Economic Geography* 69:274–92.

Bebbington, Anthony, H. Carrasco, L. Peralbo, G. Ramon, J. Trujillo, and V. Torres. 1993. Fragile lands, fragile organizations: Indian organizations and the politics of sustainability in Ecuador. *Transactions of British Geographers* 18:179–96.

Bell Blawis, O. 1971. *Tijerina and the land grants.* New York: International Publishers.

Berger, J., and J. W. Sinton. 1985. *Water, earth, and fire: Land use and environmental planning in the New Jersey Pine Barrens*. Baltimore: Johns Hopkins University Press.

Berman, M. 1981. *The reenchantment of the world*. Ithaca, NY: Cornell University Press.

Berry, W. 1970. *The hidden wound*. Boston: Houghton Mifflin.

Bertrand, R. 1996. A study of white maize on the Gallegos Ranch in the San Luis Valley of Southern Colorado. Unpublished research report. Rio Grande Bioregions Project Archives. Colorado College, Colorado Springs.

Biehl, J. 1991. *Rethinking ecofeminist politics*. Boston: South End Press.

Blaikie, P., and H. Brookfield, eds. 1987. *Land degradation and society*. New York: Methuen.

Bobrow, S. 1992. *The community land trust: A strategy for Ganados del Valle to acquire and secure land for agro-pastoral development*. M.A. thesis, Community and Regional Planning, Rural Development Concentration, University of New Mexico, Albuquerque.

Bodine, J. 1968. A tri-ethnic trap: The Spanish-Americans in Taos. In *Spanish-speaking people in the United States: Proceedings of the 1968 spring meetings of the American Ethnological Society*, ed. American Ethnological Society. Seattle: University of Washington Press.

Bowden, C. 1977. *Killing the hidden waters*. Austin: University of Texas Press.

Bradford, G. 1989. *How deep is deep ecology?* Ojai, CA: Times Change Press.

Brayer, H. 1941. The place of land in Southwestern history. *Land Policy Review* 4 (December): 15–20.

Briggs, C. L., and J. R. Van Ness, eds. 1987. *Land, water, and culture: New perspectives on Hispanic land grants*. Albuquerque: University of New Mexico Press.

Brooke, J. 1997. In a Colorado valley: Hispanic farmers battle a timber baron. *New York Times,* March 24.

Brown, F. L., and H. Ingram. 1987. *Water and poverty in the Southwest*. Tucson: University of Arizona Press.

Brown, W. 1983. Roots: Black ghetto ecology. In *Reclaim Earth! Women speak out for life on Earth,* ed. S. Leland and L. Caldecott, pp. 73–85. London: The Women's Press.

Bullard, R. 1990. Dumping in black and white. In *We speak for ourselves: Social justice, race, and environment,* ed. D. Alston, pp. 4–8. Washington, D.C.: The Panos Institute.

———. 1990. *Dumping in Dixie*. Boulder: Westview Press.

Bullard, R., ed. 1993. *Confronting environmental racism: Voices from the grassroots*. Boston: South End Press.

Cabeza de Baca, F. 1954. *We fed them cactus*. Albuquerque: University of New Mexico.

Caldecott, L., and S. Leland, eds. 1983. *Reclaim Earth! Women speak out for life on Earth*. London: The Women's Press.

Calpotura, F. 1991. People united for a better Oakland: Leading the way on lead. *The Minority Trendsletter* 4:14–16.

Camarillo, A. 1979. *Chicanos in a changing society.* Cambridge, MA: Harvard University Press.

Campa, A. 1963. *Treasure of the Sangre de Cristos: Tales and traditions of the Spanish Southwest.* Norman: University of Oklahoma Press.

Carlson, A. W. 1967. Rural settlement patterns in the San Luis Valley: A comparative study. *Colorado Magazine* 44 (2): 111–28.

——. 1969. New Mexico's sheep industry, 1850–1900: Its role in the history of the territory. *New Mexico Historical Review* 44 (1): 25–49.

——. 1975. Commentary: Long-lots in the Río Arriba. *Annals of the Association of American Geographers* 65 (4): 593–94.

——. 1990. *The Spanish-American homeland: Four centuries in New Mexico's Río Arriba.* Baltimore: Johns Hopkins University Press.

Carson, R. 1962. *Silent spring.* Boston: Houghton Mifflin.

Cassutt, K. 1990. Sierra Club member. Interview with Laura Pulido, Santa Fe, New Mexico.

Catton, W. R., Jr., and R. E. Dunlap. 1980. A new ecological paradigm for post-exuberant sociology. *American Behavioral Scientist* 24 (1): 15–47.

Caufield, C. 1985. *The Rainforest.* New York: Vintage Books.

Chase, S. 1991. *Defending the Earth: A dialogue between Murray Bookchin and Dave Foreman.* Boston: South End Press.

Chavez, J. R. 1984. *The lost land: The Chicano image of the Southwest.* Albuquerque: University of New Mexico Press.

Cheney, J. 1989. Postmodern environmental ethics: Ethics as bioregional narrative. *Environmental Ethics* 11:2.

Cheney, J., ed. 1985. *Lesbian land.* Minneapolis: Word Weavers.

Christensen, J. 1995a. Nevada's ugly tug-of-war: A visit to the heart of the Sagebrush Rebellion. *High Country News,* 30 October, 1.

——. 1995b. Nevada's most rebellious. *High Country News,* 30 October, 12.

Churchill, W., ed. 1991. *Critical issues in Native North America,* vol. 1. IWGIA Document no. 68. Copenhagen: International Work Group for Indigenous Affairs.

Clark, I. G. 1987. *Water in New Mexico: A history of its management and use.* Albuquerque: New Mexico University.

Cleaver, H. 1997. The "space" of cyberspace: Body politics, frontiers, and enclosures. Internet file available at http:/www.eco.utexas.edu:80/Homepages/Faculty/Cleaver/index.html.

Cockburn, A. 1988. Trees, cows and cocaine: An interview with Susanna Hecht. *New Left Review* 173 (January–February): 61–70.

Cockburn, C. 1977. When women get involved in community action. In *Women in the community,* ed. M. Mayo et al., 61–70. London: Routledge.

Cockerill, P. W. 1947. Rural economic problems in low income areas in New Mexico. In *Archdiocesan Rural Life Conference on Rural Problems of New Mexico,* ed. Archdiocese of Santa Fe. Rio Grande Bioregions Project Archive, Hulbert Center for

Southwestern Studies, Colorado College, Colorado Springs, "Agricultural Studies and Agroecology" vertical file collection.

Collard, A., and C. Joyce. 1988. *Rape of the wild: Man's violence against animals and the Earth*. Boston: South End Press.

Cone Newton, K., and F. Ortega. 1991. Beyond ankle-biting: Fighting environmental discrimination locally, nationally, and globally. *The Workbook* 16:98–123.

Commission for Racial Justice. 1987. Toxic wastes and race in the United States. New York: United Church of Christ.

Conklin, H. 1954. *The relation of Hanunuo culture to the plant world*. Ph.D. diss. Department of Anthropology, Harvard University.

Cook, A., and G. Kirk. 1983. *Greenham Common women everywhere*. Boston: South End Press.

Cooper, C. C. 1960. Changes in vegetation, structure, and growth of Southwestern pine forests since white settlement. *Ecological Monographs* 30 (2): 124–64.

Cooperrider, C. K., and B. A. Hendricks. 1937. *Soil erosion and stream flow on range and forest lands of the Upper Rio Grande watershed in relation to land resources and human welfare*. Technical Bulletin 567. Washington, D.C.: U.S. Department of Agriculture.

Cordoba, J. M. 1976. *No lloro pero me acuerdo*. Dallas: Taylor.

Cowan, J. 1990. *Mysteries of the dreamtime: The spiritual life of the Australian Aborigines*. Atlanta: Avery Publishers.

Crawford, S. 1988. *Mayordomo: Chronicle of an acequia in northern New Mexico*. New York: Anchor Books.

Cronon, W., ed. 1996. *Uncommon ground: Rethinking the human place in nature*. New York: Norton.

Cultural Survival Quarterly. 1988. Volume 12, numbers 1 and 2.

Curry, R. 1976–77. Watershed form and process: The elegant balance. *CoEvolution quarterly* 12 (winter): 14–21.

———. 1995. The state of the Culebra watershed: The impact of logging on the southern tributaries. *La Sierra: National Edition* 14 (1:fall/winter): 10–11.

Curry, R., M. Soulé, D. Peña, and M. McGowan. 1996. *Critical analysis of Montana best management practices and sustainable alternatives*. Technical consultants' report presented in October to the Costilla County Land Use Planning Commission. Costilla County Conservancy District, San Luis, Colorado.

Daggett, E. 1973. *Chama, New Mexico: Recreation center, its history, industries, recreations*. Albuquerque: Starline Corporation.

Dankleman, I., and J. Davidson. 1988. *Women and environment in the Third World: Alliance for the future*. London: Earthscan Publications.

Darling, F. F. 1951. The ecological approach to the social sciences. *American Scientist* 39:244–54.

Dawson, P. 1995. Armed, crazy, and lost in the Wild West. *High Country News*, 15 May, 6.

d'Eaubonne, F. 1994. The time for ecofeminism. In *Ecology*, ed. C. Merchant, 174–97. Atlantic Heights: Humanities Press.

deBuys, W. 1985. *Enchantment and exploitation: The life and hard times of a New Mexico mountain range*. Albuquerque: University of New Mexico Press.

deBuys, W., and A. Harris. 1991. *River of traps: A village life*. Albuquerque: University of New Mexico Press.

de la Torre, A., and B. M. Pesquera, eds. 1993. *Building with our hands: New directions in Chicana Studies*. Berkeley: University of California Press.

Deneven, W. M. 1967. Livestock numbers in nineteenth-century New Mexico and the problem of gulleying in the Southwest. *Annals of the Association of American Geographers* 57 (4): 691–703.

Derrida, J. [1987] 1991. *Of spirit: Heidegger and the question*, trans. and eds., G. Bennington and R. Bowlby. Chicago: University of Chicago Press.

Deutsch, S. 1987. *No separate refuge: Culture, class, and gender on an Anglo-Hispanic frontier in the American Southwest, 1880–1940*. New York: Oxford University Press.

Devall, W. 1988. *Simple in means, rich in ends: Practicing deep ecology*. Salt Lake City: Peregrine Smith.

Devall, W., and G. Sessions. 1985. *Deep ecology: Living as if nature mattered*. Salt Lake City: Peregrine Smith.

Diamond, I., and G. Orenstein, eds. 1990. *Reweaving the world: The emergence of ecofeminism*. San Francisco: Sierra Club Books.

Dickens, P. 1992. *Society and nature: Toward a green social theory*. Philadelphia: Temple University Press.

Division of Research, Department of Government, University of New Mexico Press. 1946. *The soil conservation problem in New Mexico*. Albuquerque: University of New Mexico.

Dortignac, E. J. 1956. Watershed resources and problems of the Rio Grande Basin. Technical report, Rocky Mountain Forest and Range Experiment Station, U.S. Forest Service, U.S. Department of Agriculture Experimental Station, Ft. Collins, Colorado.

Dunbar-Ortiz, R. 1980. *Roots of resistance: Land tenure in New Mexico, 1680–1980*. Los Angeles: University of California, Chicano Studies and American Indian Centers Publications.

Dyson, F. 1979. *Disturbing the universe*. New York: Harper and Row.

Eastman, C., and J. Gray. 1987. *Community grazing: Practice and potential in New Mexico*. Albuquerque: University of New Mexico Press.

Eastman, C., G. Carruthers, and L. Leifer. 1971. *Evaluation of attitudes toward land in north central New Mexico*. Bulletin 577. Agricultural Experimental Station. Las Cruces: New Mexico State University.

Ebright, M. 1994. *Land grants and lawsuits in northern New Mexico*. Albuquerque: University of New Mexico Press.

Ecologist, The, eds. 1993. *Whose common future? Reclaiming the commons*. Philadelphia: New Society Publishers.

Enloe, C. 1993. *The morning after: Sexual politics at the end of the cold war.* Berkeley: University of California Press.

Evans, W. 1990. New Mexico Department of Game and Fish. Interview with Laura Pulido, Santa Fe, New Mexico (July).

Evernden, N. 1992. *The social creation of nature.* Baltimore: Johns Hopkins University Press.

Fabian, J. 1983. *Time and the other: How anthropology makes its object.* New York: Columbia University Press.

Fausto-Sterling, A. 1985. *Myths of gender.* New York: Basic Books.

The first thousand days of the next thousand years: The Wildlands Project at three. 1995. *Wildearth* 5:3–89.

Feyerabend, P. 1988. *Farewell to reason.* New York: Verso Books.

Fisher, M. P., and R. Luyster. 1990. *Living religions.* New York: Prentice Hall.

Fite, G. 1966. *The farmers' frontier, 1865–1900.* Norman. University of Oklahoma Press.

Flores, E. T. 1983. Chicanos and sociological research: 1970–1980. In *Chicanos and the social sciences: A decade of research and development,* ed. I. D. Ortíz, 19–45. Santa Barbara: Center for Chicano Studies, University of California-Santa Barbara.

———. 1986. The Mexican-origin people in the United States and Marxist thought in Chicano Studies. In *The Left Academy: Marxist scholarship on American campuses,* vol. 3, ed. B. Ollman and E. Vernoff, 103–38. New York: Praeger.

Forrest, S. 1989. *The preservation of the village.* Albuquerque: University of New Mexico Press.

Fox, W. 1989. The deep ecology-ecofeminism debate and its parallels. *Environmental Ethics* 11 (2).

Fox Keller, F. 1985. *Reflections on science and gender.* New Haven: Yale University Press.

Frake, C. O. 1962. Cultural ecology and ethnography. *American Anthropologist* 64 (1): 53–59.

Friedmann, J., and H. Rangan. 1993. *In defense of livelihood.* West Hartford: Kumarian Press.

Friends of the Trees, eds. 1988. International green front report. Chelan, WA: Friends of the Trees.

Fuss, D. 1989. *Essentially speaking.* New York: Routledge.

Gaard, G. 1993. *Ecofeminism: Women, animals, nature.* Philadelphia: Temple University Press.

Galarza, E. 1972. Mexicans in the Southwest: A culture in process. In *Plural society in the Southwest,* eds. E. H. Spicer and R. H. Thompson. New York: Interbook.

Ganados del Valle. n.d. *The grazing proposal and the issues.* Mimeo. Los Ojos, New Mexico: Ganados del Valle.

Gans, H. 1962. *The urban villagers.* New York: Free Press.

Garcia, M. 1981. *Desert immigrants.* New Haven: Yale University Press.

García, R. 1988. *A philosopher in Aztlán: Studies for ethno-metaphysics in the Indo-Hispanic (Chicano) Southwest.* 2 vols. Ph.D. diss, Department of Philosophy, University of Colorado-Boulder.

García, R. A. 1991. *Rise of the Mexican American middle class: San Antonio, 1929–1941.* College Station: Texas A&M University Press.

——. 1992. Creating a consciousness, memory, and expectations: The burden of Octavio Romano. In *Chicano discourse,* ed. T. Mindiola Jr., and E. Zamora, 6–31. National Association for Chicano Studies, University of Houston, Mexican American Studies Program, Houston, Texas.

Gardner, J. L. 1951. Vegetation of the creosotebush area of the Rio Grande Valley in New Mexico. *Ecological monographs* 21 (3): 379–403.

Gardner, R. 1970. *Grito! Reies Tijerina and the New Mexico land grant war of 1967.* Indianapolis: Bobbs-Merrill.

Garland, A. W. 1989. *For our kids' sake: How to protect your child against pesticides in food.* New York: Natural Resources Defense Council.

Gedicks, A. 1993. *The new resource wars.* Boston: South End Press.

Geertz, C. 1969. Two types of ecosystems. In *Environment and cultural behavior,* ed. A. P. Vayda. Garden City, NY: The Natural History Press.

——. 1983. *Local knowledge.* New York: Basic Books.

Gelbach, F. R. [1981] 1993. *Mountain islands and desert seas: A natural history of the U.S.–Mexican borderlands.* College Station: Texas A&M University Press.

Ghai, D., and J. M. Vivian, eds. 1995. *Grassroots environmental action: People's participation in sustainable development.* London: Routledge.

Gibbs, L. 1995. *Dying from dioxin: A citizen's guide to reclaiming our health and rebuilding democracy.* Boston: South End Press.

Gilkes, C. T. 1988. Building in many places: Multiple commitments and ideologies in black women's community work. In *Women and the politics of empowerment,* eds. A. Bookman and S. Morgan, 53–76. Philadelphia: Temple University Press.

Goldman, M. 1993. Tragedy of the commons, or the commoner's tragedy? *Capitalism, Nature, Socialism* 4 (4): 49–68.

Golley, F. B. 1993. *A history of the ecosystem concept: More than the sum of the parts.* New Haven: Yale University Press.

Gomez-Ibañez, D. 1977. Energy, economics, and the decline of transhumance.

Gonzalez, N. L. 1969. *The Spanish-Americans of New Mexico: A heritage of pride.* Albuquerque: University of New Mexico Press.

Goodwin, E. 1991. Building coalitions for our Earth. *Woman of Power* 20:32–35.

Goonatilake, S. 1984. *Aborted discovery: Science and creativity in the Third World.* London: Zed Books.

Granado, L. 1992. Interview with Malia Davis, Denver, Colorado (February 17).

Griffin, S. 1978. *Woman and nature: The roaring inside her.* New York: Harper Colophon.

————. 1989. Split culture. In *Healing the wounds: The promise of ecofeminism*, ed. J. Plant, 7–17. Philadelphia: New Society Publishers.

Griswold del Castillo, R. 1979. *The Los Angeles barrio, 1850–1890*. Los Angeles: University of California Press.

————. 1988–1990. Southern California Chicano history: Regional origins and national critique. *Aztlan* 19 (1): 109–24.

Grossberg, L. 1993. Cultural studies and/in new worlds. In *Race, identity, and representation in education*, ed. C. McCarthy and W. Crichlow, 89–108. London: Routledge.

Grumbine, R. E. 1992. *Ghost bears: Exploring the biodiversity crisis*. Washington, D.C.: Island Press.

Guha, R. 1989. Radical American environmentalism and wilderness preservation: A Third World critique. *Environmental ethics* 11 (1): 71–83.

————. 1990. *The unquiet woods: Ecological change and peasant resistance in the Himalayas*. Berkeley: University of California Press.

Gutiérrez, G. 1994. Mothers of East Los Angeles strike back. In *Unequal protection: Environmental justice and communities of color*, ed. R. D. Bullard, 220–33. San Francisco: Sierra Club Books.

Gutiérrez, P., and J. Eckert. 1991. Contrasts and commonalities: Hispanic and Anglo farming in Conejos County, Colorado. *Rural Sociology* 56 (2): 247–63.

Gutiérrez, R. 1989. Review of *Land, water, and culture: New perspectives on Hispanic land grants*. *Journal of the Southwest* 31 (3).

Hamilton, C. 1990. Women, home, and community: The struggle in an urban environment. In *Reweaving the world: The emergence of ecofeminism*, ed. I. Diamond and G. Orenstein, 215–22. San Francisco: Sierra Club Books.

————. 1993. Environmental consequences of urban growth and blight. *Toxic struggles: The theory and practice of environmental justice*, ed. R. Hofrichter, 67–75. Philadelphia: New Society Publishers.

Haraway, D. 1989. *Primate visions: Gender, race, and nature in the world of modern science*. London: Routledge.

————. 1991. *Simians, cyborgs, and women: The reinvention of nature*. London: Routledge.

Harding, S. 1986. *The science question in feminism*. Ithaca, NY: Cornell University Press.

Harper, A., A. Cordova, and K. Oberg. 1943. *Man and resources in the Middle Rio Grande Valley*. Albuquerque: University of New Mexico Press.

Harper, D. 1987. *Working knowledge: Skill and community in a small shop*. Chicago: The University of Chicago Press.

Harris, L. D. 1984. *The fragmented forest: Island biogeography theory and the preservation of biotic diversity*. Chicago: University of Chicago Press.

Harris, M. 1976. *Cultural materialism: The struggle for a science of culture*. New York: Harper.

Hartsock, N. 1987. Rethinking modernism: Minority vs. majority theories. *Cultural Critique* 51 (3): 187–206.

Havelock, E. 1963. *Preface to Plato.* Cambridge, MA: Harvard University Press.

Hawley, A. 1944. Ecology and human ecology. *Social Forces* 22 (4): 398–405.

———. 1981. Human ecology: Persistence and change. *American Behavioral Scientist* 24 (3): 423–44.

———. 1984. Human ecological and Marxian theories. *American Journal of Sociology* 89 (4): 904–17.

Hayles, N. K. 1995. Searching for common ground. In *Reinventing nature: Responses to postmodern deconstruction,* eds. M. Soulé and G. Lease. Washington, D.C.: Island Press.

Hecht, S., and A. Cockburn. 1989. *The fate of the forest.* New York: Verso.

Hernández, I. 1992. An open letter to Chicanas: On the politics and power of origin. In *Without discovery: A native response to Columbus,* ed. Ray González, 153–66. Seattle: Broken Moon Press.

Herdon, G. 1991. *Cut and run: Saying goodbye to the last great forests in the West.* Telluride, CO: Western Eye Press.

Hirschhorn, L. 1984. *Beyond mechanization: Work and technology in a post-industrial age.* Cambridge: MIT Press.

hooks, bell. 1984. Sisterhood: Political solidarity between women. In *Feminist theory: From margin to center,* 41–49. Boston: South End Press.

———. 1990. *Yearning: Race, gender, and cultural politics.* Boston: South End Press.

———. 1992. Out of the academy and into the streets. *Ms. Magazine,* July-August.

Howell, B. J. 1983. Implications of the cultural conservation report for social impact assessment. *Human Organization* 42 (4): 346–50.

Hudson, W. E., ed. 1991. *Landscape linkages and biodiversity.* Washington, D.C.: Island Press.

Hufford, M. 1994. *Conserving culture: A new discourse on heritage.* Champaign: University of Illinois Press.

Humphrey, R. R. 1953. The desert grassland, past and present. *Journal of Range Management* 6 (3): 259–64.

———. 1987. *90 years and 535 miles: Vegetation changes along the Mexican border.* Albuquerque: University of New Mexico Press.

Hurtado, A. 1989. Relating to privilege: Seduction and rejection in the subordination of white women and women of color. *Signs* (summer): 833–55.

Hynes, H. P. 1991. The pocketbook and the pill: Reflections on green consumerism and population control. *Issues in Reproductive and Genetic Engineering* 4 (1): 47–52.

Ingram, H. 1990. *Water politics: Continuity and change.* Albuquerque: University of New Mexico Press.

Jackson, D. D. 1991. Around Los Ojos, sheep and land are fighting words. *Smithsonian* 22 (April): 37–47.

Jackson, J. B. 1994. *A sense of place, a sense of time.* New Haven: Yale University Press.

Jackson, P., and J. Penrose, ed. 1994. *Constructions of race, place, and nation.* Minneapolis: University of Minnesota Press.

Jackson, W. 1987. *Altars of unhewn stone: Science and nature.* San Francisco: North Point Press.

Jaimes, M. A., ed. 1992. *The state of Native America.* Boston: South End Press.

Jervis, T. 1990. New Mexico Audubon Society. Interview with Laura Pulido, Los Alamos, New Mexico (July).

Jones, H. 1932. Uses of wood by the Spanish colonists in New Mexico. *New Mexico Historical Review* 7 (3): 3–27.

Jones, J. A., and G. E. Grant. 1996. Peak flow responses to clear-cutting and roads in small and large basins, Western Cascades, Oregon. *Water Resources Research* 32 (4): 959–74.

Jordan, T. G. 1974. Antecedents of the long-lots in Texas. *Annals of the Association of American Geographers* 64 (1): 70–86.

———. 1993. *North American cattle ranching frontiers.* Albuquerque: University of New Mexico Press.

Jung, C. G. 1960. *Synchronicity,* trans. R.F.C. Hull. Princeton: Princeton University Press.

———. [1961] 1989. *Memories, dreams, reflections,* ed. A. Jaffe and trans. R. and C. Winston. New York: Vintage Books.

Kamel, R. 1985. Is a Women's Peace Movement taking root? *American Friends Service Committee Women's Newsletter* 6 (1): 1.

Kane, G. S. 1994. Restoration or preservation? Reflections on a clash of environmental philosophies. In *Beyond preservation: Restoring and inventing landscapes,* eds. A. D. Baldwin Jr., J. DeLuce, and C. Pletsch, 69–84. Minneapolis: University of Minnesota Press.

Kelly, K. 1989. The self-organizing mind of plants. *Whole Earth Review* 64 (fall).

King, Ynestra. 1981. Feminism and the revolt of nature. *Heresies* 13:12–16.

———. 1983a. The ecofeminist imperative. In *Reclaim Earth: Women speak out for life on Earth,* eds. L. Caldecott and S. Leland, 9–15. London: The Women's Press.

———. 1983b. All is connectedness. In *Keeping the peace,* ed. L. Jones. London: The Women's Press.

———. 1983c. Toward an ecological feminism and a feminist ecology. In *Machina ex dea,* ed. John Rothschild, 118–29. New York: Pergamon.

———. 1987. Letter to the editor, *The Nation,* December 12.

———. 1988. Ecofeminism: On the necessity of history and mystery. *Woman of Power* 9:42–44, 71.

———. 1990a. Ecological feminism. In *What is ecofeminism?,* ed. G. Kirk, 38–43. New York: Ecofeminist Resources.

———. 1990b. Healing the wounds. In *Reweaving the world: The emergence of ecofeminism,* eds. I. Diamond and G. Orenstein. San Francisco: Sierra Club Books.

Kirk, G. 1989. Our Greenham common: Not just a place but a movement. In *Rocking the ship of state: Toward a feminist peace politics,* eds. A. Harris and Y. King. Boulder: Westview.

——. 1992. Blood, bones, connective tissue: Women resist ecological destruction. In *A diplomacy of the oppressed: Women's international organizing.* London: Zed Press.

——. 1994. Women resist ecological destruction. In *A diplomacy of the oppressed: New directions in international feminism,* ed. G. Ashworth, 69–89. London: Zed Books.

——. 1997a. Ecofeminism and environmental justice: Bridges across gender, race, and class. *Frontiers: A Journal of Women Studies,* 2–20.

——. 1997b. Standing on solid ground: Toward a material ecological feminism. In *Materialist feminism: A reader in class, difference, and women's lives,* eds. R. Hennessy and C. Ingraham, 345–63. London: Routledge.

Knowlton, C. 1964a. Coming crisis in the Southwest. *Western Review* 1 (2): 5–8.

——. 1964b. One approach to the economic and social problems of northern New Mexico. *New Mexico Business* 17 (September): 3, 15–22.

——. 1967. Land-grant problems among the state's Spanish-Americans. *New Mexico Business* 20 (6): 1–12.

——. 1969. Changing Spanish-American villages of northern New Mexico. *Sociology and Social Research* 53 (2): 455–74.

——. 1986. Cultural impacts of New Mexico and West Texas reclamation projects. *The Southwestern Review* 5 (1): 13–29.

——. 1989. Spanish and Mexican land grants: A key to the past. Paper presented in April at the 31st Annual Conference of the Western Social Science Association, Albuquerque. Rio Grande Bioregions Project Archive vertical file collection, Colorado College, Colorado Springs.

——, ed. 1968. *International water law along the Mexican-American border.* El Paso: University of Texas at El Paso.

——, ed. 1976. Spanish and Mexican land grants in the Southwest: A symposium. *Social Science Journal* 13:3, special issue.

Kobayashi, A., and L. Peake. 1994. Unnatural discourse: "Race" and gender in geography. *Gender, Place and Culture* 1:225–44.

Krauss, C. 1993. Blue-collar women and toxic waste protests: The process of politicization. In *Toxic struggles: The theory and practice of environmental justice,* ed. R. Hofrichter, 256–71. Philadelphia: New Society Publishers.

——. 1994. Women of color on the front line. In *Unequal protection: Environmental justice and communities of color,* ed. R. D. Bullard. San Francisco: Sierra Club Books.

Kroeber, Alfred L. 1969. Relations of environmental and cultural factors. In *Environment and cultural behavior,* ed. A. P. Vayda. Garden City, NY: The Natural History Press.

Kutsche, P., and J. R. Van Ness. 1981. *Cañones: Values, crisis and survival in a northern New Mexico village.* Albuquerque: University of New Mexico Press.

Lamar, H. R. 1962. Land policy in the Spanish Southwest, 1846–1891: A study in contrasts. *The Journal of Economic History* 22 (4): 498–515.

Lane, B. 1988. *Landscapes of the sacred: Geography and narrative in American spirituality.* New York: Paulist Press.

Lansky, M. 1992. *Beyond the beauty strip: Saving what's left of our forests.* Gardiner, ME: Tilbury House.

Lawlor, R. 1991. *Voices of the dreamtime: Awakening in the aboriginal dreamtime.* Rochester, VT: Inner Traditions International.

Leál, L. 1989. In search of Aztlán. In *Aztlán: Essays on the Chicano homeland,* eds. R. A. Anaya and F. Lomellí. Albuquerque: University of New Mexico Press.

Lee, C. 1987. *Toxic wastes and race.* New York: Commission for Racial Justice, United Church of Christ.

Leff, E. 1995. *Green production: Toward an environmental rationality.* Democracy and Ecology series, vol. 2, ed. James O'Connor. New York: Guilford Press.

Leiss, W. 1974. *The domination of nature.* Boston: Beacon Press.

Leonard, A., ed. 1989. *Seeds: Supporting women's work in the Third World.* New York: The Feminist Press.

Leonard, O. 1970. *The role of the land grant in the social organization and social processes of a Spanish-American village in New Mexico.* Albuquerque: Calvin Horn.

Leonard, O., and C. P. Loomis. 1941. *Culture of a contemporary rural community: El Cerrito, New Mexico.* USDA, Bureau of Agricultural Economics, Rural Life Studies no. 1. Washington, D.C.: U.S. Government Printing Office.

Leopold, A. 1968. *A sand county almanac.* New York: Oxford University Press.

Levidow, L. 1992. The eleventh annual meeting of the International Association for Impact Assessment. *Capitalism, Nature, Socialism* 3 (1): 117–24.

Libecap, G. D., and G. Alter. 1982. Agricultural productivity, partible inheritance, and the demographic response to rural poverty: An examination of the Spanish Southwest. *Explorations in Economic History* 19 (April): 184–200.

Library of Congress, American Folklife Center. 1983. *Cultural conservation: The protection of cultural heritage in the United States.* Washington, D.C.: Library of Congress.

Lopéz, B. H. 1979. *Of wolves and men.* New York: Charles Scribner's Sons.

Lorde, A. 1984. Age, race, class, and sex: Women redefining difference. In *Sister Outsider,* ed. A. Lorde. Trumansburg, NY: Crossing Press.

MacCameron, R. 1994. Environmental change in colonial New Mexico. *Environmental History Review* 18 (2): 17–39.

McCourt, K. 1977. *Working class women and grassroots politics.* Bloomington: University of Indiana Press.

McCannell, D. 1984. Reconstructed ethnicity: Tourism and cultural identity in Third World communities. *Annals of Tourism Research* 11:376–89.

MacCurdy, E., trans. and ed. 1938. *The notebooks of Leonardo da Vinci,* vol. 1. New York: Reynal and Hitchcock.

McNeely, J. A. 1990. An international perspective on conserving cultural diversity: How the variety of human experience can help promote sustainable forms of using natural resources. Paper presented in June at the First National Conference on Cultural Conservation, Folk Life Center, Library of Congress, Washington, D.C.

Manning, E. 1995. Tables turned on Catron County leader. *High Country News,* 30 October, 3.

Marglin, S. A. 1990. Sustainable development: A system of knowledge approach. *The Black Scholar* 21 (1): 35–42.

Martínez, R. O. 1982–1983. Internal colonialism: A reconceptualization of race relations in the United States. *Humboldt Journal of Social Relations* 10 (1): 163–76.

——. 1987. Chicano lands: Acquisition and loss. *Wisconsin Sociologist* 42 (2/3): 89–98.

——. 1988a. The politics of ethnicity in social science. Paper presented in May at The Estate of Social Knowledge: A Symposium on the History and Historiography of the Social Sciences. Department of History, Johns Hopkins University.

——. 1988b. The rediscovery of the "forgotten people." In *Times of challenge: Chicanas and Chicanos in American society,* ed. National Association for Chicano Studies, 115–24. Houston: Mexican-American Studies Center, University of Houston.

——. 1991. The politics of ethnicity in social science. In *The estate of social knowledge,* eds. J. Brown and D. van Keuren, 228–52. Baltimore: Johns Hopkins University Press.

Martinez, S. 1991. Ganados del Valle. Interview with Laura Pulido, Los Ojos, New Mexico (August).

Mead, M., ed. 1953. *Cultural patterns and technical change.* Paris: UNESCO.

Mealy, R. 1990. Charles Lee on environmental racism: Clean environment without social justice? In *We speak for ourselves: Social justice race and environment,* ed. D. Alston. Washington, D.C.: The Panos Institute.

Meinig, D. W. 1971. *Southwest: Three peoples in geographical change, 1600–1970.* New York: Oxford University Press.

Merchant, C. 1980. *The death of nature: Women, ecology, and the scientific revolution.* San Francisco: Harper and Row.

——. 1992. *Radical ecology: The search for a livable world.* London: Routledge.

Meyer, C., and F. Moosang, eds. 1992. *Living with the land: Communities restoring the Earth.* Philadelphia: New Society Publishers.

Meyer, M. 1984. *Water in the Hispanic Southwest: A social and legal history, 1550–1850.* Tucson: University of Arizona Press.

Mies, M. 1993. Liberating the consumer. In *Ecofeminism,* ed. M. Mies and V. Shiva, 251–63. London: Zed Books.

Mies, M., and V. Shiva. 1993. *Ecofeminism.* London: Zed Books.

Mills, C. Wright. 1959. *The sociological imagination.* New York: Oxford University Press.

Mirandé, A. 1985. *The Chicano experience.* Notre Dame, IN: University of Notre Dame Press.

Miss Ann Thropy. 1991. Overpopulation and industrialism. In *Earth first! reader,* ed. J. Davis. Salt Lake City: Peregrine Smith.

Monasterio, F. O., et al., eds. 1987. *Tierra profanada: Historia ambiental de Mexico.* Mexico City: Instituto Nacional de Antropologia e Historia and Secretaria de Desarrollo Urbano y Ecologia.

Monroy, Douglas. 1993. *Thrown among strangers: The making of Mexican culture in frontier California.* Berkeley: University of California Press.

Montaño, M. 1991. *Barbacoa de Cabeza: Folk foodways and cultural hegemony in South Texas.* Ph.D. diss., Folklore, University of Pennsylvania, Philadelphia.

Montejano, D. 1988. *Anglos and Mexicans in the making of Texas, 1836–1986.* Austin: University of Texas Press.

Morales, M. 1990. Canjilon resident. Interview with Laura Pulido, Canjilon, New Mexico (August).

Morrison, T. 1987. *Beloved.* New York: Alfred E. Knopf.

Moses, M. 1993. Farmworkers and pesticides. In *Confronting environmental racism: Voices from the grassroots,* ed. R. D. Bullard. Boston: South End Press.

Mosk, S. A. 1942. The influences of traditions on agriculture in New Mexico. *The Journal of Economic History.* December, 34–51, supplemental issue.

Mott, L., and K. Snyder. 1987. *Pesticide alert: A guide to pesticides in fruit and vegetables.* San Francisco: Sierra Club Books.

Murphy, P. D. 1988. Sex-typing the planet: Gaia imagery and the problem of subverting patriarchy. *Environmental Ethics* 10 (2:summer): 155–68.

Naess, A. 1973. The shallow and the deep, long-range ecology movements: A summary. *Inquiry* 16:95–100.

———. 1989. *Ecology, community and lifestyle.* New York: Cambridge University Press.

Nagy, M. 1991. *Philosophical issues in the psychology of C. G. Jung.* Albany: SUNY Press.

Nazarea, V. In press. Introduction. In *Ethnoecology: Situated knowledge, located lives,* ed. V. Nazarea. Tucson: University of Arizona Press.

Nelson, L. 1990. The place of women in polluted places. In *Reweaving the world: The emergence of ecofeminism,* ed. I. Diamond and G. Orenstein, 173–88. San Francisco: Sierra Club Books.

Nesmith, C., and S. Radcliffe. 1993. (Re)mapping Mother Earth: A geographical perspective on environmental feminisms. *Environment and Planning: D* 11:379–94.

Netting, R. McC. 1977. *Cultural ecology.* Menlo Park, CA: Cummings.

New Mexico Department of Game and Fish. 1980. *Edward Sargent fish and wildlife area management plan.* Santa Fe: NMDGF.

———. 1984a. *Rio Chama fish and wildlife area management plan.* Santa Fe: NMDGF.

———. 1984b. *Bill Humphries wildlife management plan.* Santa Fe: NMDGF.

Nickerson, T., ed. 1945. That their fields shall prosper and their flocks increase: Problems of the Rio Grande watershed, a symposium. *New Mexico Historical Review* 15:117–40.

Norberg-Hodge, H. 1991. *Ancient futures: Learning from Ladakh.* San Francisco: Sierra Club Books.

Norgaard, R. B. 1994. *Development betrayed: The end of progress and a coevolutionary revisioning of the future.* London: Routledge.

Northern Rio Grande Resource Conservation and Development Project. 1969. Amendment of the northern Rio Grande resource conservation and development project action plan. Rio Grande Bioregions Project Archive, Hulbert Center for Southwestern Studies, Colorado College, Colorado Springs, "Environmental History" vertical file collection.

Noss, R. F. 1993. Sustainable forestry or sustainable forests? In *Defining sustainable forestry,* ed. J. T. Olson. Washington, D.C.: Island Press.

———. 1994. A sustainable forest is a diverse and natural forest. In *Clearcut: The tragedy of industrial forestry,* ed. Bill DeVall, 33–40. San Francisco: Sierra Club Books.

Noss, R. F., et al., eds. 1994. *Saving nature's legacy: Protecting and restoring biodiversity.* Washington, D.C.: Island Press.

Nostrand, R. L. 1992. *The Hispano homeland.* Norman: University of Oklahoma Press.

Oberg, K. 1940. Cultural factors and land-use planning in Cuba Valley, New Mexico. *Rural sociology* 5:2.

Odum, E. 1971. *Fundamentals of ecology.* 3d edition. Philadelphia: Saunders.

Oelschlaeger, M. 1991. *The idea of wilderness: From prehistory to the age of ecology.* New Haven: Yale University Press.

Olguín, R. 1984. *The politics of criticism as a criticism of politics: The mutual concerns of political theory and ethnic studies.* Ph.D. diss., Department of Political Science, Stanford University, Stanford California.

———. 1989. Epistemology of ethnic studies. Lecture presented in September to the Colorado College Ethnic Studies Faculty Seminar. Colorado College, Colorado Springs.

Omolade, B. 1989. We speak for the planet. In *Rocking the ship of state: Toward a feminist peace politics,* eds. A. Harris and Y. King, 171–90. Boulder: Westview.

Onians, R. G. [1951] 1989. *The origins of European thought.* New York: Cambridge University Press.

Ortíz, R. D. 1980. *Roots of resistance: Land tenure in New Mexico, 1680–1980.* Los Angeles: Chicano Studies Research Center and American Indian Studies Center, UCLA.

Paehlke, R. C. 1989. *Environmentalism and the future of progressive politics.* New Haven: Yale University Press.

Pardo, M. 1990. Mexican American women grassroots activists: "Mothers of East Los Angeles." *Frontiers: A Journal of Women Studies* 11 (1): 1–7.

Paredes, A. 1977. On ethnographic work among minorities. *New Scholar* 2:1–32.

Peet, R., and M. Watts. 1993. Introduction: Development theory and environment in an age of market triumphalism. *Economic Geography* 69.

Peña, D. G. 1988a. The andropositivist vernacular and the question of methods in Chicano Studies. Paper presented at the Annual Meeting of the National Association for Chicano Studies, Albuquerque, New Mexico.

——. 1988b. The "green" Marx: Capitalism and the destruction of nature. Unpublished paper. Department of Sociology, Colorado College, Colorado Springs.

——. 1989. When rivers burn: Environmentalism and new social movements in Mexico. Paper presented in April at the Annual Meeting of the National Association for Chicano Studies, Los Angeles, California.

——. 1990. Women, agriculture, and the environment in the Upper Rio Grande. Unpublished field research report, Rio Grande Bioregions Project, Hulbert Center for Southwestern Studies, Colorado College, Colorado Springs.

——. 1991. An American wilderness in a Mexican homeland. Paper presented in April at the 33d annual meeting of the Western Social Science Association, Reno, Nevada.

——. 1992. The "brown" and "green": Chicanos and environmental politics in the Upper Rio Grande. *Capitalism, Nature, Socialism* 3 (1): 79–103.

——. 1993a. Agroecology of a Chicana/o family farm. Paper presented in April at the 35th Annual Conference of the Western Social Science Association, Corpus Christi, Texas.

——. 1993b. *Revenue potential and ethical issues in the management of the Culebra Mountain Tract as a common property resource.* Unpublished technical report, Costilla County Conservancy District and La Sierra Foundation, San Luis, Colorado.

——. 1993c. "Forest crimes" in the subaltern life of the commons: A site ethnography of power-in-spacing. Paper presented in April at the 35th Annual Conference of the Western Social Science Association, Corpus Christi, Texas.

——. 1994a. Restoring and managing the homeland commons: The Culebra mountain tract as a common property regime. Paper presented in April at the 36th Annual Conference of the Western Social Science Association, Albuquerque, New Mexico.

——. 1994b. Pasture poachers, water hogs, and ridge runners: Archetypes in the site ethnography of local environmental conflicts. Paper presented at the 36th annual meeting of the Western Social Science Association, Albuquerque, New Mexico (April).

——. 1997a. *The terror of the machine: Technology, work, gender, and ecology on the U.S.–Mexico border.* Border and Migration Studies series. Austin: CMAS Books/University of Texas Press.

——. 1997b. Biotechnology and rural Latino communities: A critical first look at imminent threats. Paper presented in July to the Rural Latino Studies Working Group, Julian Samora Research Institute, Michigan State University, East Lansing, Michigan.

——. 1997c. Ecological services provided by the *acequias* of the Upper Rio Grande: Preliminary report. Unpublished research report. Rio Grande Bioregions Project, Colorado College, Colorado Springs.

——. 1998. Cultural landscapes and biodiversity: The ethnoecology of a watershed commons. In *Ethnoecology: Situated knowledge, located lives,* ed. V. Nazarea. Tucson: University of Arizona Press.

———. In press. *Gaia in Aztlán: The politics of place in the Río Arriba.*

Peña, D. G., and J. Gallegos. 1993. Nature and Chicanos in southern Colorado. In *Confronting environmental racism: Voices from the grassroots,* ed. R. D. Bullard, 141–60. Boston: South End Press.

———. 1997. Local knowledge and collaborative environmental action research. In *Building community: Social science in action,* ed. P. Nyden, A. Figert, M. Shibley, and D. Burrows, 85–91. Thousand Oaks, CA: Pine Forge Press.

Peña, D. G., and M. Mondragon Valdéz. 1998. The "brown" and the "green" revisited: Chicanos and environmental politics in the Upper Rio Grande. In *The struggle for ecological democracy: Environmental justice movements in the United States,* ed. D. Faber. Democracy and Ecology series, vol. 7, ed. J. O'Connor. New York: Guilford Press.

Peña, D. G., and R. Martinez. 1991. The tribology of natural resources: A study of friction in motion. Paper presented in April at the 33d Annual Conference of the Western Social Science Association, Reno, Nevada.

———. 1993. *Upper Rio Grande Hispano farms: A cultural and natural history of land ethics in transition, 1598–1998.* Unpublished research proposal. Rio Grande Bioregions Project, Hulbert Center for Southwestern Studies, Colorado College, Colorado Springs.

Peña, D. G., R. O. Martínez, and L. McFarland. 1993. Rural Chicana/o communities and the environment: An attitudinal survey of residents of Costilla County, Colorado. *Perspectives in Mexican American Studies* 4:45–74.

Peña, S. 1992. Interview by Malia Davis. Denver, CO., 28 February.

Pennick, E. J. 1990. Land ownership and black economic development. *The Black Scholar* 21 (1): 43–46.

Pepper, D. 1993. *Eco-Socialism: From deep ecology to social justice.* London: Routledge.

Perrone, B., H. Stockel, and V. Kreuger. 1989. *Medicine women, curanderas, and women doctors.* Norman: University of Oklahoma Press.

Plant, J. 1990a. Revaluing home: Feminism and bioregionalism. *Home! A bioregional reader,* eds. C. Andruss, J. Plant, and E. Wright, 21–25. Philadelphia: New Society Publishers.

———. 1990b. Searching for common ground: Ecofeminism and bioregionalism. *Reweaving the world: The emergence of ecofeminism,* eds. I. Diamond and G. Orenstein, 155–61. San Francisco: Sierra Club Books.

Plumwood. V. 1993. *Feminism and the mastery of nature.* London: Routledge.

Political Ecology Group. 1996. Immigration and the environment in the U.S.: Myths and facts. *Race, Poverty and the Environment* 6 (4) and 7 (1): 37–38.

Posey, D. 1981. Ethnoentomology of the Kayapo Indians of central Brazil. *Journal of Ethnobiology* 1 (1).

———. n.d. *The science of the Mebengokre: Alternatives to destruction.* Brasil: Museu Paraense Emilio Goeldi.

Potts, B. 1988. *Witches heal: Lesbian herbal self-sufficiency,* 2d edition. Ann Arbor: DuReve Publications.

Pulido, L. 1990. The Los Angeles Chicano community and environmental politics: What institutional environmentalism can learn from grassroots struggles. Unpublished research report, Graduate School of Architecture and Urban Planning, University of California, Los Angeles.

———. 1993. Sustainable development at Ganados del Valle. *Confronting environmental racism: Voices from the grassroots,* ed. R. D. Bullard, 123–39. Boston: South End Press.

———. 1996. *Environmentalism and economic justice: Two Chicano cases from the Southwest.* Tucson: University of Arizona Press.

Quillen, E. 1993. Now that Denver has abdicated . . . who will coordinate and inspire the West? *High Country News,* 3 May, 1, 6–9.

Quinby, L. 1990. Ecofeminism and the politics of resistance. In *Reweaving the world: The emergence of ecofeminism,* eds. I. Diamond and G. Orenstein, 122–27. San Francisco: Sierra Club Books.

Race, Poverty and the Environment. 1996. Vol. 6, no. 4 and volume 7, no. 1. Special issue on "The Border."

Rangan, H. 1993. Romancing the environment: Popular environmental action in the Garhwal Himalayas. In *In defense of livelihood,* eds. J. Friedmann and H. Rangan, 155–81. West Hartford: Kumarian Press.

Rappaport, R. A. 1968. *Pigs for the ancestors.* New Haven: Yale University Press.

———. 1979. *Ecology, meaning and religion.* Berkeley: North Atlantic Books.

Reagon, B. J. 1983. Coalition politics: Turning the century. In *Home girls: A black feminist anthology,* ed. B. Smith. New York: Kitchen Table, Women of Color Press.

Reardon, B. A. 1985. *Sexism and the war system.* New York: Teachers College Press.

Redclift, M. 1987. *Sustainable development: Exploring the contradictions.* London: Routledge.

Redman, L. 1947. Soil conservation and its relation to the community and the family. In *Archdiocesan Rural Life Conference on Rural Problems of New Mexico,* ed. Archdiocese of Santa Fe, Rio Grande Bioregions Project Archive, Hulbert Center for Southwestern Studies, Colorado College, Colorado Springs, "Agricultural Studies and Agroecology" vertical file collection.

Richardson, A. 1990. State of New Mexico Economic Development and Tourism Department. Inverview with Laura Pulido. Santa Fe, New Mexico (July).

Rifkin, J. 1991. *Biosphere politics: A cultural odyssey from the Middle Ages to the New Age.* New York: Harper Collins.

Rívera, J. A. Forthcoming. *Water and democracy in the Southwest: The Acequia Papers.*

Rívera, J. A., and D. G. Peña 1997. Historic *acequia* communities in the Upper Rio Grande: Policy for cultural and ecological protection in an arid land environment. Paper presented in July to the Rural Latino Studies Working Group, Julian Samora Research Institute, Michigan State University, East Lansing, Michigan.

Rochin, R. I. 1993. Hispanic Americans in the rural economy: Conditions, issues, and probable future adjustments. *National Rural Studies Committee: A proceedings,* ed. E. N. Castle, 62–75. Corvalis: Western Rural Development Center, Oregon State University.

Rock, M. 1976. The change in tenure New Mexico Supreme Court decisions have effected upon the common lands of community land grants in New Mexico. *The Social Science Journal* 13:13.

Rodda, A. 1990. *Women and the environment.* London: Zed Books.

Rodgers, W. H. 1982. Bringing people back: Toward a comprehensive theory of taking in natural resources law. *Ecology Law Quarterly* 10:205–52.

Rodriguez, R. 1991. Interview by Malia Davis. Denver, CO, 4 December.

Rodriguez, S. 1987. Land, water, and ethnic identity in Taos. In *Land, water, and culture: New perspectives on Hispanic land grants,* ed. C. L. Briggs and J. R. Van Ness, 314–403. Albuquerque: University of New Mexico Press.

———. [1989] 1994. Art, tourism, and race relations in Taos. In *Discovered country: Tourism and survival in the American West,* ed. S. Norris, 143–60. Albuquerque: Stone Ladder Press.

———. 1990. Ethnic reconstruction in contemporary Taos. *Journal of the Southwest* 32 (4): 541–55.

Romano, O. 1970. Social science objectivity and the Chicanos. *El Grito* 4 (1).

Romo, R. 1983. *East Los Angeles: History of a barrio.* Austin: University of Texas Press.

Rosaldo, R. 1989. *Culture and truth: The remaking of social analysis.* Boston: Beacon Press.

Rosenbaum, R. 1981. *Mexicano resistance in the Southwest.* Austin: University of Texas Press.

Rothman, H. 1992. *On rims and ridges: The Los Alamos area since 1880.* Lincoln: University of Nebraska Press.

Rothman, H. 1989. Cultural and environmental change on the Pajarito Plateau. *New Mexico Historical Review* 64 (2): 185–212.

Rowley, W. D. 1985. *U.S. Forest Service grazing and range lands: A history.* College Station: Texas A&M University Press.

Rubine, E. 1997. Shared spaces: The division of labor and gender on Upper Rio Grande Hispano farms. Paper presented in April at the 38th Annual Conference of the Western Social Science Association, Albuquerque.

Said, E. 1993. *Culture and imperialism.* New York: Alfred Knopf.

Saldívar, R. 1990. *Chicano narrative: The dialectics of difference.* Madison: University of Wisconsin Press.

Sale, K. 1985. *Dwellers in the land: The bioregional vision.* San Francisco: Sierra Club Books.

Salmon, E. 1997. Ethnobotany of the *acequia.* Paper presented in April at the 38th Annual Conference of the Western Social Science Association, Albuquerque.

Saloutos, T. 1992. Land policy and its relation to agricultural production and distribution, 1862 to 1933. *The Journal of Economic History* 22 (4): 445–60.

Sanchez, C. L. 1993. Animal, vegetable, and mineral: The sacred connection. *Ecofeminism and the sacred,* ed. C. J. Adams, 207–28. New York: Continuum Books.

Sanchez, G. I. [1940] 1967. *Forgotten people: A study of New Mexicans.* Albuquerque: Calvin Horn.

Saragoza, A. M. 1988–1990. Recent Chicano historiography: An interpretive essay. *Aztlan* 19 (1): 1–77.

Sargent, F. G., P. Lusk, J. A. Rívera, and M. Varela. 1991. *Rural environmental planning for sustainable communities.* Washington, D.C.: Island Press.

Savory, A. 1989. *Holistic resource management.* Covelo, CA: Island Press.

Schapiro, M. 1992. Browns and greens: Europe's new eco-fascists. *Amicus Journal* (winter): 6–7.

Scheffer, V. B. 1991. *The shaping of environmentalism in America.* Seattle: University of Washington Press.

Schroeder, R. 1993. Shady practice: Gender and the political ecology of resource stabilization in Gambian garden/orchards. *Economic Geography* 69:349–65.

Scott, W. 1967. Spanish land-grant problems were here before Anglos. *New Mexico Business* 20.

Scurlock, D. 1993. Pinyon-juniper in Southwest history: An overview of historical use of, impact on, and change through time. Manuscript prepared for the P-J Ecotone Study, NSF Grant, Biology Department, University of New Mexico, Albuquerque.

———. 1995. Environmental history. *Ecology, diversity, and sustainability of the Middle Rio Grande Basin.* USDA Forest Service Technical Report, RM-GTR–268, eds. D. M. Finch and J. A. Tainter. Fort Collins: Rocky Mountain Forest and Range Experiment Station.

Seager J. 1993. *Earth follies: Coming to feminist terms with the global environmental crisis.* London: Routledge.

Sears, P. B. 1964. Ecology: A subversive subject. *BioScience* 14:11–13.

Secretary of Agriculture. 1936. *The Western range.* Washington, D.C.: U.S. Government Printing Office.

Shepard, P., and D. McKinley. 1969. *The subversive science: Essays toward an ecology of man.* Boston: Houghton Mifflin.

Shiva, V. 1988. *Staying alive: Women , ecology, and development.* London: Zed Books.

———. 1990. Development as a new project of Western patriarchy. In *Reweaving the world: The emergence of ecofeminism,* eds. I. Diamond and G. Orenstein, 189–200. San Francisco: Sierra Club Books.

———. 1992. *The violence of the green revolution: Third World agriculture, ecology, and politics.* London: Zed Books.

———. 1993a. *Monocultures of the mind: Perspectives on biodiversity and biotechnology.* London: Zed Books.

———. 1993b. Women's indigenous knowledge and biodiversity conservation. In *Ecofeminism,* coauthored with M. Mies. Shiva. London: Zed Books.

———. 1997. *Biopiracy: The plunder of nature and knowledge.* Boston: South End Press.

Shiva, V., et al., eds. 1991. *Biodiversity: Social and ecological consequences.* London: Zed Books.

Simmons, M. 1988. The rise of New Mexico cattle ranching. *El Palacio* 93:7.

Sjöö, M., and B. Mor. 1987. *The great cosmic mother: Rediscovering the religion of the Earth.* San Francisco: Harper and Row.

Smith, B. 1983. Fractitious, kicking, messy, free: Feminist writers confront the nuclear abyss. *New England Review/Breadloaf Quarterly* (summer): 581–92.

Smith, C., and E. Manning. 1997. The sacred and the profane collide in the West. *High Country News* 29 (May 26): 1.

Smith, D. 1987. *The everyday world as problematic: A feminist sociology.* Boston: Northeastern University.

———. 1990. *The conceptual practices of power: A feminist sociology of knowledge.* Boston: Northeastern University.

Smith, E. R. 1953. History of grazing industry and range conservation in the Rio Grande Basin. *Journal of Range Management* 6 (6): 405–9.

Smith, G. W. 1990. Political activist as ethnographer. *Social Problems* 37 (4): 629–48.

Snyder, G. 1990. The practice of the wild. San Francisco: North Point Press.

Soil Conservation Service, Division of Regional Planning, Southwest Region. 1936. *The sociological survey of the Rio Grande watershed.* Rio Grande Bioregions Project Archive, Hulbert Center for Southwestern Studies, Colorado College, Colorado Springs, "Environmental History" vertical file collection.

Soulé, M., and G. Lease, eds. 1995. *Reinventing nature? Responses to postmodern deconstruction.* Washington D.C.: Island Press.

Southwest Organizing Project, ed. 1995. *Intel inside New Mexico: A case study of environmental and economic injustice.* Albuquerque: Southwest Organizing Project.

Speck, F. G. [1935] 1977. *The Naskapi: The savage hunters of the Labrador Peninsula.* Norman: University of Oklahoma Press.

Spicer, E. H. 1972. Plural society in the Southwest. In *Plural society in the Southwest,* ed. E. H. Spicer and R. H. Thompson. New York: Interbook.

Spoehr, A. 1956. Cultural differences in the interpretation of natural resources, *Man's role in changing the face of the Earth,* ed. W. L. Thomas Jr. Chicago: University of Chicago Press.

Spretnak, C. 1986. *The spiritual dimensions of green politics.* Santa Fe: Bear and Company.

———. 1990. Ecofeminism: Our roots and flowering. In *Reweaving the world: The emergence of ecofeminism,* eds. I. Diamond and G. Orenstein, 3–14. San Francisco: Sierra Club Books.

Starhawk. 1990a. Bending the energy: Spirituality, politics, and culture. In *Turtle talk: Voices for a sustainable future,* eds. C. Plant and J. Plant, 32–39. Philadelphia: New Society Publishers.

———. 1990. Power, authority, and mystery: Ecofeminism and earthbased spirituality. In *Reweaving the world: The emergence of ecofeminism,* eds. I. Diamond and G. Orenstein, 73–86. San Francisco: Sierra Club Books.

Steinel, A. J. 1926. *History of Agriculture in Colorado.* Fort Collins: State Agricultural College Press.

Steward, J., ed. 1955. *Irrigation civilizations.* Washington, D.C.: U.S. Government Printing Office.

Stoller, M. 1985. La tierra y la merced. In *La cultura constante de San Luis,* ed. R. Teeuwen. San Luis, CO: The San Luis Museum, Cultural and Commercial Center.

Sutton, P., ed. 1990. *Dreamings: The art of aboriginal Australia.* New York: George Braziller.

Taylor, L. 1988. The importance of cross-cultural communication between environmentalists and land-based people. *The Workbook* 13:90–100.

Teitel, M., and H. Shand. 1997. *The ownership of life: When patents and values clash.* Firestone, CA: The C. S. Fund.

Thrupp, L. 1993. Political ecology of sustainable rural development: Dynamics of social and natural resource degradation. In *Food for the future: Conditions and contradictions of sustainability,* ed. P. Allen. New York: John Wiley.

Toledo, J. R. In press. *Morning Star: The autobiography of a Jemez Pueblo Indian artist,* ed. S. Scarberry-García. Albuquerque: University of New Mexico Press.

Torres, P. 1990. Río Arriba County Extension, Interview with Laura Pulido, Española, New Mexico (August).

Tuana, N., ed. 1989. *Feminism and science.* Bloomington: University of Indiana Press.

Tucker, E. A. 1992. The early days: A sourcebook of Southwestern region history. USDA Forest Service cultural resources management report, no. 12. Albuquerque: U.S. Forest Service, Southwestern Region.

Tyler, D. 1988. Ejido lands in New Mexico. *Journal of the West* 27:24–35.

United States Census Bureau. 1989. Income in 1989 of households, families, and persons by race and Hispanic origin, New Mexico. Summary of social, economic and housing characteristics. Washington, D.C.: United States Government Printing Office.

United States Forest Service. 1996. *Final environmental impact statement: Rio Grande National Forest Plan,* Denver: United States Department of Agriculture, U.S. Forest Service.

United States Senate. 1994. Testimony of Maria Varela before the U.S. Senate Committee on Energy and Natural Resources. Hearings on proposed range land reform (May 14), Albuquerque. Washington, D. C.: U.S. Government Printing Office.

United States Senate Committee on Energy and Natural Resources. 1994. Testimony of Maria Varela, Co-director of Ganados del Valle. Hearings on proposed rangeland reforms. Albuquerque, New Mexico (May 14).

Upper Rio Grande Working Group. 1987. *Upper Rio Grande waters: Strategies.* Proceedings of a conference on traditional water use. Albuquerque: Southwest Hispanic Research Institute, Natural Resources Center, Native American Studies Center.

Valdéz, A., and M. Valdéz. 1991. *The Culebra River villages of Costilla County: Village architecture and its historic context, 1851–1940.* Denver: Colorado Historical Society.

Valdéz, M. 1990. Interview with Devon G. Peña, San Luis, Colorado (September). Rio Grande Bioregions Project Archive, Hulbert Center for Southwestern Studies, Colorado College, Colorado Springs, "Oral Histories" collection.

Van Dresser, P. 1964. The bio-economic community: Reflections on a development philosophy for a semiarid environment. In *Indian and Spanish-American adjustments to arid and semiarid environments,* ed. C. Knowlton, 53–74. Lubbock: Texas Technological College Press.

———. 1972. *A landscape for humans.* Albuquerque: Biotechnic Press.

Van Ness, J. R. 1987. Hispanic land grants: Ecology and subsistence in the uplands of northern New Mexico and southern Colorado. In *Land, water and culture: New perspectives on Hispanic land grants,* ed. C. H. Briggs and J. R. Van Ness. Albuquerque: University of New Mexico Press.

Varela, M. 1995. Ganados wins Sierra Club Foundation settlement. *Noticias nuevas de Ganados del Valle* (spring-summer): 1.

Walter, E. V. 1988. *Placeways: A theory of the human environment.* Chapel Hill: University of North Carolina Press.

Watts, M. 1983. *Silent violence.* Berkeley: University of California Press.

Weber, K. R. 1991. Necessary but insufficient: Land, water, and economic development in Hispanic southern Colorado. *Journal of Ethnic Studies* 19 (2): 127–42.

Weigle, M. [1975] 1989. *Hispanic villages of northern New Mexico.* Santa Fe: The Lightning Tree Press.

Weiner, N. 1948. *Cybernetics: Or, control and communication in the animal and the machine.* New York: Wiley.

———. 1950. *The human uses of human beings.* London: Eyre and Spottiswoode.

Westphall, V. 1965. *The public domain in New Mexico.* Albuquerque: University of New Mexico Press.

———. 1983. *Mercedes reales: Hispanic land grants of the Upper Rio Grande region.* New Mexico Land Grant Series, vol. 1. Albuquerque: University of New Mexico Press.

White, R. 1994. Sacred places: The West's new booming extractive industry. *High country news,* March 7.

Widdison, J. G. 1958. *Historical geography of the Middle Puerco Valley, New Mexico.* M.A. thesis, Department of History, University of Colorado, Boulder.

Wildearth 1995. The first thousand days of the next thousand years: The Wildlands Project at three. *Wildearth* 5: 3–89.

Wilkinson, C. F. 1992. *The eagle bird: Mapping the New West.* New York: Pantheon Books.

———. 1993. *Crossing the next meridian.* New York: Pantheon Books.

Wilmsen, C. 1997. *Fighting for the forest.* Ph.D. diss. Department of Geography, University of Wisconsin, Madison.

Wittfogel, K. 1968. The theory of Oriental society. In *Readings in anthropology.* 2d edition. Ed. M. Fried. New York: Basic Books.

———. 1972. The hydraulic approach to pre-Spanish Mesoamerica. *The prehistory of the Tehuacan Valley*, vol. 4 of *Chronology and irrigation*, ed. F. Johnson. Austin: University of Texas Press.

——. 1981. *Oriental despotism*. New York: Academic Press.

Wolf, T. 1995. *Colorado's Sangre de Cristo Mountains*. Niwot, CO: University of Colorado Press.

Women's Pentagon Action. 1998. Unity statement. In *Women's lives: Multicultural perspectives*, eds. Gwyn Kirk and Margo Okazawa-Rey, 402–4. Mountain View, CA: Mayfield.

Woolf, J. 1995. How the West was won, and won, and. . . . *High Country News*, 15 October, 6.

Wooton, E. O. 1908. The range problem in New Mexico. NMC Station Bulletin, no. 66. Las Cruces: New Mexico Extension Service.

Works, M. 1992. A place for things: Material culture and sociospatial processes in northern New Mexico. Paper presented at the annual meeting of the American Association of Geographers. San Diego, California (April).

Worster, D. 1985. *Rivers of empire: Water, aridity and the growth of the American West*. New York: Pantheon Books.

——. 1988. Appendix: Doing environmental history. In *The ends of the Earth*, ed. D. Worster. New York: Cambridge University Press.

——. 1993. *The wealth of nature: Environmental history and the ecological imagination*. New York: Oxford University Press.

——. 1994. The legacy of John Wesley Powell. *An unsettled country: Changing landscapes of the American West*. Albuquerque: University of New Mexico Press.

——. 1995. Nature and the disorder of history. In *Reinventing nature? Responses to postmodern deconstruction*, eds. M. Soulé and G. Lease. Washington D.C.: Island Press.

Wozniak, F. A. 1995. Human ecology and ethnology. In *Ecology, diversity, and sustainability of the Middle Rio Grande Basin*. USDA Forest Service Technical Report, RM-GTR–268, eds. D. M. Finch and J. A. Tainter. Fort Collins: Rocky Mountain Forest and Range Experiment Station.

Wright, A. 1992. *The death of Ramón Gonzalez*. Austin: University of Texas Press.

Zavella, P. 1987. *Women's work and Chicano families: Cannery workers of the Santa Clara Valley*. Ithaca: Cornell Unversity Press.

Zeff, R. L., M. Love, and K. Stults, eds. 1989. *Empowering ourselves: Women and toxics organizing*. Falls Church, VA: Citizens Clearinghouse for Hazardous Wastes.

Zeitlin, I. M. 1987. *Ideology and the development of sociological theory*. Englewood Cliffs, NJ: Prentice Hall.

Zimmerer, K. 1993. Social erosion and social (dis)courses in Cochabamba, Bolivia: Perceiving the nature of environmental degradation. *Economic Geography* 69.

Index

abstractionism, 86, 89
academy: and social movements, 194–95
Acequia Advisory Board, 185
acequia associations, 10, 184, 185
acequia systems, 9, 18, 40, 68, 169,
   248n. 2, 260–61, 264–65, 274,
   276nn. 15, 18; biodiversity and, 101–
   3, 166–68, 239–40; and communities,
   158–59; as cultural landscape, 143,
   145–46; environmental change and,
   46–48; managing, 240–42; water allocation in, 159, 236–39; watersheds
   and, 141–42; women and, 50–51
Acoma, 68, 105–6
agriculture, 9, 112, 151, 185, 187; division of labor in, 50–51; Hispano,
   126–27, 262–65; sustainable, 18,
   184, 261–62
agroecology, 166–68
agropastoralism, 34, 43, 44, 65, 141,
   261–62
Albuquerque, 47, 109, 165, 173n. 10,
   186
American Folklife Center, 42
American Friends Service Committee
   (AFSC), 206, 208, 209, 213, 230n. 3
American Medical Association (lscama),
   213–14
American Water Development, Inc.
   (AWDI), 69, 261
Ancient Forest Rescue, 171, 184, 272
"Ancient Songs in a Modern World,"
   104
Angel Fire, 152, 174n. 14
Anglo-Americans. *See* Euro-Americans

animals, 111; ethics and, 25–27
anthropogenesis, 4, 48, 56n. 22
Antonio Martinez Land Grant, 152
Antonito, 79, 80–81, 82, 83, 101–2,
   109, 114–15
archetypes: psychic, 110–11, 117n. 2
Archuleta, Pedro, 96
Army Corps of Engineers, 264
Arriba, Río, 6, 7, 17
Arroyo Hondo, 10
Arroyo Seco, 10, 152
ASARCO Superfund site, 206, 209, 213,
   219
Audubon Society, 127, 183
Australia, 88, 180
autonomy, 72, 145
Aztlán, 79–80, 117n. 2

Battle Mountain Gold (BMG), 9, 51,
   172n. 12, 184, 242, 259, 267, 268;
   lawsuit against, 251–58
biocentrism, 40–41, 189
biodiversity, 164; and *acequias,* 18, 101–
   3, 239–40, 242, 261–62; and biocentrism, 40–41; of crops, 262–63;
   and cultural landscapes, 56n. 22, 166–
   68, 170–71
bioregion, 92; Upper Río Grande, 7–10
bioregionalism, 15, 16, 44, 52–53, 59–
   60, 61, 92, 189, 192, 253; cultural distinctiveness and, 33–34; deep ecology
   and, 29–30; defining, 28–29; ethics of,
   94–95; political economy and, 34–35,
   36–37; sacred places and, 31–32;
   values and, 93–94

biotechnology, 112–13
Black Mesa, 98
Blanca, Mount, 258
BMG. *See* Battle Mountain Gold
Bond, Frank, 38, 147, 150
Brazil, 122–23
Brown, Wilmette, 202, 213
Bubby, Brian, 104
Bureau of Land Management (BLM), 157, 173n. 8, 258, 275n. 7
Burns, Tom, 38–39

Cahuilla, 104
California, 182, 185–86
capitalism, 15, 49, 72, 88, 135, 154, 155, 178; domination of, 17, 94; and environment, 224–25; and knowledge, 64–65; and legal system, 255–56
Capitalist Nonsustainable Model (CNM), 65
carrying capacity, 155, 165–66
Catholicism, 203, 204, 206–7, 211, 212
Center for Third World Organizing (CTWO), 185–86, 187, 210, 212–13, 217, 230n. 4
Centro del Obrero Fronterizo, 196
Centro de Orientación de la Mujer Obrera, 196
ceremonies. *See* ritual(s)
Ceremony (Silko), 110
Chacón arroyo, 25
Chama, 39, 136
Chama Valley, 124–25, 169
Chavez, Cesar, 185
Chicano/as, 6, 172n. 3; activism of, 203–12; environmentalism of, 182–87, 191–92; and environmentalists, 144–45; resource use by, 10, 16; as violent and lawless, 153–54
Chicano Movement, 204–5, 212
Chicano Studies, 12–13, 14, 194–95
Chipko movement, 122
classism, 203, 228

class structure, 17, 30, 47, 155, 178, 182, 207
Coalition for Justice in the Maquiladoras, 183–84, 196
colonial period, 158–60, 165–66, 173n. 10
Colorado, 50, 59, 182; Chicano/as in, 70–72; ecofeminism in, 203–12; ecological politics in, 16–17; government in, 63–64; rural-urban migration in, 45–46; water politics in, 185, 249, 251–58, 260
Colorado Division of Wildlife (CDOW), 156
Colorado's Sangre de Cristo Mountains (Wolf): Chicanos and, 153–57
Colorado State Historical Society, 255
commercialization, 39, 47, 147, 164, 165
Committee for Environmental Soundness, 269
commons, 9, 35, 36, 124, 134, 149, 151, 154, 158, 159; enclosure of, 11, 44, 46, 155; forests on, 161, 163; grazing on, 128, 146, 147–48; restoration of, 16, 75, 268; self-management of, 171–72; values of, 266–67
communities, 33, 34, 39, 58, 73, 98, 201, 249; acequia-based, 158–59; Chicano/a, 70–71, 77–78n. 1; ecological legitimacy and, 123, 128–29, 134; as ecosystems, 60–61; environment and, 46–47; land-grant, 15–16, 173n. 8; property rights and, 250–51; ritual and, 99–100; rural, 14–15, 38, 45; social action research in, 69–70; Upper Rio Grande, 124–25; values of, 266–67
Community Justice Organizing, 206
Concerned Citizens of Questa, 184
Concerned Citizens of South Central Los Angeles, 186, 187
Conejos, 84–85
Conejos County, 70, 82

Conejos River, 81, 100
conservation: ethics of, 38–41
conservation biology, 5, 170, 171–72
conservation movement: American, 147, 150
Cooperativa Agrícola del Pueblo de Tierra Amarilla, La, 131
Coronado, Francisco Vasquez de, 68
corporations, 150–51, 195–96
cosmology, 86, 88, 91, 109, 110–11
Costilla County, 70
Costilla County Committee for Environmental Soundness (CES), 57n. 38, 184, 187
Costilla County Conservancy District (CCCD), 51, 185
Costilla Creek watershed, 9, 45–46
crops: heirloom, 262–63
Cross Community Coalition (C.C.C.), 206
Crow Dog, Leonard, 111
CTWO. See Center for Third World Organizing
Cuervo y Valdéz, Gov., 158
Culebra Coalition, 184
Culebra Cooperative Growers, 187
Culebra Creek watershed, 9, 18, 141, 156–57, 172, 173n. 12
Culebra Mountain Tract, 155, 162–63
Culebra Peak, 272–74
Culebra River, 46, 129, 156, 260, 261–62
cultural determinism, 43–44
cultural distinctiveness, 28, 29, 32, 33, 34
cultural ecology, 36, 37, 49, 54n. 3, 94–95
culturalism, 134–35, 137; and ecological legitimacy, 121–22, 132; and moral authority, 122–23
culture(s), 36, 37, 49, 54n. 3, 90, 144, 169, 266–67; American, 148–49; goddess-centered, 201–2; Hispano, 73–74, 132–33, 136; land-based, 18–

19, 107–8; and nature, 31, 33; romanticizing, 35, 121–22
Cumbres Lake, 101
curanderismo, 204, 205, 213
cybernetic theory, 112–13

Dalton, Henry, 95
dances: Native American, 104–5
Davis, W.W.H., 161
deBuys, William, 38, 46, 149–50, 152–53, 166, 175n. 25
deep ecology, 29–30, 33, 48–49, 54–55n. 7
deforestation, 47, 48, 90, 161
Denver, 186, 187, 203–5
Department of the Interior, 66
development, 64, 71, 106, 109, 123, 258, 267–68
disturbance, 13, 19–20n. 4, 143–44
ditchriders. See mayordomos
division of labor, 50–52
domination, 13, 77; of Catholic church, 206–7; and ecofeminism, 177–79, 181; and environment, 188–89; gender and, 216–17; and history, 217–18; of nature, 193–94, 221–24; U.S. government, 64–65
Dream Journeys, Dreamings, 88
duality, dualism, 89, 135

Earth First!, 30, 31, 171, 184, 189, 272
ecofeminism, 17, 52, 54–55n. 7, 195, 218–19, 220, 225–26, 227–28, 229–30; activism of, 181–82, 188–89; in Colorado, 203–12; definitions of, 177–79, 228–29; ethics of, 201–2; militarism and, 179–80; politics and 180–81; projects of, 191–92; on sexism, 193–94
ecological legitimacy, 121, 128, 132, 133–34, 137; moral authority and, 122–23; resource management by, 126–27, 129–30

ecology, 6, 19–20n. 4, 21n. 16, 60, 170; and biotechnology, 112–13; and Chicano Studies, 12–13; humans and, 4–5, 49; knowledge of, 3–4; and rural communities, 14–15; and urban areas, 81, 82

Ecology-Feminism Center, 177

economic development, 44–45, 186–87

economics, 71–72, 82, 128–29, 130, 135–36, 182, 188, 224–25

economy, 6, 113, 125; global market, 14, 195–96

ecopolitics, 14, 169–70

ecosystems, 3–4, 13, 21n. 19, 28, 35, 60–61, 81, 143–44, 162

education, 73, 74

elites, 155, 220

Embudo, 164, 184

Enchantment and Exploitation (deBuys), 149–50, 152–53

Encinias, Art, 169

enclosure, 11, 44, 46, 155, 163

environment, 46–47, 61, 179–80; degradation of, 188–89, 224–25

Environmental Defense Fund, 183

environmental history, 143–44; of Río Arriba, 145–57

environmentalism, 6, 14, 16, 102, 108, 131; Chicanos and, 15, 17, 144–45, 177, 182–87, 191–92; economics and, 135–36; mainstream, 188–89, 219–21; women and, 50, 57n. 38, 179, 181–82. *See also* ecofeminism

environmental justice movement, 14, 17, 121, 182, 196, 227

Environmental Protection Agency, 184

environmental regulations: Spanish-Mexican, 158–60

erosion, 17, 164

Escuela Tlatelolco, 205, 230n. 2

Española, 38

Espejo expedition, 68

essentialism, 122, 137–38

ethic(s), 5, 89, 90, 97, 109, 110, 113; bioregional, 29–30, 94–95; conservation, 37, 38–41, 158, 162; ecofeminist, 201–2; environmental, 16, 101, 149–50, 157; homeland, 92–93, 98–99; hunting, 25–26, 156–57; land, 17, 49–50; of place, 168–69, 170, 172

ethnicity, 55n. 11, 217–18, 219

ethnobotany, 74, 187

ethnophilosophy, 32, 34, 39, 91, 92, 100

ethnoscience, 37, 92–93, 190, 253

Euro-Americans, 31–32, 46, 55n. 14, 102, 125, 135

exoticism, 37, 46, 48–49, 57n. 33

families, 45, 72–73

farming, farms, 9; traditional, 235–47. *See also* agriculture

farmworkers, 183, 185

feminism: and race, 214–16

Fiesta de Porcingula, La, 116–17

fire regime, 161, 163

First National People of Color Environmental Leadership Summit, 183

Fitzgerald, Jim: ""Mirror Project," 108–9

folkways, 34, 40, 73–74; as local knowledge, 41–43

Forbes, Inc., 161

Forbes, Kip, 154

Forbes, Malcolm, 8, 154, 156

Forbes, Steve, 154

Forbes Ranch, 9

forest resources, 160–62

Forest Spirits, 40

Fuerza Unida (United Force), 183

Gallegos, Corpus A., 51, 266–67

Gallegos, Dario, 242, 260

Gallegos, Jerry, 263

Gallegos Ranch, Corpus Aquino, 240, 260, 262–63, 265–67

Ganados del Valle, 10, 51, 75, 123, 124,

136, 137–38, 139n. 14, 186, 191; operation of, 130–32; stewardship by, 129–30, 133–34
gardens, gardening, 51, 74
gender, 17, 30, 37, 187; and activism, 214–17, 228; and agriculture, 50–51; and division of labor, 51–52
General Mining Act (1872), 76
gentrification, 31–32, 152, 153
Globeville (Colo.), 206, 209, 213
government agencies, 61, 65–66, 76, 150; land and water control by, 63–64, 69
Graham, Ray, 131, 134
Granado, Lorraine, 216, 224, 225; activism of, 206–9, 213, 214, 217–18, 228; on domination, 221–22; and mainstream environmentalism, 219–20
grazing, grazing land, 10, 123, 127–28, 139n. 6, 150, 234; commercialization of, 39, 165; condition of, 147–48, 248n. 4; Ganados del Valle and, 130–34, 139n. 14; impacts of, 17, 164–66
Great Britain, 179, 180
Greenham Common peace camp, 179, 180, 181
Greenpeace, 171, 183, 184
Gregg, Josiah, 161
grounded theory, 71
Guadalupe County, 70

habitats, 48, 162, 164
Hardin, Garrett, 159
healing, 74. *See also* health; medicine
health, 185, 195, 209, 214–15, 219
heritage, 97–98, 121–22
Hispanos, 16, 17, 123, 135, 138n. 4, 150; and American land use, 148–49; cultural preservation and, 132–33, 136; environmental history and, 146, 147; forest use and, 160–61; resource management by, 126, 129–30; in Up-

per Rio Grande, 124–25; water allocation by, 158–59, 250. *See also* Chicano/as; mexicano culture
history, 95; environmental, 143–44, 146–57
homeland, 16, 79, 80–81, 100–101, 108–9, 111, 114–15, 190; commons of, 35, 36; ethics of, 39–40, 48, 92–93, 98–99; and mass civilization, 97–98
homesteading, 67–68
human ecology, 60, 61
human rights, 222–23
humans: and nature, 4–5, 31, 48–49, 56n. 22
hunting, 25–26, 156–57
hydrological cycle, 68–69

identity, 20–21n. 11, 100, 132, 204–5, 207, 217–18
ideology, 36–37, 62, 248n. 5
Idyllwild School of Music, 104
illness, 181–82
immigrants, immigration, 31–32, 189
India, 122, 275n. 1
indigenous peoples, 81, 204, 205
industrialization, 10, 18, 34, 113, 162, 209
Instituto Tonantzin, El, 75
Intel Corporation, 186
intercropping, 142, 262–63
International Union for the Conservation of Nature (IUCN), 48
irrigation systems, 101–3, 141, 260–61

Jaramillo, Teresa, 269–70
Jémez Pueblo, 83, 116–17
Jung, C. G., 111, 115, 117n. 2

Kettleman City (Calif.), 186, 187
King, Ynestra, 178, 201
kinship networks, 45, 72–73
Kit Carson National Forest, 10, 162

knowledge, 7, 52, 106, 195; destruction of 64–65; local, 18, 33, 41–43, 55n. 9, 142–43, 170, 254; place-centered, 34, 37; reductionist, 5–6; situated, 11, 12, 13, 95; valid, 190–91

Krassa, Bob, 256

Labor/Community Strategy Center, 186

Lacandón Maya, 40

La Madera, 10

La Manga Timber Sale, 10

land, 16, 89, 96, 112, 123, 132, 141–42, 145, 171, 172n. 3, 181, 250, 274–75; culture and, 135, 149, 150; degradation of, 47–48, 128–29, 139n. 11, 148–49, 151–53, 154; distribution of, 67–68; ethics of, 49–50; government and, 63–64, 75–76, 150–51, 155, 157, 160, 162, 163–64; ownership of, 164–65; *partido* system and, 38–39; restoration of, 44–45, 262

land grants, 44, 75–76, 132, 152; communities on, 15–16, 47; forest use and, 160–61, 163, 173n. 8; and water rights, 184–85

landraces, 167, 262–63, 276n. 12

land rights, 124, 126–27, 158

Land Rights Council (LRC), 51, 57n. 38, 187

landscapes, 19–20n. 4, 39, 91, 143; biodiversity and, 56n. 22, 166–68; cultural, 145–46, 170–71

land speculation, 38–39, 125, 152

land trust, 132, 134

Laredo, 25

La Vega, 156

"Law of Thirst," 159, 276n. 16

laws of the Indies, 158

leadership: women's, 50–51, 57n. 38

Lee, Bill, 83–84

legal system: property rights and, 250–51; water and, 18, 249–50

leisure industries, 152. *See also* recreation; ski areas; tourism

Leopold, Aldo, 38, 39, 90, 98, 150

Levi Strauss, 183

livestock, 47, 129, 158, 165–66

locality. *See* place

Local Woman, 271–72

lococentrism, 192, 193

logging, 9, 10, 17, 18, 147, 160, 171, 173n. 8; Forest Service and, 150–51, 163–64; in Sangre de Cristos, 154–55, 161–63; on Taylor Ranch, 271–72, 273–74

long-lot. *See* riparian long-lot

Lopéz, Felix, 84–85

Los Angeles, 21n. 19, 81, 82, 100, 186

Los Cerritos, 81–82

Lucero, Josephine, 254

Lucero de Godoi Land Grant, 152

Manby, Alfred, 39, 150

Manes, Christopher, 30–31

manitos, 70, 78n. 2

maquiladoras, 183–84, 195–96

marginalization, 13–14, 136, 194–95

Martínez, Maclovio, 254

mass civilization, 89–90, 97–98

mayordomos, 50–51, 236, 238, 241, 254

medicine, 74, 204, 205, 213–14

mestizaje, 18, 43, 90, 98

Metropolitan State College, 205, 207, 208

mexicano/a culture, 44; conservation ethics and, 38–41; environmental change and, 46–47; women in, 50–51

Mexico: maquiladoras in, 183–84, 195–96

migration, 4, 45–46, 94, 152

militarism, 179–80, 181

Mined Land Reclamation Board (MLRB), 254–55

mining, 9, 17, 18, 90, 113, 242, 243, 254–55, 261; Forest Service and, 150–51; impacts of, 184, 277n. 20

Minority Activist Apprenticeship Program (MAAP), 210, 211
"Mirror Project" (Fitzgerald), 108
misanthropy, 30–31, 33
modernization, 44, 174n. 15
Mojave, 104–5
Molycorp Molybdenum, 9, 173n. 12, 184
Mora County, 70
moral authority, 122–23
mosaics, 4, 13, 19–20n. 4
Mothers of East Los Angeles, 186, 187
Multiple Use Sustainable Yield Act, 76
music: Native American, 104–5
mythology, 82–83, 86, 87, 88, 89, 90, 95, 103

National Association for Chicano Studies (NACS), 95–97
National Chicano Human Rights Commission (NCHRC), 204, 230n. 1
National Forest Management Act, 76
nationalism, Chicano/a, 58–59
National Wildlife Federation, 183
Native Americans, 16, 32, 113, 172n. 3, 183, 185. *See also various tribes; pueblos*
nature, 111; culture and, 31, 33, 135, 144; domination of, 177–78, 193–94, 221–23; exoticism and, 48–49; farming and, 242–43; humans and, 4–5; love of, 25–28; music and, 104–5; and myth, 87, 90; and people, 189–90; philosophy and, 88–89; role of, 269–70; subordination of, 5–6; women and, 223–24
Nature Conservancy, 183
Navajo, 86, 87, 88, 91, 98, 138
Neighbors for a Toxic-Free Community, 186, 206, 209
Nelson-Cisneros, Victor, 103
New Mexico, 50, 59, 123, 158, 165, 173n. 8, 174n. 15, 182; Chicano/as in,
70–71; environmental history of, 146–57; ethnic conflict in, 144–45; government in, 63–64; grazing, 130–32; land use in, 128–29; *partido* system in, 38–39; politics in, 16–17; rural communities in, 45, 124–25; water in, 68, 69, 184–85, 249
New Mexico Department of Game and Fish (NMDGF), 130–31, 137
New Mexico State University, 131
North American Bioregional Congress, 29

Oakland, 185, 186, 231n. 5
Ogburn, Robert, 251
Ojo Caliente, 10
Oñate, Juan de, 165
orchards, 74, 262; heirloom, 265–67
Ortega, Praxedis, Jr., 259
overgrazing, 17, 47, 48, 125, 126, 127, 146–47, 165–66, 173n. 10

Paéz Hurtado, Juan, 158
Pajarito Plateau, 146, 147
Paley, Grace, 180
Parrish, Essie, 105
partido system, 38–39
pastoralism, 133–34
Pastores, 186
patriarchy, 222, 223
Peabody mine, 98
Peace and Dignity Journey, 204
Peña, Sonia, 223, 224, 225, 227, 228, 231n. 5; activism of, 210–13, 215–16; and mainstream environmentalism, 219–21
People for Clean Air and Water, 186, 187
People United for a Better Oakland (PUEBLO), 186
pesticides, 185, 190, 195
philosophy, 86–89, 99
place(s), 34, 36, 108, 176n. 28; contested, 11–12; ethic of, 168–69, 170,

172; and identity, 20–21n. 11, 85; sacred, 28, 31–32; value of, 83, 192, 269–71

plants: ethical treatment of, 26, 27

Plato, 5, 83, 86–87, 88, 89, 90

poaching, 156, 157, 175n. 20

political economy, 32, 34–35, 36–37, 60, 90

politics, 6, 13, 36, 179; ecofeminism and, 180–81; ecological, 16–17, 35; water, 18, 68–69, 184–85

pollution, 9, 10, 195–96, 219, 253, 267, 277n. 20

poverty, 7, 17, 124–25, 126, 127, 139nn. 7, 11, 207

production, 65, 72, 89, 195–96

property rights, 9, 88, 124, 156, 164–65, 170, 250–51

Pueblo Indians, 146, 147, 149, 173n. 8, 185, 250. *See also by name*

Puerco, Rio, 164, 165

Questa, 9, 151, 173n. 12, 184

race, 30, 178, 182; and feminism, 214–16; and power issues, 216–17

racism, 46, 180, 203, 208; environmental, 183, 185–86; and feminism, 216, 228

railroads, 46, 47, 129, 146–47, 165, 171

Rainbow Bridge, 32

rangeland condition, 147–48, 164–66

reality, mythic, 82–83

Recopilación de leyes de los reynos de las indias, 158

recreation, 32, 151–52, 174n. 14

Red River, 9, 151, 152, 173n. 12, 174n. 14

resistance, 109, 122–23, 136–37, 156–57, 204

resolana, 43, 56n. 27, 74, 98, 118n. 5, 174n. 15

resort development, 9, 10

resource management, 125, 126–27, 129–30, 135–36, 150–51, 155

Río Arriba bioregion, 18, 40, 44, 52–53, 54n. 3, 158, 168; conflict in, 144–45; development in, 46–47; environmental history of, 145–57; forests in, 161–62; grazing in, 39, 164–66; land use in, 49–50, 157, 159–60; local knowledge in, 142–43; political economy and, 34, 37. *See also various communities*

Río Arriba County, 70, 125, 131–32, 139n. 14

Rio Costilla Cooperative Livestock Association, 75–76

Rio Grande, 164, 185, 195–96

Rio Grande Bioregions Project, 52–53, 141

Rio Grande Institute, 184–85

Rio Grande National Forest, 162

Rio Grande Pueblos, 83. *See also by name*

riparian long-lot, 143, 152, 166–68, 175–76n. 26, 262, 276n. 10

Rito Seco, 9, 242, 254, 258–59, 260

ritual, 83, 91, 98, 99–100, 111, 116–17

roads, 148, 155, 160, 161–62, 174n. 15

Rodriguez, Roseanne ""Rocky," 225; activism of, 204–5, 213–14, 215, 218, 226, 228, 229; on environmentalism, 219–20, 221; on spirituality, 223–24

romanticism, 35, 125, 137

Romer, Roy, 154

Romero, Brenda, 104

rubbertappers, 122–23

rural areas, 31–32, 38, 42–43, 92, 94, 152, 153. *See also various communities*

Salvador, Lilly, 105–6

San Antonio, 183

Sand County Almanac, The (Leopold), 90

San Francisco Peaks, 105
Sangre de Cristo Land Grant, 9, 11, 46,
    161, 175n. 19
Sangre de Cristo Mountains, 76, 115–16,
    149; forests in, 160–63, 272; land in,
    154–55; sheepherding in, 243–47; ski
    resorts in, 9, 10
San Luis (Colo.), 9, 51, 173n. 12, 184,
    185, 243, 251, 253, 260, 269, 276n. 9;
    sustainable development in, 267–68
San Luis National Historic District, 255
San Luis Peoples Ditch (and Company),
    238, 248n. 3, 260, 264, 276n. 8; law-
    suit by, 251–58
*San Luis Peoples Ditch et al. v. Battle
    Mountain Gold,* 18, 251–58
San Luis Valley, 69, 171, 272; acequia
    systems in, 235–47, 260–61; Chi-
    canos in, 153–56; environmentalism
    in, 186–87
San Miguel County, 70
Santa Barbara Tie and Pole Company,
    153
Santa Fe, 47, 106, 125, 152, 158, 165,
    173n. 10
Santa Fe National Forest, 162
science, 3, 178, 190; reductionist, 5–6,
    20n. 6, 258
second-home lots, 9, 161
Secretary of Ecology, Oceans, and Natu-
    ral Resources (SEMARNAP), 184
self-determination, 69, 228
self-management, 171, 172n. 3
sense of place, 16, 28–29, 30, 33, 37, 82,
    168, 192–93
settlement patterns, 141, 166–68
sexism, 180, 193–94, 215, 216, 226
sheep, sheepherding, 37, 146, 235–36;
    Churro, 186; and Ganados del Valle,
    130, 131; rangeland and, 147–48,
    248n. 4; in Sangre de Cristos, 243–47
Shoshone Reservation, 101
Sierra Club, 10, 131–32, 183

Silko, Leslie Marmon: *Ceremony,* 110
ski industry, 9, 151–52, 174n. 14
Ski Rio, 9
slavery, 89, 107
Smith, Dorothy, 61, 62
Smith, George W., 61, 62, 63
Smith, J. Russell, 124
social action research, 69–70
social class. *See* class structure
social justice, 218, 220, 226–27
social movements, 194–95
social relations, 62, 72, 74
Socrates, 5, 86, 90
Soil Conservation Service, 66
soil types, 141–42
Southwest Network for Environmental
    and Economic Justice (SNEEJ), 51,
    183–84, 186
Southwest Organizing Project (SWOP),
    51, 183, 186, 187
Spanish-Mexican culture. *See* Hispanos;
    mexicano culture
spirituality, 109–11, 179, 202, 223–24,
    226, 229
Spretnak, Charlene, 178, 202
Starhawk, 178, 202
State Engineers Office (Colorado), 264
stewardship, 127–28, 129, 133–34, 165,
    274–75
storytelling, 25, 56n. 27, 73–74, 237,
    238; sheepherding in, 243–47
Superfund sites, 206, 213, 277n. 20
survival, 13–14, 79–80
sustainability, 10, 15, 17, 18, 65, 129,
    190–91, 267–68
sweat lodge ceremonies, 98, 111
symbology, 83, 98, 109, 111, 117n. 2
synchronicity, 115–16

Talamantez, Inéz, 96, 97
Taos, 10, 16, 30, 32, 108, 125, 132; de-
    velopment issues in, 106, 187; land
    speculation in, 39, 152

Taos County, 70
Taos Ski area, 10, 152, 174n. 14, 185
Taos Valley Acequia Association (TVAA), 185
Taylor, Jack, 154, 156, 163
Taylor, Zachary, 163, 272
Taylor Ranch, 9, 155, 271–72
technology: cybernetic, 256–57; irrigation, 260–61
Tewa Basin Project, 41, 43
Texas, 182, 183–84, 185
Texas Center for Policy Studies, 183
Texas Farmworkers Union, 183
textual analysis, 61–63
Tierra Amarilla, 39, 108–9, 139n. 7, 186
Tierra Amarilla Land Grant, 10
Tierra Wools, 186, 187
timber cuts. *See* logging
tourism, 16, 106, 108, 125, 133, 152, 255
toxic waste, 9, 183, 184, 185–86, 219
Traditional Sustainable Model (TSM), 65
truths: universal, 5–6
Turtle Island Bioregional Congress, 29

unemployment, 124, 125, 156
United Farmworkers of America, 185, 211
U.N. Conference on Environment and Development, 181
U.S. Fish and Wildlife Service (USFWS), 156
U.S. Forest Service, 10, 66, 76, 150–51, 157, 160, 162, 163–64
University of California-Davis, 185
Upper Chama River Valley, 10, 124–25
Upper Río Grande bioregion, 7, 8–10, 16, 17, 61, 141, 143–44, 150, 168, 185; communities in, 124–25; ethics in, 49–50; political battles in, 36–37
Upper Rio Grande Hispano Farms Study, 51
urban areas, 48, 92, 94, 109, 182; eco-

systems and, 19, 21n. 19, 81, 82; place and, 192–93

Valdéz, Pat, 268, 269, 276n. 18
Vallecitos Federal Sustained Yield Unit (VFSYU), 10, 173n. 8
value(s), 83, 93–94, 107, 266–67
Varela, María, 187

Waste Management, Inc., 186
water, 16, 275n. 5, 276n. 16; allocation of, 158–59; politics of, 18, 68–69, 240–41, 264–65
Water Information Network, 185
water policies, 75–76, 158–59
water rights, 124, 169, 249; Hispano, 126–27, 158, 236–39, 240–42, 248n. 3; lawsuits over, 251–58; protection of 184–85, 186
watersheds, 9, 28, 54n. 3, 175n. 25, 258–59, 275n. 4; and communities, 249, 257; damage to, 34, 47–48, 162, 164, 173n. 12; management of, 145, 169–70, 171–72; protection of, 141–42; resource extraction and, 150–51
Westphall, Victor, 165
wilderness, 35, 36, 48, 90, 94–95, 135, 144, 145, 190
Wilderness Society, 183
wildlife, 156, 164, 240, 259
Wildlife Management Areas (WMAS), 131, 139n. 14
Wise, Walter, 257
Wolf, Tom: on Sangre de Cristos, 46, 153–57
women, 96, 103; as activists, 226–29; domination of, 177–78; and environmentalism, 179, 181–82, 187; leadership of, 50–51, 57n. 38; and nature, 223–24
Women's Pentagon Action, 179, 180, 181; Unity Statement of, 196–99
Women's Studies, 194–95

Contributors

Malia Davis received her B.A. in sociology from Colorado College in 1992. She instructs and directs field-based Wilderness Leadership courses for the Colorado Outward Bound School and is also a practicing massage therapist in Colorado Springs.

Joseph C. Gallegos is a fifth-generation farmer working on ancestral lands in San Luis, Colorado. He is active in the environmental justice and sustainable agriculture movements. Mr. Gallegos is the secretary of the Costilla County Conservancy District and *mayordomo* of the San Luis Peoples Ditch, the oldest water right in Colorado. Mr. Gallegos has published several articles on environmental justice and collaborative social action research. He is currently writing an autobiographical novel.

Reyes García is an associate professor of philosophy at Ft. Lewis College in Durango, Colorado. He is a fifth-generation rancher on his family's land in the Conejos Land Grant in Colorado's San Luis Valley and is completing work on *A Philosopher in Aztlán,* a book of essays on environmental ethics in the Indohispano Southwest.

Gwyn Kirk is an associate professor of women's studies at San Francisco State University. She is a founder of the Greenham Common women's peace camp. Professor Kirk is coauthor with Alice Cook of *Greenham Women Everywhere* (South End Press, 1983) and has published extensively on ecofeminism, peace politics, and environmental justice.

Rubén O. Martínez is an associate provost at the University of Southern Colorado in Pueblo. A native of Arroyo Seco, New Mexico, Professor Martínez has published numerous articles on race relations, minorities and higher education, and rural sociology. He is coauthor with Adalberto Aguirre of *Chicanos in Higher Education* (George Washington University Press, 1993). With Devon Peña, he codirects "The Upper Rio Grande Hispano Farms: A Cultural and Natural History of Land Ethics in Transition, 1598–1998," a research project funded by the National Endowment for the Humanities.

Devon G. Peña is an associate professor of sociology at Colorado College. He is author of *The Terror of the Machine: Technology, Work, Gender, and Ecology on the U.S.–Mexico Border* (CMAS Books, University of Texas Press, 1997). Professor Peña directs the Rio Grande Bioregions Project and is completing work on a study of historic *acequia* farms with support from the National Endowment for the Humanities. He lives and works on a ranch in El Rito, Colorado.

Laura Pulido is an assistant professor of geography at the University of Southern California in Los Angeles and has published widely in the area of environmental politics and race. Her most recent book is *Environmentalism and Economic Justice: Two Chicano Struggles in the Southwest* (University of Arizona Press, 1996).

Vandana Shiva is the director of the Research Foundation for Science, Technology, and Natural Resources Policy (Dehra Dun, India) and past recipient of the Right Livelihood Award, the alternative Nobel Peace Prize. Dr. Shiva's most recent books include *Ecofeminism* (coauthored with Maria Mies; Zed Books, 1993) and *Biopiracy: The Plunder of Nature and Knowledge* (South End Press, 1997).

Nina Veregge is an architect and historical geographer whose research focuses on urban landscapes of the U.S.–Mexico borderlands and Central America. She is presently a Ph.D. candidate in the Department of Geography, University of Colorado, Boulder.